MY DARK BROTHER

Dr Elena Govor, a Russian-born Australian writer and historian, was born in Minsk and later lived in Moscow, where she studied the history of Russian-Australian contact. In 1990 she came to Australia, the country of her childhood dreams, and now lives in Canberra, where she received her doctorate in history from the Australian National University in 1996. She has been widely published both in Russia and Australia: among her recent books are *Russian Sailors and Travellers in Australia*, co-authored with A Massov (Moscow 1993), and *Australia in the Russian Mirror: Changing Perceptions 1770–1919* (MUP 1997). Currently she is working on the history of Russian émigrés in Australia, as well as on the tragic story of her own family's experience of revolution, Stalinist repression and war.

MY
DARK
BROTHER

THE STORY OF THE ILLINS,
A RUSSIAN-ABORIGINAL FAMILY

Elena Govor

UNSW
PRESS

To my son

Ralphie Kabo and the young Illins

— the Australians

A UNSW Press book

Published by
University of New South Wales Press Ltd
UNSW SYDNEY NSW 2052
AUSTRALIA
www.unswpress.com.au

©Elena Govor 2000
First published 2000

National Library of Australia
Cataloguing-in-Publication entry:

Govor, E.V. (Elena Viktorovna).
My dark brother: the story of the Illins, a Russian-Aboriginal family.

Bibliography.
Includes index.
ISBN 0 86840 594 9.

1. Illins family.
2. Russians — Australia — Biography.
3. Immigrants — Australia — Biography.
4. Aborigines, Australian — Queensland — Atherton Tableland — Biography. I. Title.

304.894047

Cover Leandro Illin at Greenvale Station, *ca* 1927
(courtesy of Flora Hoolihan, Townsville)

CONTENTS

~

FOREWORD

Elena Govor and her husband Vladimir Kabo are among Russians who have developed an intense interest in Australia and who have then come to see the land of their study and imagining. Such people are more numerous than most of us had known before Melbourne University Press published in 1997 Elena Govor's book *Australia in the Russian Mirror*. Govor and Kabo are also among Russians who, after experiencing life in Australia, have decided to make this country their home. Vladimir Kabo describes their odyssey in his own book, published in 1998 by Aboriginal Studies Press, *The Road to Australia*. Fate, will and intellect had made him the foremost scholar in the Soviet Union on the subject of Australian Aborigines. As an intellectual from a Jewish family, incarcerated in Stalin's prisons, he began to reflect on the similarities between the Gulag and early human society, and when he was released he became a member of Leningrad's Institute of Ethnography. He had to wait more than thirty years, until 1990, to fulfil his wish to see the continent whose first inhabitants occupied his mind. He was accompanied by Elena, his young wife, who (like many other Russians, she discovered) had dreamed when young of Australia, had read Vladimir's book *The Origins of the Australian Aborigines* at the age of fourteen, had published her own *Bibliography of Australia (1710–1983)* and composed the standard Russian bibliography on Oceania, and who agreed to marry him when, as a widower slightly acquainted with her, he proposed in a letter.

'What do you know about your bride-to-be?' Vladimir's sister Lyuba asked him.

'She's very fond of Australia', he replied.

'I know quite a bit about love and how people get married', said Lyuba, 'but this is the first time I've ever heard of two people forming a union on the basis of their love for Australia.'

They loved Australia at first sight, as Vladimir had loved Elena — loved, in his ecstatic words, 'green hills with the shadows of clouds scudding over them, forests of gums, translucent and filled with sunlight, the riotous gold of wattles, pebbly riverbeds in deep, shady gullies'. They even love suburban Canberra, where they have lived since 1991, and where they became Australians, proud of the citizenship certificates handed to them by smiling officials at a homely Australia Day ceremony (who also gave them each a native tree to plant in the soil of their new country), and proud of their Australian son, Ralphie.

The introduction to this book has an epigraph from E.T.A. Hoffmann: 'The most astonishing things are those that actually happen. There is nothing more surprising or improbable than real life.' These words are familiar to readers of *The Road to Australia*. Vladimir copied them into a diary at the age of twelve or thirteen, a diary which was to vanish in the furnaces of the Lubyanka prison, but only after the passage had stuck in the mind of an interrogator, who observed 'That's very true'.

My Dark Brother is indeed a tale full of astonishing things. As the author says, 'at times it is a historical, anthropological, or literary study; at times, a documentary novel'.

Nicholas Illin and his son Leandro had small parts in her earlier book. Nicholas is a Russian intellectual who has travelled to Queensland; Leandro does his best to persuade Australian authorities to authorise a Russian settlement in the Northern Territory, and in 1915 he becomes one of only six European men in Queensland given permission to marry an Aboriginal woman.

Now we meet the two Illins as richly presented characters, in a story that goes from the Russia of Chekhov, Turgenev and Dostoevsky to the Australia of Eddie Mabo. Yes, Eddie Mabo: it was Leandro's Aboriginal son-in-law Richard Hoolihan who awakened Mabo to the subject of land rights.

Elena Govor has found a rich treasury of sources about the Illins in three continents, which she interrogates subtly and hard. The making of the book has been a family activity. Kabo's anthropology helps Govor to bring alive the Aboriginal culture of Leandro's wife Kitty, mother of his five children, who dies young but remains vividly alive in the memory of her husband until he dies in 1946 and in the memories of their children, sensitively recorded by the author. The descendants' memories of both Aboriginal and Russian progenitors are remarkably rich. Govor tests them against documentary evidence and, as a detective historian, she is often surprised at their accuracy. She makes good use of inaccuracies also: one strength of the book is its exploration of the notion of a myth. Ralphie accompanied his mother on field-work at the age of four, and heard the myth of the Rainbow Serpent from an Aboriginal elder at the very spot where people believe the events of the myth happened.

If, like me, you are apprehensive that the term 'documentary novel' may signal that genre of historical fiction, or faction, in which the reader can never be sure whether people and events rest on historical evidence or are made up, you need not worry. When the author is speculating, she tells us so. She applies a novelist's mind to a vast range of scrupulously collected evidence, from the works of Tolstoy to immigration records in Argentina, to the *Cairns Post*, as well as to records of interviews with many people, young and old. The book does read like fiction. Well-documented improbabilities abound. I sometimes felt I was reading a fancifully crafted saga, crossing oceans and generations — by Peter Carey, say. I needed all the footnotes to remind me that this is not fiction at all, that it all did happen.

The author herself is a constant, unobtrusive presence in the book as she cuts cleverly between her own research and the events of one or more generations ago. She begins and ends with the present, dedicating the book to Ralphie Kabo and the young Illins, heirs to both the spirit of Russia and the Rainbow Serpent. She sees her son and his young Aboriginal friends as destined 'to build the new Australia free from racial prejudice and thus fulfil Leandro Illin's dream'. Her rendering of that dream and its human consequences is a powerful work of creative imagination, and an inspiring text for anybody who cares about reconciliation.

K.S. Inglis

ACKNOWLEDGEMENTS

~

I would like to express my gratitude above all to Flora Hoolihan — granddaughter of the Russian intellectual, daughter of the Ngadjon Aboriginal woman, grandmother of the young Aboriginal Australian intellectuals — she has opened her heart to share with us the unique and painful story of her family. Among other members of the Illin family who especially contributed to the book are Henry Illin and his family, particularly Alec Illin and Leanne Illin; Ernest and Maud Hoolihan and their children — Derek, Dynzie, Allison and Hilary; Margaret and Frank Gertz and their family; Richard Hoolihan, Glenda Illin, Vera Ketchell, Essie Morganson, Nola Smallwood and Hazel Illin. I am grateful to Jessie Calico, the Ngadjon Aboriginal elder, for telling me the myths of her people and to Emma Johnston (née Raymond) for providing some information about her Ngadjon country.

Material from the Honduran and American branches of the Illin family also significantly contributed to the book, particularly contributions from Ellen Dale Flores, Leandro Illin Jnr, Somerled Mackay Jnr, Hector Mackay, Olga Rodgers, and René Mackay.

I wish to express my deep appreciation to Marian Hill (at the Australian National University), who for years patiently edited drafts of this book, as English is not my native language. Marian was more than just an editor for me — she was my first supporter in moments of despair and the first tactful critic, contributing her precise style of expression and her vast knowledge to this book. She also helped me to transcribe all tape-recordings of my interviews.

Roderic Campbell, the editor, further improved the manuscript with his highly professional and constructive editing. His contribution as a stylist, a creative writer and experienced linguist was vitally important in dealing with the diverse voices and sources used in the book. He also contributed to the translation of many of the Russian poems cited and the Spanish sources.

I am grateful to the Australian Institute of Aboriginal and Torres Strait Islander Studies, which, although unable to fund my research, provided me with facilities to write the book as a visiting scholar there and gave me access to the resources of its library. I also acknowledge the support of the Queensland State Archives, particularly of archivists Margaret Reid and Dianne Duroux, and manager Moira Bligh, who made a thorough search of the documents relating to the Illin family in the files of the Chief Protector of Aboriginals. Among those who provided me with advice and help in my research are Nikolai Dmitrovsky, R.M.W. Dixon, Peter Kershaw, William A. Douglass, Ric Throssell, Roy Phelps, George Butcher, Brian McNamara, Kevin Windle. I also appreciate the support of Bill Homenko, Peter Gadaloff, Igor Gadaloff, Sheila Gadaloff, Basil Strelnikoff, and George Balias, who are all descendants of the first Russian settlers of 'Little Siberia' in the Atherton Tablelands; and of Delphia Atkinson, Bim Atkinson, Giles Atkinson, and Henry Atkinson, all members of the Atkinson family. For their support and helpful suggestions, I am also grateful to Professor Ken Inglis (ANU) and Peter Browne (UNSW Press).

I would like to begin the list of people who provided assistance with Russian materials with Lena Nitkina, who, under the constant pressure of Moscow crises, having two children to look after and two jobs to work at, for years patiently and honestly fulfilled all my requests: she made telephone inquiries, collected materials from the researchers, prepared copies, found reliable people to carry the papers to Australia. Among those who assisted me in the research — which, besides ordinary archival and library references, often included preparation of handwritten copies — are Professor Aleksandr Ia. Massov, Zaiara Veselaia, Dr Anton Valdine, Natalia M. Iudenich, Dr Olga Artemova, Sergei V. Chernov, Professor Boris A. Starkov, Dr Stanislav Dumin, Dr Galina Kanevskaia, and (at the Russian State Library) Nadezhda Ryzhak. I also owe deep appreciation to the enthusiastic support of Valentina Provodina, director of a tiny local museum in the village of

ACKNOWLEDGEMENTS

Turki (Saratov province), situated near the village where Nikolai Ilin, one of the heroes of my research, was born.

I am deeply grateful to my husband, Professor Vladimir Kabo — the first reader of, and advisor on my drafts. His interest in my research, his professional, moral and financial support were essential during all these years.

My son Ralphie Kabo shared with me my fieldwork in Queensland when he was four years old, and, I hope, has learned a lot from our trip, once even being privileged to hear the myth of the Rainbow Serpent from Ngadjon Aboriginal elder Jessie Calico at the very spot in the Ngadjon country where it is believed the events of the myth took place. He and his young Aboriginal friends, to whom this book is dedicated, are to build the new Australia free from racial prejudice and thus fulfil Leandro Illin's dream.

PICTURE CREDITS

~

I owe a debt to the generosity of the descendants of Nicholas and Alexandra in Australia, in Honduras and in the United States of America, who have made available to me the photographs of their family for use in this book.

All photographs of Nicholas and Alexandra and their descendants in this book (apart from my own photographs, taken in 1996) are held in the possession of family members in the different branches of the family, who have provided them and given permission for their use here: the Hoolihan family, the respective Illin families, the Mackay family, the Smallwood family; in particular, Flora Hoolihan, Ernie Hoolihan, Maud Hoolihan, Richard Hoolihan Jnr, Glenda Illin, Leandro Illin Jnr, Vera Ketchell, Somerled Mackay Jnr, Essie Morganson.

Other illustrations have been collected from various sources, and are credited separately.

~

The Sail

A lone white sail shows for an instant
Where gleams the sea, an azure streak.
What left it in its homeland distant?
In alien parts what does it seek?

The billows play, the mast bends, creaking,
The wind impatient moans and sighs ...
It is not joy that it is seeking,
Nor is it happiness it flies.

The blue waves dance, they dance and tremble,
The sun's bright rays caress the seas.
And yet for storm it begs, the rebel,
As if in storm lurked calm and peace! ...

~

Mikhail Lermontov 1832
(translated by Irina Zheleznova)

INTRODUCTION

~

The most astonishing things are those that actually happen.
There is nothing more surprising or improbable than real life.

E.T.A. Hoffmann

Derek, a young man with an open smile, black curly hair and dark skin, on coming to our place in Canberra introduced himself: 'Nicholas Illin was my Russian great-great-grandfather'. Nicholas Illin (1852–1922), a Russian intellectual, and his son Leandro (1882–1946), who emigrated to Australia in 1910, had been the subjects of my research for some time already. This encounter with Derek was the result of my attempt to trace their descendants in Australia. It was a real surprise to me to discover that these descendants, because Leandro's wife was an Aboriginal woman, consider themselves Aborigines. At our first meeting I told Derek about my studies and plied him with questions. He, an urban Aboriginal, a cook from Townsville, told me what he knew. He did not preserve any 'Russianness' and had only vague knowledge of Russian history and the circumstances of Nicholas's life in Russia and his emigration; Derek even mixed up tales about Nicholas and Leandro. From the point of view of academic history his tales were far from the 'facts' on which a 'serious' historian is supposed to rely: 'Leandro sang the

French anthem on the street in Russia, someone has warned him that he could be arrested for that and he had to flee. He left for Southern America alone at eleven. He wrote to his parents and they came to him ...'.

But then Derek suddenly said something which — I felt — has been preserved in their Aboriginal family for generations as a sacred belief: 'My great-grandad Leandro taught his children to be proud, he told that all the people, black and white, are equal; he taught us to help the downtrodden and underprivileged and to distinguish between right and wrong'. It struck me like lightning — this simple philosophy was the essence of the credo of the Russian intelligentsia. The difference was that while Russian intellectuals seldom managed to apply this philosophy for the practical benefit of the people, the Illin family seemed to provide me with the results extending over the period of a century of the practical implementation of these ideas. In Leandro's marriage to an Aboriginal woman and his raising of an Aboriginal family, at a time when racist attitudes in Australia were not only prevalent but enshrined institutionally, we see just one aspect of these ideas being put into practice by one man. Indeed, this philosophy had a remarkable practical application: in helping this family to live with dignity and self-respect through those harsh years. And among the descendants of this family mythologisation of their ancestors' deeds seemed to have played an essential part in this process. Parting with Derek that day, I realised that my respect for facts alone, that my traditional view of history as the analysis of the 'facts' belonging to the past, had cracked. Facts seemed to mix with myth here and both shaped the present and the future.

The life of their Russian ancestor, Nikolai Dmitrievich Ilin, or Nicholas Illin as he subsequently called himself, as it can be traced now from the available sources, is an amazing combination of fact and myth. Born into a provincial family of a military nobleman, he came to destroy its century-old traditions. Instead of pursuing a military or civil career he, from his youth, was obsessed with the ideas of truth and justice. But his passionate nature, as I see it now, never allowed him to realise his ideas in full. Often he, with his moral extremism, went too far in his fight for 'the truth'; then, to escape from his endless failures, he as 'a hunted wolf', in his own words, would rush from one end of the globe to another — from St Petersburg to the United States of America, to Turkestan, to St Petersburg, to the United States of

America again, back to St Petersburg, then to Argentina, Patagonia, Australia, Colombia, and finally Honduras — patching, in his imagination, the rough material of life with his idealistic vision of himself and of the surrounding world. And in this dizzy flight, which lasted for over fifty years — a flight from himself, I believe — he would be followed by his only true supporters: his wife and children. They would preserve their own truth of him, which might contradict the 'facts'; they would pass it on to their children and grandchildren. And they, the Australian Aborigines and the Central American Hondurans, in turn further developed this combination of truth and myth in the light of their own traditional cultures.

Nicholas's personality is not simple by any means. The opinions of him are so polar that they hardly seem to relate to the same man. He himself believed that he possessed an 'extremely complaisant and always jovial disposition'. In his autobiographical prose and poetry he depicts himself as an idealistic fighter for truth and justice. His descendants — he has over three hundred of them scattered all over the world — remember him with love and pride. 'My grandfather, we called him *Deda*, was a very patient man and showed us much love, as my *Baba* (grandmother) did also. They both were just very, very nice people, very gentle, and very sweet' (Ellen [Nellie] Dale Flores, granddaughter, United States of America). 'He was enlightening the people, he was preaching too much what [the authorities] did not want the people to know' (Flora Hoolihan, granddaughter, Australia). 'My grandad Nicholas, he was a barrister of law, and a doctor, and a poetry writer' (Harry Illin, grandson, Australia). 'He was doctor in international laws, poet, writer, jurist and journalist' (Sam Mackay, great-grandson, Honduras).[1]

His Russian contemporaries had quite a different attitude towards Nicholas: 'a strange dreamer', 'cheat or psychopath', 'nasty wretch' (Ilia Repin, the famous artist); 'petty creature corroded with vanity and an aspiration for European fame', 'morally deformed personality' (anonymous critic); 'I think that he is not only a wrong man, but simply insane, he is ill, there is no other explanation for such muddle-headedness in his enterprises' (Nikolai Ge, the artist). Leo Tolstoy also considered him to be a lunatic, adding that 'in lunacy, as in intoxication, what was concealed before becomes apparent'.[2]

Modern Russian scholars consider him 'an easily carried-away schemer', 'vulgar and mean-spirited person', and they all suspect that gain was a driving force behind his actions.[3] Nicholas did not leave indifferent even my Russian research assistants, who hand-copied his writings for me from the Russian archives. 'He provoked a mixed reaction in me, first I felt that I would not have the psychological strength to figure out the essence of all the affairs of such a, to put it mildly, nervously depressed and immoderate man but then I became keen on him and even felt compassion towards him ... How well I know this type of a Russian male failure who struggles through life and is never able to evaluate the situation adequately. ... Still one can envy his persistence and courage. But poor, poor family!' (Olga Artemova). Another could not help commenting on the margins of his transcripts of Nicholas's texts: 'He must be fibbing here', 'He must have invented this, it cannot be true'.

The facts of his life suggest that he was an extremely impulsive man, who constantly got into conflicts and troubles, and several times had to start from scratch, being a gambler both in the literal and figurative meaning of the word — a gambler driven by passions and ideas. Obviously he was prone to hyperbole, but, unlike many Russian intellectuals who were apt to condemn him, his rhetoric was followed by action and the main achievements of his stormy life were his work-hardened hands and his children, who carried out his ideas in real life.

The more facts and judgements I received about Nicholas Illin, the more difficult it was for me to tell where the truth was. The hero was not just double-faced or poly-faced. He was something different. To my frustration, the truth did not emerge from the analysis of the hero as a historical personality. And then, reading his autobiography, with its skilfully placed emphases and omissions, I was struck by a thought that was both simple and a paradox. What he has left behind for us — his deeds, writings, and other people's memories of him — is not a heap of chance materials in which the historian's task is to separate the truth from myth and lie. It needs a quite different approach. He was a writer. Well, a strict literary critique would say that Illin was a failed writer. That is true but, nevertheless, he did leave one literary masterpiece — his own life, an elaborate combination of fact and fiction. If his life is considered as a literary work, then everything fits together. Such an approach opens an avenue to study the story of Nicholas Illin and his family, giving equal respect to historical documents, to the family tales of his Aboriginal and Honduran descendants, and to his own literary and biographical writings. For over two centuries in this family the historical 'facts' have been continually cycled through literature and myth, enriching the real lives of succeeding generations of family members with the creation of a history in which myth and fact have become intertwined in a rich background tapestry, continually evolving to this day.

Indeed, does not what we believe to be the truth of our past and present, the 'facts', have elements of myth? These elements are in our attitudes to the past, to our ancestors; they are in our shaping of the present for our descendants. It is not correct to treat these elements of myth as simple distortions, as faults of memory; they have their own value responding to the most essential needs of our soul, sorting out from the flow of historical events the facts that are most important from the point of view of the myth's creators and recipients.

The balance between myth and fact in the life of one man, in a family history, is only a particular instance of the balance between fact and myth in history in general. European historical tradition pretends to objectivity, considering that the only trustworthy research is research based on so-called historical facts and documents. But the objectivity of historical facts and documents, of historical memory, is an open problem itself. It is obvious now that whole fields of history written in the past and believed to be trustworthy have turned out to be mythologised, ideologised or presented from various particular positions, such as a Eurocentric one, or a racist one, or a male-oriented one, and so on. Now modern historians revise them: take, for instance, the history of the colonisation of Australia or Siberia. But who can be sure that historians of the future will not disdain the honest, modern historical writings as yet another myth? This mythologisation seems to be an inevitable process, and I believe that myth has its own value, being an essential part of history. In a way myth has the same reality as fact, but it is a spiritual reality. As the construct of collective consciousness, myth is just as much objective fact as so-called historical fact. History based on myth (for instance, Aboriginal Dreaming) and history based on documented fact (the European tradition, for example) are two parallel histories, each in its own right, and I would not despise either of them.

Using the word 'myth' in the field of a family history which deals with events not more than a couple of centuries ago, I certainly do not claim that this type of 'myth' is as developed as the classical myths of antiquity. What I describe as a 'myth' is the result of mythologisation of recent history. I believe that 'myth' is a more relevant expression here than 'legend', as, amazingly, these 'myths' are constructed in accordance with the essential patterns of ancient myths. For instance, ancestors assume features of typical cultural heroes, possess dual natures, conquer evil, or perform journeyings which, in traditional society, would lead to the sacralisation of the landscape (see 'The czarina's goblet' and 'The Russian cultural hero in the Australian landscape' in this book).

My research into the Illin family is an attempt to learn how myth and fact interweave in the lives of ordinary people through several generations and how their ethnic traditions might colour their historical memory. It also tells how a life considered to be a failure in one sense became, owing to a myth, a victory in the future. At the centre of the book is a comparison between two principal characters: Nicholas Illin, who seemed to surround himself with 'ideas' and legends, and his son Leandro, who put these ideas into practice, and thus gave grounds for the creation of the new myths.

The diversity of my sources has determined the genre of the book: at times it is a historical, anthropological or literary study; at times, a documentary novel. It is polyphonic: the voices of several generations of the Illins — a Russian intellectual, a Russian-Australian labourer, an outback Aboriginal girl, and the new generation of Aboriginal intellectuals — all mingle with one another to convey to the reader the unique experience of this family.

* * *

I embarked on this research not knowing what I might meet on the way. In July 1996 I visited Queensland following in the tracks of Nicholas and his family, and met the numerous descendants of Leandro. They, and especially Flora Hoolihan, his eldest daughter, shared with me the wealth of family tales of their Russian and Aboriginal ancestors. Flora who, having grown up in the outback, never went to school and could hardly read English, let alone Russian, preserved through the years of her wandering life as her most treasured possession part of Leandro's archives, including Russian manuscripts of her grandfather Nicholas. The other part of the archives travelled for years around Queensland with the family of Leandro's son Richard Illin, and I gained access to it on the Atherton Tablelands, where the Illins started their farm in 1910 and from where Leandro's Aboriginal wife Kitty came. They knew how to preserve their past.

Then, full of impressions and family tales, I started the hunt for facts in Russian and Australian archives and libraries. I aimed to verify each word of the family tales by facts and thus to understand the laws according to which these tales have been created. Even for me, who grew up in Russia and knew the research world there, obtaining the Russian materials was a hard job. Living in Australia since 1990, I could not visit Russia myself and I had no money to pay Russian archives for the research. All my hopes rested on the help of my Russian colleagues and friends. At times, when one attempt after another failed and months of fruitless waiting turned into years, I began to suspect that the materials concerning Nicholas were enchanted, that he did not want us to dig further for 'the truth'. And in some cases I had to give up, leaving open the question 'what was the truth'. But my Russian search did bring considerable results and, besides the copies of Nicholas's numerous writings, I made a lucky acquaintance with Valentina Provodina, the head of the local museum in Turki, not far from the village of Ilinka, where Nicholas was born. There are plans now to open an exhibition in the museum devoted to him and thus to reunite him with his countryfolk, in the name of whom he conducted his struggle 'for the people'. The names of all my numerous helpers in Russia are listed in the acknowledgements.

Nicholas Illin left descendants, not only in Australia, but in Honduras (Central America), where his son Romelio (1886–1976) and daughter Ariadna (1890–1971) founded large families, numbering over a hundred descendants, and in the United States of America, where some of those descendants have moved (in Appendix 1 at the end of the book most family members referred to in the course of this book are listed by name, with a brief note on their place in the family to help identification; a separate Appendix contains family trees). The recollections of these Honduran descendants, family tales, and some documentary evidence and photographs contributed considerably to this book, too. Unfortunately, I had no opportunity to visit this part of the family and thus, inevitably, the account of their life cannot be as thorough as that of the Australian side.

Most rewarding was my painstaking research in Australian archives and libraries, which enabled me to tell in detail the story of Nicholas's son Leandro — the second hero of the book. I first read about him nearly twenty years ago in Russia, when I had just started my studies of Russians in Australia; I read a 1912 Russian newspaper account of Leandro's trip to the Northern Territory to explore it as a potential place for a Russian colony. The article did not give his name and was just signed 'N.Il.'. Who could foresee then that one day, in Australia, I would discover the manuscript of Leandro's travel diary for this very trip in 1912! Then came dozens of his letters to the authorities in connection with the treatment of his Aboriginal family and other Aborigines, his numerous contributions to the *North Queensland Register* and the *Herbert River Express*. Leandro, who throughout his Australian life was nothing more than a labourer and who died in oblivion, turned out to hide under, what he called, his 'ungainly appearance' the talent of an outstanding democratic writer of whom Australia can be proud.

But Leandro was more than a writer; he was a remarkable character as well, copy and opposite of his father at the same time. Although both were guided by the same ideas, the life of each of them went differently and Leandro, unlike his father, managed to put those ideas into practice. While Nicholas was a public servant and a St Petersburg lawyer, Leandro became a 'bush lawyer' in the best meaning of the word and a people's councillor. While Nicholas aspired to change the whole world, Leandro accepted life as it was. While Nicholas carried his family through five continents, Leandro stayed with his family in one area. The story of Leandro's family does not fit into the pattern of a traditional family history, telling who married whom, and where they lived. It is the story of a family whose genesis was in the love of two people from different sides of the globe — the Russian man Leandro and the Ngadjon Aboriginal Kitty Clarke — but it is more than that, too. It is also the story of a family that emerged out of Leandro's passionate belief in the forthcoming universal brotherhood of people and his courage in defending the principles of honesty and justice. He needed this courage throughout his life — to endure the battles with the officials to protect Kitty from deportation to a reservation and to marry her at a time when such marriages were prohibited by the authorities; to part forever from his own parents in order not to separate his Aboriginal stepson from his mother Kitty; to raise six young Aboriginal children in outback Queensland after Kitty's tragic death; to struggle for the rights and dignity of his children and all Aborigines whom he met throughout all these years, till his death in 1946. And day after day he, a lonely fighter, discredited and crushed by the authorities, would rise again and again, struggling for justice and literally saving the honour — I am not afraid of this word — of the Australian nation when it was still suffering outbursts of racial prejudice whether it was towards Russians, or Aborigines, or Italians.

The events of the past were not the only aspect of my research. More and more I became captivated by the modern life of Leandro's Aboriginal descendants — their ethnic self-identification, their connections with their Aboriginal past, their attitudes to their European ancestors. Even though in this book I often refer to the members of the Illin family as Aborigines, the reality is more complex. They might consider themselves as people with Aboriginal descent rather than as 'Aborigines'; or, as Glenda Illin, Leandro and Kitty's granddaughter, recently told me: 'I am I'.

But what most impressed me in this family was their everlasting aspiration for justice, which they had inherited from Leandro and Nicholas. Several of them have stood at the cradle of the movement for Aboriginal rights in Queensland since the 1960s and some occupy important positions in different Aboriginal organisations, and they now constitute the new generation of the indigenous intelligentsia. It is symbolic that even Eddie Mabo — one of the most important figures in modern Australian history — was 'awakened' years ago by Leandro's Aboriginal son-in-law Richard Hoolihan. The seeds sown into Australian soil by the Illins, these Russian rebels, have yielded their first crop ...

IN SEARCH OF THE HERO

HERO AND ANTI-HERO

From early morning Ilinka, the country seat of the Ilin family, has been full of excitement. Two girls have come from the village to help the old cook with the meals, and several others are cleaning the house. The wine cellar has been opened, and Evgenia, Kolia's mother, with the help of the gardener Efim, is choosing flowers for her dress and to decorate the rooms of the house. Kolia, a four-year-old fair-haired boy, has been dressed up this morning in white pantaloons with laces and a blue frock with embroidery and warned not to go down to the river.

Ilinka, with its abundant, fertile park extending down the slope towards this river, stands almost lost among the endless fields and meadows of the southern Russian black-earth belt, the steppe. There was an orchard, too, descending in terraces down to the river-banks. The river has a frightening name, Shcherbedina, but for Kolia it was the kingdom of frogs, tadpoles, and dragonflies. Kolia liked to play there although the best fun he had was watching the village boys — just a bit older than he was — drive the flocks of ducks with their ducklings down to the water and, taking off their pants and smocks, splash around in the river looking for crayfish or trying to catch fish with a wicker-trap. Oh, Ilinka had so much — even Kolia's favourite champignons, grown in the hothouse.

Never mind about not being able to go down to the river. Today Kolia has found lots to interest him in the house instead — the mysterious, cool darkness of the wine cellar; the songs that the maids sing, cleaning the house; the radiant excitement of his *mamenka* Evgenia. But the best moment of all is when Dmitrii, his *papenka* (dad), having finished giving orders to the servants, sits down in the rocking chair on the veranda with his pipe and Kolia can immediately climb up and claim his attention. Sometimes on such occasions *papenka* would tell him about their ancestor Dmitrii who burnt the Turkish fleet, or about his own father, Nikolai, Kolia's grandfather, who fought Napoleon and lost his arm in the Battle of Borodino in 1812. Or he might — a delightful moment! — allow Kolia to touch the weapons hanging on his study wall, while telling him about his first battle with the Turks. This was at Kulevcha in 1829, when he and his friend, both young cadets in charge of the standards of their detachment, by their own courage inspired their privates not to waver under the Turkish attack and the Russians finally won the battle.

But on this particular day *papenka* has decided to read Kolia the story of Columbus, from the *Universal Traveller*. Listening to the story, Kolia gazed as if enchanted at a coloured picture in the book — blue sea, white sails, yellow sand, green palms and dark natives surrounding Columbus. Could he have known that this land (later to be called Honduras) capturing his imagination now would one day become his own last resting-place? That his own descendants would mix with the descendants of the Indians and Spaniards pictured there?

Kolia is the first to spot a carriage on the road winding down below through the green meadows. This is their long-awaited visitor — a painter whom *papenka* has commissioned to paint their family portraits. In years to come this painting will preserve the excitement and solemnity of this day: Kolia standing by his *mamenka* on their sunny lawn ... the smell of the oil paints ... his effort to stand still.

The painter, although no more than a provincial artisan, has managed to catch the most important feature in Evgenia's face — her strength of mind. Not even the attributes of feminine refinement — the soft folds of her elegant morning dress, her bonnet adorned with flowers, a tender rose in her hand — it seems, were able to change this impression of fortitude. It was this fortitude, after all, that had brought her, the daughter of noble Polish counts, to this god-forsaken spot. Her fortitude and love.

On that day years ago in Poland she had stood on the balcony of their house while the Russian Elizavetgrad Hussar regiment was riding through the town. How united, strong and brave they seemed to be! The hussars resplendent in their blue jackets braided with rows of golden cords and buttons, and white, fur-edged pelisses slung over their shoulders, and their high, white busbies, with shining sabres and carbines, and white field-kits emblazoned with the czar's crown. Their thoroughbred horses decorated with blue broadcloth saddles and tassels.

She noticed Dmitrii Ilin at once. He was at the head of his detachment, sitting on the horse as if glued there. And then he smiled up at her and she waved back and at that moment she already knew that if he called her to go with him she would go. She would go even though her family looked upon the Russians as invaders who had partitioned her motherland. They had crushed the Polish uprising in 1831, when she was a child. And long before that, in 1812 her father, Colonel Count Jan Potocki, had joined Napoleon Bonaparte's army when he invaded

Russia. This time, in 1848, the Russians were passing through on their way to crush the revolution in Hungary.

Despite all this, she would go with this man if only he would come for her. And he came. They both knew, however, that her family would never let her marry a Russian. So, she did what her favourite heroines from novels did — she eloped with Dmitrii and later secretly married him.

Almost 150 years later her great-granddaughter Nellie relates what happened. 'The story is that she sent the maid to look for some strange-coloured sugar; the woman did, and that gave her a lot of time to pack up some things and go off with lieutenant Ilin.'

Whatever happened after that, she was too proud to complain and her fortitude — which she will need soon now, very soon — never deserted her. Following the premature death of her husband Dmitrii, when Kolia is just six, she will call on this fortitude to survive and to raise her beloved boy. But all that is still to come. For now, Kolia, his head golden in the sun, stands beside her gravely watching the painter.

The painter depicted Kolia as a little adult, in the style usual for a provincial portrait of the time. Even Kolia's blue frock with its belt echoes in colour, fashion and decoration his father's hussar uniform. Was not it about himself that the adult Kolia would write years later: 'A five-year-old child with the carriage and manners of a self-possessed adult dandy — such is the ideal modern child'. The serious expression on his face is not like a child's, and only the tilt of his little fair head gives an impression of delicacy, while the hoop he grasps in his hand tells us that he is supposed to be a boy.

The wheel of this boy's life will turn, like the revolutions of the hoop in his hand, and sixty-five years later it will bring him to the other end of the globe, to the bank of a nameless, dried-up creek, which later will become known as Illin's Gully. There, on another sunny day like this one, his dark grandsons Ginger, Dick and Tom, his Australian Aboriginal grandsons, will be running up and down a bush track bowling a wheel, just like the way he used to bowl his hoop. But, barefoot, scantily dressed, sleeping on dry grass in a humpy, these boys will have nothing, in comparison with what he had at their age. He was a young landlord, an owner of dozens of human souls; despite that, they will be richer — they will have freedom. And, watching them there, he will realise that these boys playing and laughing on this bush track are his main achievement in life. The wheel of fortune, the roulette wheel, the wheel of life ... Indeed, nearly all his life will lie between these two sunny days in Ilinka and Illin's Gully.[1]

On that sunny day in Ilinka nobody would have suspected that Kolia, this delicate boy who poses with such a solemn expression for the family portrait, has come into this family, not to continue the family traditions but to break with them, to be the last landlord of Ilinka; that his coming into this family has been in order to expiate the sins of his forefathers ...

* * *

Nikolai Dmitrievich Ilin (or Kolia), later known as Nicholas Illin, one of the heroes of our story, was born on 27 November (9 December) 1852 in the village of Ilinka in Balashov district, Saratov province, halfway between Tambov and Saratov.[2] His ancestors — hereditary military noblemen — had moved here from Tambov province by the 1790s.[3] Ilinka, named after them, was their family estate and had over a hundred serfs. The serfs had to work for their landlords for half of the week, in exchange for strips of land and communal pasture their land-lords provided for their use.

The Ilins' estate was its own world. Evgenia maintained a distance between Kolia and the peasants. She never forgot that 'she was an aris-tocrat and always acted like that, like she was better than anybody', according to her great-granddaughter Nellie. Dmitrii's sudden death seemed to prove that Evgenia's decision to break with her family was a mistake, but there was no going back; she had Kolia to take care of, and there was the estate to look after and preserve for him. She was still very young and before long had married a neighbour, a local landlord, who Kolia described as 'a hardly literate and rough person'.

This marriage further contributed to his spiritual separation from his mother, although that began earlier. He had grown up dreamy, impressionable, hot-tempered, and lonely. Evgenia understood him well, better than he understood himself, and she foresaw the dangers which would await him in adult life. But the only way she knew to deal with this was for him to be brought up *comme il faut*, that is, to behave properly, according to the conventions of their class and time. And she recognised that he would not do this unless he was compelled to. In bringing up Kolia she tried to combine two approaches: that of the mother and that of a father, whom the stepfather could not replace. It

did not work out, giving neither the degree of security that he expected from a mother, nor the acceptance of authority that Kolia's father
could have instilled. There was no happy childhood full of the romance
of the old country-house. His later verdict was harsh: 'My mother was
a woman of little education; she loved me a lot, but by her despotic
nature and unreasonable upbringing she gave a wrong direction to my
development'.[4] It might be that the key to his further misadventures
was hidden in his relationship with her. And from his childhood came
his thirst for equality in love, for love without fear, which he did not
enjoy as a boy. It would take him years to find a woman who fulfilled
these aspirations.

When the time came to study, as there was no proper school nearby, Kolia was sent to Tambov, nearly 200 kilometres away, which meant
several days' journey in a horse-drawn troika, to the sound of its bell
tinkling continuously as they travelled through the woodlands and
across the steppe. After the spaciousness and village pleasures of Ilinka,
and mixing there with people who, although branded by his mother as
inferior, were spontaneous and natural, Kolia found himself in the quite
different world of the Russian provincial town.

Flora Hoolihan, Kolia's Aboriginal granddaughter has preserved a
keepsake of that time, which has survived miraculously. It is a photograph of a middle-aged man and on the reverse side there is a faded
inscription: 'To dear friend and comrade Nikolai Ilin with fond memories from his cordially affectionate ...' — but the signature was impossible to decipher with certainty. Months later, browsing through
Chekhov's plays, I came across a photograph of Chekhov with a group
of actors. The face of one of them, V.N. Davydov, seemed strangely
familiar. I returned to Flora's photo — indeed, it was him, and the half-
obliterated letters of the signature finally formed into the words 'Ivan
Gorelov (stage-name Davydov)'. Vladimir Davydov (1849–1925) was a
famous Russian actor who made his name performing in plays by
Chekhov and Tolstoy and in other classics. He and Nikolai Ilin became
friends while studying in Tambov, when Davydov was still Ivan
Gorelov. After graduating from school, their lives followed different
paths: Gorelov travelled the roads of Russia performing in provincial
theatres, while Nikolai rushed about between St Petersburg, America
and Central Asia in search of truth. One cold winter's day in 1886,
twenty years after leaving Tambov, they embraced each other in St
Petersburg and exchanged photos ...

The Tambov they had known in the 1860s was a gloomy place, according to Davydov, who later wrote of the town: 'Tambov depressed me. ... The town was sinking in thick mud. ... The street lamps, sunk to one side and never lighted, were the town's only decoration. The boredom in the town was inconceivable. ... Tambov dwellers spent all their free time, every evening, playing cards and gossiping. There was no library and no permanent theatre there.'[5]

Tambov School was a *gimnaziia*, a select school for boys from the privileged classes. It was supposed to provide a thorough education in such diverse subjects as literature, history, Western languages (French and German), Latin, mathematics, and natural sciences.

Still, Nikolai's opinion of it was quite low: 'I was the top pupil in all grades, but I received relatively little knowledge at the school, let alone any spiritual development, in spite of the fact that I graduated from the school with the gold medal. From the fourth grade I had been showing the teacher of literature piles of my writings, but the old man read my notebooks very seldom and just automatically gave me the highest mark in literature. It was practically impossible to get any guidance from him for my literary writings as he, being eighty years old, hardly moved, and, moreover, was rarely sober.'

Nikolai by no means exaggerated. Davydov develops this picture even further.

'I FOUND MYSELF IN A BEDLAM', says Davydov, 'bearing the name of Tambov School. ... In my time it was the receptacle of everything bad and its ways were those of a seminary, although it was mainly noblemen's children who studied there. ... The premises were terribly cramped, dirty, and damp. ... The director of the school, the good soul Artiukhov, was spineless and that is why there was no discipline at all. The teachers, schoolboys, and under-teachers did what they wanted. Anyone who felt like it, would steal. ... We hardly learnt anything at all there. There were no teaching aids, there was nothing to read, no homework. The hubbub in classes was such that even if one wanted to pick up and learn something it would be impossible. ... We grew up left to our own devices, but with a good knowledge of life.'

Nikolai, however, was deprived even of this school of real life. In his autobiography he wrote: 'At home I was under the constant supervision of my aunt, an old maid, who vigorously opposed my acquaintance or exchange of ideas with anyone at all. I knew only textbooks and the small shop-library of a certain Shemaev. It had a few hundred predominantly ridiculous books and while I studied at the school I read literally all of them.'[6]

It took me quite a long time to learn how misleading it could be applying a stereotyped pattern for a reconstruction of the actual past of such a character as Nikolai Ilin. For instance, from reading the brief outline of his biography in a biographical dictionary I was nearly led astray into seeing his early years as those of a 'typical' youth of this epoch. Thus, 'graduated from Tambov School with gold medal' suggested an aspiration to knowledge and a perfect education. 'Joined Medical and Surgical Academy in St Petersburg' — this suggested he, like other progressive young people of that time, wanted a practical education which would allow him to serve his people. 'Became involved in a student conflict and had to leave for America' without finishing his course in the Academy[7] — this surely must have been to escape arrest after involvement in radical student activities. The Academy was a notorious hotbed of the revolutionary student movement, and many of its students suffered persecution by the authorities. My imagination, then, was ready to identify him with a doctor-revolutionary like Bazarov, hero of Turgenev's *Fathers and Sons* (1862). Luckily, I was stopped by Nikolai himself, who, in his autobiography, created a quite different outline of his personality, which provided a new dimension to these facts.

'MY MOTHER WARNED ME BEFORE I TOOK THE SCHOOL-LEAVING EXAMINATIONS [in 1868] that if I did not get the gold medal for coming first I should not dare to return home. I received the medal but attended the exams with a revolver in my pocket, in case of failure. After the graduation my mother asked me what I felt a vocation for and in which higher educational establishment I intended to study. I had asked myself this question several times already but had no answer. In other words, although I had a lot of knowledge in different areas, the school did not arouse in me any inclination towards a particular field of study.

'But I had to choose something and, buying a book with the programs and rules of entry of all the higher educational establishments of Russia, I chose the Medical and Surgical Academy only because the entrance examinations there began two weeks later than in the universities. This allowed me to stay longer in the country and enjoy the autumn hunting season. Thus I, a passionate hunter, could catch the autumn passage of the woodcock. It had a decisive effect on my whole life, as I could not overcome my antipathy to medical studies and I did not graduate, either from the Academy, or from any other higher educational establishment. The problem was not only my aversion to medicine, but the fact that I had grown up as if in a monastery, in complete isolation from any social life, and as soon as I went to St Petersburg I joined a group of reckless youths and spent my time extremely frivolously. As a result, I got involved in a minor student conflict and left for the United States.'

We never find out what this 'minor student conflict' was about. In Nikolai's autobiographical novel *In the New Land* Aleksei Silin (Nikolai Ilin's double) will remember this misadventure even more dramatically: 'The first years of student life were unfortunately terminated by a *flight* abroad. Then followed a back-breaking, unaccustomed struggle in the new country for the daily piece of bread, the news of an opportunity to return home, and the touching meeting at the railway station with his mother who for a time had *thought her son had perished for ever* [emphasis added].'

And then these events, as if resurfacing through 125 years of the past, came to me as they are remembered now by Nikolai's granddaughter Flora.

'MY GRANDFATHER STUDIED A BIT TO BE A DOCTOR, TOO. He did not want to be a doctor. They said that to be operating or cutting a finger you've got to be smoking. And that's what he did not want to do. He did not want to smoke.

'Well, he used to gamble. He must have had plenty of money. There was a story my father used to talk about — I don't know where it was, I was too young to remember — but, my grandad used to gamble, big, father reckoned. And this fellow came and gave some money to him to hold, and he came back and he wanted this money back, or, maybe my grandfather lent the money to this fellow. Anyway, he said he will report grandfather for being a moneylender or something, he wanted to get him into trouble. Grandfather picked up the money, in an iron box it was, and was going to hit him with the box. And then he thought quickly: "Better not. I'll be up for murder." And he gave the money back.'[8]

At last the pieces of his life seem to be coming together. But we will be wrong again if we take at face value these images he projects — that of the lonely, provincial youth suffocating without spiritual development at the rudimentary school, or of a village lad preferring hunting to all other vocations, or of a city fast-liver obsessed with gambling. Nikolai had just started his masterpiece, his life; he had just begun his life-long game of hide-and-seek with the future, and again the pendulum swings in the opposite direction.

This time Nikolai does it through his first book *Six Months in the United States of North America*, in which he told about his misadventures there in 1872. He was just nineteen then, but what a mature observer this youth turned out to be. To write as he did in that book one needs to be much more than a school swot, or a hunter, or a reckless gambler. Well, recklessness there was — 'blood rushed to my head, anger enveloped me ... nervously I clenched the axe-handle', he would write about his second day in America, when he nearly killed his employer on discovering how ruthlessly this man had swindled him. But recklessness was maybe all that this youth had in common with this other self that emerged from all those other stories. Plus, of course, the unclear cause of his flight to America. All the rest was different.

Nikolai travelled to America with his friend S., a passionate, handsome Georgian with long, curly hair, dressed in a red Russian shirt, an outstanding wrestler and gymnast, who had studied previously in the Academy of Arts in St Petersburg. Joining a flood of immigrants, they went via Hamburg, Hull, and Liverpool to New York. All the world seemed to be on the move. Watching these people, Nikolai made independent judgements on different national characters; comparing the English with the Americans, Germans and Irish, he pondered on how much the success of each group in America had to do with its national values and national character. His judgements, no matter how critical they were, were never racist, nor did he generalise about any one group as a result of bad experiences. For instance, many émigrés leaving Russia were preyed upon by Jewish criminal elements but Nikolai, unlike many of his compatriots, did not prejudge all Jews even though he was duped by Jewish crooks more than once.

Obviously, Nikolai was no provincial greenhorn who had read nothing more than 'ridiculous' books from Shemaev's library in Tambov. (Incidentally, according to the Tambov School's report, its library numbered over a thousand volumes.) He came to America expecting to find the dreamland of his schooldays — a 'country of savannas, *llanos*, virgin forests, bisons, caimans, jaguars and rattlesnakes', a country of redskins and courageous hunters, a country about which he 'just could dream as of something forbidden, inaccessible'. At the same time, however, he exhibits a profound awareness of diverse social and political issues, being particularly influenced by Eduard Tsimmerman, the Russian traveller, who praised to the skies American social and economic progress. And when at last the American shore loomed on the horizon Nikolai nearly wept with happiness.

Alas, he was to find neither of his Americas. Instead he and S. will be duped and brutally enslaved for two months by an American farmer, then duped again and again, and even stoned by a mob fired up by xenophobic bigotry. Finally, Nikolai himself will learn to lie to get a job and thus save from starvation several Russian youths living in a commune, with whom he shared a room in New York. That will be his most painful acquaintance with America's lower depths. Yet, in spite of all these misadventures, he will not condemn the country of his dreams. On the contrary, he will manage to see behind the ugly details in the foreground the significance of the background. He will accept America as it then was — with its swindlers, its capitalist exploitation, its ruthlessness towards the weak. His personal misadventures will not shatter his admiration for American principles of democracy, personal liberty, and reason, as well as for its immense technical achievements, its high standard of living, its good manners, and social and racial tolerance.[9]

Indeed, for a nineteen-year-old youth he exhibited significant maturity of mind together with an outstanding potential to become a writer or a scholar. Now at last we can see who Nikolai Ilin was in reality! But will we not be misled again if we accept this new image as the only truth? Have not all the images created by him of himself an equal right of existence in the masterpiece called his life? This masterpiece in which Nikolai as hero is interwoven with Nikolai as anti-hero — the real-life Nikolai with the double of his imagination.

* * *

Nikolai left America in August 1872 and went straight to Ilinka. He was leaving the St Petersburg of the Medical and Surgical Academy, and his student life far behind. His medical textbooks were piled into a trunk. For years to come they would travel with him all over the world until finally, washed up by a flood on the Burdekin River, they came to rest in 1927 in the Australian Never Never ...

The Ilinka he returned to was seemingly unchanged but he now looked at it with fresh eyes. The peasants' slab houses, dark under autumn rains, seemed to grow even deeper into the land. They clung to the banks of the Shcherbedina, close to each other. And their inhabitants, dressed in homespun hemp clothes in summer and sheepskin garments in winter, seemed like survivals from bygone centuries. Their one-room dwellings, in which the oven occupied nearly a quarter of the space, had tiny windows and on long winter nights were lit by burning a hemp wick dipped into oil. In winter they shared their living space with poultry, sheep, pigs, and cattle. The peasants were no longer serfs but emancipation did not seem to have improved their life at all. They lived in constant want in spite of their hard work and the fertility of the land (the black soil in this area was a metre deep). But their ploughing technique had not changed since ancient times — the plough (*sokha*) was basic, just a twisted tree-branch, pulled by a feeble horse. They grew rye, some oats, millet, wheat and buckwheat. After emancipation, although they were self-sufficient in terms of producing what they needed, they had to pay off their tiny plots of land to their former landlords and, as wages were low and they had few resources, these payments were an enormous burden for them. That led to a new type of enslavement, this time economic, to the local rich men.[10]

Nikolai settled in the Ilinka estate-house, in the same room where he lived as a child. The wheel of his life had made its first full turn. He knew his life had been unsuccessful so far: neither St Petersburg nor America had accepted him. But he was only twenty years old, and did not lose heart. He had a new project into which he could throw his energy. He would do what his family should have done long ago — fulfil his duty towards the peasants. For generations the toil of the peasants had subsidised the life-style of his family; it subsidised his education and life in St Petersburg, his travel to America. This change of attitude, which had been growing over recent years, was probably the most significant development within him at this time. He had encountered such notions in St Petersburg, where the air seemed to be permeated with ideas about the duty of the intelligentsia towards the people, towards the working classes. This was the cornerstone of *narodnik* (or Populist) ideology, and in the early 1870s many of the *narodnik*s were 'going to the people': settling in villages and working as teachers, doctors, or artisans, and at the same time 'enlightening' peasants, advocating the ideas of revolution and justice. Nikolai was not ready to take on the whole *narodnik* ideology, but its main idea of duty to the people captured his heart. He did not need to go far away to 'the people':[11] they, his former serfs, humble, oppressed, illiterate, were around him.

As soon as his mother allowed him to handle the affairs of their estate by himself he started his experiment, later described in his novel *In the New Land*. He, as his double Silin, 'the owner of a smallish estate, which he'd inherited, became possessed with the unrealisable idea — to raise peasants' wages in two or three nearby villages and thus liberate them from the oppression of the kulaks. The dream remained just a dream and Silin's money slipped into the iron-clad trunks of these very kulaks through the holey pockets of the peasants.' In *Songs of the Earth* Nikolai added that he soon quarrelled with all the nearby kulaks and had to leave.[12] This disappointment with the passivity of the Russian peasant Nikolai would feel throughout all his life but he would never blame the peasant alone, understanding that specific Russian conditions had created that type of character.

This was not the only thing, however, that would induce in him a sense of personal failure. Soon after his return to Ilinka Nikolai had started an affair with a peasant girl from Turki, a nearby village. Even though Nikolai was attempting to change the old ways in respect of the peasants, in starting this liaison he was little different from other Russian landlords. Some of these landlords, like Leo Tolstoy's heroes of *Resurrection* and *Devil* would later experience repentance, but some never bothered about the girl's fate. In October 1873 Nikolai's girl gave birth to their illegitimate son, registered as Ivan Gerasimovich Ivanov.[13] Nikolai obviously had no intention of marrying the girl — at around that same time he married his first wife. All he promised her was to take care of their son, which he did as far as he could. He never mentioned this story in his writings, but it obviously never left him: when, years later, in Australia, his son Leandro found himself in a similar situation and decided to marry an Aboriginal woman, Nikolai was the first to support him.

Nikolai's first marriage was *comme il faut*, that is, it was as befitted his station in life. His wife, a colonel's daughter, Vera (Verochka) Tomich, was a 'beautiful, smart, well-educated girl', according to how he describes her in his novel *In the New Land*, in which she appears under her real name. He also says in the novel that their fathers had served in the army together and that he had married her in order to rescue her from marriage to an old general. Whether this was true or not, their marriage — both in life and in the novel — failed in spite of the birth of their son Sergei.[14]

In the novel their growing apart is explained by the differences in their upbringing and world outlook. In real life there seems to have been a quite different cause, according to the way Nikolai's granddaughter, Nellie, tells it.

'FROM WHAT I UNDERSTAND, his first wife was unfaithful to him. A friend of his let him know that she was unfaithful, so he told her one day that he was going out of town for a couple of days and instead of that he returned in the morning and found her in bed with some man. My grandfather hired a detective to "find" him with a woman in a hotel room, so that the disgrace would not be on his wife for the divorce but on him. He protected her name. And so he was divorced from her.'[15]

For Nikolai this was a double failure: not only had his relationship with a proper lady broken down, but also his relationship with a peasant girl. He had not succeeded in leading a life *comme il faut*, as a landlord and a married man; but, equally, his attempts to fulfil his self-imposed duty towards the people also foundered, owing to his betrayal of this peasant girl and to his inability to defeat the kulaks.

Fearing that the anti-hero in him might take the upper hand, he found an unusual way to restore his peace of mind: to write his book *Six Months in the United States of North America* — about himself as an intellectual hero (never mind that there, too, he failed in his clash with real life!). But even that was not enough and Nikolai was soon searching for a way out of all Ilinka's tangles.

Suddenly a way out emerged. The authorities were looking for public servants to administer Central Asia, a vast territory newly conquered by Russia. It did not take him long to apply and in summer 1876 he left Verochka, but without formally divorcing her, and headed towards a new life. Hero was determined to win over anti-hero this time.

HERO AND HEROINE

The record of Nikolai's service in Turkestan does not say much about either hero or anti-hero.

MAY 1876
> enrolled into military-civil administration in Turkestan on the fourteenth [the lowest] rank.

OCTOBER 1876
> member of the commission enquiring into the state of Tashkent Public Library.

NOVEMBER 1876
    transferred to the Fergana region administration.
JUNE 1877–JANUARY 1879
    served as an official for the system of land tenure in the Fergana
    region.
JANUARY 1879–DECEMBER 1880
    a judicial investigator in the Margelan district.
JANUARY–JUNE 1881
    a clerk in the Syr Daria district board of administration.
FROM JUNE 1881
    a judicial investigator (temporary position) in Tashkent.
END 1881–SEPTEMBER 1882
    a clerk in the Syr Daria district board of administration.
SEPTEMBER 1882
    applied for retirement 'due to ruined health' and retired with the
    rank of provincial secretary [the twelfth, of fourteen ranks].

Six turbulent years of Nikolai's life are hidden behind the dry lines
of the official transcript of his service record, which were followed by
several more years spent in Tashkent. In his autobiography Nikolai was
very critical of his Turkestan period: 'There in the end I wasted the ten
best years of my early life, having nothing to read and no one to speak
to there. If I had any literary gift it was destined to disappear in such
conditions.' He would say the same in a poem: 'My absurd youth has
ruined all that had been sown in my heart'. Many years later in the
Patagonian mountains, reviewing his life, in his poem 'Confession' he
would ask forgiveness of the people (*narod*) for this page from his past:

I seek forgiveness for when, with that gang of officials,
        I was devouring what belongs to the people
            Despite realising such orgies
            Bring the people only suffering.[16]

But was this period of his life, under the emblem of the anti-hero, really wasted? That would only be half the truth; the other half is that this
was the maturing of the hero, both real and literary. From the young,
curious, though easily duped observer of life he turned into a fighter for
justice, a person guided by his noble ideals. He might finally leave
Turkestan defeated, but it would be as a real man, enriched with what

was most important in his life — his new wife, who was to become his lifelong friend, and their children. These years on the Russian frontier also supplied him with material for his major novel *In the New Land*, several short stories, and his long poem *The Orient Legend*.

To understand this new hero better we need to look at Turkestan as depicted in the pages of his novel *In the New Land*. A most depressing picture emerges. Russian 'civilisers' had invaded this new land with only one aim — to provide themselves with a regular, abundant illegal income from the natives and the public coffers alike. 'Evil in Turkestan became nearly the routine order of things, which none was ashamed of.' After the army's unnecessary cruelty towards the native people during the conquest, the so-called civilisers move in to corrupt them by involving them in shady schemes. The judicial system was no less corrupt and incompetent than the administration. All that was true and was depicted by his contemporaries as well, but Ilin in his novel went further; he revealed another side of life, one seldom discussed openly. As most of the officials and officers lived there without families, an air of licentiousness seemed to pervade the whole colony. And in the novel a monstrous gallery is unveiled before the reader. A school headmistress who trades in teenage girls to local debauchees. One of her clients, an engineer, when finally caught with his sixteenth girl-victim, is not condemned by public opinion and escapes punishment. A father using his young, motherless daughters as his own concubines. Officials acquiring, from the local inhabitants, young native boys or girls for sexual relations ... Dostoevsky's debauchees fade in the light of these villains. The only two positive characters, who try to expose the reigning lawlessness to the governor-general, end up either abandoning the struggle or getting killed. As for the governor-general himself, a nice old man (whose prototype was K.P. Kaufman) — in spite of his declaration that 'my doors are always open for the downtrodden', he has no power to confront the truth and instinctively hides from it.[17]

As the evil in the novel builds, we realise that a hero is required and eventually, in the middle of the novel, one does appear: Aleksei Silin, who seems to be an identical twin, or a double, of Nikolai Ilin. Indeed, this novel — one of Nikolai's best works — is strikingly autobiographical. Even though years later he would say: 'I wrote this novel driven by the need for money, preparing for each monthly issue over 100 pages and I worked without any plan, describing facts and events from memory'[18], the novel is more than just a reflection on the real-life events of his youth (as is usually the case with beginning writers). He seems purposely to give all the characters similar names to the real names of their prototypes as if, by fearlessly exposing evil, he intends some kind of public repentance for all their past sins; in all this he spares neither himself nor his wife, even occasionally going so far as to own up to some things that most probably only occurred in his dreams rather than in real life …

So, the hero, Aleksei Silin, a young man of twenty-five years, dressed in a white tunic and black trousers tucked into high hunting boots, enters the novel. Behind him, the boat trip up the Volga, the train to Orenburg and, finally, over 2000 kilometres of travel by mail carriage through the Asian steppe to Tashkent. Ahead, there is the new Orient — the world he is to conquer.

Yet, before long we discover that this young man with his 'quiet, pleasant voice, shy face and homely blue eyes' does not fit the image of the hero either: his fearless fight with a group of bandits in an ambush soon contrasts with the fear which grips him hunting for a tiger in the Syr Daria reedbeds. He, with his naïve belief that black is black and white is white, is too weak to change this world he has entered and he gradually gives in to the local ways of doing things. He learns not to be ashamed about receiving a salary for doing nothing; what's more, turning into an inveterate gambler, he is able to gamble away a month's salary in one go. And even all the disgraceful practices going on around him no longer seem to worry him.[19]

Still, there is one thing which allows Silin to resist totally submitting to this corrupt environment: the local people, whose way of life and language he becomes interested in and begins to study. The area of Tashkent and the Fergana valley was populated by farmers, so-called Sarts, descendants of Iranian and Mongolian tribes (now known as Uzbeks). Silin does not view them through rose-tinted glasses, however. It was a society with all the usual oriental, feudal vices. Its ruling élite behaved no differently from the Russian colonisers, in robbing its own people; their *sharia* (Islamic law) court hearings, for instance, seemed to Silin nothing more than a caricature of justice. The poor were infected with servility, the vice which especially sickened Silin, and, if circumstances allowed, easily became social parasites (such is the character of Omarka, who rises from being a slave to a powerful, unscrupulous boss). But Ilin/Silin managed to see beyond that. His spiritual revival began when, to escape the corrupting influence of the Russian colony in Kokand, he asked to be sent to the most remote Russian outpost, the native village of Aravan (Ravazan in the novel), on the slopes of the Tien Shan mountains.

Years later, confessing his 'tender love' for Turkestan and its people, Nikolai will write:

> These warm-hearted people
> Stirred my soul with their humbleness
> And, with their honesty and inexhaustible kindness,
> Have taught me to think more honestly.
>
> They found their spiritual source
> In the natural beauty of Turkestan
> While wise verses of the holy Koran
> Protected them from pernicious evil.[20]

Silin/Ilin conscientiously carried out his formal duties and took seriously the matters of land tenure and tax reform he had to deal with. Nikolai wrote in his autobiography: 'In Aravan, between hunting and playing cards, I thoroughly studied the economy of the local natives and submitted to the military governor of the region General [A.K.] Abramov a project for taxation reform'. The reform not only increased state profits but gave more justice to the poorest of the native peoples and involved the native people themselves in the valuation of their lands for tax purposes. After trials in two local areas, which he conducted, the reform was finally introduced in Turkestan but Silin/Ilin was not promoted as a reward; on the contrary, lacking the necessary qualities of an easy disposition and an ability to compromise, he was squeezed out of the 'System' by other officials, who treated him as an 'upstart'. He could not waive his principles; nor could he even share the philosophy of his colleague Stepanov, that one needs to accept compromise in less important issues in order to gain strength and achieve success in more important ones.[21] Silin/Ilin did not accept the first lesson that matters of the world cannot be seen as just black and white. And, what was even harder to take, at times it seemed to him that in this world there was no white left at all. This was a world of compromise, and worse — it was a yellow and brown world, the colours of the surrounding steppe and mountains, which, although different, seemed equally treacherous ...

The hero had to abandon his position, in which he had gained experience and success, and assume a totally new role of judicial investigator; but he did not stay long in this position either. Fighting for justice, Silin exceeded his commission and one day, in the absence of police, he killed a tough native criminal whom he was trying to catch red-handed. The powerful supporters of this criminal, who had penetrated into the Russian administration, achieved Silin's dismissal and further persecution.

Probably this was an autobiographical reference to Nikolai's own life. A vague family tale, as remembered by Sam Mackay, Nikolai's great-grandson, might relate to this episode. 'In St Petersburg it seems that Nikolai was a member of the police. I was told once that, while he was on duty, they had to go after a criminal who was resisting arrest and who was armed. Nikolai confronted the criminal and in order to protect his life, he used his weapon and killed the runaway. After this incident Nikolai had to hide since the criminal's family were well-off and had lots of influence.'[22]

Well, Nikolai's life in St Petersburg would have enough mysteries to contain this story as well. And, indeed, such an event could well have happened more than once ...

The reason for the haphazard character of Nikolai's service record now becomes clearer. After his dismissal Silin moves to Tashkent, and works as a private lawyer. By this time Silin is no longer a curious youth. He has turned into a fighter against injustice, and he, just as Nikolai Ilin had to, would have to flee Tashkent a few years later because of conflict with the local authorities.

But before we come to this final episode we must explore one more story. Neither Nikolai's life nor the novel would be complete without the heroine. And now she appears: the real Alexandra Konstantinovna Karlova and the imaginary heroine of the novel Alexandra Konstantinovna Karpova. Both are young and are called Sasha, a Russian diminutive name. Very little is known about the youth of the real Sasha. The personality of this woman, whom descendants remember only as an elderly, loving *Baba* (granny), seems to me no less a mystery than that of Nikolai himself. In years to come she would share with him Turkestan mud-houses, St Petersburg parlours, a Patagonian shepherd's hut, a humpy in the Australian jungle, cabins in dirty ships, a bed of grass by a camp-fire — from continent to continent, losing their children and raising their grandchildren, without reproach, through thick and thin, their life together would last till Nikolai's death-bed in Honduras.

Glenda Illin, her Aboriginal great-granddaughter, preserves a family relic, a silver spoon with three engraved Russian initials K.I.K., which stand for Konstantin Ivanovich Karlov, the name of Alexandra's father. According to Alexandra's Honduran descendants, he was born in Helsinki and served as a garrison commander in Irkutsk and later in Tashkent. Her mother, Natalia, came from Irkutsk, and Natalia's mother is believed to have been Tartar or Mongol.[23] Sasha was born in around 1860 in Irkutsk and, according to descendants, married Nikolai in 1877, when she was just sixteen. We know nothing about the real Sasha Karlova's life in Turkestan apart from the fact that her first daughter Maria (Mania) was born in around 1879 and her first son Leandr was born in 1882 in Tashkent.

Sasha Karpova, the heroine of the novel, on the contrary is depicted very graphically and with great psychological depth. We meet her first as a thirteen-year-old girl on the dusty streets of Tashkent in 1875. She is a student at the ill-fated girls' school already mentioned, whose headmistress trades her to the local debauchee, the engineer Motarov. Setting a trap, Motarov pretends to help Sasha, charms her, and then rapes her. She does not expect help from her family: her mother is a simple, strict, shrewish woman, and her father, Konstantin Ivanovich Karpov, a petty commissariat official, loves her, but is a weak man. Fearing their anger, Sasha gets more and more entangled, turning into Motarov's slave. When Sasha's fall is finally discovered, her parents severely flog her and incarcerate her for months. With acute psychological insight Nikolai depicts how, during these months of waiting for the trial of her violator, Sasha's attitude to him changes, and compassion and love begin to replace hatred. But then, coming face-to-face with him in the pre-trial proceedings, she discovers his true nature, and, being unable to bear further incarceration and the hatred of her parents, she flees Tashkent for newly conquered Kokand with a chance acquaintance, Mikhail Voskresensky, a petty official. She believes she will be able to begin a new, independent life in Kokand, but instead becomes the slave of this dissolute man.

Silin meets her in autumn 1876 in an inn on the road from Tashkent, where they are both awaiting fresh horses to continue their respective journeys on to Kokand. As Voskresensky is boasting in the next room, Silin shares a samovar and some of his food with a hungry

Sasha. This timid girl catches his imagination from the start. Although not a beauty, she is attractive, with her healthy, young, dark-complexioned face framed by curly dark hair peeking out from under her kerchief, and with large, expressive black eyes, in which fright is gradually replaced with gentleness and intelligence. In Kokand Silin visits their home occasionally and is the only one who treats Sasha with compassion and respect; she is ostracised by the rest of 'white society' because of her indecent position as Voskresensky's kept woman. Although she feels antipathy towards her always drunk and penniless 'lover', she, still a mere child, has nowhere to go, and only her genuine interest in the surrounding world of the native people helps her to survive. She gradually breaks down the mistrust of their neighbours, the local Muslim women, and is allowed to enter their secluded world. She learns their customs and language and soon earns respect as a 'woman-doctor', helping them with her knowledge and medicine.[24]

The sympathy between Sasha and Silin grows but he does not yet dare tell her he loves her and would like to marry her. And when he does tell her — after being betrayed by Voskresensky on a tiger hunt and nearly killed — it is too late: Sasha is expecting a child and is obviously too noble to burden this naïve young man with her child and herself ... They are finally united some three years later, after both had experienced a lot of suffering alone; this happens on the fateful night when Sasha with her daughter runs away from Voskresensky and Silin rescues her from a gang of robbers, killing their leader. We meet them next in Tashkent, three years after these events, a happy family of four with a young son — the double for Nikolai's own son, Leandr. Silin, having been dismissed from the position of investigating judge, works as a private lawyer. They live in a suburban cottage, surrounded by a lovingly cultivated garden, in which both of them work, and are befriended by the native people and a couple of honest Russians. But how changed our heroes are! Now Silin conducts an open, frenzied fight for justice against the network of local powerful crime bosses and corrupt public officials. Sasha, for her part, being advised by a friend to tame her husband a bit in their own interests, answers without hesitation: 'I will not influence him to do anything, however little, against his persuasions. It is impossible with our relationship as, if I manage to persuade him, I would stop respecting him after that myself'. And it is she who finally discloses to the authorities the documents intended to bring down the criminal conspiracy of corruption.[25]

Shortly afterwards Silin is arrested and, once his friends secure his release, he has to flee Tashkent for ever. The novel has a symbolic and prophetic end. Silin on top of a hill, lonely and defeated, casts a last glance down at Tashkent. There the roofs of the houses of the *nouveaux riches* rise, here by the river they celebrate with a picnic. But he is looking for his own small, white house with its avenue of ailanthus trees, where he had left Sasha and their children. He searches for it but cannot find it. There is no place for them in this town.[26] If only Nikolai, our real hero, could know how many houses created with his own hands he was to leave like that in the years to come — in St Petersburg, in Patagonia, in Australia — in his eternal search for justice ... in his eternal flight from himself ...

Sasha's image was in many ways new in Russian literature of the time. The destiny of girls betrayed by a lover or sexually exploited by a landlord was always tragic — for instance, Nastasia Filippovna from Dostoevsky's *Idiot*. And while compassion towards a prostitute sacrificing herself for the survival of the family (Sonechka from Dostoevsky's *Crime and Punishment*) was gaining ground in literature, for Sasha to have a harmonious and happy family life after her previous tragic misadventures was unheard of as the possible end of such a story. We never know whether the real Sasha actually underwent the ordeals that her namesake from the novel experienced; maybe this heroine was simply a creature of Nikolai's fantasy, or of his secret dreams, which he felt he could only express through the medium of Silin, his alter ego. Nevertheless, what scarce evidence there is does suggest that the story of their relationship was an unusual one. To begin with, you would hardly have expected the Karlovs — the family of an official — to allow their sixteen-year-old daughter to live with a married man. According to Nikolai's service records, he was still married in 1882 to his first wife, Vera Tomich, which means that he and Sasha were living in a de facto relationship — something it would have been difficult to have kept hidden from the Karlovs. To judge from his poetry, however, Nikolai was a proponent of free love. In one of his poems the heroine declares that only freedom in love makes it genuine while marriage bondage and hypocritical law in reality hide lust. The heroine without hesitation says:

> Believe, my friend, I'll always have the power
> To say that I am yours and to disdain the crowd.
> But while I wear a slave's chains
> The two of us will be eternal slaves.[27]

Sasha herself wrote in 1890 about her life as if hinting at some past troubles: 'When I tell you all my life, however unattractive it is, you will see that I nevertheless have an instinct to live in accordance with God'.

The memoirs of Nellie — granddaughter of Nikolai and Sasha — suggest that Nikolai's mother Evgenia treated Sasha as her inferior.

'WHEN MY GRANDFATHER WORKED IN THE EASTERN PART OF RUSSIA AS A JUDGE, my grandmother was very young and had Mania [Maria], who was an infant. They had to travel all across Russia to go to the east, where my grandfather was, and her mother-in-law went with her. They went by stage coach and in one place, where they stopped to rest, my grandmother was very, very tired and she fell asleep holding the baby. There was a couple in charge of the place where they stopped, and the wife said to my great-grandmother: "Why don't you hold the baby so that she can rest, she's very tired", and she answered: "Oh, she's nothing but a peasant. She can take it". So the woman jumped up and grabbed hold of her and tried to choke her. The woman's husband grabbed her and took her away.

'Later on he told them the story of why she'd acted that way. She had been a slave there on some place and had an affair with the owner's son and had a child by him. The owner's son was sent off to study, to school or whatever it was, and he came back a year later and went straight back to this slave girl. She had another child by him. By this time the owner was very angry, and had the two children taken and thrown to the boars to be killed, and they did it in front of the mother. The slave-mother ... lost her mind, so they married her to this innkeeper and gave them liberty and told them to get out of that place. They did. And the woman was very angry at what happened to her and that my grandfather's mother should talk like that about my grandmother.'[28]

Nevertheless, whatever people around them might think of them, Nikolai and Sasha found what was most essential in one another — love, support, and understanding. And now, after the failures of Turkestan, the new world of St Petersburg lay ahead of them ...

ь рано обрютели.

еть с тѣмъ, безъ опасенья

ить проступокъ роковой,

военныхъ упражненьямъ,

защищать свой край родной.

и въ своей землѣ свободу

мог спокойно наслаждать

миръ любимому народу

пышныхъ дѣла ограждать.

———

Хе, всѣ мы молоды бывали.

Надъ нѣмъ дѣдъ старый не ворча

Кому изъ насъ недокучалъ

и въ родительской морал

WHAT IS TRUTH?

SOW THE NAME ...

Disillusioned in both his attempts to conduct his life *comme il faut* — his first marriage and his career — Nikolai determined to break with the traditions of his class. In this state of mind he began his game with the names of his children, a game which would take up its own momentum and continue for over a century.

His own name and surname were the most ordinary — there are thousands of Nikolai Ilins in Russia. The origin of the surname (meaning 'son of Ilia') is the Hebrew name *Eliyāhū*, which means 'Yahweh is God', and is the name of the biblical prophet known in English as Elijah. This name is widely used in Indo-European languages. Presaging the eternal obsession with truth and justice of our Ilins, this prophet fought for the pure worship of Yahweh. For the Russian surname Ilin (Ильин), with its soft 'l' and stress on the second syllable, there is no exact transliteration into Roman characters. In French it might be spelled as 'Ilyine' but in Australia Nikolai chose the rarer form of 'Illin'. His Australian descendants pronounce it with the stress on the first syllable and, as such, it does not sound like a Russian surname at all. His descendants did not realise how common the name is in Russia and, for instance, they were hoping that the Russian athlete Ilin who took part in the Olympic Games in Australia in 1956 might be a relative. The first name Nikolai (Nicholas) has its history, too. For centuries the Ilin family kept an ancient, small icon of St Nicholas the Miraculous, the image of their protector. Generations of Ilins carried this icon for protection, worn on the breast, in many battles, the last to do so being Dmitrii, Nikolai's father. It is likely that Dmitrii named his son in honour of St Nicholas the Miraculous, as Nikolai was born almost on this saint's day.

Probably it was the fact that his own name was so common that decided Nikolai to give his children unusual names, going against the strict rules of the Russian church, which demanded that a child be given the name of her or his saint-protector, according to the church calendar. Nikolai ignored church dogma when choosing protectors for his children. While his first children had conventional Russian names — Ivan, Sergei and Maria — with the following ones he took the initiative into his own hands.

He named his son, born on 9 (21) July 1882 in Tashkent, Leandr. This name, rarely used in Russian, originates from the Greek name Leandros, itself derived from two Greek words meaning 'lion-man'. Obviously Nikolai, who knew some Greek and Greek mythology, wanted his son to be a real man, strong as a lion. In the romantic Greek tale, Leander was a young man who lived at Abydos, on the Asian side of the Hellespont (now the Dardanelles). He loved Hero, a priestess of Aphrodite, from Sestus, on the other side of the channel. Every night Leander swam to his beloved across the dark sea, from Asia to Europe, guided by a lamp in Hero's tower. One stormy night a high wind extinguished the beacon and Leander was drowned. His body was washed ashore beneath Hero's tower, and she, in her grief, threw herself into the sea.

Leandr Ilin did grow into a strong and courageous man, but his strength was more than the physical strength of the lion — it was the strength of the spirit. And he knew how to love, and struggle for his love, no less than his Greek namesake did. As a child he was called by the diminutive names Lena or Lenka. While in South America his name became Leandro, a form which he preserved when he went to Australia, although some people in Australia called him Andrew.

Leandro's name has passed on in the family — in his younger brother Romelio's family as well as his own. Romelio's son and grandson, living in the United States of America, both have this name. Leandro's son Harry gave his own son this name, too. But this young man at the age of eighteen, to the grief of the family, drowned at Crystal Creek, near Townsville, as if repeating the destiny of the Greek hero. The tradition did not stop there, however. The nephew of the drowned Leandro, born nine years later with the same birthdate, was named after him, as Leanne, the drowned Leandro's sister, relates: 'with God's gift of life his nephew was born on the same date as Leandro and was named after our brother'.[1] The name underwent further transformation, taking a feminine form, as Leandra — the name of one of Harry's granddaughters.

Nikolai's next son, born around 1885, received the name Karterii. This is a rare Russianised name, also borrowed from Greek, from the word meaning 'strong', 'courageous', and 'patient'. And indeed patience and courage were two qualities which distinguished the short life of this boy (nicknamed Pusha). He suffered from severe heart disease and spent most of his time patiently lying in bed. At five years of age he amazed the whole family once when he was arguing with his younger brother over a toy; he suddenly gave in, saying 'Let it be, you take it', and 'quietly stepped aside full of self-respect with his hands behind his back'. Another family tale concerns his gift of foresight about his own death when still only a boy.[2]

For his youngest son, born on 10 (22) July 1886, Nikolai chose yet another unusual name — Romelii. This name is from a Greek word signifying 'strength' and is probably the Russianised form of the Latin name Romulus, the legendary founder of Rome, the son of the god of war, Mars. Nikolai's son was called Roma at home, and in Argentina his name took the Spanish form of Romelio. He lived a long life full of adventures, and his name did indeed foretell his destiny in the sense that he would become more strongly connected than his siblings with Latin American culture, finally founding a Spanish-speaking dynasty in Honduras.

Ariadna, the name of Nikolai's second daughter, born on 22 May (3 June) 1890, also comes from a Greek name — Ariadne. The name is derived from Greek words meaning 'much liked'. Another meaning of this name is 'fidelity in marriage'. Ariadne in Greek mythology was the daughter of the Cretan king Minos and granddaughter of Helios, the sun god. She helped Theseus, whom she loved, go through the Labyrinth in which the Minotaur lived, by providing him with the magic clew, or ball of thread. By following 'Ariadne's clew', Theseus managed to kill the Minotaur and get out of the maze. He took Ariadne with him when he left Crete but later abandoned her on Naxos, sailing away when she was asleep. Dionysus, the god of wine and vegetation, found Ariadne there and married her. He placed Ariadne's wedding crown in the sky, where it can be seen as a constellation.

Nikolai's Ariadna, who was called in the family Ara and later Mamara (*mama* Ara), was a woman with a strong personality and, similarly to her Greek namesake, she experienced grief and happiness in love. Two of her Honduran granddaughters now have her name.

It is believed that Nikolai had one other daughter, who had the Russian name Vera, which means 'faith'. Although she died as an infant, her name has lived on too, preserved by the Aboriginal part of the family.

It seems that the history of his descendants proves the truth of Nikolai's own variant of an old proverb 'sow the name, reap the destiny'. As for Nikolai and Alexandra themselves, their names live on now in their descendants in Australia, Honduras and the United States of America — three of their descendants have the name Nicholas or Nikolai and twelve have the names Alexandra, Alexander, Alejandra or Alejandro.[3]

ST PETERSBURG TANGLE

Still, to give children unusual names is not sufficient on its own, the main thing is to raise them in accordance with the beliefs of their parents. This was especially so for the Ilins now that they had moved from the abundant south to misty, gloomy St Petersburg. Nikolai wrote in his autobiography: 'in 1881, after a conflict with a local influential person, I left Tashkent and arrived in St Petersburg with a huge family (I married for the second time in Tashkent). I had neither means, nor acquaintances in St Petersburg.'[4] Owing to the widespread corruption, it was rare indeed for someone to come from Central Asia without a fortune — but with Nikolai it was the case. By that time as well Ilinka had, according to him, been sold off to pay for the debts of his parents. Family photos suggest that they came to Petersburg in around 1884–85.

To make a living, Nikolai began to write fiction for periodicals. He first wrote for the progressive periodical *Books of the Week* his autobiographical novel-chronicle *In the New Land*, exposing the abuses and corruption among the Russian colonial authorities in Turkestan. 'In the ... novel *The Fugitives*', Nikolai says, 'and in the short story "Against All Expectations" I depicted the real life in Turkestan that I knew well and, to avoid misleading the reader, I deprived it of romantic or legendary colouring.' Both works were published in the popular magazine *Picturesque Review*.[5] His historical novel *The Fugitives* dealt with an episode from the anti-Russian Kokand uprising of 1875 in all its complexity, showing the atrocities committed on both sides. In the centre of the novel is Tikhon, a Russian peasant with an unusual destiny: deprived of his fiancée by his landlord, he rebelled and was sentenced to hard labour in Siberia, escaped and found his way to a Central Asian war-lord who had a number of Russian fugitives in his service. Tikhon converted to Islam but, compelled to fight against the Russian army, he chose to return to his countrymen in spite of all the humiliation he had experienced in Russia. This theme of a deep, spiritual attachment of a Russian fugitive to his native land was a prophetic one for Nikolai himself — in his thirty years away from Russia Nikolai would not find peace for himself anywhere in the world, and his death-bed request would be to ask his son Romelio to return to their motherland ...

The story 'Against All Expectations' was about the tragic lot of a young Polish man in Russian service who aspired to be treated by the

Russians as one of their own but remained Polish inside. This story might have had some autobiographical background as Nikolai, it seems, never forgot about his own Polish blood. And again, prophetically, years later these themes — this adaptation to an alien country, this duality of ethnic origin — would become burning questions for his children and grandchildren scattered across the world.

In St Petersburg Nikolai tried out the legal field as well. He summed up his observations of the numerous violations of judicial procedure in Turkestan in his 'Judicial notes' published in the *Judicial Newspaper* in 1886, in which he appealed for a radical reform of legal procedure in the area. From 1886 Nikolai began to work as a private attorney in the law-court in St Petersburg, primarily defending cases involving poor people.[6]

Neither Nikolai's publications nor his work brought in enough to support their growing family and Alexandra did what was rarely done by married women of her social standing: she started her own business at their home — a fashionable sewing workshop with dress-making courses. But in spite of a constant shortage of money the family lived in style. Their last address in St Petersburg was Nikolaevskaia Street (now Marat Street), house 16, flat 39, not far from the central Nevsky Avenue. This was in a six-storey apartment building intended for middle-class residents. They employed a cook, housemaid, and nurse, a tutor for the children, an assistant for Alexandra's courses and an assistant clerk for Nikolai. In summer they rented a five-room *dacha* (country-house) as well. Moreover, they paid for an English governess (rare enough even in well-off families) for their children and for violin lessons for Leandro.

Nikolai took into his family his two eldest children, from his previous relationships: his illegitimate son Ivan from the village of Turki and Sergei (Serezha), Vera's son. He was hoping that all his boys, in recognition of the military glory of his ancestors, would be admitted to the naval college at public expense, but it did not happen. Instead, young Alexandra found herself the stepmother of two teenagers, Ivan being just thirteen years younger than she was. Flora still remembers hearing how it brought a lot of tension to the family, as the eldest children disliked her. Alexandra could not manage Ivan, who was unruly, and the servants would often cover for him. The end came when he was caught stealing and in 1887 was sent to the St Petersburg agricultural colony for young criminals to be reformed. Sergei brought his share of troubles to the family, too. In the summer of 1890 he became seriously ill. 'We have a big misfortune', Nikolai wrote. 'Serezha's legs and arms are paralysed. He lies flat on his back unable to move.' It was a long time before he recovered.[7]

But, however many troubles the parents had, the children seemed to be happy. On Easter night 1912 Leandro, asleep on a dinghy off the northern coast of Australia, dreamed of those bygone days. A dream full of everlasting happiness.

'I SAW MYSELF A LITTLE BOY, IN RUSSIA. My sister [Maria], brothers and our friends are going to church. Mother is advising us to be careful when coming out from church, as it is cold yet. The snow is still there. We all run downstairs, rushing to church to get a place as it will be all full up. ... While walking, the noise is horrible — everybody wants to say something, everybody laughs, but when in church, the noise is finished. We enter — everyone makes a serious face, but after a few minutes everyone is busy. Brother John [Ivan] goes to sing. The boys are talking to the girls. One of my brothers is trying to make me believe he can hypnotise anybody at all by looking at the back of his or her head and making him look back. ... But I hear the chorus and the priest singing 'Christ Resurrected!' ... There starts a great movement in the church. Everybody starts kissing one another. The clergymen come out on to the street to consecrate the Easter eggs etc. The bells are ringing quickly and I hear the artillery gun [firing] to announce to everybody the great joy of God's Resurrection ...

'I dreamed I was at home in our big dining room. The samovar is on the table, heaps of painted eggs, Easter cakes and the *paskha* (this is made out of very fresh cheese cooked with all sorts of sweets in it. This must be on every table during Easter.). Father and Mother met us at the door and gave us the traditional kisses. We kiss one another, exchange eggs. When my turn came Father and Mother gave me a porcelain egg — swan — I went for a dish with water to put it [in] to swim ...'[8]

* * *

This might seem like a traditional, Russian, happy family, but it was not. In Central Asia Nikolai's misadventures had been, in spite of their seriousness, coloured with the excitement of frontier life and with his and Alexandra's romance, but now in St Petersburg all was different. The devilish city full of social contrasts, described by Pushkin and

Gogol, Dostoevsky and Nekrasov, stretched its web over Nikolai. The tangle began to grow by 1890.

This Petersburg tangle would hold him in its grasp for nearly three years more. In Nikolai's life this seems to be the most mysterious period, its culmination determining the years to come. There is a lot of contradictory material about this period: Nikolai's book *The Tolstoyan Diary*, his and Alexandra's letters, his poetry, stories remembered by their children and grandchildren, and, finally, remarks his contemporaries made about Nikolai. Nonetheless, these diverse materials do not allow me to tell with confidence what the truth is. And, symbolically, the starting-point for this period was Nikolai's encounter with the painting *What Is Truth?*.

In February 1890 Nikolai and Alexandra saw this painting by the famous Russian painter Nikolai Nikolaevich Ge (1831–94) at an exhibition. Nikolai was so impressed with it that he literally wept standing in front of it and Alexandra could hardly drag him away. The painting depicted the spiritual opposition between Christ and Pontius Pilate, and one episode in particular: when, to Christ's impassioned words 'I was born and came into the world for this one purpose, to speak about the truth. Whoever belongs to the truth listens to me', Pilate replied with the searching question 'And what is truth?' and then left the room as if not expecting a reply (John 18:37–38). Ge's Pilate was not a philosopher but a complacent official guided by commonsense. Christ, his opponent, personified the majesty of sacrifice in the name of an idea. But what an unusual Christ appears in the painting! He seemed to have nothing of the traditional image of the God-man — not his glory but neither, on the other hand, did he have his gentleness, all-forgiveness and love. This was an ugly figure of an exhausted, haunted man, with an emaciated, sallow face and hair sticky with sweat. But it was not just a realistic depiction of suffering. Nikolai was especially impressed with the Christ's eyes 'through which from this powerless meagre body emanated superhuman energy and the serene and unshakeable conviction of his rightness and moral strength'.[9]

That night Nikolai wrote to Ge: 'If I were a Pagan, after seeing your Christ I would be baptised'. And indeed that night he reread the New Testament, which he had not opened since his schooldays. As for the painting, it was soon prohibited by order of the czar from being exhibited in Russia, but Nikolai could not forget it. In May he suddenly suggested to the painter that he himself could organise an exhibition for the painting abroad. According to *The Tolstoyan Diary* Nikolai made this decision spontaneously, without even discussing it with his wife. Ge accepted the offer and visited the Ilins at their *dacha* near St Petersburg. The painter did not disappoint Nikolai's expectations — this 'tall, grey old man' dressed in threadbare, peasant clothes, Leo Tolstoy's friend and follower, seemed to bring peace to Nikolai's restless soul. The Ilins nicknamed Ge *dedushka* (grandad) and everyone, old and young, immediately adored him.[10]

Now, nothing could stop Nikolai from going abroad, which meant leaving Alexandra to face the disarray of his family problems with a new-born Ariadna on her hands and with just enough money to live on for two months. He did not change his decision even after Serezha became paralysed and his application for early release of Ivan from the agricultural colony, for which Nikolai had solicited over several months, was suddenly hindered by Arakin, the deputy minister of Justice. Nikolai knew that this was revenge. Ivan's case, indeed, was just one end of the elaborate St Petersburg tangle, which Nikolai wanted to cut at one stroke. Behind the scenes there was his conflict with the authorities, financial troubles, and, according to the Illins' family tales, his involvement in underground political activities. Later he will be accused of undertaking the exhibition of this painting to make money, but his reasons seem to be quite different: it was sacrifice in the name of Ge's Christ, fulfilling Christ's behest 'Go your way, sell whatever you have and give to the poor, and you will have treasure in heaven; and come, take up the cross and follow me' (Mark 10:21). 'Treasure in heaven' for Nikolai would be liberation of his passions, and, in his heart of hearts, he hoped for brotherly help for him and his family from his new idols — Ge and Tolstoy — in exchange for his sacrifice in the name of their ideas.[11]

But was there not another cause for his decision to leave? *The Tolstoyan Diary* begins with him being on the brink of a nervous breakdown in February 1890. Even the sound of the doorbell startled him. It is reminiscent of the state of mind of someone fearing an arrest. Could this relate to the story recorded by Sam Mackay, and mentioned earlier, of an accidental killing of a criminal? Nikolai only hints in his book that he had exposed some 'big-wigs', who tried 'to swallow' him in revenge, and the case had turned into a 'matter of honour' for him. Then, just on the eve of departing abroad with the painting, he writes about a new blow: 'The thunder struck over me. ... Something stung me painfully and deviously. ... The honest name is defamed, the family is ruined.'[12]

The tales preserved by his family depict this troublesome time in the light of a definite belief that the cause of his troubles was his struggle for justice and his underground political activities. I first heard about this from Leandro's Aboriginal descendants. Derek and Dynzie, grandsons of Nikolai's granddaughter Flora, told me: 'Nicholas stood for the lower class, he told peasants about their land rights; the authorities were persecuting him for this and that is why he had to leave Russia'. Then Flora herself added some flesh to the bones of the story.

'MY GRANDFATHER WAS SOME SORT OF A LAWMAN. Spoke out against government ruling, always was fighting for the underdog, the unfair things. ... He used to tell the people what rights they had and what they were entitled to, land, school, whatever. ... He was enlightening the people, he was preaching too much what [the authorities] didn't want the people to know anything about.'

Flora's brother Dick told his children that 'Nicholas fought for the serfs and it was against the government, their ruling'. They have a vague recollection of one of the cases he fought for as a lawyer — 'They would not give a one-legged man a pension who lost [his leg] at the war. Grandfather fought the case and got the pension for him.'[13] Nellie, Nikolai's granddaughter, contributed her version.

'MY GRANDFATHER WAS SENT ONCE AS A LAWYER (he was a doctor of Law, it is what they studied) to the United States to see how democracy would work in Russia. Well, when he got back he said that democracy was the thing for Russia, not the czarism or communism, and he was not liked for that. He wrote articles in the newspapers which nobody liked either. It was only him defending democracy.'[14]

Finally, there is the story recorded by Romelio as he heard it from Nikolai.

'MY FATHER WAS A LAWYER in St Petersburg, who preferred handling the legitimate claims that the workers and other poor employees in the city had against the factories and other firms, and he became so specialised in this field that he had almost continuous success. The factory owners were furious and they complained to the minister for Justice, asking him to put a stop to it. The minister replied, "Gentlemen, for the moment there is nothing I can do because Illin is acting within the law. But at the first opportunity that presents itself, even for the slightest omission, I shall withdraw his licence to practise and punish him severely."'

In an interview for a Honduran newspaper Romelio went further and referred to his father as 'an extremist-revolutionary' who, as a lawyer, 'defended workers who were accused of subversive activity'.[15]

The events of summer and autumn 1890 as reconstructed from archival documents show the situation in a quite different light. In August the minister for Justice rescinded Nikolai's licence to practise as a private attorney. This measure was normally used in cases of criminal misconduct, but Nikolai suspected that, in his case, it was because he was taking Ge's banned painting abroad. Nevertheless, on 15 August 1890 Nikolai left with the painting for Europe, taking with him also his son Leandr. However, while Nikolai was organising exhibitions of the painting in Hamburg and Berlin, events in St Petersburg took a turn for the worse. It turned out that his trip abroad with the banned painting 'just poured oil on the flame which began to burn earlier'. The driving force behind the scenes was the powerful public procurator, Alexander Kuzminskii, who became Nikolai's bitter enemy and wanted revenge for some perceived slight. It seems that Kuzminskii unaccountably — perhaps, as Nikolai believed, acting out of wounded pride — blamed Nikolai for the collapse of proceedings he had instituted in his role of public procurator against someone for giving false evidence in a case involving one of Nikolai's clients. Not long before that, Nikolai had already had his licence to practise withdrawn for two months, on Kuzminskii's recommendation, as a punishment for having been in conflict with another attorney, Gerke. Now, in another incident, Nikolai 'made a formal blunder' in one of his cases and, even though Nikolai argued it 'had nothing to do with his morals', Kuzminskii denounced him to the Ministry of Justice as an 'unreliable person' (*neblagonadezhnyi*), demanding that his licence to practise be declared void, which was done.

All this suggests that, at least by 1890, it was Nikolai's professional 'blunder' and, probably, his quarrelsome disposition — rather than his alleged underground political activities or his exposure of 'big-wigs' in his later writings and tales — that brought him into conflict with the authorities.

Alexandra, on learning about the situation, shared her despair with Ge, who lived at Yasnaya Polyana with the Tolstoys. Leo Tolstoy immediately wrote to his friend Alexandra Kalmykova in St Petersburg:

'HIS WIFE TRIED TO GET TO THE BOTTOM OF THINGS at the Ministry, after [Ilin] left, and the news went from bad to worse: his licence to practise is void and they say that they would not allow him to return, and if he did return he would have to go into exile. The poor woman is terrified, she burns letters and papers expecting a search and wants to go abroad. She has four children. ... Please, help her. I have nobody in St Petersburg besides you, and none better than you could help her; reassure her and find out what is the matter. She is a good woman, and hard-working.'[16]

Throughout October and November Tolstoy kept mentioning in his letters and his diary about how he and Ge wanted to give some practical support to the Ilin family. Tolstoy even made a direct appeal to Kuzminskii (who, incidentally, was his relative, the husband of his favourite sister-in-law Tania). Upon receiving his answer, Tolstoy wrote in his diary: 'A harsh letter from Kuzminskii. Yesterday I understood what is happening to him, ... the higher he rises, the colder, more callous and more harsh his conduct as an official becomes, and he grows further and further away from people's love ... and his only consolation is the awareness of his power.'[17]

Nikolai's trouble over his right to practise law was soon to be aggravated by his misadventures abroad exhibiting the painting — misadventures that would lead to the rupture with Ge and Tolstoy.

NIKOLAI, ALEXANDRA AND COUNT TOLSTOY

Tolstoy's attempt to support Alexandra in autumn 1890 did not occur by chance. The Ilins had become newly converted Tolstoyans after reading, in May 1890, Tolstoy's short story *The Kreutzer Sonata*. At that time the story was banned under censorship, and readers circulated it in handwritten copies. Securing a copy for a few days, people would invite their friends over to listen to the story being read out loud. Nikolai writes about their first impressions.

'I AM SPENDING THE THIRD DAY IN OUR *DACHA* together with my wife and two ladies, our close acquaintances. We spent all this time reading *The Kreutzer Sonata*, which recently became famous, and in endless debates and discussions about it. Our everyday life has been turned upside down; we forget to eat and drink, we stay awake at night. A strange thing this is: each of us, individually, knew everything depicted by Tolstoy and yet reading this story, how can I say it — reading it opens up to you new, unknown truth. ... I swear to God that hardly anybody has experienced from the book more than we did after reading this work. Yes, we have to ... scrape off the dirty layers of modern civilisation's habits and customs; we have to reveal in ourselves a human being, which indeed was created in God's likeness. How lucky we are that our eyes were opened while our children are young... This rebirth will be a hard struggle for ourselves but we will manage to guide our children along this pure and straight way.'[18]

Nikolai perfectly depicts the shock his contemporaries experienced upon reading *The Kreutzer Sonata*. In this masterpiece Tolstoy discussed issues of everyday life for every man and woman — love and sex, marriage and children, jealousy and adultery. The ordinary story of Pozdnyshev revealed, under Tolstoy's skilful pen, all the falsity of an outwardly conventional family life based on sex alone. The climax of the story, when Pozdnyshev in a fit of jealousy kills his wife, constituted a formidable warning to the reader, who could see that this tragic outcome was brought about by just the sort of everyday family conflicts the reader might experience in her or his own life. The story did not just portray the nightmare of the family life of modern man, it also offered a way out: not to marry or, if one did marry, to live in chastity.

The impression made by *The Kreutzer Sonata* on Nikolai and Alexandra was reinforced by the Tolstoyan Ge's visit to their *dacha*. Shortly after Ge's departure Nikolai wrote to him: 'Sasha diligently reads Leo Tolstoy and constantly in her actions adjusts herself to what he thinks, to what you would do in the present case'.[19] Nikolai, in his book *The Tolstoyan Diary*, has shown how their attitude to the teachings of Tolstoy developed further. According to *The Diary* by September 1890, when Nikolai was abroad with the painting, Alexandra had become a convert to Tolstoy's teaching of chastity. She wrote to her husband: 'Yes, my dear friend, only now I realise all the abomination of our previous life; now that this saintly man [Tolstoy] has opened up for us the new pure life. How clear and pure my inner world is now; and I can look anybody straight in the eye, there is nothing to be ashamed of, nothing to hide. And before? Muck and muck! ... Oh, what disgust I feel now when I remember how abominably we have lived these thirteen years together.'[20]

In *The Tolstoyan Diary* Nikolai sees their past quite differently, however: to him, it was 'thirteen nearly ideally happy years spent together', 'when we hardly ever had a serious disagreement, even over trifles'. He sees no one else to blame for Alexandra's defection but Tolstoy himself and, from having been his disciple, Nikolai immediately turned into his most vehement accuser. Tolstoy's ideas 'have affected me personally, and my family happiness, and threaten to destroy it', he writes, in despair after receiving Alexandra's letters.[21] From then on it was as if his eyes were opened, and he attacked *The Kreutzer Sonata* and its creator with all his polemical fury.

Why did Nikolai get so agitated at Alexandra's new enthusiasm for chastity? Why had they both been shocked after reading *The Kreutzer Sonata*? Nikolai does not write about it directly in *The Tolstoyan Diary* but there is a clue in the story of Nikolai and Alexandra's own life and love. Reading *The Kreutzer Sonata*, Nikolai seemed to see his own life — it was a chain of failures in his relations with women, which might have been the result of his 'monastic' youth in Tambov arranged by his aunt and of the permanent influence of his mother's domineering personality. First, there had been the relationship with the peasant girl — although society treated this kind of relationship as normal, he always knew it was not, and reading Tolstoy had confirmed his guilty conscience. Then his accidental, foolish marriage to Verochka, their growing alienation from each other and his suspicion of her infidelity. And that night when he was returning home, fearing that his suspicions might come true ... How could Tolstoy have known all that? And his flight to Turkestan ... These women he left behind continued to haunt him, to prey on his conscience. And then his sudden love for sixteen-year-old Alexandra, whom he moulded not just into a lover but into a devoted friend. And now she dares to say that everything was wrong?

'Eternal idealist', Nikolai writes, irritated about Alexandra's enthusiasm for chastity. But was it only a deep need for moral self-perfection that made her apply Tolstoy's preachings to herself so completely? Might the reason for it be more down-to-earth? Nikolai's previous relationships had become known to her and they seemed to haunt her all her life as much as her own past haunted her, whatever that was like before she married him. Sam Mackay relates: 'Before marrying Alexandra, Nikolai wed a lady named Vera, who liked dressing in red. ... This previous lady in the life of Nikolai was the reason for Alexandra to hate red dresses, which she never wore so Nikolai would not remember his former wife.'[22]

Her position as stepmother to Nikolai's earlier children only made matters worse. So did the way Nikolai's snobbish mother slighted her, either for her inferiority ('Oh, she's nothing but a peasant') or for her 'Tartar' blood. This tension must have been very strong to be recalled by her descendants even now, over a hundred years later. Added to that were her own troubles, with the births of six children, and her constant worries over their health — 'Ara [Ariadna] has been ill for ten days already, I pray God that she will survive' — and the terminally ill Pusha. Their endless financial troubles, too, and Nikolai's inability to provide for the family. First, his premature retirement from public service, and his conflict with Tashkent authorities; then, their life in St Petersburg on the income from the monthly instalments of his 'accusatory' novel — a dubious source of income for a beginning writer in czarist Russia. And then his new employment as a private attorney and new conflicts. And — we can only suppose — there was his addiction to gambling, and his everlasting belief that he would be lucky somewhere else, far away: 'Let's give up Petersburg and go away, give up and go' was his fixed idea for years. Not surprisingly, in running dress-making courses at her house, Alexandra was not following the fashionable preachings about the beneficial influence of working life on the idle upper-classes but was responding to bare necessity — providing a constant income for the family in case of new misadventures on her husband's part.

The events of 1890–91 were the final blow for her: the cancellation of Nikolai's licence to practise as a lawyer, and her humiliating visits to the authorities, together with the rumours that he would be prosecut-ed, while at the same time Nikolai has gone abroad with the painting, leaving her with no money. Then, on top of this, his new misfortunes abroad increase their debt to Ge to 3000 roubles. And Nikolai kept sug-gesting one new project after another to her: sell her dress-making courses, emigrate from Russia, open a vegetarian canteen in St Petersburg ... In a moment of despair she unbosomed herself to Ge: 'Kolia torments me unbearably. We lived together for a long time but knew each other very little. Still I have to bear all for the sake of the children. Leo Nikolaevich's teachings are my only salvation. They con-sole me, otherwise I would not be able to survive.'[23] And, indeed, from reading Tolstoy, who alone in his writings seemed to understand all her worries, a simple solution came to her — to live in chastity, to stop bearing new children. In this way at least she would partly lessen the unbearable responsibility which she was carrying for the huge family, being herself just thirty years old. What is more, she could achieve this without hurting Nikolai's feelings, she felt, by following the teachings of the man they both worshipped — Leo Tolstoy.

The anxiety which Nikolai experienced learning about Alexandra's serious conversion to Tolstoy's teaching of chastity suggests that he felt guilty in his relationship with her, even though he reiterated to himself that they had an 'ideally happy' marriage. Have not his writings about her been a peculiar attempt to charm away the real problems that he heaped on this young woman? For instance, Sasha from his novel *In the New Land* looks towards her life with Silin without any fear, deeply respecting his moral persuasions, and being sure that he, with his abilities and eagerness to work, will be able to provide for the family anywhere. In *The Tolstoyan Diary* Nikolai writes about Alexandra as a cheerful, kind, even-tempered, energetic woman with 'immense commonsense' who never complains. In his poetry she, his lyric heroine, 'revives his spirit', tired from the struggle for justice. The real Alexandra was not exactly that. From her almost illiterate, clumsy letters of this period to Ge there emerges a simple, suffering woman, with a deep faith in God, searching desperately for a spiritual father, whom she seems to find in Ge. She has no illusions about her Kolia: 'he was spoilt by his upbringing and he had nobody to awaken his good instincts. I myself was unable to do it, and anyway I am not so well developed for it' she confesses to Ge without any false shame. Nikolai knew the truth and his guilty conscience haunted him especially deeply on this trip. His letters to Ge and Sasha were full of frightening despair, and he at times thought of suicide.[24] As a result, owing to the worrying truths of *The Kreutzer Sonata*, Tolstoy became a scapegoat.

But Nikolai's fears were baseless; he had no need to engage in complex theoretical argument against Tolstoy's ideas just to persuade Alexandra to change her mind, nor, in particular, to convince her that *The Kreutzer Sonata*'s ideas of life in chastity had anything to do with honest and loving couples (such as themselves). There was, indeed, in their life something stronger than all the theories — their love and spiritual unity. This can be felt throughout *The Tolstoyan Diary*. It begins with their elated mood before their outing together to the exhibition where Nikolai was to see Ge's painting, a mood that clearly persisted after they had seen the painting: 'We spent the evening in heart-to-heart talk about Christ, the painting and the New Testament. We read it together. It was for the first time since I left school.' He writes in *The Tolstoyan Diary*, when he learns that the painting was banned: 'I could not stay alone any longer in the city flat and left on the evening train to Siverskaia, where my family had been living at the *dacha* for a week: at least I will be able to share my impressions with my wife'. Similar spiritual unity is seen in the way they address each other, in which 'My friend' predominates. Even in his poem written during the trip Nikolai says 'My beloved friend — my wife!'.[25]

Indeed, there is nothing more enigmatic than a woman's feelings, and, however great the hardships that fell to the share of Alexandra, married to such an extraordinary man as Nikolai was, she never stopped loving her Kolia and being happy in this love. And when Nikolai returned home, after eight months of misadventures abroad, worn out, prematurely aged and broken, he recorded these touching words in *The Tolstoyan Diary*: 'It is the seventh day since I have been back in my quiet haven. And, as before, they all love and caress me — even more it seems, if it is at all possible, than they did before.'[26] The following year he would flee abroad, again leaving Alexandra alone with the children, this time for five long years ...

As for Nikolai's criticism of Tolstoy, it developed along the following lines. After Alexandra became obsessed with Tolstoy's teachings on chastity, Nikolai wrote in *The Tolstoyan Diary*: 'Before, at times, I doubted if I have the right to demand of Tolstoy that he himself live according to his doctrine. Now it became obvious for me that it is my sacred and indispensable right.' His argument was that Tolstoy, since he claimed the role of a prophet–preacher, must himself live according to his preachings and that people have the right to be interested in his private life. To his readers Nikolai poured out all the 'facts' obtained at third-hand about Tolstoy's 'hypocrisy'. He picks up rumours — that Tolstoy has a two-year-old child, which means that he himself does not follow his own doctrine of chastity; that Tolstoy eats on silver; that he works, not for self-improvement, but for exercise only; that he has transferred his estate to his wife; that he continues to live with her in spite of the fact that they have totally contradictory views of the world.

Now Nikolai begins to see *The Kreutzer Sonata* in the most extreme, negative light. 'Pozdnyshev with all his words, thoughts and doings has buggered up the grand effect created by all that Tolstoy's other heroes said, thought and did ... And what rich material there is in Yasnaya Polyana itself! To follow step by step the spiritual degeneration of the former creator of Anna Karenina into the present scribbler of *The Kreutzer Sonata*; ... to investigate his home life; to investigate what led him to such an indiscriminate and foul rejection of the possibility of pure family happiness; ... to describe this motley crowd of pious hypocrites who flow there, not only from all over Russia but from abroad, to put on an act ... And would it not be a great, noble, selfless exploit for him to do this job, to reveal the roots on which *The Kreutzer Sonata* has ripened.'

An original piece of advice, indeed. But Nikolai goes even further, declaring that Tolstoy is no more than a too fastidious 'general of literature'.[27]

Nikolai's manner of arguing gives the impression that he was like a man possessed when he wrote all this. Tolstoy never declared that he claimed the role of a prophet–preacher; on the contrary, in his writings he did not conceal that he was a man with all his foibles, which he was struggling to overcome. This struggle lasted until the end of his life and finally resulted in his leaving home shortly before his death in November 1910.

The tragedy of Tolstoy's last days deeply affected the whole of Russia, indeed, the whole world. While Nikolai, at the very time that that tragedy was playing itself out in Russia, was starting his life from scratch for the fourth time, erecting a slab hut in the depths of the Australian jungle and cutting ancient trees to plant an orchard ...

We will never know if Nikolai finally admitted that he was wrong to accuse Tolstoy of hypocrisy. Both men sacrificed their own lives for the furtherance of their ideas. And yet, in one point Nikolai did score a moral victory: his and Alexandra's love defeated all Tolstoy's theories about chastity as an ideal.

FATHER AND SON

Nikolai's misadventures abroad with the painting involved a second character, for whom this ordeal became a watershed in his spiritual development — Leandr, his eight-year-old son.

Not long before their departure, on Leandr's name-day, Nikolai devoted an exhortative poem to him:

> In order that I name you, child,
> Desired, darling son of mine,
> Be a citizen of conscience;
> Preserve in your heart ideals
> Of good and truth; and share even
> The last crumb you have with your young brother;
> And in the face of strong scoundrels
> Better to break, but never bend.[28]

This simple, 'home-made' poem written by the head of an out-wardly prosperous family says much about the essence of Nikolai's rela-tions with his children. Natural love between a 'child' and a father enters a new phase: the boy has to merit the distinction of being a 'desired son'. Reserved fatherly love combines with sacrifice: not every father would wish his son to 'break' rather than 'bend', that is, to perish rather than betray his ideals. (Years later Leandr would say 'Men die to uphold their principle', and this would not be just words for him.) The father is deeply conscious of the necessity of this moral extremism and does not hide from his young son the troubles and injustices of the sur-rounding world, in which power is in the hands of mighty 'scoundrels'. This general feeling of trouble and premonition of forthcoming ordeals is expressed in the exhortation to share '*the last* crumb' with his 'young brother'. Here, 'young brother' means 'the people' — the underprivi-leged and downtrodden. Even the traditional wish to 'Preserve in your heart ideals / Of good and truth' Nikolai supplements with the behest to be 'a citizen of conscience' — in other words, do not limit 'good and truth' to the circle of people close to you, but actively, consciously implement these ideals in society and the state.

Such moral expectations of children were quite usual among the Russian democratic intelligentsia of the time. Still, they were rarely realised in full, being often outweighed by commonsense. In the Ilin family, however, this rejection of compromise had been accepted unre-servedly and fully implemented for many years in their everyday life. Leandr, although not the eldest son, was Nikolai's first 'real' son — the son he had named, raised from infancy, and from whom he had almost never been separated. In his heart of hearts Nikolai hoped that, while his own attempts to act according to his principles sometimes went astray, this boy would be able to correct his father's mistakes — to turn them into an ultimate good. And, amazingly, he did.

To have such a strong impact, these ideas could not have emerged as a result of simple moralising. Indeed, Nikolai's views on child upbringing were pioneering for the time:

'POOR CHILD BORN IN THE LEARNED AND CLEVER NINETEENTH CENTURY; poor child, worthy of pity! The young eye asks for green fields, the sun, the blue sky; lungs ask for air; muscles for space, activi-ty; nerves for impressions, ... freedom, childish enterprise. And the lit-tle heart, it also asks for things — it seeks warmth, kindness, compassion, as well as an understanding of, and consideration for the interests of the child. But none of these, not lungs, nor muscles, nor nerves, nor heart, receive the nourishment they need. Instead, a child from a tender age undergoes training in accordance with the clever century. The slightest attempt to play, to show his strength is damped with a cold *tenez-vous droit, soyez tranquille* [behave yourself, keep quiet], in its Russian, German or English form. ... By nine all that is childish in him is already squeezed out and crushed. ... And no one notices that, together with playfulness, the buds of will and enterprise have been pulled out, too; that the school of *comme il faut* has killed his curiosity and activity; that cultural urban conditioning has destroyed his sensitiveness from the very beginning. As a result, all the buds of God's gifts are stripped from this beautiful plant and, instead of a developing human being, there is just a growing, moving dummy. Schooling, with its unbearable load of different substitutes for knowledge that are mainly unnecessary for mind and for heart, takes the child's development further in the same direction, completing the process.'

Nikolai believed that an ability to understand 'the soul of a child' — to listen to the child, to be interested in the child's impressions — was indispensable to create the children's sincere love, respect and friendship for their parents.

And for a young man with a heart open to impressions and passions, 'thirsting for noble activities, for dangers, for exploits' — for such a young man, Nikolai argued, it is most important to be able to apply his abilities in real life.[29] Is he not speaking about himself? Is not his entire adult life an attempt to compensate for the shortcomings of his childhood and youth? Now that he has become a father himself, he does not want to repeat these mistakes with his own children; he is determined to raise them according to his ideals.

* * *

But let us return to eight-year-old Leandr, a lively, smart, cheerful, dark-complexioned boy with big, black eyes. Nikolai has decided to take him abroad to help with the organisation of the exhibition as an English interpreter, offering Leandr an opportunity to really put his knowledge into practice (he has learnt the language from a governess) and be a real help to his father. But that means a serious trial, too — he is to part with his mother, family, and home for the first time. A touching parting when the *Maria-Louisa* sails, as Nikolai tells it.

'LEANDR, PREVIOUSLY CHILDISHLY MERRY AND CARELESS, GREW QUIET AND BECAME SERIOUS ...

'"Good-bye, my precious little one, take care of daddy, help him", are his mother's parting words. The ship slowly pushes off.

'My heart was wrung', Nikolai says, 'I looked up at Leandr. The boy does not take his eyes off his mother and two tears shine on his cheeks; he is about to burst into sobs.

'"Lena, darling! That's not like you! You, such a brick, you are going to upset your mother with tears!"

'"I won't, daddy ..." And with a trembling hand the child wiped the tears across his cheeks, tried to smile, and started waving goodbye with a handkerchief.'[30]

Thus, on the occasion of his first serious trial Leandr receives the same advice from both parents: to think of, to care about someone else. And his mother's words 'take care of daddy, help him' — instead of what would be quite natural for his age, 'listen to daddy, behave yourself' — are the ones that count. And life will confront the two of them, the father and son, with situations when the help of young Leandr is to prove vital indeed.

Telling about the organisation of the exhibition in Hamburg, Nikolai mentions Leandr in passing: 'One can hardly tell all the details, and they made such a back-breaking day that by the evening Leandr and I were completely exhausted'. But one can feel that the father's attitude towards his son, as to an equal, is quite natural; similarly, that it is natural for Leandr to provide his father with real help — are they not comrades-in-arms in an important common cause![31]

As the time went by and the exhibition brought only losses Nikolai became more and more depressed, thinking of suicide, and, who knows, maybe Leandr's presence stopped him from taking the fatal step. 'Lenushka is happy and merry, and I feel so sorry for him, tears just suffocate me when I look at his joy and think about you all. But what a nice and clever boy he is, what a kind soul; all who meet him are delighted.' By November the state of their finances was so bad that he and Leandr would be living on 'bread and butter, and whatever turns up'.[32] 'I had so little money', Nikolai writes, 'that in Berlin I had to parade in a summer coat in very cold weather, and paid for it with a bad cold.' Leandr was dressed no better. In such clothes, in December 1890, they left Hamburg for America, via England, as steerage passengers; it was as cold in their berths as it was on deck. Ice floes dotted the sea; a sharp, icy wind cut them to the marrow. Nikolai writes:

'I WORRIED TO DEATH ABOUT LENA, who stoically endured cold and hunger. Yesterday I noticed that tears were running down his bluish cheeks.

'"Lena, are you crying, my darling? Are you very cold?"

'"No, daddy, I am not crying at all, the tears are coming out just because of the frost", the boy answered, hardly able to move his blue lips; but I knew he was crying and just did not want to confess that he was cold; moreover, to make him wrap up into something I had to be very strict with him as he kept on wanting me to put on more warm things.'[33]

Indeed, this boy who grew up in a well-to-do family, surrounded by a nanny, governess, tutor, servants and, most importantly, by the loving care of his mother, had endured the first ordeal of his life with credit, and more was to follow.

While transferring in England to the *Servia*, a transatlantic ship, Nikolai discovered that a bundle with decorations for the painting was missing. Nikolai left Leandr to look after a dozen pieces of their luggage loaded on the steamboat which took passengers to the *Servia* and went back to search for the bundle on the wharf. He did not notice the steamboat pushing off with Leandr on board — '"Wait, stop! My boy, my son is there!", I cried in German and in Russian, rushing madly along the wharf', Nikolai relates. At first the people around him laughed at him, but finally he was taken to the *Servia* on a tugboat. 'All my thoughts were with Leandr, who must have had a terrible fright finding himself alone on the ship which was about to sail off across the ocean.' Rushing about, searching for Leandr, Nikolai 'was a bit surprised that none of the passengers could tell me where the boy was. He must have been looking for me, waiting, crying; if he was on the ship at all ... A lost eight-year-old child should have attracted general attention', Nikolai thought. And just then he heard: 'a calm childish voice calling out "Daddy!" and I turned around and saw a huge pyramid of trunks, boxes and packages with the tiny figure of my Lena on top of it. Calmly climbing down, the boy explained that all this time he was guarding our luggage, not losing sight of it when it was transferred from the luggage boat to the *Servia*, and now, on his orders, it has been stored in one place.

'"And were you not scared when the boat set off without me? ..."

'"Why should I be scared? You knew what you were doing; I was sure that you would return in time ..." the boy answered quite calmly.'

And at that moment the missing bundle was brought up.[34]

The father certainly shouldered a great responsibility taking the boy on this hazardous, essentially adventurous trip, risking his health, making him endure cold and hunger. But maybe all this was compensated for when, one morning after a storm, they saw 'a wonderful picture. Masts, funnels, yards, ropes, pulleys, folded sails, deck — absolutely everything was covered with ice about two inches thick, ... in short the *Servia* had turned into a fantastic, crystal vessel.' And how could they forget the moment when, in the first rays of the rising sun, they had a magnificent view of New York harbour, and the New World emerged in front of them in all its beauty and might. Nikolai summed up his reflections on arrival in New York: 'My Lenka ... is shouting "Hurray", his little eyes shine, his face glows; come what may he will never be a walking dummy.'[35]

And America allowed Leandr to show his worth in full. On landing, Leandr takes up the duties of Nikolai's interpreter. 'Well, is this swarthy boy a Russian too?' the customs officers enquire, surprised at his dark complexion. But as soon as he started speaking 'the Yanks were won over'. And before long, when Nikolai went away to negotiate the customs duty for the painting, Leandr was sitting beside the director of the customs-house, who treated him to sweet pies and showed him pictures in an illustrated American magazine.

At the exhibition opening in Boston Leandr, dressed in a red or a blue Russian shirt with a sash and velveteen pants, started to work as a cashier. 'Leandr copes perfectly with his new duties', Nikolai writes. 'Ladies are fond of him. Many tell me that they are more interested in my son than in the painting itself.' This lively, handsome Russian boy who spoke fluent English was, in the opinion of the Americans, good publicity for the exhibition. Nikolai, who was in a desperate financial situation, took advantage of this, too: 'Now I stop at nothing'. Leandr became so confident in his new capacity that Nikolai left him to manage the exhibition all by himself while he went for a few days to New York.[36]

The boy even made his own friends. In Boston Madame R—s, an aristocrat and one of the most wealthy of Americans, was so charmed with Leandr that she first brought 'her little friend' refined dainties and then sent him an invitation to visit her, in which she wrote: 'I see in you an excellent boy, who promises to grow up into a worthy citizen of your country'. Another American lady, from Chicago, watching Leandr at work, told Nikolai that 'this trip provided the boy with a perfect practical schooling ... as real education was to learn about life and people'.

This was a natural point of view for Americans, who often began their careers in the practical school of life, with mastering a trade rather than with university education.[37]

Finally, it was time to leave America. Leandr undoubtedly knew that their enterprise had failed, that they were broke, that his father was expecting serious trouble on their return to Russia. Even so, when the worn-out and completely impoverished Leandr and Nikolai once again set off across the Atlantic travelling steerage, the boy, in spite of all their misadventures, did not lose his self-sacrificing love for his father. Nikolai wrote that on this voyage their situation was even worse than on the first one as he and Leandr were constantly subjected to 'the most insulting tricks, abuses, blows' from the Irish, who believed them to be Jews. 'For me such an attitude is a chance occurrence', Nikolai reflected, 'but a Jew experiences it all his life. How can he not become hardened and not be filled with hatred towards the people around him in return!' The crisis came when Nikolai, protecting Leandr from an Irishman who had struck him, confronted the Irishman with an open clasp-knife. The Irishman retreated and Nikolai and Leandr were left alone after that. For Nikolai it cured him of his Tolstoyism, with its preaching of 'non-resistance to evil by violence'. For Leandr it was a unique experience to be in the shoes of someone persecuted just for his ethnic origin.

But the confrontation with the Irishman was not the end of their misfortunes. Nikolai, who by the time of this confrontation had a bad cold, collapsed with a severe nervous breakdown; by night he had become delirious, and for a week he lay between life and death, often unconscious. Thoughts of Alexandra and his children, and especially Leandr, haunted him all the time. He asked his Jewish fellow-travellers to take Leandr to the Russian consul in Liverpool, in the event of his death.

But Leandr did not lose heart and maybe it was his love that saved his father. 'The boy looked after me with a touching attention, with thoughtfulness unusual for his age. When, at night, I was parched with thirst, he, hardly dressed, half-awake, would get up, disappear somewhere and bring me water. I believed that he got it nearby, but later I discovered that he had to go upstairs, and on a cold, often stormy night, wait for an appropriate moment, then run across the deck washed over by waves, pump a cup of water and, shivering and wet, return to me.'[38]

In Liverpool a new ordeal awaited them. They were stuck there for five days, penniless, 'sleeping in a doss-house and nearly starving'. For

49

FATHER AND SON

hours they would wander the streets. Let's listen to Leandr's discretion and tact when speaking with his father in this critical situation:

"'Daddy, I am hungry", the child tells me and I have just three shillings for five days, for food and for a bed.

"'Look at these beautiful toys, Lena," I say, pretending that I did not hear his words. The boy, lost in reverie, looks at the shop window.

"'Daddy, isn't it time to eat? ... "

"'Oh, yes ... Let's go down this street first." We go down "this street".

"'Daddy, dear, I am hungry, I want to eat ..." Tears are pouring down. I buy a roll and calculate how to hold out till the money comes [from Russia].'[39]

Luckily, the money finally arrived and, at last, 'forgetting about all the ordeal, worries, misfortunes and hazards, my boy and I were rushing to St Petersburg, burning with impatience to see our dear ones and endlessly varying in our dreams the circumstances of the forthcoming reunion'. And they were not disappointed. They plunged into the sea of love of their family. But if Nikolai, who looked strikingly aged, provoked mostly compassion, Leandr became the real hero of the day — 'a young Yankee for sure', Nikolai wrote about him on the last pages of his *Tolstoyan Diary*.[40]

These eight months away from home and the ordeals they came through together brought Nikolai and Leandr a great deal closer. Nikolai's admonition to the boy from a year before did come true — Leandr from 'the child' grew into 'the son'. The practical school of life into which his father plunged him, not suspecting himself how hard and harsh it could be, certainly taught him a lot. But the main result of this journey was not the accumulation of practice and knowledge, as the Americans saw it. The main result was specifically Russian — the moral and spiritual maturing of the child. After all, was not this — moral gain as the consequence of ordeals caused by impracticality — a distinctive characteristic of the Russian intelligentsia?

THE TOLSTOYAN DIARY

Nikolai's final split with Ge and his disillusionment with Tolstoy, which resulted in the publication of his most controversial work *The Tolstoyan Diary*, had its roots in the failure of his exhibition enterprise. The financial aspects of this enterprise gave grounds for accusations against Nikolai, and the situation was indeed confusing. Ge had originally suggested that Nikolai should exhibit the painting at his own expense and take the profits for himself. In an emotional moment Ge said 'Take the painting and do with it what you wish — sell it, exhibit it as you choose', as moral satisfaction was all he needed. Nikolai accepted, but he wanted to share the profits. It seems they both, 'the Tolstoyans', wanted to outdo each other in their generosity and aversion to money. And each believed that he was benefiting the other. Not a word was said about who would be financially responsible if the exhibition made a loss rather than a profit. In June 1890 Pavel Tretiakov (owner of the famous art gallery in Moscow), on Leo Tolstoy's suggestion, bought the painting for 5000 roubles. Nikolai sincerely believed that he had a moral, if not a legal, right to use this money for the organisation of the exhibition. On his departure for Europe he took 2000 roubles from Tretiakov's money. However, this was not enough and Nikolai, if his book is to be believed, wanted to take some money from an employees' fund, which he planned to repay somehow after his return. Moreover, he had his own debts, but expected to recover some of his money from his own debtors and to finalise financial matters with Ge on his return to Russia.[41]

Nikolai was supposed to go straight to America, and Tolstoy had written a number of letters asking his American friends and followers to support the exhibition. On arrival in Hamburg, however, Nikolai decided to stay in Germany first, where he toured Hamburg, Berlin, Hanover, and Elberfeld (Wuppertal) with the exhibition. The painting was well-reviewed by newspapers but the public did not come in great numbers and the financial outcome of the exhibition was disastrous. The money (2000 of Tretiakov's and 1200 of Nikolai's roubles) was spent in three months on travel, insurance, rent of the exhibition halls, advertising, and receptions. Soon Nikolai found himself in desperate need and appealed to Ge for help. Ge sent him a further 1000 roubles and Nikolai went to the United States of America. In January–March 1891 he held exhibitions of the painting in Boston, Providence and Baltimore, but again without any financial success. Ge's resentment towards Nikolai's impracticality and financial ruin was growing, and Nikolai, learning about this, in turn grew resentful of him. In March 1891 Ge suddenly asked Nikolai to bring the painting back to Russia and sent some more money for the return trip and insurance.

On arrival in St Petersburg in April 1891 Nikolai was shocked by Ge's cool attitude to him. In a bitter letter he argued: 'for eight months the child and I endured drudgery, lice tormenting us, we suffered hunger, shivered from cold and stank. ... It is not my fault that we had no material success; I believed from what you had said when you gave me the painting that it was not material success you were after but moral satisfaction, and I provided for you not just the satisfaction, but triumph, laurels. For this and for my hard work I indeed deserved at least a sincere "Thank you", but you have not said it to me.' As for the money, Nikolai at first believed that, of the 3000 roubles remaining from what Tretiakov had paid, at least some was due to him to cover his losses and debts arising from the exhibition. Ge, on the contrary, considered that he could collect this money himself, which he did, but, moreover, he expected that what Nikolai owed him would be returned, which amounted to over 3000 roubles. Ge finally, according to Nikolai, admitted why he was so displeased with him: 'I believe that the financial failure of the exhibition happened because you were occupied with something else other than the exhibition'. Might it be that rumours about Nikolai's passion for gambling had caused Ge to make such an accusation? Nikolai's last resort was to call Leandr and ask him to testify before Ge that he did nothing else apart from the exhibition. But it was not enough.

Now the Ilins feared the worst. In a letter to Ge Nikolai wrote that he acknowledged that while, legally, he had no right to ask anything of Ge, he believed that after all he had suffered he had a moral right to appeal to Ge to at the very least not put him in the dock, and — knowing how Ge loved Leandr — to save his son from the debts of his father. Alexandra, too, forgetting that just recently she had extolled Ge as her only friend and support, as her spiritual father and beloved 'grandad' for her children, poured out her accusations to him: 'How cunning you have been to cheat Kolia and me, to milk us of all that you could for your vanity and your pocket. I have noticed your falseness for a long time already ... Now I see clearly who you are.'[42] These were the Ilins' last letters to Ge, but not their last word on the matter. Although Ge remitted the debt, Nikolai shortly afterwards published his ill-famed book, *The Tolstoyan Diary*.

The Tolstoyan Diary is indeed a book of unusual genre. It is a peculiar combination of a private diary with a travel journal interwoven with lengthy philosophical and polemical discourses. In addition to this, despite having the form of a diary, the book is not a diary at all; the bulk of the text was obviously written mostly from memory, and backdated, after Nikolai had split up with Ge on his return to Russia. For instance, according to the first entry in *The Diary*, dated 10 March 1890, it was on this day he saw Ge's painting at the exhibition and the same night wrote a letter to him. In reality, the painting had already been banned and removed from the exhibition on 7 March 1890 while Nikolai's letter, which has survived, was written on 26 February 1890. Similar discrepancies can be detected with other dates and events. Many early 'entries' are noticeably coloured by his later deep resentment against Ge and those close to him. In spite of this, I am sure Nikolai did not distort the real flow of events as there was a witness before whom Nikolai would not allow himself consciously to pervert the facts, a witness who shared with him all the ordeals of that troublesome year — Leandr, his son. And finally this book, be it a diary or a backdated diary, tells a lot about Nikolai's personality: he said exactly what he wanted to say.

The reaction of the critics was not long in coming. The few right-wing, anti-Tolstoyan periodicals remarked that the book disclosed 'the falseness of Tolstoy's spiritually crippled hypocrisy', but the rest considered it nothing more than a lampoon. The reviewers' indignation was caused, not by Nikolai's criticism of Tolstoy's ideas (such criticism was a commonplace in Russia at that time), but with the meanness he showed, particularly his unrestrained targeting of Tolstoy's private life. Not surprisingly, Nikolai's own personality, which occupied the main place in the book, provoked a storm of accusations. The reviewers stigmatised him as a 'petty creature corroded with vanity and an aspiration for European fame', as an 'ignoramus who covers his private reckonings and shady transactions with vulgar rotten reasonings'. They believed the author to be 'morally deformed', distinguished by a 'disordered mind and disposition'. Some seemed to be sincerely puzzled about Nikolai's altruistic decision to organise the exhibition at his own expense. 'It is hard to imagine anything more tragicomic than this Mr Ilin ... His romanticism and naïvety are unbelievable ... He ruins his family, gets up to his ears in debt, experiences together with his child destitution and hunger — and all this just to show the painting to the world.' Ilia Repin, a famous Russian painter, was indignant about the book: '*The Tolstoyan Diary* is a base thing. This cheat or psychopath very naïvely complains that he did not manage to fleece Ge completely. During the six months of his tours he milked Ge for over 4000 and, as the latter had no fifth, this naïve swindler Ilin in unison with his wife printed a lampoon on Ge and Tolstoy, and what a lampoon!! He is sure to make a fortune with the book — it sells like hot cakes. To hell with this nasty wretch!'[43]

A cheat or else a crank — Ilin's contemporaries saw no other reasonable explanation. The Russian art scholar Vladimir Stasov, who published a study of Ge and had at his disposal the Ilins' correspondence with Ge, inclined to the first alternative. He argued that all the 'facts' in the book were falsified and the book aimed to attract public attention with its scandalous nature; he treated all Nikolai's ordeals as nothing more than 'Ilin's tragicomedy'.[44] Tolstoy and Ge, on the contrary, believed Nikolai to be insane. Ge wrote to their mutual acquaintance Iakubovskii: 'I pity Ilin as I have come to the conclusion that he is not quite in his right mind ... I did not read his book and, in order not to have hostile feelings towards him, I am not going to.' 'I think that he is not only incorrect, but simply insane, he is ill, there is no other explanation for such muddle-headedness in his enterprises. Usually these people are clever, at least skilful, but he is very bad. Well, let's forget about him.'[45] Tolstoy, years later, remembered about Ilin when, in a letter to his friend Chertkov, he was discussing Kenworthy: 'Yes, he [Kenworthy] is insane ... His stupid aspersions on you and his attempt to impute to you something unthinkable even for an inveterate scoundrel are disgusting. He reminds me of Ilin, who took Ge's painting abroad. He is a lunatic but in lunacy, as in intoxication, what was concealed before becomes apparent.'[46]

Modern scholars writing about Ge treat Ilin's book as nothing more than a libel on Ge and Tolstoy and believe Ilin to be a 'schemer' who aimed to make money first on the exhibition and then by concocting the book.[47] As such he was destined to remain in the history of Russian art and literature; but the reality is more complex.

Why not believe Nikolai's claim that his offer to organise this hardly profitable exhibition abroad at his own expense, while leaving his family without money — inexplicable from the point of view of commonsense — was an earnest sacrifice in the name of Ge's Christ? And when he, completely impractical at carrying out such an enterprise, underwent unbearable sufferings, there was none besides Leandr to follow him; the others, even his idols Ge and Tolstoy, preserved their commonsense and did not become fully embroiled. He wrote to Ge from America: 'You, dear Nikolai Nikolaevich, have reproached me for my nervousness. Nervousness, like all the rest, has its boundaries too. If a man is beaten beyond what he can bear, then nervousness and despair appear. My life is completely broken and I look forward to its end as something desirable.'[48] Nikolai was not a God-man as Christ was, and, when his limits were reached, he, in response to what he considered betrayal, hit back as an ordinary mortal would.

I look at the pages of this particular copy of *The Tolstoyan Diary* in my hands. The book has its own fate, too. This copy wandered with its author all over the world for a long time. Once, on learning about the death of Arakin, an enemy of his in Russia, Nikolai recorded between the lines of the book a sarcastic stanza on the death of the 'debunked scoundrel'. Otherwise, he hardly ever returned to the book, as his real life pushed his theorising of the past further and further away. And finally real life directly intervened.

There is an inscription inside the book in Romelio's hand: 'I apologise that this book is in such a poor state. When we were in Australia there was a cyclone, which destroyed our house, and these books have been damaged. That is the only copy that I have.'

The cyclone struck the Atherton Tablelands in March 1918. It carried away part of the book, the end part with the back cover, and threw it down somewhere on the ridges of Bellenden Ker. The remaining pages in a frayed cover made a new journey with the Illins to Colombia, Honduras and, finally, the United States of America. In January 1996 Romelio's son, Leandro, brought me a copy of these pages. He, who hardly knew Russian letters, carefully preserved this relic of his grandfather, not suspecting how his thought, his voice was crying out passionately on these pages and appealing to his descendants, to all of us: 'Listen to me, understand me'. The voice broke in the middle of a word on the missing pages and then again and again attempted to prove its case ...

* * *

Nikolai himself wrote in his autobiography: 'I hesitated to publish *The Tolstoyan Diary* for a long time, but the desire to make public my painful sufferings overcame practical considerations'. Indeed, the opportunity 'to unbosom himself' was more important to him than the inevitable hostility of the critics and public. Now, after publication, the time had come to confront the result. There is a strange passage in Nikolai's letter to Semen Vengerov, the literary historian. 'To tell the truth I do not know myself what to think about my book, what it is worth ... Now I have only one feeling: that I did not make it up, but recorded what I survived and felt, what happened. Maybe I was false when I felt, thought, understood this, maybe I did it badly, dishonestly, but for God's sake, tell me this sensibly, without bias.'[49]

He truly did not know whether he had 'made up' the story or not; whether it was his real ego or the imaginary alter ego whose experience he was describing. He truly did not know who he was — the one who felt the pangs of conscience or the one who frenziedly continued to prove his truth — and which one was hero and which, anti-hero. He truly did not know how the white (his tears in front of the painting, his devotion to Ge, and reading of *The Kreutzer Sonata*) turned into the black: his life now — ruined, jobless, ostracised. And how could that spring of 1890 turn into the gloomy autumn of 1892?

But, what was worse, winter was approaching, and winters in St Petersburg were not like those of his childhood in Ilinka; here, they were endless and dark ...

'A HUNTED WOLF THAT'S DOOMED TO DIE'

The Tolstoyan Diary was published in February 1892 and several months later Nikolai suddenly fled Russia, finally ending up in Argentina. It was five years before Alexandra and the younger children managed to join him there. What caused these dramatic events was unclear to me and, amazingly, quite different explanations emerged in the tales I heard from the different branches of the family.

Leandro's children have preserved various versions of the story of the flight. Flora, his daughter, mentioned this flight several times in her letters. 'He spoke out against the czar ruling. He had to run. They were going to kill him.' 'He put his own words to the French national anthem, *Marseillaise*, and sang it in the street; he had to jump and run because they were going to kill him right after. The people helped him to get away. ... He did not even go home after that. This is what Father told us.' Ernie, her son, remembers about the *Marseillaise*, too: 'One day he got up on a box in the street and sang his own words to the *Marseillaise*'. Harry, Flora's younger brother, had a less clear memory; the only thing he remembered for sure was the death threat. 'He left Russia because he was trying to help poor people there. He could see that a war was going to come up. He could not do much good and he had to get out because if they had got him they could cut his head off.'

Lullie, Flora and Harry's younger sister, said that the family had to flee 'because even though they were rich they were for the poor people, they had to leave because they were going to be killed, there was an uprising there' (these words are remembered by Nola, her daughter). The daughters of Dick, Leandro's eldest son, have another version, which he told them. 'Great-grandad [Nikolai] went to court to fight for some people he believed were in the right. He won the case and he was still down in his office when the soldiers came to his house and told they had come there to get him. But great-grandma knew they were coming and sent our grandfather [Leandro] to go and warn him not to come home that night. And they left with the clothes they had on ... Great-grandad had to get out of Russia or he would have been killed.'[50]

Nellie provides in detail the circumstances of the flight itself. 'My grandfather had to leave Russia because a friend of his told him that they were coming to arrest him and advised him to go away. Well, he packed up a couple of things and took all the money they had at home and left my grandmother with all the kids and fled from Russia. It was winter-time and there was snow on the ground. He put a sheet over himself and crawled through the snow across the border to Germany, and then he kept on going until he got to Argentina.'[51]

And finally came the version as recorded by Romelio, Nikolai's son.

'MY FATHER WAS IMPRUDENT ENOUGH TO BUY SOME COLD-METAL PRINTING-TYPE, which was strictly prohibited and considered an equivalent offence to having a firearm without permission. No doubt, the secret police investigated. My father received a surprise summons to present himself at the Third Department (political police). There, he was taken to the chief's private office. Imagine his surprise when he recognised the police chief as a friend of his from his childhood and school years, Alexander Buturlin, who embraced him affectionately and said: "Nicholas, you never expected to find me here, but you see how different people's paths through life are! But let's come to the point, so as not to waste time: I have an order for your arrest. For the sake of our childhood friendship I want to give you an opportunity to save yourself, provided you do what I tell you. Take the first train leaving today for the frontier, with your legal passports. If you delay until tomorrow I won't be able to help you."

'And, with a quick handshake, he said, smiling sadly: "Do you understand that I am acting contrary to my official duties? I wish you success. But hurry."

'After arriving home and telling all this to my poor mother, who he was leaving with three children (us), he then collected up the last few coins, and some jewellery such as wedding rings, my baptismal cross, watches, and so on. He put his passport in order and, leaving his poor unprotected family broken-hearted, he wasted no time in getting to the noisy station and taking the train which departed for the border with Austria.'

The remainder of the story is a most vivid account of the border crossing. On arrival at Brody, the border station, Nikolai, in spite of having a legal passport, accepted the offer of a local Jewish smuggler to take him across the border illegally at night. They were caught by a border-guard patrol, but Nikolai managed to persuade them that he was on business there and they let him go; he even discovered among the border guards Ivan, a son of one of his former serfs. On the second attempt he made, accompanied by the Jewish smugglers, he finally succeeded in crossing the border.[52]

Nikolai's poetry seems to confirm his, or, rather, his lyric hero's revolutionary aspirations, although always without any concrete details.

> A pure love for truth
> Was burning in my heart,
> Desired, sacred truth ...
> I longed for fight, I longed for light
> I hated lies and sham ...

In his autobiographical poem 'Father and son' the hero tells how they, the fighters for truth, were betrayed by 'the grey crowd', which did not support them at the decisive moment. In another autobiographical poem 'Confession' he confesses that:

> When an intrepid friend
> Came to lead the people
> I did not dare go with him ...[53]

Nevertheless, in the foreword to the collection of this revolutionary poetry (published without censorship) Nikolai depicted his departure abroad quite differently, without any reference to revolutionary involvement. 'Following the publication of *The Tolstoyan Diary* [the author] seemingly burns his boats and takes as it were a new spiritual direction. He goes abroad, stays for a year in Switzerland and then goes to Argentina.'[54] The possibility that his departure was caused by his split with St Petersburg society confirms Ge's remark about attitudes to Nikolai in March 1892, after *The Tolstoyan Diary* was published: 'It seems that his past is not good at all, as he is not received and is spoken about either little or disapprovingly'.[55]

By 1893 the details of Nikolai's flight circulating in St Petersburg were far more prosaic. Ge wrote to Iakubovskii in July 1893: 'I have learned by chance from the deputy procurator that poor Ilin has been caught; he has made so much trouble that legal action was taken against him. In the meantime he fled to Vienna while his family is left to the mercy of fate.'[56]

These different versions obviously do not hang well together. The easiest way to work round them might be to consider the stories that Nikolai told to his children about his past as distortions of the real events; but I have learned to respect these stories, however unusual they may seem at first glance. For instance, in one of her first letters Flora wrote this about her father, Leandro: 'he left Russia when he was eleven years old and went all by himself to where his father was in South America. Grandmother sent him because grandfather was there alone, the rest of the family came after two or three years.' I could hardly believe this story. Then, a year later, I received further details of the same story preserved by Nikolai's Honduran descendants: 'Alexandra (*Baba*) sent Leandro with money in a sack to Argentina, accompanied by a woman, but she stole all the money'. The 'sack with money' was a detail making the whole story nearly believable. And, finally, the facts came too. According to passenger lists, Alexandra went to Argentina in 1897 with the two younger children, Romelio and Ariadna, but without Leandr.[57] That means that Leandr did go alone to Argentina to look after his father when he was just eleven ... It is hard not to believe that with the Ilin family anything was possible!

Still, whichever we believe of these versions of the reason for his flight — whether a 'criminal offence' or political involvement, or whether it's the story of the '*Marseillaise*', possession of printing-type, or defending somebody's case in court — it is hard to reconcile them with Nikolai's fear of being killed. These offences are not serious enough for execution, even in czarist Russia.

But could not the key to it be in another family tale recorded by Sam Mackay from Honduras?

'NICHOLAS PARTICIPATED IN THE COMMUNIST MOVEMENT, but as time passed he realised that communism was not what he really thought it would be, and backed away from [the movement]. He participated in politics with Lenin, Trotsky and Kerensky. Kerensky escaped to England. Trotsky went to Mexico, where he was followed and killed. Lenin stayed in Russia and Nikolai went to Europe. Then he took off to Argentina in 1898, when he found out the communists were after him to kill him for withdrawing from their movement. Nikolai wrote a book against the bolshevists.

'After his departure to Argentina, communist Russian agents arrived in Argentina seeking to kill Nikolai. They caught him and took him to the seaside, apparently knocked him dead and threw him into the sea. They thought he was dead, but he survived because of the low tide at the time he was thrown into the sea. These Russian agents went back to their country and declared Nikolai dead. Since they considered Alexandra a widow, the government granted her permission to leave Russia along with Romelii [Romelio] and Ariadna, their children.'[58]

This story, with all its obvious later additions and inexactitudes, does have an important rational kernel — if we consider that the word 'communists' (which only came into use for the political organisation after the revolution of 1917), means here just 'revolutionaries', or 'radicals', the story seems quite possible. It happened in Russia (Dostoevsky wrote his famous novel *The Possessed* about such revolutionary revenge); it happened abroad, even in Argentina. The Russian painter Sergei Praottsev, a contemporary of Nikolai, was a former revolutionary who had collaborated with the secret police in Russia. Praottsev escaped to Argentina but soon the Russian revolutionary community there heard about his activities as an informer; the Russians made several attempts to assassinate him for his betrayal and Praottsev had to hide in the Paraguayan jungle.[59]

Nikolai had to hide in Argentina, too. According to his granddaughter Nellie, 'he was working for the Botanical Gardens of the Museum [in Buenos Aires] and went to Patagonia to get away, so he would be safe'.[60] The fact is that, even in Patagonia, he settled with his family in the most remote mountainous region, on the border with Chile — actually on the no-man's land between the two countries. This tale about Nikolai being pursued by the members of some revolutionary organisation with which he no longer wants to associate is possible; but the second part of the story — Alexandra only being allowed to leave Russia five years after Nikolai is declared dead — to some extent seems to contradict it.

But even this part of the story, however fantastic, seems to have some basis. Other members of the family have heard it, too. Nellie relates: 'Well, he lived in Patagonia for many years and secretly communicated with my grandmother. She had to stay in Russia for seven years until they declared her a widow whose husband had died. So, then my grandmother got a permit and went to Argentina.' Stasov, in his book about Ge published in 1904, remarked about Nikolai: 'by now long ago deceased'. Commentaries to Tolstoy's collected works even provide the year of Nikolai's death — 1895.[61] But in this version again there is a loose end. Neither Nikolai's political activities nor a criminal offence of a common nature gave grounds, according to Russian laws, for depriving his wife and children of the right to leave Russia legally, so that there would be no need to declare him dead and wait for five or seven years.

Such dramatic revolutionary involvement as Nikolai was supposed to have had could not remain unrecorded somewhere in the Russian archival dossiers. Over several years I applied to scholars in Russia for help and gradually all possible sources of information have been checked: printed directories of radicals and political offenders, the archives of the czarist secret police (*Okhranka*) in Moscow and St Petersburg, Tambov School documents.[62] And nothing was found. Our Nikolai Ilin did not appear in any records of political suspects or offenders. Alexander Buturlin (the man who, according to one of the tales, was Nikolai's school-friend and, as secret police chief, warned him of his impending arrest) turned out to be a phantom, too — he never studied in Tambov with Nikolai, and was not in charge of the secret police.

Yet another dead-end ... What *was* the truth, I asked myself, and where should I look for it? I felt that we would never learn that truth unless Nikolai himself let us know. I could do nothing more but wait. Until he did.

INTERMEZZO

THE CZARINA'S GOBLET

~

Among the Illins' family tales was one, over two centuries old, about a brave sailor. I first heard it from Nellie, Nikolai's granddaughter.

'ONE OF GRANDFATHER'S ANCESTORS, DEMETRIO, WAS IN THE NAVY WHEN THE WAR WAS WITH TURKEY. His commander said that if one of them would go and set fire to the sails at the end, with the wind blowing the way it was, that it would set fire to all the sails and they could win the battle. So, Demetrio and a friend of his, they went. They had a few drinks to get courage, went and set fire to the sail and it was like the commander said, they won the battle because all the sails caught on fire. His friend was killed, so he was the only one left to face the glory of what they had done in the battle.

'The czarina ordered him to present himself in front of her, which he did, but he had been drinking quite a lot, being congratulated by his companions and whatever. So by the time he got in front of the czarina he bent down in front of her and fell flat on his face. She was angry, which is natural. She picked up a goblet and said: "I'm drinking to his health and give it to him so he can keep on drinking". Well, that goblet was in the family possession and my grandfather [Nikolai] had it. Eventually they [the Russians] gave honours to him for what he had done by naming a ship *Lieutenant Demetrio Illin* (the way I understand it) and my grandfather donated the goblet to go in this ship. He took Leandro or Romelio, I don't know which of those, when the ship came to visit Buenos Aires, and they went aboard and saw the goblet there, but later on this vessel took part in a fight with the Japanese and was sunk by them, so the goblet went down with the ship. That was the end of it.'

Sam Mackay from Honduras provided further details, adding a Spanish as well as a mythological flavour to the story.

'DIMITRI SERGEEVICH ILLIN WAS A LIEUTENANT OF THE RUSSIAN NAVY. His mother was a countrywoman from Saratov. Dimitri Sergeevich burned the Turkish fleet in Shesma's Gulf [Gulf of Çesme], and ... was named Shesma's hero. The czarina, queen of Russia, was celebrating the victory, and toasted in honour of Dimitri; she finished her drink and asked a domestic to call Dimitri to give him the wineglass but

Dimitri was drunk in a tavern celebrating the victory. In that condition Dimitri was taken to the czarina and in front of her he kneeled down and vomited at her feet. Still, after this incident, the czarina gave him her wineglass so he could continue celebrating. Dimitri died poor in the village of Illinka because he vomited at the czarina's feet.

'Eighty years later, after his death, a warship was made with his name *Lieutenant Dimitri Sergeevich Illin*. The captain of this ship was Captain Virilov. Nikolai Illin gave his wineglass to Captain Virilov before Nikolai left Russia. There is a monument of Dimitri in Tambov city.'[1]

On the other side of the globe Nikolai's Aboriginal great-grand-daughters Glenda and Vera showed me what they believed was a medal presented by Catherine the Great to 'Ilin, the hero who bombed up the ships at the war'. It was an ancient oval icon of St Peter and St Paul, which, they remembered, 'once had a purple ribbon on it'.[2]

* * *

Hearing these stories, I realised that they had survived for so long and grown into a myth not by chance — that this myth was destined, by some inner logic, to have a concealed meaning for the story of the Ilins. But first I had to check whether there was a real historical hero who had inspired the emerging myth. Indeed there was. And, moreover, the real facts of his life seemed to belong to a myth too.

Dmitrii Sergeevich Ilin, born in 1738, graduated from the naval cadet school. In 1769 he received the rank of lieutenant. With the Russian navy he travelled from St Petersburg around Europe to the Aegean Sea shores of Turkey to take part in the Russian war with Turkey. There, the Russians blockaded the Turkish fleet, which was twice the size of their own fleet, after the first battle in Çesme gulf. Two Russians, Lieutenant Dmitrii Ilin and Prince Vasilii Gagarin, and two Englishmen in Russian service, Elphinstone Dugdale and Thomas Mackenzie, volunteered to take four Russian fireships and set the Turkish fleet on fire. General I.A. Gannibal[3] was in charge of the technical part of the attack. The risk for those on the fireships was enormous. They had to approach the enemy vessels under artillery shelling, couple the fireship to an enemy vessel, light the fireship, which was stuffed with explosives, and then escape in a rowing boat.

On the moonlit night of 26 June (7 July) 1770 the attack began. Ilin was the only one of the four to succeed in nearing a Turkish battleship and in setting it on fire. His courage and composure impressed those witnessing his actions: having started the fire, he left his fireship unhurriedly and, standing back a bit, stopped to watch the results. At that moment the chain of explosions started. Flames illuminated the terrible picture — the water was strewn with corpses and wreckage. The Turkish ships were standing so close to each other that fire soon spread through the whole fleet, its effect worsened by the explosions of ammunition stores and by constant shelling from the Russian battleships. By the morning the Turkish fleet, over seventy vessels, had been completely destroyed; out of 15,000 men in the Turkish navy only 4000 survived. After decades of decay in the Russian navy this was its first triumph, and it was achieved by courage alone.

The commander-in-chief of the Russian fleet, Count Aleksei Orlov, the notorious courtier and a favourite of Catherine II, reported the details of the victory to the czarina. She said that Lieutenant Ilin should be decorated with the order of St George, 4th degree — the order given for exceptional bravery. The Russian poet Mikhail Kheraskov celebrated the battle and Ilin's exploit in a grandiloquent ode. Ilin continued his service in the navy for several years but in 1777 he had to retire as a captain first-class because of epilepsy. He spent the rest of his life in poverty and obscurity. After his death, on 19 (31) July 1802, in the remote village of Zastizhie (Tver province), the desperate poverty of his two daughters, Catherine and Alexandra, moved another Russian writer, Gavriil Gerakov, who approached young Czar Alexander I to obtain pensions for them. Between 1886 and 1910 the Baltic Fleet had a mine-cruiser *Lieutenant Ilin* named after Dmitrii Ilin, and in 1916 a new destroyer, *Lieutenant Ilin*, was built (later renamed the *Garibaldi*).[4]

The personality of Dmitrii Ilin, as preserved in history and in the family tales, can indeed, it seems, be treated as that of a mythological hero, and, moreover, of a hero with a dual nature: the illustrious, 'high' hero combined with its opposite, the trickster, jester, or fairy-tale fool. In Nellie's story Ilin emerges from nowhere as a figure that has connections with fire — a distinctive attribute of a cultural hero — but his fire is a destructive fire, unlike that of Prometheus and similar 'high' cultural heroes. His exploit — conquering 'monsters' (the Turks, here) is a usual occupation for a mythological hero — has cosmic features of death and rebirth; our hero not only escapes death himself but also revives the glory of the Russian navy. Ilin impressed his contemporaries with his exceptional boldness bordering on recklessness or, rather, foolhardiness. The family tale retained by Nellie develops this foolhardiness in terms of a 'low' hero, almost a folk fool: 'So, Demetrio and a friend of his, they went. They had a few drinks to get courage, went and set fire to the sail ...'.

The culmination of the story — the czarina's goblet given to Ilin — further reveals the dual, ambivalent nature of the hero. Incidentally, the goblet[5] appears in the story at three crucial moments, each time as a part of the major mythological opposition between top and bottom. It first appears as a dubious gift of the czarina at the moment when top and bottom have switched roles: Dmitrii, just when he is about to be elevated to the top by the highest blessing, falls down vomiting; nevertheless, he is elevated and rewarded but as a carnivalesque jester would have been. Thus, the hero's profanity, his involuntary attempt to break the social hierarchy, to lower the czarina to his level, is answered by the clever czarina in the same grotesque language: he receives the goblet, which personifies his own dual nature — high and low — after which the social hierarchy is restored. The second time the goblet appears it is as Nikolai's gift to the ship's museum — as an attempt to preserve Dmitrii on top, in a serious, heroic way. Finally, according to the story the goblet sinks with the ship during the war; it literally goes to the bottom. This is perfectly determined by the logic of the myth, although it contradicts historical facts, as the ship did not sink during the Russo-Japanese war. Moreover, the goblet itself survived in a museum collection.

In Sam's variant the life story of the hero is the travelling from bottom ('his mother was a countrywoman') to the top (heroic exploit at the battle), back to the bottom ('died poor in the village') and to the top again ('there is a monument of Dimitri'). Even Ilin's drunkenness and epilepsy (which the ancients thought bestowed second sight) are usual trickster's characteristics, which allow the trickster to see the 'true' nature of things not blunted by the hierarchy of the social cosmos.

Nikolai's descendants, who lost connections with Russia a century ago and have a very vague knowledge of Russian history, managed to preserve this story for 230 years precisely because it was constructed like a myth — a living myth that gradually became enriched with local details. Moreover, Dmitrii Ilin as a mythological hero assumes features, not of a real ancestor, but of a mythological ancestor, when the descendants believe that he is their direct ancestor but cannot figure out their actual relationship with him. For instance, Nellie refers to him just as 'an ancestor', Sam considers him to be Nikolai's great-grandfather, and Sam's brother, René Mackay, refers to him as Nikolai's father; while Nikolai himself in his autobiography wrote about Dmitrii as his 'cousin grandfather' (in other words, the brother of his grandfather). A thorough search conducted in Moscow, St Petersburg and Saratov archives proved that if Nikolai and Dmitrii are related at all it is only because there might have been some common ancestor sometime before the seventeenth century.[6]

I was frustrated again. Yet another dead-end! But if we treat Dmitrii as a mythological ancestor does it not all fit together, even another of the beliefs of the modern Illins — their belief that they are related to Russian royalty? Glenda Illin, Nikolai's Aboriginal great-granddaughter, told me about it in a matter-of-fact way. 'Dad used to tell us that we were related to Russian royalty', she said, 'but we did not think that we were any better than anybody else.' This time it was more than family tales, as indeed different branches of Russian Ilins, related to Dmitrii, the Çesme hero, retain the legend that they came from Ruriks, the ancient Russian czars. The founder of their branch was Prince Constantine, the younger brother of the famous, thirteenth century warrior-saint Prince Alexander Nevsky (see the Illin family tree, in Appendix 2).

Mythology has its own truth, or at least its own logic, and one day, when I had already abandoned any hope of finding 'facts' concerning this story, I received the e-mail from Natalia Iudenich that I had been awaiting for so long. Iudenich, a retired engineer and amateur genealogist, who, between visits to archives, grows potatoes on her vegetable plot to survive the coming winter, discovered an amazing document while researching in the naval archives in St Petersburg. It proved that, in 1776 at a solemn ceremony when Catherine II presented awards to the Çesme heroes, Dmitrii did not manage to kneel properly in front of the czarina. She, nevertheless, gave him the goblet from which she drank his health, but that blunder or his epilepsy caused his premature dismissal from the navy soon afterwards.[7]

But that was not all. Iudenich also discovered a letter from our Nikolai Ilin in Argentina to the upper-deck crew of the *Lieutenant Ilin*

— a desperate appeal for help. In this letter Nikolai explained that in 1886, after the cruiser was built, newspapers had asked descendants of the hero to provide his portrait. Following this appeal, he had informed the cruiser's captain Aleksei Birilev (so, Virilov from Sam's tale is a real person!) that a fire at Ilinka had destroyed all their family portraits, leaving him only two relics of his grandfather Dmitrii: the czarina's goblet and an ancient icon of St Nicholas. Although it was his only treasure he had decided to donate the goblet to the ship. In return, Birilev had promised (on the czar's behalf, Nikolai believed) to provide for the education of his sons at the naval college and to return him their family estate, Ilinka, sold for debts. None of what he had promised ever came to pass.

Meanwhile, Nikolai confessed, after the financial failure with the exhibition of Ge's painting:

'I BECAME MORE AND MORE ENTANGLED IN POVERTY and, being evicted with my family from the flat, I spent 1900 roubles belonging to my client in the hope that I would have enough time to repay the amount I embezzled. Unfortunately, the client suddenly demanded the money and, refusing to give me even a fortnight's grace, lodged an appeal in court. I had two alternatives: either to escape or to desecrate the name of Ilin, honest and glorious for generations. I could hope for the jury's compassion, even for acquittal, but I could not avoid publicity and disgrace. Then I fled abroad.

'It is twenty-one months since then. My family drags out a miserable existence in St Petersburg. My wife with her needle feeds them all. I, in Argentina, have chosen to suffer drudgery, together with my twelve-year-old son. ... Often we have no food for days and my boy courageously hides his hunger. ... If not for the disgrace that is associated with banishment how happy I would be to exchange this existence for exile — even to Sakhalin — but together with my family!! For twenty-one months I hoped to manage on my own and to achieve some success that would enable me to save enough money for my family to travel out here; but now I am a broken man and take this liberty to implore you, gentlemen: 'Help my poor wife as brothers in Christ, as nobleman to nobleman, as officers of the cruiser *Lieutenant Ilin* for the little great-grandchildren of the patron of your ship.'[8]

How naïve and touching it was, that appeal to the memory of the legendary lieutenant (who was not even his grandfather) — as if he was appealing to his own missed destiny ...

* * *

Well, we have found 'the truth', and thus destroyed all other legends. Or have we? Do we need to accept it as the only truth? I do not want to. I do not intend to repeat Pontius Pilate's question addressed to Christ, hunted to death for his truth. Nikolai had his own truth, too. Whatever his crime was, he expiated it with suffering such as no one could imagine. He pleaded in his 'Confession':

> Forgive my sins, my motherland,
> As I repent committing them.
> I've paid for them all through my life —
> A hunted wolf that's doomed to die.[9]

And maybe he cried in front of Ge's painting because he, more than anyone else, recognised in this hunted and despised Christ his brother, his own, well-concealed alter ego. Nikolai's attempt to realise this alter ego in real life failed; he lost nearly everything — motherland, his good name, part of his family and money. Yet he found the strength to start a new life on what he was left with — his faithful wife and three children — at the other end of the globe, in a shepherd's slab hut in the Andes.

FROM
FARM TO
COLONY

UP IN THE PATAGONIAN MOUNTAINS

The waters of the stream fighting their way down between the boulders were cold and green. Nicholas — he was now known by this name, no longer as Nikolai — loved to camp here by this stream on his way home from hunting expeditions to Lago Futalaufquén. The stream started off high in the Andean glaciers, then, like its numerous brothers, rushed down the eastward slopes; below, in the valley, the streams all joined to form Rio Futaleufu and Rio Yelcho and flowed back through the mountains to the west, in the direction of the Pacific Ocean. According to a treaty between Argentina and Chile, the international boundary was supposed to lie along the crest of the Cordillera of the Andes between the watersheds of eastward- and westward-flowing rivers. But the whimsical passage of these streams, which might diverge and flow in both directions at once, was the cause of an international boundary dispute between Argentina and Chile and nearly cost Romelio his life: it would have done, had it not been for Ariadna.

When Nicholas's family came from Russia in 1897 and settled here, on the eastern slopes of the Cordillera but well to the west of the watershed, this was a no-man's land. Nicholas's naturalisation as an Argentinian soon played a crucial role in the border dispute since the Argentinian government then extended its border nearly 50 miles west of the watershed, as far as the Illins' cattle-run stretched, claiming that this territory was already occupied by Argentinian subjects. Life on the disputed border taught the Illins to act quickly.

Sam Mackay, Ariadna's grandson, relates what happened in 1905: 'a Chilean soldier riding a horse appeared as Romelio was working in the field. When the soldier saw Romelio, he took out his sabre and went after him. ... Ariadna, who was just fifteen, ran home to get a weapon to give it to Romelio, but when she got back, the soldier was about to kill Romelio, so Ariadna had to shoot and kill the soldier.'[1] War is war ...

But now, looking at the green, impetuous waters of the stream, Nicholas did not think about the treacherous world of people; his heart was filled with that delightful feeling of a poem about to be born. Years ago, when fleeing from Russia, he wrote as if prophetically about these mountains and his initial despair:

Up in the mountains, abandoned and alone,
In vain you'll search for peace and calm.
How to forget the dreams of youth?
How to forget the yearnings of the past?

As an uprooted flower carried by a wave
Will never again grow on bare rock,
So the great spirit of your youth will fade
In your tormented, morbid heart.[2]

This nameless stream, which century after century had fought its way along the dark canyons, seemed to open up a new philosophy to him. 'Why do you hurl yourself on the boulders, which you never will be able to overpower?', he asked the stream. 'Would it not be wiser to take a quieter route around the rocks, along the valleys, as either way the end will be the same — you will disappear into the ocean.' And today the stream seemed to bring him its answer.

I don't fear the gloomy rocks
My waters crush them by degrees:
The way to freedom — ever open,
Who tries to stop me will be swept away.

...

Nothing, however great, will resist the passion
Of my sacred aspirations. I race ahead,
I trust myself, myself alone,
And, however long it takes, I will win.[3]

'The way to freedom — ever open' he said to himself and at that moment he believed that, whatever had happened in the past, his life was not a mistake. This peaceful day beside the stream was no abdication, no defeat but a spiritual rebirth.

Alexandra's recent trip to Russia had been a painful trial for both of them. She went to see their eldest daughter Mania (Maria), left behind in St Petersburg, who was married to a Russianised German road-engineer, Wilhelm Pettersen, and had two daughters, Antonina (Tonia) and Valentina (Valia). When, after a year away, Alexandra returned to their shepherd's hut in the Andes, she and Nicholas realised that they had burned their boats forever: 'In the company of Russians I am an alien now', Alexandra declared in Nicholas's poem. Even so, sometimes he would be carried away to his motherland — in his dreams. Then, he would return to the land where he left behind the aspirations of his youth, where he left his children and the lonely grave of his little Karterii:

> There, beside a child's grave
> In a far but native land
> Where you, my dear nestling, have your eternal sleep
> I'd like with all my heart to be with you ...[4]

Before, at the moment of despair, he used to lament:

> Mocking destiny has given me the freedom
> To waste my painful days away from the motherland.

But now he saw his tragedy as being attributable to something far greater than a banal embezzlement: it was the outcome of his conflict with the official Russia of 'Pilates'. And he nearly believed himself, declaring that, with 'a penitential line I could receive back from the Russian authorities all my former comforts', though he would not do this because he could never bring himself to ask his enemy for mercy. All that was left for him now was to sing his newly acquired freedom:

> None of your business who I am!
> My heart is free — that is the main thing.[5]

It cannot be, he would say to himself, looking at the restless stream below, that his passion for freedom and justice was a trifle; one day it should achieve results — if not in his own life, then in the lives of his children or his grandchildren.

This feeling of freedom came to him only gradually. He did not care to remember the trials of his first years abroad. First, there was the period in Switzerland. This was a place of refuge for Russian radicals of all political persuasions, but after spending some time there he felt himself suffocating in the mire of their discords. Just when his desperation was compounded by his lack of money he received a commission to study Jewish colonies which had been established in Argentina by Baron Hirsch. The commission came from Osip Notovich, the editor of the Russian newspaper *Novosti*, which had never been highly regarded by the democratic elements in Russia; nevertheless, Nicholas agreed to take this job. Argentina needed farmers, and the Jewish Colonisation Association, established by Baron Maurice Hirsch, a capitalist and phi-lanthropist, aimed to settle Jews, mainly refugees from Russia, on the land there. They were to acquire new skills and to create a new way of life, with dignity and prosperity, free of persecution. Nicholas was to chronicle this new experiment in the first young colonies — Mauricio, southwest of Buenos Aires, and Moises Ville, north of Santa Fe. His research did not last long, however, for he soon quarrelled with Notovich, and Nicholas found himself not only penniless in Argentina but, worse, hopeless. He tried farming, worked as a stevedore, as a labourer, a wandering photographer and a pedlar[6] — and all this time he never forgot about Sasha, alone with the children in St Petersburg. In a moment of despair he sent her his photograph — a sad and aged face with inward-looking eyes — inscribed with his poem.

> Beneath the pleasant southern sun
> Lonely and alone
> Your tired-out barque awaits,
> My true friend.
>
> Its rigging still unbroken,
> Still strong the sails,
> Only the horizon and sky
> In rough weather are overcast.
>
> But as soon as the sail trembles
> When the wind gusts,
> Renewed in vigour, the barque sets forth
> For fresh seas.[7]

Like Lermontov's lonely white sail far from its homeland, seeking what lies at the heart of the tempest — the rebellious sail of his youth is no more, now that the tempests of real life have pursued his barque from sea to sea until, exhausted, it is washed up on an alien shore ... And

Sasha, his only true friend, far-away in St Petersburg, sent him their most valued treasure — young Leandr, with money in a sack. Betrayed and robbed by the woman who accompanied him, the boy did manage to reach Argentina, to find his father and to rescue him … from himself. Years later, as the hero of Nicholas's poem 'Father and son' reappraising his life, he will say to his father:

Life's turbid wave will never carry off
The pure precepts of the early days
That you and Mother taught.
As rapid ebb-tide waves
Will never carry off a barque
Chained to a granite wall.[8]

And that will not be just words: the barques led by his children will find their proper way in real life, unlike his Lermontovian rebel sail …

However, for now his twelve-year old boy, who, according to Nicholas himself, 'had experienced sufferings far beyond one of his years', shares what has befallen his father. 'With a small camera, we wander in the heat of the tropical sun across scarcely inhabited pampas, unable to speak the local language, visiting half-civilised gauchos and offering our services. Often we have no food for days and my boy courageously hides his hunger. Frequently dead-tired and suffering heat exhaustion, we lie down on the bare land, hiding our heads in the shadow of our wheelbarrow and only the cold night air revives us.'[9]

But eventually they had some luck. Nicholas's good education in humanities, languages and science allowed him to find a 'clean' job as a librarian and assistant-manager of the anthropological section in the Museo de La Plata. The museum acted as a research institute and Dr Francisco Moreno (1852–1919), its founder and director, was a geographer and enthusiast of the study and settlement of the vast, unexplored areas of western Patagonia, which influenced Nicholas's interest in these areas, too. In La Plata, a quiet, cultural centre near the ocean, all the tension experienced by Nicholas over the previous years now poured out in a poetical explosion. His main creation was the elaborate *The Orient Legend*, based on the Turkestan folklore he had enjoyed while living there. It took him back to when he was young — to his and Sasha's falling in love.

And finally she arrived from Hamburg, in June 1897, on the

Mendoza and accompanied by Romelio, now aged ten, and Ariadna, who was seven (plus a mysterious Marie Ilina, thirty-two years old, of whom we never hear again). Nellie, Ariadna's daughter, has preserved the excitement of their unusual reunion.

'SO THEN MY GRANDMOTHER GOT A PERMIT and went to Argentina. She went to see the people that helped her because they knew my grandfather. They settled her somewhere. My mother was seven years old by then. She ran to my grandmother one day and said that there was a man walking down the street who looked just like her father, whom she knew from the photograph. "It must be him, it must be him", she said. So my grandmother ran outside and it *was* him. So that's how they got together again.'[10]

Ariadna, Romelio and Leandro (the boys now used these forms of their names) — that was all that remained of their big family. The others were in Russia: the eldest children, Ivan, Sergei and Maria, had stayed on there; Karterii and the infant Vera were buried there.

For a while the family enjoyed life in La Plata. To have a clean, intellectual job was a rare occurrence for an émigré — the majority of Nicholas's compatriots in Argentina were destined to work as labourers. This quiet, comfortable life was not for him, though, and his rebel sail was once more lured out in search of tempests ...

Nicholas became disenchanted with Argentina's dictatorship and anti-democratic state system; about his decision to move on, he wrote: 'Discovering that it was not worthwhile leaving my motherland in order to live in such conditions abroad I retreated with my family to the wild Patagonian Andes, where the government, according to presidential decree, promised to give the settlers blocks of land free of charge.'[11] Well, maybe this was only half the truth, as the main reason for this new flight, this time from comfortable La Plata, was the necessity to hide from his mysterious enemies, as Nellie mentioned in her memoirs, or ... again from himself.

'Gypsies, gypsies for sure', Alexandra laughed, helping to load onto the ox-cart the trunk with Nicholas's books and manuscripts, which she had managed to bring from their St Petersburg flat to Argentina. This ox-cart with its high wheels took them across the continent. The pampas, which reminded Nicholas of the Russian steppe around Ilinka, were replaced by endless, arid plateaux gradually rising westwards. Strong winds raised clouds of sand, and the primitive mud-and-straw huts belonging to local shepherds they met along the way scarcely offered them any protection. Now they were to learn the primitive life-style of the gaucho — beans or corn flavoured with oil was the main diet, and *maté* (herbal tea), and for a bed several sheepskins and a poncho on the earthen floor. Day after day they continued on their way west, to the Andes looming high on the horizon, to their Promised Land. South of the upper reaches of the Chubut River they reached Esquel, a tiny frontier township, continuing southwest from there towards the Welsh colony Diez-y-séis de Octubre (16th of October, also called Trevelin). The Welsh came here, to this barren land, about fifteen years earlier and by the turn of the century had changed it into a flowering oasis.

The Illins chose land to the south of the Welsh colony, in the Corcovado valley just at the foot of the Andes, which was abundant with water. Nature in its unspoiled might and beauty brought peace to Nicholas's tormented soul. To the west rose mountain chains with snow-white tops and several volcanoes. The steep slopes were covered with the ancient trees of Araucania — cedars and bamboo groves mixed with beeches — and in autumn would flame red and yellow. Mountain streams, waterfalls, and glacial lakes with mirror-like emerald water contributed to the enchantment. Later this picturesque belt of forests and lakes on the eastern mountain slopes would become known as 'The Argentine Switzerland' and nowadays parts of it are declared national parks. But for the Illins their immediate preoccupation was how to survive in this wilderness.

Nicholas with his young sons built a hut (in winter it was nearly as cold here as in Russia). Then they bought some horses, cattle and sheep, established a vegetable garden and orchard and started their pioneering life full of adventures.[12] The only thing Nicholas did not have to worry about here was his younger children growing up into walking dummies, hidebound and conventional. Life on the frontier provided them with perfect opportunities to develop their potential in a natural environment. As for schooling, he himself taught them reading and writing, and studied Russian literature and history with them, both from the democratic point of view. A local teacher contributed to the Spanish side of their education. The sons, both sharing Nicholas's aspiration for justice, grew up different — Leandro, an extrovert, was always on the move, rushing outside, into the wide world; while the more sentimental and quiet Romelio, an introvert, mostly stayed at home with the family. As for Ara (Ariadna), she had no other examples but her brothers, and she grew up a real frontier tomboy — different from them all, though. Nellie tells about her youth.

'MY MOTHER LEARNT TO RIDE HORSEBACK, TO SHOOT AND CARRY A GUN with her, because there was a lot of pumas there. She was capable of doing anything that a man was capable of doing.

'One time my grandmother and mother went to visit a neighbour that was kilometres away. When they were coming back there had been a flash flood, a river that was near them rose and they couldn't cross it — it was too deep. So they had to stay on one side, their home was on the other side. They had not taken anything to eat, so she killed one of the horses and that's what they survived on for a week. They ate the horse, until the waters went down and they could get home.

'My grandfather used to make a trip every year to Buenos Aires to take all kinds of rare plants to the Botanical Gardens. One year he took my mother with him, she was about twelve years old. On the way back winter had come early, and they had to travel by horse to get home and it was very, very cold. So my grandfather used to put her on the ground and cover her with a blanket and throw snow over her, pack her up so she could be warm. The horse fell once and my mother had broken ribs and a broken leg. Well, he patched her up, they made it back home safely.'[13]

Besides collecting rare plants, Nicholas hunted a lot up in the mountains together with his sons. Henry, Nicholas's grandson, remembers that he worked as a taxidermist for museums as well. Hunting had always been an exciting pleasure for Nicholas, somehow compensating for the way that in his youth at Ilinka there had been little change of scene. His sons, who from their early days had had more than enough changes of scene, took a more pragmatic view of hunting: the furs provided a way getting some cash. Leandro earned money by trapping Colpeo foxes.

But, as soon as their ranch in Corcovado was established and Romelio was strong enough to help Nicholas as a herdsman, Leandro was able to fulfil his long-held dream, which was to cross the Andes and to see the Pacific Ocean. He began to take commissions from their neighbours, especially the Welsh, who did well, and was engaged to drive cattle, sheep, and pack mules loaded with wool, across the Andes to the Chilean markets. 'I have travelled very much, and sometimes very slowly ...' he wrote much later. 'I had trips of five months, sometimes through deserts, and once I travelled ten consecutive months over the Andes on the same horses.' Along mountain passes, past volcanoes and glaciers, through the uninhabited, dry, western slopes of the Chilean Andes he made his way to Puerto Montt and then north, past Lago Llanquihue, to the Chilean markets of Valdivia and Temuco.

Mountain forests were followed by yellow rocks and alpine meadows with incredible ultramarine lakes while the mountains with snow-crests lying ahead seemed always to be blue. Black-and-white condors with their three-metre wing-span glided for hours over Leandro's herd. Red, sensitive guanaco stood still, like graceful statuettes on the rocks, and then raced downwards. At night the light of his camp-fire kept pumas away and the stars of the Southern Cross showed him the direction to take. And then morning came and the snow-crests turned red, filling his heart with admiration — and loneliness. Leandro never questioned his father's choices but sometimes he thought that he would give away all the wild beauty of this alien land for one day in the pine forest of his childhood, close to their *dacha* in Siverskaia, near St Petersburg.

Sometimes Leandro travelled eastwards, towards the Atlantic Ocean, across endless prairies with never-ceasing winds. He wrote that he knew well all the southern territories of Argentina and all ports down the Patagonian coast. His travels from Buenos Aires took him up the Rio Parana to Rosario, Santa Fe, Victoria, Corrientes, Posadas, Misiones — to the hot Argentine north, as well as to the neighbouring countries of Uruguay, Paraguay and Brazil.[14]

Leandro, to survive these hard journeys, had to put into practice Nicholas's theoretical democratic ideals about the equality of all people and respect for their way of life. He learned a lot from local Tehuelche and Araucan Indians, the latter being especially numerous on the Chilean side of the Andes. He always ate the local food and was never put off by it, whether it was horseflesh or maize. In general, so far as both Leandro and Romelio were concerned, their Argentinian Spanish, their skill in using the lasso and bolas, their dress and behaviour — playing local songs on a mandolin soon became one of their favourite pastimes — made the brothers gauchos rather than immigrant-outsiders. Leandro always highly valued the predominant racial tolerance of the Patagonian frontier. The local English were the only ones who did not abide by this. Leandro wrote about this years later. 'I have seen Anglo-Saxons in South America who after 30 to 40 years in the country and making huge fortunes [were] not able to speak Spanish and called every Argentinian "peon" or "nigger" and rode the racial horse.'[15]

For Nicholas it was not so easy to accept the surrounding life-style, the surrounding world. His passion for justice never let go of him, even in the Andes. Years later he would write to an Australian newspaper about one such clash.

'FOR MANY YEARS I WAS A NATURALISED ARGENTINE SUBJECT, and lived in the territory Chubut, far from all civilisation by many hundreds of miles. Having knowledge of the Spanish language I corresponded with liberal newspapers in the capital (Buenos Aires) and communicated without restraint all the abuses committed by the local authorities (which were many), who were suitably situated on account of great distances from the federal government. Once there appeared a constable with an order of arrest from the local "commissario" (sheriff) without explaining the reason for my arrest. The constable conveyed me 60 miles to the police station. My eldest son followed me and immediately sent telegrams to the Ministers and President of the Republic, pointing out to them that the 20th paragraph of their constitution does not allow them to keep anybody under arrest for more than 24 hours without explaining the reason of the arrest, and that nobody can be deprived of their liberty for more than 24 hours without a judicial inquest or trial. A few hours later came telegraphic orders to set me free, and the commissario was called back and another sent instead.'[16]

Indeed, there were enough problems in Argentinian life to provoke Nicholas's criticism: from the political regime itself ranging all the way down to a Patagonian missionary who 'enslaved and impudently exploited natives under the pretence of converting them to Christianity while acquiring from the corrupt Argentine government a colossal land concession ... and made a huge fortune in the name of love for his brother'. According to Nicholas: 'Argentina is an ultra-imperialist republic. The constitution is a dead letter: the parliament has no opposition and fulfils the orders of the actual dictator — the president. ... An oligarchy, a bunch of *Distinguidos* (estate-owners) rules the country overriding everything and everyone. The administration is conducted with unlimited arbitrariness. The court is a banal parody of justice.'[17]

Argentina, 'a republic', turned out to be not much better than his autocratic motherland. The difference was that, in Argentina, he had some opportunity to struggle against the local corruption while he could do little about Russia — only write about her in his poems, without much hope of ever seeing them published. The Russian destiny now, from his Patagonian perspective, seemed more and more clear to him. During his years of exile in Argentina he wrote at least fifty poems, including several long poems. Some of them might be considered now as crude and wordy but in some, especially those written in the form of folk poetry, he did manage 'to rise with his Muse to the heights of poetic Parnassus'. The formal quality of his poetry seems not to have occupied his mind a great deal, as the Muse which came to him was the Muse of struggle and revenge. He declared himself to be a 'Poet of destruction' and used his 'castigating pen' 'to whip the scoundrelly clique' which ruled Russia, to awaken his suffering motherland to struggle.[18]

At the centre of Nicholas's poetry is *narod* — the Russian people, its working masses. Throughout his life Nicholas lived among many different peoples. He never idealised any of them but, on the other hand, he never treated members of any national group with racial prejudice — whether they were Jews, Americans or Central Asian Uzbeks. Even during the Russo-Japanese war he did not adopt the chauvinistic attitude towards the Japanese which the Russians were swept up with; he gave the brave and honest Japanese military men their due. But only the Russians occupied a special place in his heart. He clearly saw all their faults. They were 'downtrodden resigned slaves', famous in history for one quality only: their patience in suffering. And, worse, this 'grey crowd' in its savagery and ignorance was easily deceived and apt to help its oppressors crush its real brothers — the revolutionaries. In spite of all this, Nicholas had a deep love for the people just as they were. Moreover, they were the crucial element in his image of his motherland. In opposition to official Russian history he wrote his own version in a long poem, 'History of the Russian State', in which he admired Russia's free, ancient past and believed that the Russians would finally awake and reclaim their old freedom. He did not spare even his own ancestors, the Ruriks (belonging to whom was a point of pride for any Russian), who, argued Nicholas, by bringing ancient Russia its statehood deprived its people of their freedom and dignity.[19]

Now, especially after the abortive Russian revolution of 1905, his views of the situation in Russia underwent a significant development in comparison with his previous attitudes. If, before, he had had some illusions about the positive role which some honest officials could play, now — in his view from the Patagonian wilderness — nothing seemed to restrict his criticism of, or, rather, his aversion to, the upper classes as a whole. His mocking 'High society commandments' discloses their repulsive moral credo. Among these 'commandments' the most revealing are the following:

7. For the extremely important purpose of decorating yourself with braids and trinkets spare neither your honour, nor your wife, nor your daughters, since they all are your own property ...

9. Praise your Orthodox Czar at crowded meetings and in all your papers ... But at friendly gatherings abuse him without mercy for his stupidity, since he fails to satisfy your bestial cupidity.

No one belonging to the powers that be could elicit his sympathy — the officials choking Russia in their deadening grip; those serving its corrupt, servile 'justice'; priests who have forgotten about God; generals squabbling for the czar's trinkets and disgracing the Russian flag in battles, as they are apt to fight only against their own unarmed peasants and workers; the political police corrupting people to such a degree that in any gathering of three the third is sure to be a denouncer; liberal 'reformers' who build their reforms on the bones and blood of the working classes. And at the head of this gang is the main criminal — the czar, 'a villainous butcher'.[20]

Nicholas believed that the only way for his people to end their sufferings and slavery would be to unite in a 'bloody struggle' against their oppressors. In his poem 'To the dying fighter' (1906) the fatally wounded terrorist does not repent killing several innocent victims as it was done in the name of the supreme aim of liberating millions of the czar's victims. In another poem Nicholas mentioned that 'dynamite rather than sentiments' was the only way to get at the powers that be. And the czar above all others, Nicholas believed, deserved execution. His views were more radical than those of other Russian democratic intellectuals of the time: for the final outcome of the struggle, he naïvely believed that as soon as the czar and his gang were removed the kingdom of light, freedom, equality and joyful toil would establish itself.[21] About a decade remained before the correctness of his views was tested.

In the meantime the life of their little family in Corcovado went on its own way. In around 1908, while Alexandra was spending a year in Russia visiting Mania, at the age of just eighteen Ariadna married Wilhelm Steinkamp, a son of their German neighbour. On 6 September 1909 she gave birth to a boy. Continuing the family mythological naming-tradition, they named him Hector, after the great, chivalrous Trojan warrior, a hero of the epic poem, the *Iliad*. According to vague family tales Nicholas and Alexandra did not approve of Ariadna's union and wanted to take her away; but Ariadna and Wilhelm soon separated in any case.[22] Ariadna's marriage was the least of their worries, however.

Their worst problem was the trap into which they had fallen, having been misled by the Argentine government. The initial presidential decree, which had promised settlers in the Patagonian wilderness huge blocks of land free of charge on condition that slight improvements were made, was cancelled and the Illins, like their Welsh neighbours, found themselves unable to realise their right of ownership. The years of hard toil were in vain; the corrupt Argentine 'democracy' had gained the upper hand.

Nicholas was nearly sixty already but he decided to start once again, in a new place, in a new country, on the opposite side of the globe. It did not take him long to choose Australia once he had seen some booklets about it, which advertised it as a country of justice and of abundant fertile land. And there was one more consideration. Nellie relates: 'After my grandfather found out about Australia, he thought that that was a good country to bring Russians to for a colony. And after my grandmother came back from Russia they packed up and went.'[23] It was May 1910.

PATAGONIA TO AUSTRALIA VIA PARIS AND MONTE CARLO

Nicholas was crossing the Atlantic Ocean for the sixth and final time, but for the first time his family was travelling with him, and the final lines of his old poem came back to his memory. When he'd sent this to Sasha how different things were then: he was alone, despairing. And now they were all together, embarked on a new adventure.

> But as soon as the sail trembles
> When the wind gusts,
> Renewed in vigour, the barque sets forth
> For fresh seas.

> And full of bright hope
> It will choose a new way ...

The new way lay ahead, towards the unknown Australia. Nicholas was determined to 'colonise' it with the help of his family, with the help of other Russians. Indeed, he seemed very purposeful. According to his account in a St Petersburg newspaper:

'ON ARRIVAL IN LONDON we visited the Queensland government agency and without any obstacles were enlisted as emigrants on the first ship departing to Australia. It was the *Omrah*, of the Orient Line.

'A ticket to Brisbane for an ordinary third-class passenger costs £17. As emigrants we paid as follows: my sons and daughter £5 each; myself, as a man older than forty-five – £12; my wife, as the mother of able-bodied emigrants – free of charge.'[24]

Nellie's memoirs give the story another dimension, showing that Nicholas's determination had a telling set-back, without which, however, he would not have been himself.

'THEY WENT ON A SHIP TO ENGLAND, and from England to Paris, and actually they stayed for a few days there before taking a ship to go to Australia. He had some money, so he said he was going to go over to gamble with this money and make a fortune. Well, the only fortune he got was that he lost all this money but he had bought a train ticket, round-trip ticket, from Paris to Monte Carlo, and a good thing he had, because he came back broke. Well, they took a ship there and went to Australia.[25]

His last visit to Europe was conducted under the auspices of his two passions: gambling and poetry. Neither was for the money itself but for the intoxicating moments of power over routine. While his 'Muse of Chance' betrayed him this time, his 'Muse of Poetry' found a welcome reception in Paris. In 1910 Paris was becoming a centre for Russian culture and for Russian political emigration. Sergei Diaghilev organised his famous Russian seasons there — performances of Russian opera and ballet, supported by the group of Russian intellectuals, The World of Art. There were posters adorning the streets of Paris during these years of the graceful ballerina Anna Pavlova, or the bass Fedor Chaliapin in the costume of ancient Russian czars, or posters in folk-art style for the ballets *The Firebird* and *Petrouchka*. Russia was in vogue and the cream of Russian intellectual modernists headed to conquer Paris then — the poets Konstantin Balmont, Anna Akhmatova and Nikolai Gumilev, and the artists Marc Chagall, Vassili Kandinsky and Lev Bakst. In cheap studios on Montmartre, in cafes and salons they mixed with the French intellectuals, contributing a Russian aura to the refined air of Paris. What a feast it was for the Illins after years as herdsmen in Patagonia.

But that was not enough for Nicholas, his heart was far away, in suffering Russia. It did not take him long to get in touch with Russian political émigrés. Bolsheviks, mensheviks, esers (socialist-revolutionaries), maximalists — there was a variety of them sharing socialist ideas, but each was also involved in endless struggle with each other. Nicholas's clear poetical voice seemed to return them to the lost heroism of the final goal, for instance, in his version of 'Workers' Marseillaise' (this is the mysterious French anthem figuring in his descendants' tales!):

> We will inspire bloody terror
> In tyrants with our might.
> We will overpower oppressors
> Through our toil.

> We will cast down the idol from the throne
> And the czar will take flight.
> We will trample the crown to dust
> And smash the altar.

> By common effort all peoples
> Will build a bright temple of toil,
> And the star of equality and freedom
> Will rise over it.[26]

In Paris Nicholas met Nikolai Glebov, a menshevik, and a participant in the Russian revolution of 1905, who lived in exile under the pseudonym of Stepan Golub and was involved in the publication of the journal *Proletarian Banner*. He became interested in Nicholas's life story and liked his poems. They agreed that a book of his poetry would be published in Paris at Nicholas's expense while all the proceeds from its sale would support the publication of the *Proletarian Banner*. Stepan Golub kept his promise and while Nicholas was beginning to 'colonise' the Atherton Tablelands his book *The Songs of the Earth* was published in Paris with an introduction by Golub. He had an impression of the Ilins as a 'likeable and close family' and portrayed Nicholas as a 'poet-grandfather'. But what appealed to Golub most was Nicholas's ability to oppose the contemporary decadence of the symbolist poet Konstantin Balmont, and the like, with a sincere, passionate, clear idea of freedom and social justice. Beneath the cold Andean peaks he, it seems, had preserved in their pure state the nineteenth century democratic ideals that in Europe and Russia had been corrupted by the new fashionable trends. Even the title of his book *The Songs of the Earth* opposed the symbolist Balmont's aspiration to be named 'Poet of the Sun'. Golub expressed only one regret that 'these songs would remain inaccessible in Russia, where the poet himself would like to direct them most of all, where these songs are the most necessary'.[27]

Nicholas's personal copy of *The Songs of the Earth* had, like the *Tolstoyan Diary*, its own destiny. From Australia it travelled with Nicholas to Colombia and Honduras, and after his death it was in the possession of Romelio. Years passed and one day in the 1960s Romelio's son Leandro came home very excited: a Russian ship had come for the first time to Honduras. They were the first real Russians, his lost brothers, the missing link to help him to reunite himself with the unknown motherland of his ancestors. The sailors were, indeed, nice fellows and accepted him as one of their own. Telling them about Nicholas, Leandro gave them *The Songs of the Earth*. When Romelio found out about this he was very upset, but nothing could be done to retrieve the book; the ship had gone. Hearing the story from Leandro in 1996, I understood him but was upset too — it might have been the last copy of the book to survive, as none of the libraries seemed to have it. Luckily, Nadezhda Ryzhak from the Russian State Library in Moscow discovered a copy in the collection of Nicholas Rubakin, a famous Russian book-collector. The copy came to me in Australia and I sent one copy of it to Leandro in the United States of America and another one to Nicholas's motherland — to the Turki Museum. Nicholas did come home to his countrymen, eighty-six years later.

At last all the excitements and disappointments of their brief visit to Europe were over and they boarded the *Omrah*. This was a large steamship of 8282 tons, which made regular voyages between London and Australia. It had over 100 passengers, mainly emigrants from Britain, whose occupations were recorded in the list of passengers as farmers, labourers or farm-hands. The Illins — Nicholas, Alexandra, Leandro, Romelio, and Ariadna (with her son Hector, although he did not appear on the passenger list) — were recorded as 'farm-hands', too, travelling as assisted migrants.[28] One other Russian family — Mary, Boris and Ludmila Daniel — was aboard the ship.

On 22 July 1910 the *Omrah* sailed from Tilbury Docks on the Thames. A crowd of people was watching her departure. Later,

Leandro recorded his impressions of this moment: 'Poor tired people! I could read on their faces the wish to leave London, to go somewhere in search of luck.' For the next forty-six days the Illins left all their troubles behind and could relax and watch the world. The *Omrah*, under the command of Captain H.G. Staunton, was a clean and comfortable ship and the Illins were pleasantly surprised that, in the third class, 'they enjoyed comforts similar to those of the second class on the best Russian steamships'. The horrifying memories of Nicholas's trips with Leandro, shivering from cold in steerage, were in the past. On 26 July they sailed through the Strait of Gibraltar, and in another day they were in Marseilles, then Naples and Taranto in Italy, where bags of European mail for Australia were loaded on the ship. On 3 August they arrived at Port Said, absorbing for a few hours the picturesque atmosphere of the orient. Leandro wrote about an encounter he had there.

'I WENT INTO A JEW'S SHOP TO BUY SOMETHING AND PAID HIM WITH A SOVEREIGN. He had to give me change back, and he gave me some counterfeit coins. I refused to take them, but he boldly insisted on ringing them in on me. I refused again, so he put them back into the cash-box, turned them a time or two, and tried to give them to me again, until I threatened to call a policeman. I got my own back then.'[29]

Years later the practices of the Queensland government would remind him of the way this trader behaved.

At dawn the next day they passed through the Suez Canal. On the way to Ceylon the weather was cool as the monsoon was blowing and they entered Colombo at noon on 13 August. The memory of this day still lives in the Illin family. Ernie Hoolihan had heard about it as a boy from Leandro, his grandfather. Lush tropical vegetation, coconut palms, the waving masts of the numerous ships in the harbour, and native boys surrounding the *Omrah* and begging for coins. The swift flight of a dark body diving into the water and the smiling face of the lucky one who caught the coin ... They left Colombo the following night and for a long time the flashes from the lighthouse on the south of the island sent a farewell to the *Omrah*.

After crossing the equator the Southern Cross, their old Patagonian friend, appeared over the horizon. Some passengers grew sad and lonely on this long passage to Australia, but not the Illins — they were all together, they had their countryfolk, the Daniel family, to speak to, and little Hector amused them all making his first awkward steps on the rocking deck.

On 23 August, after the ten-day voyage across the Indian Ocean, they finally arrived in Australia, at Fremantle. Their first impression of the country made them enthusiastic. They might have agreed with the words of the Russian agricultural expert Nikolai Kriukov, who visited Fremantle in 1903:

'WE ARE IN AUSTRALIA, AT LAST! ... Light-blue sky, bright sun, perfect harbour, a town with beautiful, new stone buildings, well-dressed people moving in all directions and not one policeman — these were the first impressions. Involuntarily I remembered the first disembarkation, in Vladivostok: black gangway, black cheerless buildings on the shore, cold mist, no movement and a policeman in the foreground probably himself wondering why he was fixed to this spot. And the ordered jingle of spurs rather than the sounds of people bustling about.'[30]

The *Omrah* continued her voyage around Australia. Adelaide, usually quiet and English-like, was exuberant with life on the Saturday when they called there — workers and labourers enjoyed a short working-day and all shops, restaurants and theatres were open till late. Melbourne, the temporary federal capital, was occupied with discussion about the likely site for the new capital — Yass–Canberra or Dalgety. In Sydney, where they arrived on 1 September, golden wattles blossomed along the shores of Port Jackson. The city was celebrating the newly established Wattle Day, a day to mark Australians' devotion to their new country. Fascinated with this new world, the Illins watched the sunset over the bay from the deck of the *Omrah*, which was moored at Circular Quay.

Their strongest impression of this first encounter with Australia was the absence of poverty.

'BEGINNING WITH THE FIRST AUSTRALIAN PORT (Fremantle) and in all the following, we were inspired more and more deeply with an impression that was quite unknown, not just for someone who has come from Russia but even for us who have seen Europe and both Americas. It was the impression of "wholesale satiety". Whether in ports, on the streets or in theatres, on weekdays or on holidays, my eye half-consciously was looking out for the shabby, tired fellows who are so well-known to me, but in vain. They were not there. And I have to confess that, after I had visited the main Australian cities and disembarked in Brisbane, I still involuntarily continued to look for the misery that to our mind is inevitable (it should be there somewhere!) but did not encounter it.'[31]

On 5 September 1910 the *Omrah* arrived in Brisbane. As Nicholas relates: 'We were transferred from the *Omrah* by a river steamboat to the Immigration Depot — a clean, spacious barracks with one half allocated to males and the other to females. ... We could stay in the Immigration Depot for seven days free of charge and during that time had no reason to complain, neither of the food nor of the accommodation.' For many Russians, with no money and without English, the only way out of the Depot led to the railway construction sites all over Queensland. The Illins had different plans: they wanted to work on the land. Nicholas, as a former medical student, went to see Mr Mellish, the director of the Department of Public Health. He, according to Nicholas, 'took great interest in us and personally led me to the director of the Department of Public Lands, Mr Graham'.

'WE ENTERED HIS OFFICE, BUT HAD TO WAIT ON ONE SIDE for half-an-hour while Mr Graham, seated at his desk, was talking openly with a toil-hardened colonist who was sitting in front of him smoking a cigar.

'The colonist plied him with questions and received unhurried, detailed answers. Only when he had finished asking all his questions did this man get up from his seat, an easychair with arm-rests, and in a relaxed manner take his leave from this high official, as equal with equal. When I replaced the colonist in the easychair, I immediately discovered that I, similarly to my predecessor, was on an equal footing with my interlocutor.

'From the questions that I was asked and from explanations that I received I became convinced that, here, work is conducted conscientiously, judiciously, without humbug, not for the sake of appearances, and without excessive formality and delays.'[32]

Following the laws which govern the creation of a legend, Nicholas, when writing to Russians, elevated the ranks of these officials a little.[33] This is not surprising, as Mellish and Graham were for him the first officials to personify the Australian style of treatment of the working man and of handling affairs, which differed so much from Nicholas's former experience as a public servant in Russia. It was Graham who advised them to go to the Cairns area and the Illins followed his advice.

As they were leaving the Immigration Depot on the bank of the Brisbane River to head north to Cairns, the young jacaranda in front of it was wearing its first purple-blue blossom. It seemed that the blue of the sky rested on the thin branches, promising hope and love. And it was love that interfered with the Illin family here, causing the first split:

Leandro decided to delay his departure to the north for a few weeks longer.

Nicholas wrote about the onward journey:

'WE TRAVELLED FREE OF CHARGE BY RAILWAY TO THE SMALL PORT OF GLADSTONE. From here we had to pay £3 each to get to Cairns by a small ocean steamer. She delivered us there comfortably in two days. This voyage between the eastern shore of the Australian continent and the chain of coral reefs parallel to the shore with numerous picturesque islets between which the steamer zig-zags is the most pleasant trip in the quiet season.'

The sea was quiet, with a slight swell and transparent as crystal, exhibiting its underwater world of corals. Yet even in these peaceful surroundings Nicholas was absorbed with social issues. 'There were about thirty passengers in the second class (corresponding to our third class) and five or six in the first. Passengers of the second class — labourers and peasants — looked like the passengers of the superior class on our boats and enjoyed similar comforts.'

Among the passengers Nicholas noticed an American missionary from New York Bible House, who had come to preach among the 'wild tribes'. Nicholas, if we are to believe his story, immediately clashed with him, revealing in front of the other passengers the predatory nature of missionaries in Argentina. The next day, when Nicholas spotted the missionary attempting to sell some bibles to the passengers, he interfered and asked:

'"WHAT WOULD CHRIST DO IF HE CAUGHT YOU DOING THIS?" There was no answer. "Remember what he did to the sellers of doves. And what might he do to those who trade in the Holy Word!" "Oh! You are an anarchist ... anarchist! Now I see ..." and, backing away from the surrounding passengers, the preacher disappeared into the first class and did not show himself until Cairns.'

They stayed for a few days in Cairns, 'a small attractive township', waiting for their luggage, which had been loaded by mistake on another steamer, and finally, with free immigrant tickets, took a train to the Atherton Tablelands, where they were going to settle. At first the train travelled through the beautiful, coastal tropical areas with their pineapple and banana plantations.

'IT HEADED TOWARDS THE RANGES AT FULL SPEED, making a running start to take the first slope. If the attempt was unsuccessful, the train would back up and make a new run. The engines are not very powerful. The railway is narrow-gauge because its construction was very difficult and involved considerable expense. Zig-zagging, the train climbs upwards, cutting into the marvellous, dark green tropical forest. Now it hangs over an abyss, at the bottom of which a silver stream winds its way among fallen rocks; now it rushes across a bridge, invisible to the passenger, over the deep chasm of a dried-up mountain creek; now it disappears into one of the sixteen tunnels situated within the space of just 12 miles; then it reappears under the dazzling rays of the tropical sun, and the excited passenger can see the town and the shore far below, with the cultivated fields through which the glittering river winds ... And past the sharp edge of the shore with whimsically scattered buildings begins the wide, boundless surface of the quiet, enigmatically indifferent sea blending into the blue of the sky.'[34]

They enjoyed the views as yet unaware that the threads of fate were even now being twined into their first knots, linking them, via this stretch of track, and certain other new Australians: unaware how people whose destinies are in small ways intertwined unknowingly cross each others' paths. A few months after this journey Leandro and Romelio would be working here on the railway, in No. 10 Tunnel, repairing the damage caused by the cyclone, while at the other end of the tunnel young Jane Mailer and her family were stranded in Cairns, waiting for it to clear. Many years afterwards Jane Mailer, who had by now become Mrs Waters, would buy the Illins' farm and rename it Watersvale ...

The train, meanwhile, again approached the dense, dark wall of tall, tropical rainforest. And then the township of Tolga emerged from it as the gateway to the Atherton Tablelands — the gates to a new world.

THE 'CHERRY ORCHARD' ON THE ATHERTON TABLELANDS

The table was smooth, well-planed, and still retained the smell of walnut. Nicholas put a pile of clean paper on it. It was not raining today and through the open window the peaceful evening looked in on his room. Now that the scrub was mostly cleared between his house and the Russell track, it had extended his horizon. It was more than two years since they had chosen the selection. Now it was time to sum up his life. Nicholas decided to do it in the form of a letter to the popular St Petersburg newspaper *New Times*. His calloused hands that of late were more used to an axe, a saw, and a spade felt awkward with the pen at first. But the habit returned and the first even and accurate lines soon lay on the page.

LETTERS FROM AUSTRALIA

Australia is far, very far from Russian people, but Russians have discovered it. Each Japanese boat brings to the eastern ports of this country several dozen of our countrymen. ... I believe that these notes will hold some interest for those Russian readers who rush to try their luck in the far-away 'foreign lands', searching for better conditions of life. My family and I came here for the same reason.[35]

Was it really so? In his heart of hearts he knew that it was not just 'better conditions of life' he was looking for. In contrast to many of his countrymen, who had their dreams of finding overseas a terrestrial paradise, of lands flowing with milk and honey, Nicholas preferred to avoid what came too easily, money especially. He had already been burnt by the money that had poured into the pockets of his ancestors from their serfs; he had dirtied his fingers with the money that he received as a public servant for collaboration with the powers that be. Now he recognised only one way to achieve things — by hard toil with his own hands on the unspoiled land. He was, as it were, consciously seeking out hardship, which was to protect him on his life's path and to distance him from his former mistakes.

Thus, such hard toil was a way of getting his own back for the missteps of his past — for his failure in Ilinka, where the stigma of 'lord soul-owner' stuck to him forever; of getting back at that vacillating, devilish St Petersburg, where white and black melt into one another and blend with eternal northern twilight; for allowing himself temporarily to be deceived by an Argentinian regime in which freedom was tempered with dictatorship.

Still 'getting his own back' is not enough to explain Nicholas, as he was an artist in a world which was rapidly shrinking under the pressure of new technology and rationalism. It was the artists who tried to break the mad circles of rationalism, through modernist art — whether it was the naïve tropical jungles of Henri Rousseau, the ecstatic dancers of Henri Matisse or the South Sea paradise of Paul Gauguin. Nicholas was a modernist, too, but his paintings were his life. Now, for the first time its colours were deep, clean and genuine: white was white, red was red, black was black. But the main colours were the green of trees and grass, the blue of the sky and the gold of the sun.

And these new, clean colours required a new genre, not a poem, but a documentary narrative of a settler in a wild new country.

> We arrived in the township of Tolga. We had to stay here awaiting the selection of our lots. In the township that consisted of just a hundred scattered houses there turned out to be four hotels, which existed to service travelling farmers and labourers. Board in the hotels, consisting of breakfast, lunch, dinner and accommodation, costs £1 per week ...
>
> Having discovered that, after the selection of the lot, one cannot settle on it immediately as it is covered with dense forest, we rented the usual accommodation for a working family: a cottage of four rooms with a kitchen. The price of such accommodation is from 4 to 7 shillings per week. ...
>
> In the Land Office in Atherton my sons and I were shown the plans of two parcels of land divided into portions. In the first one nearly all portions have been taken; in the second one (Gadgarra group) only one portion has been claimed. Fearing that soon the lots may be taken in Gadgarra, too, we told the manager that we would like to take three portions ... This verbal agreement was enough. As we have not seen the lots themselves, we have chosen on the plan the portions whose value was a bit higher than the rest, hoping that they will be better. After paying the first fee of £5 for the portion, we got the receipts in the Land Office and the first stage of formalities was over.

It took them half a day on horseback to get from Atherton to their lots. From the small village of Peeramon — the last outpost of civilisation — they took the Russell track (now it is known as Topaz road), which was carved through the forest by goldminers, who had lived in Boonjie since the late 1880s. The track was 10 feet wide with dense tropical forest standing on both sides, its canopy extending to practically cover the roadway. The sun could barely penetrate through the lush foliage to the muddy, red road. Luckily, it was the dry season now and the track was passable. They were warned to avoid the stinging tree with its broad leaves covered with tiny stinging hairs. A person who was stung by this tree could suffer pain and fever for several months. Horses were also extremely susceptible to it and, if stung, could crush themselves and their rider to death. In the worst, most narrow places it was necessary to lead the horses along the road in single file.

When the Illins finally reached Nicholas's lot, number 31, pegged out on the side of the Russell track, they realised that this venture into pioneering might have taken them a bit too far. The jungle was so dense that they could not go further than a few metres into it. There were no neighbours; no living soul was around and there was only the booming, trumpet-like grunts of cassowaries coming from the crater of the extinct volcano further along the track. And suddenly they saw a brown kangaroo hopping across the road; it swiftly climbed up a tree and disappeared into the jungle, jumping from branch to branch. They had heard about kangaroos but never imagined them doing such tricks. So, the first resident to meet them on their lot was a Lumholtz's tree-climbing kangaroo, which inhabits only this area. Nicholas's eyes lit up, remembering his hunting adventures in Ilinka, and in Aravan and Patagonia. Now it was Australia's turn.

They moved further along the track to inspect Romelio's and Leandro's lots. Soon they saw a big clearing to their right. The embers of a camp-fire were still smoking, and the ground was covered with heaps of nutshells. A dark shadow glinted behind the trees, at the edge of the scrub, and disappeared. All was quiet, only the cassowary continued its lonely calls. This place had the ominous name of Butchers Creek. The small party continued on its way following a land map and soon discovered Romelio's portion 63, which was northeast of Russell track at the foot of a high hill, while Leandro's portion 61 was even deeper into the jungle with its only access being along a steep mountain road known as Cairns track. Now, remembering this first inspection, Nicholas continued his 'Letters from Australia'.

> Dense, venerable half-tropical forest covered our lots and the whole locality. We hired axemen to fell the first 15 acres, as my children, although having grown up used to back-breaking labour, had no idea of the local methods of tree-felling. While they were building a small shed to live in and dug a well, the 15 acres were felled. To fell an acre costs 45–50 shillings.

They decided to concentrate their efforts on Nicholas's lot first and they all settled there together. Their first dwelling was built in a style borrowed from the local Aborigines. Leandro remembered that they built 'a tent-shaped frame then put palm leaves over and cover[ed it] with a thick thatch of lawyer-cane leaves'.[36] By the end of October, five weeks after their arrival in Tolga, they had moved into the slab shed built by Leandro and Romelio. The unpacked trunk with Nicholas's books and papers served as a table. Some blocks sawn from the felled logs substituted for chairs. Beds were made of sacks tied to the forked ends of sticks driven into the earthen floor. Clothes hung along the wall on hangers made of sticks tied to nails. A camp oven with an iron grid completed their basic furnishing of the hut. For a lamp they had a candlestick, the first lamp for several miles around ... Their luxurious Petersburg apartments with nearly a dozen rooms, with a maid, cook, secretary, nanny and governess, seemed never to have existed.

Their nearest neighbours were the goldminers living in Boonjie, in the upper reaches of the Wairambah Creek, south of Gadgarra. George Clarke had discovered alluvial gold there in 1886. He blazed a track from Herberton to Boonjie (parts of it are still known as Clarke's track). Christie Palmerston, adventurer and writer, arrived almost simultaneously at the goldfield from the southeast, along the Russell River. For several years the goldfield flourished, with several scores of miners living there. By 1910 it had lost its former fame and provided a living for just a handful of colourful types who preferred a secluded life. One of them, a Frenchman, Charlie Civry, had escaped from the French penal colony in New Caledonia and was hiding in Boonjie. Another miner, known as Tom Anderson, had assumed the name of his friend and fled Scotland, fearing that he had killed a man in a brawl. Years later he learned that the man had survived and there were no longer any charges against him.[37] One of the other miners, Tom Denyer, an aged Scot from Boonjie, would become Leandro's stepfather-in-law; Charlie Civry was to be his brother-in-law. But that would be later.

Another of these Boonjie personalities was Fred Brown, known as Boonjie Brown. One of the first settlers in Boonjie, he established a small settlement there with a butcher's, a baker's and a blacksmith's shop to serve the miners. His brother-in-law, Harry Land, ran a farm, providing supplies. With the establishment of the township of Malanda, which began to develop soon after the Illins' arrival, the first settlers were supplied with groceries from a shop there, delivered once a fortnight by Charlie Bubke on pack-horses. A vegetable garden with pumpkins, sweet potatoes and maize planted between the stumps on the first acre of cleared forest became for the Illins their main means of survival. They also acquired a goat, to have a fresh supply of milk for Hector. Alexandra learned to bake bread in the camp oven and the men provided the household with game.

Scrub turkey and its eggs constituted the main feature of their diet in these early years. These birds build huge mounds of fallen leaves and peat, up to 2 metres high and up to 8 metres in circumference, in which they lay eggs; the heat of the decaying leaves deep inside the mound acts as a natural incubator. The male bird builds the mound kicking heaps of leaves and debris onto it with its strong legs and afterwards looks after the mound, checking the heat with its long, bare neck and increasing or reducing the temperature by the amount of debris on the top. Scrub turkey eggs are large and chicks hatched from them are well-advanced, being able to scratch their way out to the surface of the mound and look after themselves from their first hours of life. Turkey meat was tender and tasty and all the family enjoyed it. The only disappointment for Nicholas was the ease with which he could hunt for them — it was slaughtering rather than hunting. A disturbed bird would fly up onto the lower branch of a tree and just sit there looking around, its large, black body and red neck making it a perfectly visible target for the hunter.

Leandro recalled his bush experience, and the food, years later.

'I THINK I HAVE EATEN EVERY SORT OF BUSH FOOD — cassowaries, emus, climbing kangaroo, white timber grubs, carpet snake, kangaroo rat (a delicacy) and many other things, even echidna (porcupine). Some of them are excellent, some passable and some just a means of saving yourself from starving. Among the best bush tucker [is]: (1) Turkey or scrub hen chicken on the point of hatching still in the egg; (2) timber grubs in winter; (3) young cassowary; (4) joey kangaroos or wallabies (still in the pouch); (5) kangaroo rat is like rabbit stewed but like chicken grilled, (6) flying foxes, (7) porcupine.'[38]

Except for the rainforest covering the whole land, conditions might seem very attractive. In his letters to Russia Nicholas mentioned that 'the soil is perfect, the climate is one of the best in the world and rains are in abundance'. But the most impressive detail for his Russian readers was the amount of land they received — around 160 acres each. As a comparison, the lots Nicholas's former serfs received were 6–8 acres per person. Michael Gadaloff, a Russian who settled close to Illins, wrote in his letter to a Siberian newspaper with enthusiasm: 'Do congratulate me! 160 acres of splendid land in a locality with a wonderful healthy climate, within 30 miles of the sea, at an elevation of 3000 feet, and this for 35 shillings an acre and 21 years to pay it in.'[39]

The price of land was rather high in comparison with other areas in Australia. For Nicholas's lot it was the highest, at 50 shillings per acre; for Romelio's lot it was 45 shillings per acre, and for Leandro's, 40 shillings per acre, which meant yearly payments ranging from £10 for Nicholas's, down to £7 for the least expensive lot.[40] During the first years a settler did not get any income from the land but had to invest money in improvements as well as keep himself and his family, which means that he had to have sufficient initial capital or else obtain a loan from the bank. The Illins, as distinct from many poor Russian émigrés, had brought money with them. Nicholas's capital was £1500, which he invested in improvements. But even with capital it would take at least ten years of hard manual labour to clear 160 acres of land and transform it into an agricultural farm. 'You know, I feel awe-struck when I think of this tremendous amount of labour and expenses', wrote Gadaloff.

Still, Nicholas believed that Australia provided the best conditions for working-men. His first impressions were very favourable. He wrote, in French, to the under-secretary for Lands, on 15 March 1911. 'Having arrived from the Argentine Republic with the intention of colonising in this country I settled with my family on N 31, 61 & 63 Gadgarra (Atherton District) and I am thoroughly satisfied with the conditions I have found, so much so, that I have written to my former neighbours in Patagonia, who awaited news from me in order to follow my example.'[41]

The Illins were determined to get the best from their lots. And the main obstacle to that was the scrub. 'No one at that time placed any value on the scrub, it was enemy to be destroyed in the name of progress, and in a practical sense it was necessary to destroy it as quickly as possible in order to make a living', Edgar Short wrote about those years.[42] 'Scrub' or 'vine scrub' was the specific Atherton term for what is known now under the more poetic names of 'tropical rainforest' or 'jungle'. The first settlers brought the term here from drier areas, where 'scrub' meant low, stunted, impenetrable vegetation; it was also a synonym for the inhospitable outback. But the Atherton 'scrub' was very high. The thick, mighty trunks of these tall trees were intertwined with numerous vines, which wound their way through the dense canopy over 30 metres above ground-level. The ground in eternal twilight was covered with dead, rotting trunks and thick undergrowth climbing up towards the sun.

In the world that had already invented cars, steam-boats and airplanes, a man confronting the rainforest had nothing except an axe, a spring-board and his own skills. The Illins were to master them. Nicholas wrote about the local tree-felling technique.

> The forest is cut leaving high stumps as the felled trees are burnt after drying out. Trees are not cut at root level as local trees have unusually thick buttresses. Some trunks are cut 3–8 arshins [2–5 metres] above the ground. To do this, deep notches are made on the trunk and a board with a metal shoe on the end is inserted into the upper one. Standing on this board, the cutter cuts the tree. One needs skill and practice to stand steady on a shaking board barely stuck into the trunk while chopping the tree with a big heavy axe; one needs adroitness and experience to know when to jump off the board at the moment when the hewed forest giant utters a light crackle preceding its fall. For carelessness and awkwardness one often has to pay with injuries, maimings and even life, as one falling tree knocks down a number of other trees chopped only part of the way through. It is difficult for the cutter to escape from the trees falling in different directions because the ground is heaped up with felled trunks, branches and clinging vines. Felling is a kind of sport among the locals. My neighbours were surprised when my sons, especially the younger one, mastered the felling technique leaving high stumps — a matter of pride for every woodcutter–sportsman.

Indeed, the felling technique was risky, but it nevertheless saved the timber-cutters a lot of time and effort. Without it, to cut a single big tree with a circumference of two-to-four persons would take a whole day. The spring-board described by Nicholas allowed one to get to the thinner part of the trunk to chop. The 'drives' — which was when the heavy tree fell, toppling part-cut trees all in a line interwoven with vines would spread for up to an acre at a time.

The ringing of axes intermingled with the drawn-out whistle and loud cracking sound of the whip-bird coming from the depth of the forest and then suddenly Leandro or Romelio would cry out '*Beregi-i-i-s!*' (beware!) and with a thunderous crash the line of trees would fall down, sending branches and leaves into the air. After the 'drive' the ground looked like a battlefield. Separate tall stumps jutted out above the mass of felled trunks, broken branches and thick, dark-green foliage. At that moment Nicholas would take little Hector to watch for animals that were stunned in the first minutes after the fall but gradually managed to make their way out of the debris. Possums, brown and sometimes black-and-white, with rounded eyes, big rosy ears and long, prehensile tails were staring about them in bewilderment. The most fanciful of these was the green ringtail possum with its white ears and belly and thick, moss-green fur on its back and tail — a unique specimen among marsupials and mammals. Its green colour protected it in the green foliage.

The scrub was inhabited by other creatures as well — not so visible but more dangerous. These were the leeches and scrub itch-mites. The Illins, and especially Romelio and Leandro felling trees all the time, encountered them as soon as the first rains began in January. At that time nothing could stop the leeches, which came in their thousands. Unnoticed, they found their way under people's clothes and into footwear to suck from their favourite spot — between the toes. Often the men's socks, when they were taken off in the evening, were covered with blood. The sores left by the leeches healed slowly and even Nicholas's medical skills could not help to cure them. Tiny scrub itch-mites penetrated under the skin, especially on the legs, causing an insufferable itch. The local method of protection was the application of paraffin to the legs. Sometimes they met a red-bellied black snake, which although poisonous did not seem aggressive. The carpet snake — a python several metres in length — seemed more terrifying but was completely harmless. Local old-timers, following the example of Aborigines, learned to cook and eat it in the manner of eel. It was here that Leandro gained his experience in how to handle snakes, later becoming an experienced snake-catcher.

The sun set over the forest on the other side of the track. Through the open window Nicholas heard the piercing, lonely evening calls of a scrub hen. He closed the window, lit a kerosene lamp and returned to his article.

> In the forest there is some valuable timber such as cedar, red beech, white beech and bull oak. The first one is very rare, but lucky the man who discovers that tree on his lot: one at least average in size will make £100–200. There were fortunate ones who, on their lots of 160 acres which cost £300, discovered cedar and made £500–700. Still, most of the lots do not have cedar, not all lots have even red beech and white beech, which sell for between £4 and £10 on average. There are some dozens of these trees on one of our lots (two other lots have just a few), but because our lots are 12 kilometres from the railway our trees will be purchased only after all the valuable timber which is closer to the line has been bought and taken out. However, a colonist can hardly count on considerable gain from the sale of timber, it is a matter of luck, as firstly not all lots have valuable cabinet timber ...

Alas, Nicholas did not suspect that they were among those lucky men with a tree on their lots which could bring them a fortune.

Years later, in around 1936, when they had sold their land and left the Tablelands, Leandro, according to Flora, 'reading a newspaper came across the photo of a cedar tree that was cut on his former land, and it was so big, that about fifteen people could dance on top on the platform. He said, "Look at the money I would have got if I was there on that selection".'[43]

Nicholas warmed to his theme.

> ... Secondly, in spite of the tremendous wealth in timber of the area, there are only two recently established firms, with insignificant capital, that are involved in its exploitation. Because of the scarcity of their means, they base the success of the enterprise, not on the development, but on the buying up for next-to-nothing of the most valuable timber; though even this timber, for instance dark walnut, is sometimes left unsold and huge perfect trees are just burnt out to clear the land.

Nicholas would not be himself if he did not raise his voice to criticise the rapacious practice of rainforest destruction — he was one of the first Europeans to do so here — but there was no way for him to improve the situation. In December 1911 they began to burn the felled scrub on their selections, too. During the dry season, which began in June, trees dried out and now flames eagerly turned tons of dried timber into pillars of smoke that day after day hung in the sky. For several years these columns of smoke were to become a usual feature of Christmas-time in Gadgarra.

The scenery after the burns might seem ugly and depressing — charred trunks of jungle giants lay in all directions buried in the ashes among lonely, blackened, tall stumps. But for the farmer it was the first light at the end of the tunnel. Indeed, now he was about to receive the first reward for the whole year of exhausting toil, for his painful blisters and sores. The reward was the exceptional fertility of the soil formed by the volcanic sediment, jungle humus and the fresh ashes. In a few months the sown grass would grow up to human height and, according to Edgar Short, it would be a problem to find cows at milking time in this grass.[44]

Inspiring hopes in the hearts of his readers, Nicholas continued the article.

> After the burning-off the settlers usually sow grass for cows or plant maize and pumpkin with a hoe as it is impossible to plough yet, because of the numerous stumps. According to local calculations, each acre of grass may feed one cow, which during the milking period gives butter (delivered to local creameries) for approximately £1 a month. Buttermilk is used to feed pigs, which is another significant means of profit.

... He finished the article and went outside. The night sky was clear. Surprisingly for the tropics, it was frost that he was worried about just now. On the Atherton Tablelands, at more than 700 metres above sea level, there are sometimes frosts at night in winter-time. Nicholas went down the path to the place that for him was the heart of the farm, to his sacred 'cherry orchard'. Cherries did not grow in it, though; instead, it had fruit more suited to this tropical climate: bananas, oranges, pineapples and peaches. But the orchard was exactly that — a Chekhovian one, planted and lovingly cultivated with his own hands to bring people joy rather than profit.

Was it not about him, about the orchard of his childhood in Ilinka, that Chekhov said: 'Your grandfather, your great-grandfather and all your ancestors owned serfs, they owned human souls. Don't you see that from every cherry-tree in the orchard, from every leaf and every trunk, men and women are gazing at you? Don't you hear their voices? ... But if we're to start living in the present isn't it abundantly clear that we've first got to redeem our past and make a clean break with it? And we can only redeem it by suffering and getting down to some real work for a change.'

Chekhov's heroes promised: 'The earth is so wide, so beautiful, so full of wonderful places'. 'We shall plant a new orchard, more glorious than this one. And when you see it everything will make sense to you.'[45] Nicholas followed this advice in full, one of few Russians to do so. And now he was looking at his slim, vulnerable peach-tree seedlings and at the lush banana trees and pineapple plants. Fireflies flitted over the trees in their endless dance and strange tropical constellations glittered overhead. Something tore at his heart — how was he to accept this alien world, how might he find a place for his Russian soul in it; and his ideal Russian 'cherry orchard', how was he going to create that so far away from Russia, in this country where perhaps no one would dare cut it down, as happened in Chekhov's play, but where at the same time no one would appreciate it either.

The new moon, slowly rising over the tops of unfelled jungle trees, was greeted by the anxious, piercing call of an owl. Agitated, Nicholas slowly returned to his desk but soon he was himself again and neat lines flowed onto the paper once more.

WORKING-MEN'S PARADISE AND THE 'POLICE AGENT'

Nicholas's letter from Australia (quoted above) was only the tip of the iceberg when it came to correspondence he conducted with Russians in those years. After his first article, 'Russians in Australia', was published in the *New Times* in 1912, he began to receive large numbers of letters 'from all over Russia from people of different social and professional walks of life' with numerous questions about Australia. Work on the selection took most of his time and it was hard for him to write letters to individuals. So, the detailed account he gave in this letter of their experience of settling on the land was an attempt to provide a collective answer to all his correspondents.

His 'Letters from Australia' finally took the shape of a booklet, in the second part of which he discussed the general conditions of the country. A few days after completing the booklet he mailed the packet to Russia, to Vladimir Korolenko (1853–1921), the writer, publicist and public figure, who was the personification of the conscience of the Russian democratic movement. Korolenko sympathised with what the Illins had undergone and Nicholas asked him to give the article to the *New Times*, where Nicholas's first correspondence had been published in 1912. The editor of the *New Times* was reluctant to publish the material, as the text was too long, but Korolenko insisted on publication without editing, straight from Illin's manuscript. The first part of the article was eventually published, on 14 August 1913, concluding with 'to be continued'. But then the editor discovered that the second part could not be published in the *New Times* without censorship and editorial cuts, as Illin 'preached socialism, moreover, an anarchistic, unfounded socialism'.

This mass-circulation newspaper, once liberal, by 1913 had become quite reactionary and Nicholas himself felt dissatisfaction with its policy. Answering Korolenko, Illin apologised for letting Korolenko down but argued in his own defence: 'There is neither hungry, nor wretched here. ... If life itself tastes of socialism how should I distort it? ... Is it possible to blame me seriously if I did not limit myself by facts alone but delved into the causes of them? The editorial board of the *New Times* should accuse the facts which contradict its program rather than myself.'

The continuation of Nicholas's article was not published, and he finally broke with the *New Times* and sent a new letter-article to the newspaper *Discourse (Rech)*, the central organ of the Constitutional-Democratic party. This newspaper was popular among the liberal intelligentsia and the Illins subscribed to it even when living in Australia. This letter was most likely also unpublished, but luckily it has been preserved in the State Archive of Literature and Art in Moscow.[46]

Nicholas's 'Letters', taken together, became part of ongoing Russian debates about Australia. Since the late 1890s Australia had gained worldwide fame as a country where significant socio-economic reforms had taken place. Among liberal and progressive writers in Russia it was already known in clichéd terms as 'Lucky Australia' and considered a working-men's paradise. Russian émigrés were to confirm these impressions from their own experience.[47] Some of them, and especially the intelligentsia, came to Australia, as Illin put it, 'believing that the triumph of the democracy here is complete and that there is no capital [that is, capitalist system] there'. They were upset, soon after their arrival, to discover that there were the same social contradictions in Australia as in the Old World.

The optimistic Illins aspired to explore the essence of the Australian social system. Leandro believed that the inclination of the Australian people was 'to provide for themselves the best laws and liberty' and that they 'wish to go ahead of all nations with their labour platform, and are proud of their Labor Government', and have 'the freeest Parliament in the world'. Nicholas admitted in his unpublished 'Letter from Australia' that, although Australia was a democratic country, there were two social classes and there was class struggle; but, he argued, Russian idealists, disappointed with this discovery, did not want to notice that in Australia the class struggle took place under immeasurably better conditions. In his original article 'Russians in Australia' he enthusiastically wrote:

'IT IS NEARLY TWO YEARS since we settled here as colonists, establishing ourselves on the basis of labour rather than capital ... The region is just being brought to a life which is built on principles that have nothing in common either with our age-old Russian ones or with the foreign, European and American ones.'[48]

The 'principles' Nicholas referred to obviously meant progressive social and economic legislation and democracy. The Illins, as distinct from other Russians, seemed extremely optimistic in their attitudes in spite of all the hard work they'd had to do on their selections. Nicholas argued:

'WHEN MY CIRCUMSTANCES LED ME TO BE LIVING RIGHT AMONG THE PEOPLE, right at their very heart, I became convinced that there is no misery at all here, and what is considered as poverty here we would describe as an enviable well-being. For instance, a worker's family having £100 in the savings bank is regarded as poor here; to be considered as well-to-do one has to have over £1000.

'The life here, given the wages, is not expensive ... The working day lasts eight hours, minimum wages are around 8 shillings per day and for every hour of work overtime — 1s 3d. On the railway construction site my children earned 12 shillings per day. A worker in general lives here with the comfort of a Russian intellectual on an average income.'[49]

During the first years their selections did not bring any income and Leandro, Romelio and Ariadna had to look for paid jobs, especially during the wet season, when it was hard to clear the scrub. Recalling these years, in 1937 Leandro wrote: 'When I landed here in 1910 a fellow could leave a job and pick up another 10 chains away on the same day. Living was cheap and gold tinkled in all pockets.' His immediate impressions about conditions of work were, it seems, not so euphoric. He wrote in his diary for 1912 that his first Easter in Australia was spent 'working on the night shift on the Cairns ranges, near No. 10 Tunnel, clearing the rails of the ground which came down from the mountains washed by the rain', remarking a few pages further on, about an official: 'Mr N. Holtze again asked me to have a rest — (I wish him for a boss when I worked on pick and shovel work)'.[50] 'Pick and shovel work', or excavations on railway construction sites, was one of the main occupations available to Russian émigrés in these early years. Others worked in mines and on canefields. The Russian émigrés criticised the intensity of this kind of work, or 'the sweating system', as well as the absence of labour protection, especially in the mining industry. Leandro himself worked for a while in mines in Chillagoe (west of the Atherton Tablelands) and in Cobar (New South Wales) and had a narrow escape in an accident when one of the mines blew up.

This was indeed hard, physical work. And justifying the necessity for hard work was a major point made by Nicholas in his letter to the *Discourse*. Is it possible to settle well in Australia? is it possible to find a good situation there? — that was what numerous Russian intellectuals asked Nicholas. To answer, he had to think over the difference between the situation for the intelligentsia in Russia and in Australia. He defined Russian intelligentsia as people who come to Australia with ideas but without calluses on their hands. In Russia members of the intelligentsia were mainly employed by the government, which paid high salaries; once recruited, they became an integral part of the powers that be. In Australia, Nicholas found, 'some of the tasks of the Russian intellectuals have been solved already, some were still waiting to be solved but in quite different conditions'. The salaries in government employment in Australia were, in comparison with Russia, meagre, and situations were scarce. Workers received wages equal to those of 'white-collar' employees. Another unusual feature to the Russian eye was the extreme rationalisation of 'white-collar' tasks. 'The station master', Nicholas wrote, 'is also in charge of the telegraph, the post-office and the savings bank, at the same time he couples carriages, conducts shunting and issues goods.' In Russia each of these tasks would be performed by a special employee.

Nicholas realised that the strikingly high level of prosperity in Australian society was based on hard, physical work, on real work, which Russian intellectuals had for generations preached but seldom put into practice. The Russian intellectual could survive in Australia, believed Nicholas, only if he sincerely renounced his predominantly intellectual, privileged position in life and desired to become an ordinary worker. Thus, he concluded, 'for the general question "is it possible to settle well in Australia?" there is one correct answer: with energy and a willingness to get one's hands dirty — "yes"'.[51]

That was the democratic life-style in practice. In addition to its most visible aspects — people's dress and the equality in relation to the working classes that struck Nicholas immediately after his arrival — he soon made 'discoveries' about conditions in Australia which, in themselves, are revealing enough of the Russian way of thinking to be recorded in his 'Letters from Australia'. Russians believed that high barriers were inevitable between social classes in all aspects of life. In Australia Nicholas discovered a quite different pattern: 'Characteristically of Australian democracy there is only one grade of flour and bread for a poor man and a millionaire alike and there is no such thing as "the highest grade" of flour'. Moreover, he was amazed to discover that in Tolga's hotel one could see seated at the same table 'a manager of the railway and a labourer who repairs it'.[52]

The first trial of Nicholas's faith in Australian social foundations came in 1913 in connection with his application for naturalisation. On 10 October 1912, while Leandro was in Sydney, Nicholas and Romelio went to Atherton and lodged applications for certificates of naturalisation. In the statutory declaration Nicholas gave his date and place of birth. For occupation, he wrote 'Farmer (in Russia Doctor of Law)'. Then they both took the oath of allegiance before the police magistrate, Patrick Mortimer Hishon. With strong feeling they repeated the solemn words, their hands placed on the bible: 'I do swear that I will be faithful and bear true allegiance to His Majesty King George V, his heirs and successors according to law. So help me God!'

The documents were forwarded, as usual, to the Commonwealth Department of External Affairs in Melbourne. The Department requested the Chief Secretary's Office in Brisbane to obtain additional identification documents from the applicants, and the request was forwarded to the local policeman, who visited the Illins. After this visit, the Chief Secretary's Office sent the following despatch to the Department of External Affairs on 14 December 1912: 'All papers connected with [the applicant's] birth were lost while he was in Argentine. … I am forwarding herewith a document obtained from the applicant, which he states is a certificate he received when he was naturalised in Argentine'. In January 1913 Romelio received his naturalisation certificate, but not Nicholas. He immediately appealed to the Department of External Affairs in French and in Russian. The letter (translated by the Department into English) reads as follows.

Gadgarra,
23ʳᵈ January 1913

Commonwealth of Australia,
Department of External Affairs,
Melbourne

Yesterday my son received a Certificate of English Naturalisation, but I did not.

Nearly two months ago a police officer of the district appeared at my house, saying that he was charged to collect all available information with regard to my son, Romelio, and myself. As a result we gave him three documents: two certificates given to each of us by the Argentine police, and my Argentine naturalisation certificate.

Last week the above-mentioned police officer met me at the Tolga Railway Station and returned my Certificate (attached). I asked him why did he, when charged to collect information concerning me, dissemble the most serious and favourable. He could not deny that this was the utmost consideration, since the information with regard to my son, identical to that concerning me, he had sent to Melbourne. He made no attempt to give me any explanation as to his manner of acting.

I came from the Cordilleres to Australia because of the reputation for justice which I understood the Australian authorities possessed. In this instance, from his manner of treating me, the police officer mentioned showed clear negligence, to say the least. I forward documents which will leave no doubt as to my personality and character. Since my arrival in this country I have lived on my farm working continually and never going away. What do I still need to forward to become entitled to a Certificate of Naturalisation in this country? If anything more is needed or if I have forwarded less than others, I respectfully ask to be informed of it. I suppose I have forwarded more than others! I have been two-and-a-half years on my selection (No. 31 Gadgarra). I have put all my capital (£1500 sterling), and the labour of myself and family into improvements.

If at the end of three years I am not an English subject, I will lose it all. I know that to become possessed of my selection, such as it actually is now, there would not fail to be aspirants, but would it be just to shatter the hopes of one of an advanced age, having a family, and all through the negligence of a police agent.

I respectfully await an answer
Nicolas Illin

All Nicholas's personality was in this letter. Firstly, instead of writing in English, which he did not know to perfection, or only in Russian, as other émigrés did, he preferred to send a copy in perfect French as if to say 'No matter that I do not know English; still, I am a European intellectual, and your equal'. Incidentally, he acted similarly soon after his arrival on the Atherton Tablelands when he and his sons had to undergo a humiliating 'literacy test', to prove that they could read and write. He used the test to write the following in French: 'I can speak and write sufficiently in French, Spanish, Russian, Polish, German and Latin'. What was this — a message to us, to the future, or a means of protecting his dignity?[53]

Secondly, Nicholas's appeal reveals the profound disgust the Russian democrat has for the police with its 'agents' (this is particularly clear from the Russian version of the letter). Finally, the appeal showed in full Nicholas's impulsive nature, which was inclined to exaggerate and to become persuaded by his own exaggerations. Probably 'the police agent' did not send Nicholas's second certificate just because he decided that one was enough, while the processing of Nicholas's application would have been delayed because of the Christmas holidays. In any case at least eight months remained before the deadline for when the lack of naturalisation papers might affect his rights to own the land. And, obviously, the immigration authorities had no intention 'to shatter the hopes of one of an advanced age, having a family, and all through the negligence of a police agent', by depriving him of his own land.

When, several months later, Leandro's application was delayed, too (he lodged it only on 25 June 1913), his appeal to the minister of

External Affairs was written in a different style, understanding that bureaucrats in Melbourne just needed a more persuasive approach to process an application faster.

27–10–13
Peeramon
North Queensland via Cairns

To the Hon. the
Minister for External
Affairs. Melbourne

Dear Sir,
It is a good while now that I did put an application for naturalization and I was sworn loyalty to His Majesty the King. I was awaiting to get my naturalization papers as I want them badly. I am a selector of the Atherton district where I hold a portion of land as an agricultural farm.
I am compelled by law to become a British subject before three years when holding land, if not my rights become forfeited. So you can see by this I find myself in a very uncertain position. Also it hurts me financially as I have improvements done but I can not apply to the Agricultural Bank for a loan. … So you will find perhaps I am writing to you not without reason. I hope you will give your early and benevolent attention to this letter. Thanking you in anticipation I remain Sir your obedient servant
Leandro Illin

(Ex-delegate to the Northern Territory for Russians sent lately by the Federal Government).

In spite of these problems neither Nicholas nor Leandro blamed the system in general, as some other Russians often did. The Illins saw faults only with a particular bureaucrat or 'police agent' but had faith in the justice of the higher authorities.

Finally, in 1913, they were all naturalised: Romelio in January, Nicholas in March and Leandro in October. Alexandra was automatically naturalised as Nicholas's wife, while Ariadna became naturalised by her marriage to Harry Dale in July 1912. Years later Leandro wrote about his naturalisation: 'I became naturalised by deed and spirit in 1913 … I have taken an oath of allegiance and I was found fit to become a British subject, a fact I am proud of.' And, indeed, he did contribute a lot to his country of adoption. In fact, in 1911, some time before making their applications for Australian citizenship, Romelio and Leandro both applied to the Russian czar to have their Russian citizenships annulled. They did not really have to do this, but for the Illins adoption of Australian citizenship was more than just a matter of pragmatism; they also wanted to be free from their obligations to Russia.[54] The Illins still recall that Ariadna, too, was always proud of her British passport. Romelio will also remember it at a difficult time in his life, in 1943; but Australia will turn its back on him ...

LITTLE SIBERIA

In 1940, during the war, when Australia was looking for spies on its own territory and all aliens were under suspicion, the Atherton authorities discovered their own 'spy' — Nikifor Homenko, a Russian from Butchers Creek, who had failed to register with the police as an alien. At the court hearing Homenko stated that he was one of the first to start a farm here twenty-five years before and he believed that he had long been naturalised. However, he was convicted as an alien and the generous 'presiding magistrate took a lenient view of his case', so that one of the pioneers of the area was not jailed as a spy but only fined a considerable amount of money. He was lucky that the local authorities did not dig deeper, as secret police reports of the early 1920s referred to him as a north Queensland representative of the Secret Seven, 'the most silent, militant and dangerous' pro-Soviet group in Australia. In 1940 Homenko made a fresh application for naturalisation and the local constable who had to interview him found that, although he had been living in Australia since 1913, Homenko 'has not a very good knowledge of reading or writing, he can read big print but his pronunciation is very poor'. To explain to the authorities how Homenko could have survived all these years without much English, the constable wrote: 'For a number of years he resided in a locality where there were several other Russians and he therefore used more of his native language than English'. To survive for twenty-five years in Australia without much need for English one needs to have a real community around.

In July 1996 I visited Bill Homenko, Nikifor's son, on his farm along the Gadaloff road. And, telling me about their Russian neighbourhood, he said, 'That's what they used to call this: "Little Siberia"'.[55] But even he did not remember that it was Nicholas Illin who, in 1910, had founded Little Siberia in the heart of an Australian jungle.

Little Siberia in the heart of the Tableland jungle — a microcosm, like a small piece of Russia planted there by the whim of fate. With a patriarchal Nicholas Illin, and sharing a common vision with each other, there were twelve men in their twenties and thirties, seven women and over a dozen children. They came from all walks of life — peasants, workers, soldiers, professionals, office employees. They were of Russian, Byelorussian, and Ukrainian descent, and they came from all quarters of the huge Russian empire — from St Petersburg in the north to Tashkent in the south, from Volyn in the west to Vladivostok in the east. For some of them the route was via imprisonment, exile and escape, through the Far East, or Europe, or the Argentine. However hard their life in Russia had been, and however hostile the attitudes to them in Australia might be, they did not renounce their Russianness. Their children, even adopted children, could speak Russian and only lost their fluency in Russian after the death of their parents as none of them established contact with the new Russian community of so-called 'White Russians' that grew up in Australia after the revolution.

* * *

Being away from Russia for seventeen years did not make Nicholas forget about his suffering countrymen. Unable to do anything about changing the situation in Russia itself, he decided that a small Russian colony in a democratic country might be a start. While in Patagonia he had learnt about 'Australian justice', and his first thought was 'that Australia was a good country to bring Russians to for a colony'. During his one-week stay in Brisbane after his arrival in Australia, Nicholas managed to get in touch with some Russians there and discuss his plans for a Russian colony in the tropical north. In particular, he invited Michael Gadaloff (or Gadalov), who had arrived from Russia several months previously and was looking for a place to settle, to become his neighbour. As soon as Nicholas took the land in Gadgarra he renewed his invitations to Gadaloff and to some other Russian acquaintances. As a result after six months, on 15 March 1911, he was able to write: 'I have done all I can to make my Russian countrymen colonise in my neighbourhood and in consequence eleven lots in Gadgarra have been allotted to Russians'.

His campaign was obviously successful to judge from what Michael Gadaloff wrote, around July 1911, in his letter to a Siberian newspaper comparing two Russian settlements: 'In Wallumbilla [near Roma] the selectors are mostly more simple people; where my selection is they are more cultured. For instance, lately eight young men have taken three selections of 160 acres each here, some of them are involuntary citizens of Australia.'[56] 'Involuntary citizens' was a euphemism to mask the category of political émigrés who had fled political persecution in Russia. Not all of them stayed on their selection for a long time: some claimed a lot but never settled on it, some lost the battle with the tropical 'scrub' and moved to places where it was easier to live. Only the most stouthearted remained.

Michael Gadaloff's family was among those who remained. Michael Gadaloff (Mikhail Vasilevich Gadalov, 1883–1972) came from a famous, rich family of Siberian goldmine managers, traders and arts patrons. He arrived in Australia in 1909 together with his wife, Theodosia (Fedosia, née Bobroff), and three young children, Olga, his step-daughter, Valerian and Eugene. His most treasured possessions consisted of a collection of photos of his friends (intelligent, serious, open faces, or is it the old photographic technique which makes them so?), a portrait of Vera Zasulich — a romantic, terrorist heroine of the early revolutionaries — and a letter of 1901 from his first teacher, the political exile Konstantin Efimenko: 'Cherish, my friend, your honour, … cherish your human dignity, … do not develop a passion for profit, be content with what you have earned, … and from your honest earnings help anyone who is poor and needy without regard to his religion, be he a Jew, a Tartar, or a Russian'.

Michael, like dozens of his friends, had only wanted to put into effect this simple advice his teacher gave him. Awakened by the first Russian revolution in 1905, he became involved in the organisation of workers into trade-unions and was temporarily arrested and kept under police observation. His only way out was to flee the country, leaving behind his well-paid jobs as a shop-assistant and a book-keeper. He sacrificed a potentially brilliant career in the family enterprises, as well as a comfortable life in Vladivostok.

'WE USED TO LIVE IN A GOOD HOUSE situated on the side of the hill and had a particularly nice panorama from there: the harbour, the Golden Horn full of boats … My wife and I usually visited the theatre every week; there was a good theatre, one season there was a good opera and other dramas or plays discussing modern Russian life.'

In Australia Michael tried a number of jobs — on a railway

construction site and on a sawmill, living in a tent on dried meat — while his wife stayed with their children in Brisbane, sewing men's clothing at home for a factory. Her earnings were barely enough to keep the family. Yet, in spite of these initial difficulties they seemed optimistic.

'WE DO NOT REPENT EVER HAVING LEFT OUR NATIVE LAND, notwithstanding that my present social position is different to the one I occupied in Russia. ... None of us has ever yet thought that we came here on a wild-goose chase (to say nothing of the children, who cry when we, jokingly, talk of returning to Russia), in spite of the fact that my actual income — at present — is smaller than it was in Russia, life here is in no case worse. ... You do not have to tremble for tomorrow, and last, but by no means least, for your own freedom and absolute liberty. All this gives a profound reason why Russians should emigrate to Australia.'

In 1912 the Gadaloffs settled in Gadgarra on their selection deep in the scrub northeast from the Russell track (portion 57). The track to their selection followed an Aboriginal path on top of the ridge between Butcher and Caribou creeks. They were the first permanent settlers on this track and soon it became known as the Gadaloff road. Michael began his fight with the scrub just as his optimistic call for Russians to emigrate to Australia was being taken up by the Queensland Intelligence and Tourist Bureau; in its booklets to attract potential immigrants, for several years running the bureau reprinted the most favourable passages from his letter (omitting all the problems he discussed). Of his 169 acres, Michael felled 125 acres himself. Theodosia, his wife, had her own lot of suffering: it was a hard time, especially for a woman with children. Their first dwelling was a tent, the second was a tin shed, and only the third one was a sturdy, big slab-house. Twice a day she had to milk the growing herd of cows, carrying gallons of milk each year. But loneliness was the worst. She did not learn to speak English, and some neighbours remember Theodosia often sitting alone in the house, quietly crying. She died in 1922, one of the first Russians to die in this area.

Michael Gadaloff went back to Russia in 1926, married and brought his new wife, Betty, to Australia. They ran a farm, called the 'Golden Bottom', and had two sons, Igor and Ross. The 'Golden Bottom' did not bring them a fortune but it was one of the most successful farms in the area. It allowed all Michael's children to receive a good education, passing on the aspiration to knowledge to the next generation, most of whom are university graduates. Michael sold the farm in the mid 1940s and moved to Brisbane, where he retired. Not long before his death in 1972 he wrote his memoirs. Michael's grandson, Peter, an accountant from the Gold Coast, finishing up an interview with me, said: 'Grandfather was born into goldmining industry, my son is now a geologist working for a goldmine in Kalgoorlie, the wheel came full turn'.[57]

In 1915 the Homenko family settled on portion 58, next to the Gadaloffs. Nikifor Petrovich Homenko (b. 1884) and his wife Vera (née Khnikov) were born in the small Byelorussian town of Cherikov. Nikifor, a welder by trade, riveted boats in shipyards. First they moved to the Far East, and then in 1913 took a ship to Australia. Nikifor's son, Bill (Vasilii) Homenko, tells their story.

'I WAS BORN IN VLADIVOSTOK IN 1913 AND I WAS ONLY A BABY WHEN THEY CAME on the ocean boat, and they came to Darwin. But mum did not like the place, she reckoned the sun was too close, too hot. And they came to Cairns then. And from Cairns they shifted around where he could get a job. And then pop was working on that railway line that came through from Malanda to Tarzali. Some people were there and they said "Why don't you get a block, open up some land, otherwise you'll get a job here and a job somewhere else and you've got family". So he selected.

'You had to go and have a look, select, if you like it, well you pay very little and put your name down on the book. It was all scrub. We came here in 1915 and were the second one on the Gadaloff road. I can remember when pop first settled down here at the little creek, they had a little patch of scrub felled, and my brother and I used to go down the creek there and got a hiding there. They were frightened we might get drowned. Pop felled a patch of timber, burned it, grassed it, then we started milking a few cows, six or eight or something for a start. We had a little billy-can of cream, used to take it past the Butchers Creek school, back on to that Russell road up there to Malanda.'

When the Homenko boys grew up, they became teamsters engaged in pulling timber and later bought two adjacent portions, thus expanding Little Siberia.[58]

The Prochoroff family settled on the other side of the Gadaloffs at the beginning of 1916 (portion 54). Michael Prochoroff (Mikhail Prokhorov, born in 1880) was a worker. At the age of twenty-two he joined the Russian Social-Democratic Workers' Party and was engaged in revolutionary activities in Mariupol, Balashov, Orenburg, and Tashkent. In 1910 he was sentenced to two years' exile in Siberia. He fled from there to Australia, together with his wife, Maria (née Mikhailov), and his young daughter, known here as Leila. They arrived in Brisbane in September 1912. Michael tried a number of jobs in Cairns, Gordonvale, Chillagoe and Townsville, often specialising as a pattern-maker and carpenter. In the meantime they had two more girls and finally decided to settle on the land. Their choice of Gadgarra was obviously due to the presence there of a growing Russian community which included political refugees. Soon after they settled at Gadgarra their son Alexander (Aleksandr) was born, on 11 July 1916, and it is believed that he was named after Alexandra Illin, who assisted Maria Prochoroff as a midwife for the birth. Leo Tolstoy claimed that the personality of the child is formed during the first five years of life. If that is true, we have to concede that the extremely hard pioneering conditions under which the Prochoroffs lived at that time provided a stimulating environment for the young Alexander, who eventually became the first Australian-born Nobel Prize-winner. However, Australia had to share this glory with Russia, as around 1923 the Prochoroffs, who remained sympathetic to the ideas of communism, returned to Russia.

Aleksandr Prokhorov (as he is called in Russia) graduated from Leningrad State University in 1939 and had a highly successful career in physics — being one of the founders of quantum electronics — as well as in the administration of Soviet science. In 1964 he was awarded the Nobel Prize and in 1966 he became an Academician of the Academy of Sciences of the USSR (a highly select institution); in 1969 he became editor-in-chief of the *Great Soviet Encyclopedia*. Until recently, however, Academician Prokhorov remained unknown to many Australians. Professor Norman Heckenberg from the University of Queensland, who has gathered material about him for an exhibition, relates that in 1996, while at the international physics conference in St Petersburg, he wanted to talk to Prokhorov and 'see if he still had an Australian accent, but couldn't get near him — he is a grand old man of Soviet science'.[59]

Across the road from the Gadaloffs was portion 38, rugged land with the crater of an extinct volcano on it. In July 1911 this portion was selected by Gabriel Ivanoff (Gavriil Mironovich Ivanov, born in 1883), who originated from the same Balashov district where Nicholas Illin was born. A peasant's son, he joined the revolutionary movement, was imprisoned and sentenced to Siberia for life in 1909. It did not take him long to flee to Harbin, where he worked as a teacher under an assumed name, and then, in June 1910, he went to Brisbane. Probably there he met the Illins and decided to join them in Gadgarra. Although he lost his battle with the scrub and surrendered this selection in early 1912, he remained in touch with Little Siberia, working nearby on the railway construction works and at sugar-mills and finally took another selection near Babinda. He was, it seems, an active member of the Union of Russian Workers in Brisbane, and in 1915 he agitated against conscription in Cairns. In 1917, after the February revolution, he was one of the first to return to his 'mother country', which he 'could not forget'. According to his passport application he wanted to go there 'attending to my old parents and to serve my country in its time of trouble'. It might be that the Illins asked him to look for their relatives in Saratov as communication was becoming more and more difficult. Gabriel Ivanoff left Australia in May 1917, with dozens of other Russians heading to the Far East.

He did not have to wait long to find himself in the midst of Russian troubles. He escaped alive but lost all his Australian documents including his passport. It was only in 1921 that Ivanoff, stranded in Russia, managed to send a desperate plea to the Australian authorities through Gadaloff, who did his best to rescue his former neighbour from Russia and return him to 'sunny Queensland'. Finally, they managed to persuade the Australian authorities to send new documents for Ivanoff to Moscow.[60] I could not, however, find any document confirming that he succeeded in returning to Australia. If he did stay in Russia, he would probably have suffered under Stalin's repressions in the late 1930s, as did many of the Russian émigrés to Australia who managed to return to their motherland.

The Russian history of portion 38 at Gadgarra continued, though. Ivanoff left it in 1911 after clearing 10 acres of scrub. The land remained abandoned for a year-and-a-half, and the clearing became covered with prickly scrub. At that time, 1913, the Strelnikoff couple arrived in Brisbane. Soon they were in Little Siberia, where they took this abandoned block. Vasil Strelnikoff (Vasilii Ivanovich Strel'nikov, 1875–1965), although originating from Central Russia, worked for years in Tashkent, as a conductor on the railway and then as a manager of a hotel. The local corruption and theft so colourfully described by Nicholas in the 1880s had continued its reign in this remote corner of the Russian empire. Vasil, according to his son, 'did feel very strongly for the people that were poverty stricken and was all for honesty' and, disgusted by this atmosphere, finally decided to emigrate to Australia.

In the 1960s Strelnikoff wrote his memoirs. In recalling his first ten years in Gadgarra, he devoted half of the story to one episode alone, an episode which in its importance seemed to outweigh all the other hardships he had experienced — impenetrable scrub, a path to his selection along which you could travel only on horseback, life in the tent, building a house by himself, the devastating cyclone of 1918. This episode showed the injustice of the local authorities towards him. Soon after his arrival he was arrested by Constable Seary as a 'common criminal' in Peeramon, fingerprinted, handcuffed and thrown into the prison. Vasil's English was very poor at that time — 'as soon as I picked [up] my *Teach yourself* book I would start to go to sleep' — and he did not understand at all why he had been arrested. At the court hearing it came out that the police considered that he had overloaded his horse by transporting 100 pounds of timber planks on it (local farmers would carry 200 pounds without being arrested). He was fined one shilling, but it was not that which worried Strelnikoff. He wrote: 'I told [Seary]: "You know I have not committed any crime. Why then are you sullying my name?" He smiled and made no answer, and I felt I had been so humiliated for no reason at all'. Now, eighty-five years later, his son concludes the story.

'THEY JUST WANTED TO MAKE A SHOW OF HIM because he was a new settler from a non-English speaking country. Papa was so upset at the behaviour of Seary that he wanted to pack and go back to his homeland. Nevertheless, they finished up friends. Papa used to make a home-brew, kvass; Seary used to have so much of Papa's kvass that he could hardly ride his horse home.'

In Australia Strelnikoff became a member of the Union of Russian Workers. After the revolution he no longer associated with the Russian radicals but, nevertheless, remained tarred with the same brush. While he battled with the scrub and established his farm, World War I and the Russian revolution came. Strelnikoff's aspiration to receive freehold rights over his land, a condition for which was naturalisation, was denied as the immigration authorities decided not to naturalise Russians at all. By that time his wife, Mary, had become ill with rheumatism because of the damp climate of Gadgarra, but they could not sell or sub-let the selection and go to a drier location. They had become hostages of the land in which they had invested all their energy and money. Strelnikoff lodged one application after another, but even solicitors' appeals to the commonsense of the authorities — 'he disclaims all association with the unruly Russian elements, refusal of his naturalization certificate means practical ruin to my client' — could not change this Australian 'democracy' which could, at a stroke of the pen, outlaw whole nations.

This tragic situation lasted for years. But it might well have had its roots in a quite other kind of reality — a virtual reality, as it were. Strelnikoff's block, it will be recalled, had on it the crater of an extinct volcano (which would later be named after him). Strelnikoff could not suspect that, when he cleared the scrub around the crater, he was committing a sacrilege — as this was a sacred place of the powerful Rainbow Serpent, which then took its revenge. But about that, later.

In 1923, after eight years of battling with the authorities, Strelnikoff was at last naturalised and moved to Mareeba. He sold the farm in 1930 and worked as a carpenter and as a cook. His children — Alevtina (a daughter, born in 1924), and Basil (a son, born in 1925) — received a good education. They brought home Australian culture while Vasil taught them the revolutionary songs of his youth: 'Arise, you working people, fight the enemy, you hungry ones ...'. Even now, all these years later, Basil can still sing these songs, but what is more important is that he and his sister inherited their parents' generosity and aversion to injustice and dishonesty, and their obsession with knowledge; many of their own children are university graduates. 'I especially value in this country that people do not act unjustly', Vasil wrote in his memoirs, and in a letter in 1947 to Michael Gadaloff he summed up his Australian experience: 'The one who wants to work honestly will not be hungry in this country'.[61] His only request to Gadaloff was to buy him some black caviar and Russian-style herrings in Brisbane ...

Romelio's block bordered on that of the Balias couple, while Leandro's neighbour was John Nikonets. They were early settlers, too. Vladimir Balias (1875–1944) came from a western Ukrainian village and spoke Russian and Polish. He had served in the Russian Imperial Guard in Moscow, and the memory of that time is still alive in his family. According to his son George: 'It was quite a story to listen to him, they had those beautiful jewels and sabres, there was a lot of sabre fights for practice'. But this brilliant life was not his destiny as, in the aftermath of the first Russian revolution of 1905, the polarisation and animosity among the guardsmen was growing, even in this élite detachment, and many of them left the unit fearing the forthcoming persecutions. Vladimir took the road to the Far East, to Harbin. He was accompanied by his wife Alicia (née Bosnikov), a former nurse who came from Odessa.

They came to Australia in April 1910 and, after working for several months on the railway in Blackbutt, he preferred to move to the north, where the Illins were inviting settlers to join the new Russian colony. He joined them at the end of 1910 and took a selection at the corner of what later became known as Russell and Gadaloff roads (portion 62).

In January 1911 a local land commissioner reported to Brisbane about the arrival in the area of the exotic Russian settlers: 'With the exception of L. Illin none of them is able to speak more than a few words of English. They are, however, educated in other languages, and I would ask that I be directed as to the educational test to be applied to them ... These people have already located themselves on the land allotted to them. They have so far done a good deal of improvement work and no doubt will prove themselves good settlers.'

At his 'literacy test' (translated by Leandro Illin) Vladimir Balias kept silent about the causes of his defection from the Russian Imperial Guard and described himself as a farmer. He did in fact become one of the most successful farmers in the area, owing to his earlier agricultural experience. Before that happened, however, allegations made against Alicia Balias had attracted the attention of Queensland authorities to the extent that a police inspector was despatched in November 1911 from Cairns to Gadgarra to interrogate her.

It was alleged by a certain Russian, F. Kechelly, that she was wanted by the Russian authorities as she 'poisoned a woman of Russia' at Harbin in Manchuria, and 'ran away from Harbin prison'. After visiting her, the inspector reported:

'ON THE 13TH INSTANT [November 1911] I proceeded to Yungaburra to complete my inquiries and I ascertained that the only Russians residing in that district are Illins who have a selection at Gadgarra and the woman Balas mentioned in the attached letter. She is living alone on a selection at Gadgarra and her husband is working on the railway line at Peeramon which is about 8 miles from Gadgarra and 7 miles from Yungaburra. I interviewed this woman Balas at her selection at Gadgarra. This woman can speak very little English and consequentially she is very hard to understand. … This woman appeared to be very peculiar in her manner and her actions slightly demented.'

It appears that, after this visit, the authorities were unable to conduct a proper investigation and abandoned the case. Meanwhile the Baliases, unsuspecting of all the allegations, continued to clear their selection.

Their name has found its way onto the map of Gadgarra, too. Butcher Creek started at the Balias farm — George still has the most vivid memories of it: 'I nearly got drowned in that creek when I was three-year-old, I fell in it and could hardly get out'. On rainy days the Gadaloff road became impassable where the creek crossed it, and in 1915 local residents applied to the Lake Eacham shire council to build the Balias Creek bridge.

George is the adopted son of Vladimir and Alicia Balias; he was born in 1922, and some believe that he is part Aboriginal. His earliest memory of Butchers Creek is the screening of silent pictures in the Community Hall across the road. He used to go round the back of the hall trying to slip inside. Since that time movie-making became his hobby and sixty years later, when he went to a Butchers Creek school reunion, he brought his movies with him and screened them in the same hall 'completing the circle of sixty years'. He also remembers his Aboriginal nanny, Diana, who came from the camp in Boonjie. In 1928 the Baliases sold the farm and moved to Malanda, and then to Tolga, where they had a maize farm. When the war broke out, nineteen-year-old George enlisted and fought in New Guinea. He returned to Australia in time to bury his father in 1944.

'I BURIED HIM, but when I came back to get the stuff I did not have a chance to get around through all of that, my unit was put in the train and we were shifted down to Brisbane. I do not know what happened to all his papers. Soon my mother died and the house was sold by public [trustee].'

The wind was turning the pages of the diary that Vladimir Balias kept for years, chronicling the life of Little Siberia. But who cared about the pile of Russian papers that fell out of an old briefcase, papers containing the answer to the mystery of the Baliases' flight to Australia and of George's origin. And now, half a century later it still hurts him: 'It's all a bit of a tangle at the moment. I do not know where I am and who I am.'[62]

John Nikonets, his Russian name was Ivan but he was known to locals as Nicka, joined the Baliases and Illins in June 1911. He led a lonely life and never married. Michael Gadaloff said that it was hard for a Russian to find a wife as 'local women did not like Russian men because of their accent, it was a very rough accent and Russians were not Anglo-Saxon, they were foreigners'. Nikonets sold his farm in 1921 and left the district as 'the damp climate' became 'unsuitable to his state of health'.[63]

Two more Russian farms were situated on the other side of the Russell road, in Malanda Parish, opposite Romelio's portion. They belonged to Lamin and Fadchuck, two quite different personalities. Vladimir Nikolaevich Lamin (1880–1951), although born in a village on the Volga, gave the impression of being a highly educated man. Nothing is known about his life in Russia and the reasons for his emigration to Australia. In 1910 he arrived in Australia with his wife Mary, tried to find job in Brisbane, then took a selection in Wallumbilla, where a Russian colony was growing under the leadership of an old Russian revolutionary, Paul Gray. Lamin did not succeed there; he surrendered the land and moved to Chillagoe, working also on cane-cutting in Mulgrave. Soon he discovered the Russian colony in Gadgarra and selected a block at the corner of Russell road and Clarke's track. The Lamins moved to their selection in 1913 and soon a hill adjoining it became known as Lamins Hill. This name is well-known nowadays, for since the land has been cleared the magnificent look-out from the hill attracts many tourists visiting the Tablelands. They sold the farm in 1924 but remained living in the area.[64] The Lamins were childless, yet before long they became related to the Illin family in a most unusual way, as we shall see later.

Felix Fadchuck (Filimon Alekseevich Fadchuk, 1884–1932), a bachelor, became a colourful local personality. Originating from a village near Kovel, in the western province of the Ukraine, he worked for a while at the post office in Kovel and then illegally crossed the border with Austria and managed to reach Argentina. It is most likely that he came into contact with the Illins there as, in 1912, he followed them to the Tablelands and took a selection on Clarke's track, next to the Lamins. After dairying became established in the area, Felix worked as a cream-carter, then as a bullock-driver. According to his Australian neighbour, Edgar Short, 'when his English failed to impress his team enough to get the desired result he was apt to lapse into Russian or even

Spanish on some occasions'. Edgar Short gave a perfect portrait of him in the context of local anti-Russian sentiments.

'FELIX, THE RUSSIAN BULLOCK PUNCHER, WAS NOT A GOOD MAN TO CROSS, though he was amiable and friendly enough if treated right. He had the high cheekbones, slightly slanted eyes, and faintly Asiatic cast of features which some eastern Slavs possess. One of our neighbours, who incidentally was not popular with anyone, disliked him intensely, and usually referred to him, in his absence, as "that yellow Mongolian B—". The day came when Felix was on his way home from Malanda with his team, and the neighbour, also on his way home, rode past. Thinking he was well out of range he greeted Felix "Good day, you yellow Mongolian B". Felix could use the long bullock whip, he could also move fast.

'Neighbour put spurs to his horse, but as horses sometimes do, it pranced up and down a couple of times before taking off, Felix got within range and swung the whip, saying: "How you like Mongolian B now?" There was no reply from the fast disappearing and bloodsoaked target, who had his shirt and skin split from shoulder to waist.'

He added that in Russia Felix was a pro wrestler, 'a fact which some men discovered to their sorrow'.[65]

* * *

We were sitting on a rusty cistern in the yard of Bill Homenko's farm. Bill's toil-worn hands were resting on his knees, his bare feet planted firmly on the land. His Australian slang and his wide-brimmed hat made him a real bushman, yet to me he seemed terribly familiar: I had met such old men when I travelled along Byelorussian roads looking for the roots of my own ancestors. Even Bill's yard itself — horses standing quietly by a hand-made post-and-rail fence, the old barn with a busy mouse appearing from time to time under the door, land muddy after the rain — seemed so familiar in a Russian way. All except the corrugated iron ...

And Bill led me into the time when Leandro lived next to him — 'That scrub you can see, it was Leandro's. There's no fence there. Scrub's a boundary from there to my boundary here, right through to Cairns track.' To the time when barefoot Russian children rode horses along the Gadaloff road, when he and his younger brother, John, were playing on the banks of Caribou Creek, which was now, like eighty years ago, quietly flowing on its way to the ocean. We were in the last outpost of the deserted Little Siberia and Bill Homenko was its last Mohican. The misty hills cleared of scrub behind him were the only reminder of three dozen Russians who once had settled this land. But could all the Russian hopes and despair with which they worked this land, the sweat and tears they poured over it, the love and pain that they experienced on it — could all that have disappeared without a trace? Although invisible, it was all here, a Russian layer in the little world of the Atherton Tablelands. And from here the threads of destiny of the Russians' descendants spread far away all over the world. It took the Prochoroffs back to Russia, some of the Illins to the Honduras and the United States of America, and all the rest, including Leandro's family, to different parts of Australia.

As I was leaving, Bill, with genuine Russian — or was it outback Australian? — generosity, gave me a bucketful of sweet tangerines ...

LEANDRO AND A RUSSIAN COLONY IN THE NORTHERN TERRITORY

Inside the former Australian Archives building on the outskirts of Canberra it seems to lack totally an aura of the past. Air-conditioning makes you comfortably cool after the midsummer heat outside; you are surrounded by microfilm machines, rows of modern folders with indexes and the latest achievement of technology — computer retrieval systems. I had been struggling with it for several days already in an attempt to find material about the early Russian émigrés in Australia. Finally, it was 1 February 1994, I decided to try the most primitive and rash method — giving it the command to show me all documents with the word 'Russian' in their title. The computer, after some hesitation, offered me over 600 entries and I bravely began to search through them all. When, an hour later, I reached the third hundred I felt that I was ready to give up, and suddenly on the screen there appeared 'Russian Emigrants for Northern Territory, Parts 1–3, 1911–1913'. Soon I was loading the microfilm into the machine and in a few minutes the modern, sterile-white screen filled with the voice of a Russian man from 1912.

'THE FULL MOON WAS SHINING — Nothing can beat the beauty of these tropical moonlight nights on the sea shore. I looked round and saw the steamer which approached like an enchanted palace lighted by electricity. ...

'During the night we had a performance by "dingoes". It is really a pleasure to wake in the night, bright and moonlit, and listen to their wild howling — You feel then that you are in the middle of wilderness near to nature. ...

'I have always, every day, drunk water from the creeks, swamps, billabongs, rivers, etc. I know Russians are not careful about their health, and if they come here they will do the same. Mr Vladimiroff tells me I will get malaria. If I do, Russians must not come here.'[66]

It was a travel diary that captivated me from the start. I felt that its author — bearing such an uncommon first name, Leandro Illin — was a most unusual personality. But how could I predict then that this diary was just the beginning of an unfolding tale that I, together with his family, would pursue for years to come.

Gradually, the whole story about the project of the Russian colony came to life. It turned out that Little Siberia was not the only outcome of the Illins' involvement with the destiny of the Russian community in Australia. The Illins had more ambitious plans, which for a time coincided with the plans of the Australian government. Since 1910 each Japanese boat from the Far East had brought dozens of Russians fleeing from their motherland to the 'Australian Paradise'. By the end of 1911 the growing number of Russians arriving began to cause serious concern among Queensland authorities. Their unusual dress provoked the curiosity of Australians, too, a curiosity combined with apprehension. What to expect from them? Attitudes towards the Russians changed from day to day: fighters for freedom, criminals, experienced agriculturalists, dirty Asiatic Russians. The Russian consulate and the authorities in Russia published official warnings intended to prevent a mass exodus to Australia, but these had the opposite psychological effect on potential emigrants, who were suspicious of everything that came from the authorities. 'They write it to discourage us from going there', the Russian workers and peasants concluded, and continued to leave in ever-increasing numbers for Australia.

On 16 November 1911 the Russian vice-consul in Melbourne, Harold Crofton Sleigh, discussed with the minister for External Affairs, Josiah Thomas, the possibility of settling the arriving Russians in the Northern Territory. Thomas, a former miner and enthusiast for the development of the Northern Territory (newly taken over by the Commonwealth), appears to have had no prejudice against Russians, considering them to be good agriculturalists. He suggested that, if two Russians from Queensland were chosen, he 'would make arrangements for them to visit the Northern Territory to spy out the land, with a view to getting as many Russians as would come to settle there'.[67]

The time of the Christmas holidays was approaching and the Russian Association, a benevolent society formed a year before, called Russians scattered all over Queensland to come to a general meeting in Brisbane to discuss plans for an agricultural settlement in the Northern Territory. A correspondent of the *Brisbane Courier* wrote: 'In fact, so deep and earnest was the interest taken in this subject that the debate was at times characterised by a warmth of expression and demeanour that was with difficulty controlled by some of the more tranquil spirits. The majority of the men are stalwart, and bear the impress of the agriculturist. Some of them may be artisans or even students, but all express determination to labour hard in the country of their adoption.'

But the *Courier* correspondent was unable to grasp the essence of the conflict here. What was happening here was symbolic of the struggle going on inside Russia itself, which was to reach its culmination in 1917: at this gathering in Australia two Russian groups with their different approaches towards the future confronted one another. Along with those who wanted to use the Australian conditions to fulfil a centuries-old dream for the Russian peasantry of a free life in a free land, there was a radical wing headed by the charismatic bolshevik, Artem, Lenin's confidant. He preferred the path of radicalisation of the émigrés, of educating them in the spirit of proletarian, class struggle; he aspired finally to turn them into champions of Marxist-Leninist ideas within the Australian workers' movement. He managed to seize the leadership of the organisation at this meeting, following which bolshevism became the dominant political tendency of the Russian Association, also known as the Union of Russian Emigrants.

Even so, the more moderate wing was quite strong. It is not surprising that they elected Leandro Illin as one of the delegates. His mature age, agricultural experience, extensive travels, knowledge of English, intelligence and independent way of thinking made him a reliable observer and a trusted champion of Russian interests in this alien country. Several months later, in a moment of hesitation, he would write down in his diary: 'I am not a learned man. ... Why did I undertake this responsibility myself? ... Will my countrymen be satisfied with my report? I never thought I was the right man for this business, but it was their wish that I should go.'[68] He was indeed the 'right man' and he proved this even before he went to the Territory.

But, first, a loose end which unexpectedly led me back to those days in Brisbane before Leandro's departure — the photo of a gentleman that Flora, Leandro's daughter, produced from her archive, the photo being inscribed by Nicholas Manowitch to Leandro in 1913. 'He was some sort of a Russian minister', Flora remarked. 'Hardly', I thought, seeing that the first Russian priest settled in Australia only in 1923. It took me nearly two years to discover that Flora was right.

Manowitch (1872–1925) was a priest, although before that he had been a socialist. He fled Russia and went to Canada, where he was ordained to the Orthodox priesthood by a bishop, but by a 'wrong' bishop, that is, one unrecognised by the official Russian Orthodox Church. From Canada he went to Dunedin in New Zealand, where he started up an Orthodox church, but was soon discovered and expelled. He had just settled in Brisbane and begun weekly services for Russians in St Mary's Church on Kangaroo Point when the Criminal Investigation Branch received information that the Russian Orthodox Church considered him to be an impostor. What happened then followed the usual methods of secret police, be it in Russia or in Australia: he was made to become an informer to avoid disclosure. Manowitch was in a good position to become an informer, being trusted by Artem and other radicals.

And there was plenty to tell the police. It was the time of the Brisbane general strike of January–February 1912, which the Russian Association supported. Moreover, Artem and the Australian Workers' Association were plotting 'that the assistance of the Russians was required to educate the Labor people in Socialistic doctrine and it was required that the Russians in the various centres should interest themselves in the movement and keep in close touch with the various unions'. The Queensland authorities felt a growing dissatisfaction with the Russians and made threats to deport them.

At that critical moment Leandro interfered. Manowitch made his report, telling how Leandro Illin had called on the Russian consul in connection with this affair:

'HE WAS INFORMED BY THE CONSUL that their actions in connection with the strike, and their suggestions of bomb making, had come under the notice of the Government, also that owing to their aggressive attitude towards the Government, it was intended that all undesirables should be deported to Russia. ... [Illin] represented to the Consul, that they were peaceable law abiding people, and that there was no reason why the Government should take such drastic actions towards them.'

At this time Leandro became friendly with G.P. Barber, Labor MLA, who made the necessary arrangements with the federal government for the Russians' trip to the Northern Territory. While they really cared about improving the situation for Russians in Australia, Leandro and his family remained committed to the cause of socialism. How, otherwise, can one explain their close association with Nicholas Rosalieff (Rozaliev, 1884–1932), a young socialist revolutionary, who fled from exile in Siberia and came to Australia. A number of post-cards dating from 1911–12 addressed to Rosalieff by his Russian comrades-in-arms, which one has to read between the lines to understand, have amazingly survived, finding a place in the collection of post-cards owned by Flora, Leandro's daughter. Another Russian radical, the anarcho-communist Alexander Zuzenko (1885–1938), who, after participation in the mutiny on the *Potemkin*, fled to Australia in 1911, considered Nicholas Illin to be his 'spiritual father'.[69]

The second delegate to go to the Northern Territory with Leandro was Konstantin Vladimiroff (Vladimirov). Newly arrived in Australia, he was a highly educated specialist in agriculture connected with agricultural colleges and the Institute of Forestry in Russia, a member of the Russian Geographical Society. For eight years he had served as inspector of Fisheries on the Aral Sea and in Turkestan. He published a number of works on agriculture and contributed reports to the Geographical Society.

Vladimiroff's personality seems to be a contradictory one. Probably he had to leave Russia because of involvement in radical activities. Anyway, he was clearly the first person to acquaint the Northern Territory wilderness with Russian revolutionary songs. According to Leandro, while the lugger they were on was struggling towards the mouth of the Daly River, 'it was raining impetuously. Mr Vladimiroff was standing on the deck in his impermeable coat singing a Russian song, which says something like this — "The clouds are running over the seas, this will be a storm we will try to stand and struggle against it".' At the same time Vladimiroff was rather arrogant, with lordly manners, and unused to physical work. Soon Leandro was to write in his diary with surprise: 'We carried our luggage to the "dinghy", a little distance. I believe Mr Vladimiroff has done this kind of work for the first time in his life.' He was never separated from his umbrella, which became an object of Leandro's constant jokes.

'I THINK WE MADE A BEAUTIFUL PICTURE. The blackfellow ahead, then myself, Mr Vladimiroff following me on a bay mare under the umbrella, and the pig trotting behind and making a horrible noise ...

'The umbrella is getting old and broken. My opinion is, that if Russians are satisfied with his report they ought to present him with a new umbrella with an inscription.'[70]

All the same, Vladimiroff possessed great self-command and was an experienced traveller and, although the frontier conditions of the Northern Territory were an ordeal for him, he endured them perfectly. In general, as a team they complemented each other well. Leandro's important contribution to the success of the expedition was his knowledge of English — a rare skill among Russian émigrés. Vladimiroff, for instance, did not know the language at all. Still, he had an important capacity — being experienced in the systematic organisation of observed facts. After the expedition he submitted to the Department for External Affairs a 'Report on the Northern Territory of Australia' (sixty-four typescript pages), which discussed in systematic form its geography, agricultural and pastoral industries, and colonisation issues. In essence, this was the first comprehensive description of the Territory, with an analysis of its problems and prospects.

Leandro's approach to his task was quite different: 'My idea is not to express opinions of other men, picking out the best, but to speak only about what I have seen'. The best form for it was a diary. A diary, and especially a travel diary, is always a balance between what is written for yourself and what is intended to be read by others. Some travellers later rewrite their diaries, reducing in proportion its private entries. Leandro knew from the very beginning that his diary would be used by the officials in the Department for External Affairs and by the Russian émigré community. Despite this, it did not make him rewrite or reduce the flow of his private thoughts. Thus, Leandro's 'Report of the Northern Territory' (ninety-two typescript pages) is an amazing combination of travel diary, report to the government, discussion of serious socio-economic issues, mixed with personal reflections — sometimes humorous, sometimes poetic — and recollections of his earlier life.[71] This art of making connections between the way he saw general issues and his own private life was an essential feature of Leandro's way of thinking. He was to exhibit this characteristic later in his letters to officials and in his correspondence to the *Herbert River Express*. To do things *comme il faut*, in 'the way it should be done', was by no means his aspiration. He recognised only two criteria for his writings: honesty and clarity. This diary was Leandro's literary debut. It was a debut for Nicholas's ideas as well: his son, brought up in Jean-Jacques Rousseau's style, in complete freedom and with the art of solving problems of real, natural life, now was entering the *comme il faut* world on his own.

On 24 February 1912 Leandro Illin and Konstantin Vladimiroff boarded the *Empire* in Brisbane. Their whole journey was organised at the expense of the federal government. They passed along the east coast and Thursday Island and on 4 March arrived in Darwin. They stayed in the Northern Territory more than two months, inspecting nearly all accessible farms between the middle reaches of the Daly River, Pine Creek, and the upper and lower Adelaide River. The first thing they did was, accompanied by some officials, to make an unsuccessful attempt by sea to reach the site of the proposed Daly River Demonstration Farm. In four days their lugger made only 37 miles against contrary winds, and finally they returned to Darwin. After that they took a train to Pine Creek, visiting on the way back Brocks Creek, Stapleton and Batchelor Experimental Farm. Their next trip was to the lower reaches of the Adelaide River, where they visited Blue Water Hole and Humpty Doo. They also inspected a number of farms around Darwin and travelled to Charles Point by sea. Their final journey was to Daly River. They travelled by train to Brocks Creek and then on horseback with Aboriginal guides to Glenavon plantation on the Daly River. This last journey took twelve days.

Describing their journeys in the Territory, Leandro seems to have been overwhelmed by its wild and pristine nature; for him it was like being present on this land at the time of creation. We came, he says:

'TO A NICE DEEP CREEK WITH WATER AS CLEAR AS CRYSTAL, 15 feet deep. As it was very hot I simply walked into the creek and drank, like a horse, as much as I could.'

'[At] the mouth of the Bamboo Creek ... I heard a noise which made me think about alligators. I went quietly and looked through the bush and saw a wonderful thing. The creek was alive with fish, nice big ones. Sometimes they jumped out of the water and made the noise which attracted my attention.'

It was a world where 'hundreds of kangaroos and wallabies followed' the travellers while they 'walked through the jungle' near Daly River; where the grasses were 'the same height as the horses'; where 'millions of geese', ducks and other birds were flying over swamps near Adelaide River and large mobs of buffalo and wild pigs rushed through the forest.[72]

Leandro's diary has a number of bright, memorable sketches of the outback life-style.

'AN OLD SETTLER of Wheel Danks Creek [somewhere near Daly River], Mr George Warr, ... met us very kindly, brought a fine, sweet watermelon from his little garden, and killed a goat for us. There were also a few aboriginals, and a dark lady played the gramophone for us. They play with the same needle for years, I believe. The wood of this machine is eaten by the white ants, and it holds together miraculously.'

Rich farmers coming out for 5 o'clock tea in 'paradisiac dresses and bare feet', 'humpy made of bark', 'stringy bark' used as bed — this world had nothing of the 'Englishness' that other Russian travellers so severely criticised when visiting Australian cities.[73] Leandro and Vladimiroff saw the white pioneers there as 'Australians'; it was a new nation. Moreover, by this time Leandro had easily adopted distinctly Australian words, which he often used without inverted commas as though they were quite natural for him — brumby, billy-can, damper, humpy, billabong, lubra, and so on.

Aborigines were an essential part of this frontier world. Leandro's diary is a valuable source for learning about the Northern Territory Aborigines at a period when their society, in spite of interference from the colonists, still preserved a number of traditional features. Leandro and Vladimiroff wrote about the social and numerical composition of Aboriginal 'camps', their traditional diet, and the role of hunting and gathering of wild rice. They also wrote about the importance of traditional religion in Aboriginal life. But the main issue that occupied their attention was the shocking picture of European exploitation and cruelty in relation to the Aborigines, which was recorded by Leandro in his journal and later submitted to the federal officials.

The Russians gained their most impressive lesson, in relation to the treatment of Aborigines, from Thomas and Roberts, the owners of Glenavon plantation near Daly River. When Leandro wanted to pay the Aboriginal guides who had brought them to the plantation with some provisions, he was reproached by the hosts for 'spoiling the blacks for them. "They would not get as much from us for a year's service", said Mr Thomas.' And on the next day when Leandro wanted to throw away a tin of spoiled salmon he was advised by Thomas to give it to the Aboriginal men. '"They will be poisoned perhaps", said I. "No matter" he replied, "there are plenty of them". When I wanted to give them tea he became really angry and said "There is plenty of water, don't you spoil my blacks!'" It was not unusual for Roberts to fire a shot to frighten 'blackfellows' approaching his fields. 'Is it not interesting to see in free Australia a man in a white cork hat in the middle of twenty blacks with his hand in his pocket holding a small Browning?', Leandro concluded sarcastically.

Twenty Aborigines who were working on the farm were paid with boiled maize and tobacco (both grown by themselves) and a pair of trousers, or a belt, or a hat for a year's work. 'This is less than twopence per man for food', Leandro calculated. Starving Aborigines had to bring their own food to the farm, which gave Mr Thomas grounds to boast to the Russians: 'Are they not silly animals? They have plenty of game and fish, and could live without work, but yet they come to work and bring some tucker.' The Russians constantly heard from the locals that they could use Aborigines' labour for nothing.

Leandro saw that the whites' invasion brought the Aborigines all kinds of evil, such as addiction to alcohol and 'nicotine', 'which keeps the natives in slavery'. 'Their English is composed specially of swear words.' Their women were used by white men, and children were kept at the mission station on Bathurst Island ('a kind of prison for unhappy half-castes'). The Russians witnessed chained, imprisoned Aborigines and watched how they were tried without understanding the nature of their trial. All this created a depressing picture for the Russians.

Nevertheless, Leandro also recorded cases of quite different attitudes towards the Aborigines by some other farmers. Mr Glasson, who lived not far from Thomas, was disliked by his neighbours because he treated Aborigines better than others did. Mr W. Milton, an intelligent farmer from Stapleton, according to Leandro: 'speaks highly of the aboriginals he has working for him — He says they can do any kind of work on the farm nearly as well as himself. Mr Milton treats them well, with clothing and food the same as his own. This shows that the natives can be useful with good people.'

Leandro, in distinction from Vladimiroff, recognised, and even admired, Aboriginal traditional skills:

'... THEY BELIEVE THEMSELVES SUPERIOR TO THE WHITE MAN, AND IN SOME WAYS THEY ARE. They can catch, find or get [any] animal they want. They will find food where white men will die of hunger. They can track anything they like, and see you when you do not see them. ... Natives are splendid walkers.'

Even so, at this time he was far from idealising the Aborigines in their current state. His view of Aborigines developed out of two quite different, and contrary approaches. His attitude was that of a Russian intellectual who aspired to the equality of all people; but at the same time he saw them as any ordinary Russian would, with a characteristic compassion for the disadvantaged mingled with the European conviction of white superiority. Consequently, it was a confused position he adopted, all the more so because what he was witnessing was an Aboriginal society in decline, the result of the European destruction of traditional Aboriginal values, and this meant there were times when he was capable of some narrow-minded observations:

'THE DIFFERENCE BETWEEN [Aboriginals] and the animals is very little. ... They cannot be treated well, as if you give them a finger they will try to get the whole hand. ... If you do not show them who is the boss, they will weary you by asking for one thing and another.'[74]

But such statements he made only on 'theoretical' pages of his diary. In practice, he was guided by a better and more reliable barometer — his own heart, which did not allow him to be either bossy or sentimental. It was more natural for him to be an unbiased observer, a humorous narrator and an honest partner in his contacts with the Aborigines. Could he suspect that European–Aboriginal relations were soon to become pivotal in his own life, and remain so!

Leandro's fascination with the frontier was mixed with an awareness of the social problems which would immediately confront Russian immigrants settling in the Territory outback. The main thing that worried him was alcohol. The common custom all over Australia of 'generosity in drinking and paying' was aggravated in the Territory, as bars were the only place where men could go and relax. Leandro argued to the federal authorities that a liquor ban in the Territory was no less important than agricultural issues, and especially for Russians: 'I know [that] Russians, as well as other nationalities, and perhaps more than others, like to visit the bars and I would like to find for them a "paradise", that is a sober community — Protect the men against themselves.'[75]

This trip enabled Leandro to have a close encounter with the world of Australian power élites. He knew about the arbitrariness of the Russian authorities, mostly from his father's experience; he knew the Latin American masquerade, where dictatorship wore the mask of democracy; now he — 'comparatively a new arrival with my eyes wide open' — was to explore the 'genuine' Australian democracy at close quarters. From the start, on their way to the Territory aboard the *Empire*, in the Territory itself, and on the *St Albans*, which took them back, the Russian delegates found themselves surrounded by high-ranking officials. Among them were Sir Josiah Thomas, the minister for External Affairs, Senators A. McDougal and Frank Brennan, Postmaster-General C.H. Wise, several members of the House of Representatives, as well as J.F. Ramsay from the Department of Agriculture, and Sir Hubert Murray, the governor of New Guinea. They also met the Territory administrative élite: Justice S.J. Mitchell, the current Administrator of the Territory, and Professor Gilruth, who came to replace Mitchell as Administrator, Director of Agriculture Clarke, Justice Mallam, ex-Police Inspector Paul Foelsche, and the director of the Botanical Gardens, Nicholas Holtze. Years later, reflecting on that time Leandro wrote: 'I can assure you they were mortals like the rest of us. Some with more ability, some with more luck, some with more backing, some perhaps with more strings to pull to get where they are; some good actors.'

Their close acquaintance with the local administration provided the Russian delegates with abundant material, which is reflected in Leandro's diary. Little by little they became acquainted with 'Darwin's punctuality' and the bureaucracy which 'could happen only on Government employment'. It took Leandro several weeks to persuade the local officials, and particularly Nicholas Holtze, to allow them to travel to Daly River overland: the officials assured the Russians that the roads were impassable, which turned out to be far from true when Leandro and Vladimiroff made the trip there at their own risk. 'Poor Northern Territory administration! I think they know as much about their Territory as I do, except by hearsay ... There was no place to wet the feet, and no creek which I could not jump over', commented Leandro.

It was characteristic of Leandro that, when he and Vladimiroff found themselves stranded in Darwin because of supposed floods, he went to Territory Administrator Mitchell.

'I ASKED HIM TO GIVE ME SOME KIND OF WORK (pick and shovel or anything), and I would wait until the better season came, and Mr Vladimiroff was agreeable to live at his own expense. ... His Honour told us that there was no work in the Northern Territory, but he promised to apply to the Government for extension of time.'

It became clear to Leandro that he and the officials spoke different languages — they were unable to comprehend Leandro's point of view: 'I do not much like living on Government's expense, doing nothing'.

The Russians felt that the local officials 'were making a joke of [them], as they did with the federal party', which was inspecting the state of agriculture in the Territory. For instance, Leandro believed that Darwin's administrators sent a group of federal inspectors to the Batchelor Experimental Farm, 'where there is nothing to see', instead of showing them a prosperous private farm, and they did this only because 'the inscription the federal party saw in big letters, "Batchelor Experimental Farm", made a very good impression, and filled their hearts with hopes'.

The poor impression the Russians had of the local administration was reinforced by a Territory old-timer and ex-police inspector, Paul Foelsche, who believed that many enterprises failed there: 'because the money was never spent by the managers on the business for which it was collected, but was nearly all spent on drinking, building fine cottages for the managers, making tram lines, telephones, sheds. The sugar cane was planted on the gravel stones and every business was carried on in the same way.'[76] The final opinion of the Russian delegates was that the poor, inadequate, wasteful management knew only how to put on a show during an inspection. Nevertheless, they continued to believe that the federal government could play a positive role in settling the Northern Territory.

The main concern of the Russians was the state of agriculture in the Northern Territory and the prospects for the Russian settlement there. Their observations, which cover many pages in their reports, are of significant value as they provide a data-filled picture and first-hand records of farmers' opinions; they had had close contact with at least two dozen local farmers and vividly portrayed them in their writings.

'I NOTICED THAT THERE WERE NO MARKETS', Leandro wrote years later, 'and products of much value could not be grown ... The main aim of most settlers seemed to be to get rid of their farms to the Government and I was approached several times and asked to recommend 'their' farm to be taken over by the Government. Most work was done by Aborigines with hoes, some settlers standing watching them with a revolver in their belts.'

But the Russian visitors were not discouraged by the modest achievements of the Northern Territory economy, believing in the potential of the country. 'The climate ... is not so dreadful as they say.' 'The Europeans can live and work in the Northern Territory but of course some precautions must be taken.' As to precautions, Vladimiroff believed that it was only possible to drink boiled water there, while Leandro undertook his risky experiment on himself, drinking water from creeks just as careless Russians would do. Luckily, this experiment did not affect his health.

The Russian delegates considered that the Northern Territory was suited neither for wage-earning nor for living in villages, as Russians usually did. The only option for Russian immigrants would be family mixed farming, including pig-breeding, supplemented by vegetable gardening and goat-breeding for the farmers' own family needs. This program would be possible only with initial government assistance to provide new arrivals with a house, stock, seeds, and a plot of cleared land. This, they believed, would be the most reasonable course, since the Northern Territory at that time was not a place to make a fortune and was unlikely to attract those with capital; they could find better places elsewhere in Australia. Still, it was a good country for people who 'do not need much money, but food and quiet living'. Leandro appealed to the federal government: 'Take the man who has nothing to lose, the people who starve ... give them assistance and they will do well'.[77]

On 6 May 1912 Leandro met with the minister for External Affairs, Josiah Thomas, at Government House in Darwin and gave him his first impressions of the Northern Territory's suitability for the Russian colony. The Russian delegates now had to return to Queensland to report to their countrymen. They were given first-class passages back on the *St Albans*, but there was an unexpected problem.

'... AS I HAVE WORN OUT ALL MY CLOTHES', Leandro wrote, 'during the trips throughout the Northern Territory, and my capital was only two shillings ... I did not want to travel first-class, ... but Mr Vladimiroff objected. I knew it was very discourteous travelling amongst well-dressed people in a suit like mine, but it was Mr Vladimiroff's fault, so I could not help it.'

Leandro himself considered that 'highfalutin' is no good for me' and admired the Greek philosophers Diogenes and Socrates, 'who preached simple life'.

On 7 May 1912, together with several federal officials, the Russians left for Queensland on the *St Albans*. Leandro visited his family in

Butchers Creek. Here he was shocked by reports in the Russian newspapers about famine in Russia. Leandro immediately wrote to the minister for External Affairs: 'I am anxious to do my best for my fellow countrymen and the Commonwealth and in my opinion I consider the Northern Territory would be a salvation from starvation for them'. Nicholas Illin felt really proud of the results of his son's expedition. 'My son has brought back a journal full of serious, interesting observations', he wrote to a Russian newspaper.

In July 1912 Leandro read his report to the Russians in Brisbane. He did not colour the truth. 'I am going to tell my Russian countrymen what I have seen … and let them form their own opinions', he stated in an interview to the *Cairns Post*, which, in describing Leandro, stressed how 'pleasingly and intelligently' he spoke. After listening to his report in Brisbane, the Russians — who were employed mainly as navvies on railway construction sites — with the passion of born peasants kneaded in their hands the samples of soils and crops Leandro had brought with him. Many became enthusiastic about settling on their own land and forming a Russian colony in the Northern Territory. In the subsequent months Leandro sent several letters and telegrams to the minister for External Affairs, Josiah Thomas, appealing to him to save starving people in Russia and direct those Russians who were already in Queensland to the Northern Territory. Meanwhile, Leandro was living in Sydney and translating his report into English; this used up all his savings, and finally, he 'could not stop any more in Sydney and had to come and work [in Cobar] in the mine underground'. He had no money to type up the report and appealed to Thomas, who gave him a small subsidy for this purpose. Leandro then went to Melbourne on the *Orsova* to submit his report to Thomas personally and they met on 25 January 1913 and discussed his report. Leandro was so anxious to help the Russian community in Australia that he considered the possibility of abandoning his farm in Butchers Creek to go to the Northern Territory: 'As Russians are still coming to Australia perhaps I would do more good going to the Northern Territory. Being myself there it will be easier to do them good and also for their settlement.' He even bought a good camera to 'be able to illustrate my further reports with photos'.[78]

These plans did not come to fruition. Clearly, after Thomas left his position in 1913, the government lost interest in the project. Although the proposals by both Illin and Vladimiroff about mixed farming and government assistance were quite realistic, they were not accepted. The Russians, accustomed to subsistence farming in extreme climatic conditions, could have been ideal agricultural settlers in the Northern Territory. Perhaps a hundred or so such colonists might have contributed considerably to the economy of the Northern Territory and facilitated its further development, as well as changing the destiny of the Russian community in Australia. The initial assistance that they asked for might soon have been returned a hundredfold. Unfortunately, this did not happen; instead of becoming farmers and landowners the Russian émigrés remained hired workers, who became more and more radical under the influence of subsequent events.

The failure of the project to which Leandro devoted more than a year of his life — at the expense of gaining capital by clearing his lot in Gadgarra — was the first serious disappointment he experienced in the Australian social and political systems. Several Russians who did go to Darwin were sent either to the Batchelor Experimental Farm ('a horrible, dreadful place, the worst I have yet seen in the Northern Territory', according to Leandro) or struggled on their own as labourers in Darwin. The sad story of one such immigrant family, the Manikovs, became a *cause célèbre* throughout Australia, contributing to Leandro's disillusionment with the outcomes of his report.[79]

In the old world of the landed classes, caught with its pretensions
and conventional assurance by a local artist — young Nikolai Ilin
with his mother Evgenia, at Ilinka, in the early 1850s.
This was the world Nikolai would later reject.

A late nineteenth century view of Turki, Saratov province — the township not far from Ilinka, the Ilin estate, where Nikolai conducted his illicit first relationship, and Ivan, his first son, was born.

courtesy of Aleksandr Massov, St Petersburg

St Petersburg years, 1880s–1890s. Despite all Nikolai's journeyings and misadventures, the Ilins lived in a comfortable neighbourhood — a flat in 16 Nikolaevskaia, now Marat St (left-hand block, *above*). However, the main burden of holding the family together fell on Alexandra, seen here in a photo from that time.

The painter Nikolai Ge, a Tolstoyan, seemed almost saintly to the Ilins when they first met him — qualities reflected in his 'Self-Portrait' (*opposite*), painted in 1892, not long before his own death, and when his relationship with the Ilins had already soured over Nikolai's handling of the exhibiting of his painting 'What is truth? Christ and Pilate' (*above*), 1890.

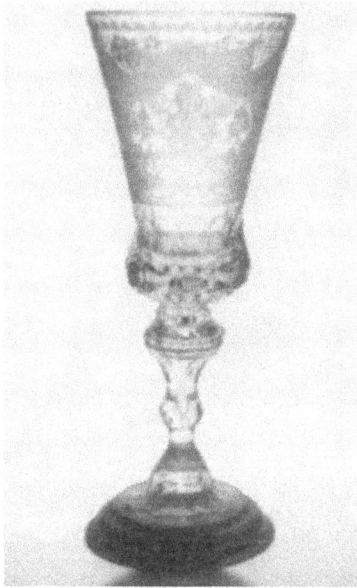

The czarina's goblet, mid eighteenth century.
In its retelling of how Catherine the Great gave her wine glass to Dmitrii Ilin,
the family story conveys some of this czarina's earthiness and her ironical wit.

The ancestral Ilin arms incorporates elements originating with
the princes of Galich; however, more recent Ilin descendants,
since the late sixteenth century, have no coat of arms.

Bixio y Cia.   Buen Orden 556

Nicholas Illin and his daughter Ariadna, early 1900s, Buenos Aires, Argentina.
Life in Patagonia provided Ariadna with outlets for her strong-willed
determination and resourcefulness; for Nicholas, finally reunited with
his family, they were good years and creatively productive.

ORIENT LINE R.M.S. OMRAH

The *Omrah* carried the Illins to Australia, yet another new life,
1910 — from a postcard, scrawled with Hector and Nellie's Russian letters.
On this ship, too, Leandro and Mila met.

Father and son: Nicholas Illin, 1910s–1920s (*above*)
and Leandro Illin, *ca* 1920, Australia (*opposite*).
An especially close relationship in which the restless ideals of the father bore
fruit in the unyielding principles by which the son conducted his life.

The author with Bill Homenko, Gadaloff Road, Butchers Creek, 1996;
and map of the Butchers Creek area, Atherton Tablelands. Homenko's farm
provides a glimpse of the last vestiges of 'Little Siberia', whose full extent
in its heyday in the 1910s–1920s can be gauged from the
Russian names on the map (*opposite page*).

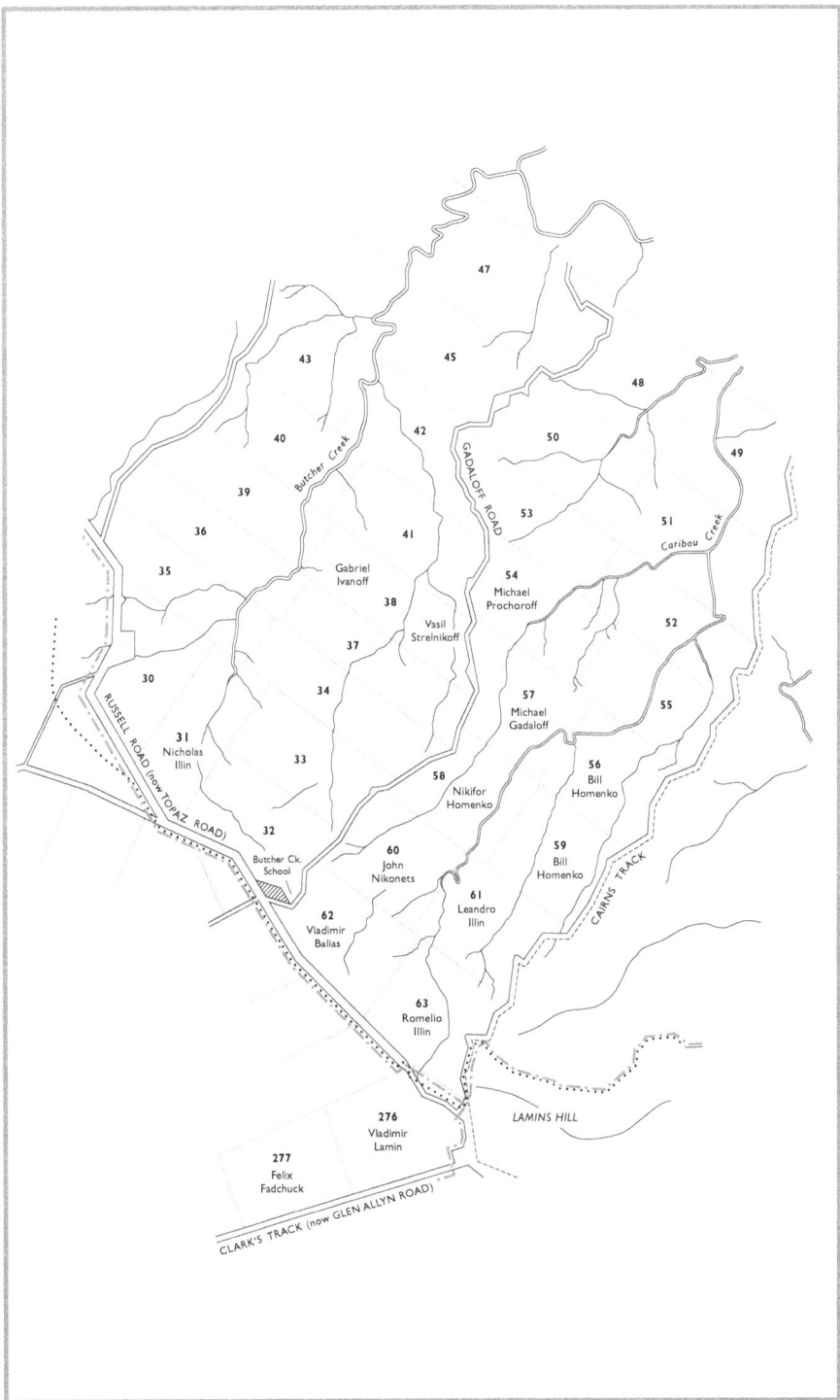

47

43   45

40   42   48

39   50   49

36   41   53   51   Caribou Creek

35   Gabriel   54   52
      Ivanoff   Michael
      38   Prochoroff

37   Vasil   57   55
      Strelnikoff   Michael
                     Gadaloff

30   34   58   56
                  Bill
31   33   Nikifor   Homenko
Nicholas   Homenko
Illin   32   60   59
         Butcher Ck.   John   Bill
         School   Nikonets   Homenko
         62   61
         Vladimir   Leandro
         Balias   Illin

         63
         Romelio
         Illin

276   LAMINS HILL
Vladimir
277   Lamin
Felix
Fadchuck

CLARK'S TRACK (now GLEN ALLYN ROAD)

RUSSELL ROAD (now TOPAZ ROAD)

GADALOFF ROAD

Butcher Creek

CAIRNS TRACK

Leandro Illin at Greenvale Station, *ca* 1927.

Kitty Illin with her dog Possum, at Greenvale Station, *ca* 1924.

Kitty Illin at Greenvale Station, *ca* 1924, with (*left to right*) Flora, Dick, Harry, Ginger, Lullie and Thomas — the first generation of this Russian-Aboriginal family.

The author and Vera Ketchell, Malanda, sorting through Vera's archive, the source of Mila's letter.

The Ngadjon elder Jessie Calico with four-year-old Ralphie Kabo,
the author's son, Malanda, 1996.

Keepers of the flame, Queensland, 1996: not only have the stories been kept but also heirlooms that now, their original meaning lost to family members, have become almost like holy relics of their Russian past. Glenda Illin (*above*), Atherton, holding an eighteenth century Russian coin, the silver spoon from Alexandra's father, the St Peter and St Paul icon, and Leandro's cap. Flora Hoolihan (*opposite page*), Townsville, with Nicholas's Russian manuscript poem.

A day at the Ingham Show, 1929: *(from left to right)* Kennedy (a friend), Ginger, Tom, Leandro, Lullie, Dick, Flora, Harry.

Harry, Tom, Leandro *(left to right)* timber-getting at Stone River, 1935.

Greenvale station, 1920s: life here was hard but there were good times, too.
LEFT — riding Nugget, *ca* 1924–25, with (*from left to right*) Flora, Tom, Lullie, Leandro, Harry and Dick.
BELOW — Tom Illin (*left*) and Maurice Dallachy sparring, with Flora and Leandro behind, *ca* 1927.

Flora Hoolihan in 1945 and Richard Hoolihan (*opposite page*) in 1929
(both photographed at Ingham).

Recalling the old days.
Harry and Flora reminisce with Mac Core (*right*)
at Mt Full Stop, 1996.

Recalling the old days.
The author interviewing Flora and Harry, with Ernest (*right*),
1996, Townsville.

Emily's stay, though short, gave the family an important connection with their Ngadjon past. Here, she is photographed with Lullie (*left*) and Flora (*right*), with Flora's children John, Margaret and Ernest in front, 1940, Stone River.

Emily, the eldest surviving Ngadjon witness to the
coming of the whites, with young David Johnston
at Boonjie, early 1950s.

Leandro's sons in war-time service in the Australian Army:
Richard Illin (*above*), 1943, and Thomas Illin (*left*), 1944.

Romelio Illin in Honduras, with his driver Jose Martinez,
at Santa Barbara, 1927.

Romelio Illin with his wife Cristina
and children Leandro, Somerled and Demetrio, 1934.

The Mackay family, late 1930s, Honduras:
(*from left to right*) Olga, Ariadna, Jack, Somerled, Hector, Nellie

Illin descendants from Australia, Honduras and America photographed in
Queensland, 1984. From left to right — (*at front*) Richard Hoolihan, Hector
Mackay (Honduras), Edwin Hoolihan; (*at rear*) Flora Hoolihan, Gloria Illin,
Dick Illin, Robert Illin, Glenda Illin, John Hoolihan, Leandro Illin (America),
Ernest Hoolihan, Janet Eaton, Margaret Gertz.

Vera Araluen (Lullie) Smallwood's family at her daughter Margaret's wedding. From left to right — (*seated*) Nola, Vera Araluen, Dynzie, Gail; (*standing*) Essie, Leslie, Alan, Margaret, Gordon, Colin, Dynzie Jnr.

Ernest and Maud Hoolihan's children celebrating Dynzie's twenty-first birthday, Canberra, 1996 — (*left to right*) Dynzie, Michael, Ernest, Derek, Allison, Maud, Hilary.

J.W. Bleakley, the Queensland Chief Protector of Aborigines, who at almost every turn, from 1915 until the 1940s, Leandro found blocking his way.

PRELUDE

UNTOLD LOVE STORY

~

It was a rainy night in Malanda and we were gathered in Margaret's kitchen when Vera Ketchell brought us a bag full of letters and papers preserved by her father Dick. Margaret, Flora's daughter, and Vera were cousins, both Leandro's granddaughters. We piled heaps of letters, which luckily had been spared by cockroaches and mice, onto the kitchen table, and the first to lie in my hand was a letter dated 3 October 1910. It began with a desperate appeal, 'Lenushka, if you knew how bad it is after you left!'

'Lenushka ...' Just what his mother would have called him when he was a child. And now it was a Russian girl addressing him with this tender name, a girl he left behind in Brisbane to join his family on the Atherton Tablelands. Eighty-six years ago, somewhere not far from where we are now Leandro read the letter over and over again, listening to this same tropical rain. It was his second month in Australia, in a new land; no one could say what destiny was awaiting him or, rather, what destiny he would choose for himself. But through all that happened to him he carried these four pages covered by half-faded, impetuous handwriting till his last days. And for fifty more years, mute, they were kept by his son, Dick. Four pages from a book without beginning or end. I believe we will not disturb his memory if we re-read these lines now.

3/X/10

Brisbane

Lenushka, if you knew how bad it is after you left! Firstly — a terrible anguish, secondly — a new trouble on my hands: yesterday evening we visited a priest (he invited us); my mother, talking about the job I want, said that I could teach French at school. You see, Lena, how ridiculous it is?! When we were walking home, I retorted to mother that I did not consider myself strong enough and did not want to have a scandal when they would sack me and would not employ me anywhere any more. She got angry and began the usual objections: if she had studied in such a select school as I and if she had

had such governesses as I had, she would not have even hesitated ... etc, etc...
Finally, we really quarrelled and mother 'in a fit of anger' said that she did
not care a fig where I might go and what I might do. At least she said this
sincerely! As for me, Lenushka, if I spoke a bit better, I probably would find
a place, but now I just do not know where to go and what to do! I was think-
ing about this all night and did not decide anything.

You ask if I meant it when I wrote 'see you soon' — yes, of course! But only
on one condition — that you recover from the madness (I don't know how else
to call it, as a normal man can't love me). Lena, one more question — very
important — write me the whole truth about the thing I dread (I do not say
the words as the letter can fall into the wrong hands). I hope you understand
me? Write me the truth and everything because to know it later will be much
worse. I do not threaten, Lena, I am just very egoistic, I care about myself.
However disgusting my life is to me, I still think that, to shoot myself, I
would not have enough — really I do not know what, folly or courage. How
to escape all this unhappiness! Lena, I beg you do not begin to speak about me
with your family; what's more, even if someone speaks about me, keep out of
the conversation, and for God's sake do not defend me; let them say what they
like about me between themselves, they can't say anything worse than the
truth.

Goodbye, Lena — write more often

M.

'M.' was all that she left for our curious eyes. Still, some facts began
to connect in a chain. The Illins arrived in Brisbane on 5 September
1910 and, according to naturalisation records, while the rest of the family left for Atherton Tablelands after a week, Leandro lingered on in
Brisbane for one month. They were determined to take possession of
the land, so what could keep him in Brisbane at such an important
moment? And M.'s letter provided an answer — love.

Her family was obviously newly arrived and impoverished, and yet
she and Leandro seem to be very intimate already; moreover, she had
managed to antagonise his family. When could it all have happened, I
asked myself. Then suddenly I remembered a line in the shipping
records of the *Omrah*: 'Mary, Boris and Ludmila Daniel', a Russian
family that came aboard in London and were travelling as 'farm-hands'.
M. had to be one of them — Mary or Mila (Ludmila) Daniel.

Impatiently, I looked at the computer screens and microfilm reader's screens but they did not want to say anything about the Daniels: they were not in naturalisation records, not in the electoral rolls, not among residents. Some time later I told the Brisbane-based, Russian historian Nikolai Dmitrovsky about my fruitless search and a miracle happened — he recollected an article about the Daniels from a Russian emigrant magazine. The Daniels were the most popular family in the Far East during the construction of the railway there. Mary's husband, Evgenii, a buoyant, energetic and fascinating personality, was a manager. Mary was the first Russian woman to invite Chinese officials to her house, which contributed to their popularity among the local population. When she travelled on the railway, the Chinese met her with a guard of honour and music; her name-day was celebrated by special church services throughout the town they lived in. The Daniels had two children, then teenagers — a son, Boris, and a charming daughter, Milochka (Mila, or Ludmila). When the railway was completed, Mary unexpectedly divorced her husband and left with the children for Australia.

On the *Omrah* the Illins met the Daniels: Mary, the ambitious woman used to luxury and devotion, now going through a crisis in her life; her son Boris, now twenty-one years old, whose age allowed them to travel as assisted immigrants; Mila, a refined, sixteen-year-old girl from a select school, disguised as a 'farm-hand'.[1] After the idle, vulgar officials that Milochka would have encountered in the East, Leandro, an honest, straightforward young man, a courageous hunter from the Andes, a passionate defender of the downtrodden, must have seemed the first real man to her as she listened for hours to the stories from his life. Unexpectedly for both, their love flared up on this long journey under the southern stars. But the voyage came to an end; in Brisbane, in the Immigration Depot, they were to confront reality. Leandro, who was twenty-eight already, obviously left her in no doubt of his feelings, but he also understood that this distressed child's need for him as a protector might be confused in her mind with real love and he just couldn't take advantage of that. In any case, what could he offer her — a shed in the jungle? Moreover, her mother was probably suspicious of the radical Illins, who were guided by ideas rather than commonsense. She had quite different plans for the future of her children. Finally, Mila and Leandro had to part.

I could not find out what happened to the Daniels after that. They disappeared as many other human grains disappear, each carrying away with it its own world ...

Later on, I asked Flora about Leandro's girlfriends. To my surprise she smiled slightly and said:

'YEAH ... I GOT TWO PHOTOS THERE SOMEWHERE ... He would not even speak of it, but he said once to us about his girl-friend. I think she was a little bit older than him, I just do not know where she came from, must be from some other place. She was supposed to be going away from Australia and she wanted father to go with her. And she had money, too, she wanted to pay his fare to go with her, but he said "No, I couldn't leave my family, I couldn't take myself away from them." No, his family was dearer to him, he'd never go away and leave them. Not for that woman, anyway. But they went away and left him later ...'

Flora, a little sad, stopped talking.[2] From the yellowish, tattered photo a reserved, intelligent, strong-willed girl was looking at us. It is unlikely that this was Mila Daniel from the *Omrah*. Mila did not seem rich enough to pay the fares for Leandro, while Flora has not heard that the girl on the photo was Russian. One more untold story ...

On the second photo produced by Flora was a girl of another type — young, pretty, flirtatious. Flora knew only that she was a waitress. Although Leandro did not drink in bars, he knew this type of girl well. It was after watching men there that he summed up the social problems confronting them in the outback. In his report on the Northern Territory in 1912 Leandro shared his concerns about the situation, mingling, as was usual for him, his own experience with reflections and suggestions.

'MEN DO NOT MARRY UNTIL THEY HAVE ENOUGH MONEY TO MAKE A HOME. This is a wrong idea (some people, especially ladies, might call me a savage) as in the old country the women do not wait until the man has plenty of money, but marry and make a home together. It is difficult to make a home without a wife. ... After long pioneering and living in a tent in the lonely bush, tired morally and physically, the man feels very often at home in the hotel, where the nice waitresses joke, and look after those poor men well, who forget at this time all their misfortunes and hardships. The earnings of these honest men go like a stream into the barman's pocket accompanied by three words, "Have a drink."

'... The women of Australia should be more patriotic, and take the lead in fighting against alcohol, and then many Australian citizens would be able to earn money and make for themselves the so desired "sweet home". The woman everywhere is the source of joy for the man (this time ladies will agree with me), or the source of grief, or happiness, or unhappiness, or of steadiness or the contrary, and all kinds of mental or physical movements depend on the woman and I am sorry to say, ladies do not like pioneering or pioneers, but prefer the town man always (whose life is never so interesting and valuable for this country as [that of] the pioneers).

'When I was a little boy I heard stories which always ended in somebody who had done something wonderful and had in recompense a girl for his wife. Poor pioneers never get any other recompense but the bottle.'[3]

He was thirty, yet the fairy-tales his nanny Pelagea used to tell on long winter nights in far-away Russia had not come true in Australia — the girl with whom he would make his own 'sweet home' at Gadgarra did not appear. In his case the usual obstacles to marriage — pioneering life and the absence of money — were aggravated by his nationality. His father gave his children the whole world yet he doomed them to the life of eternal strangers.

It took years and years for them to adjust to a new country, to be recognised by that country, whether it was Argentina, Australia, or the Honduras. Romelio, more home-bound than Leandro, could not find a wife either. His niece Nellie even suggests that the Illins left Australia for South America because of this. In Honduras Romelio did not marry before 1929, when he was about forty-three years old. It was probably the same lack of understanding in a spouse from a different cultural background that made Ariadna's first two relationships unsuccessful.

Maybe there was something else affecting the prospects for marriage for Nicholas's children. Perhaps the relationship of their parents with each other, and their conduct with the children was so harmonious in spite of all their misfortunes that the children subconsciously wanted to reproduce this in their own married life; perhaps they wanted to find features of their parents in their own spouses. A vain dream for a pioneer in the new country! Even from the few preserved fragmentary facts we can see that Leandro's attachment to his parents affected his relations with women. Still, the day came when his attachment to a woman became stronger than his attachment to his parents. He stayed with her and their children; his parents left forever.

That woman was Kitty Clarke, from the Ngadjon tribe.

"The Aboriginals Protection and Rest[...]

ORDER FOR RE[...]

ficers and Constables of Police, Prison Officers, and others w[...]

Section 9 of "The Aboriginals Protection and Restriction of the Sale of [...] the Minister may cause Aboriginals within any district to be remove[...] _Kenneth McDonald Grant_ _Yunga[...]_ Aboriginals hereinafter named be removed from _[...] River_ for the causes stated in connection with thei[...] d subject to such conditions as may be prescribed.

NAME.	
Kitty Clarke & her three children	For her ow[...] To accompa[...]

KITTY'S WORLD

IN THE COUNTRY OF THE RAINBOW SERPENT

We were standing on top of Lamins Hill. The mist was so thick that we could not see further than a couple of metres. I went a few steps away from the car and the mist enveloped me. Now nothing reminded me about my own time and space. This pervasive mist made commonsense vacillate. The world which, I was sure, did not exist any longer, was here. I could see it more and more clearly through the melting and gliding mist. Below the hill the dark-green waves of dense rainforest appeared. It was permeated with myriad raindrops sparkling in the sun, with anxious voices of unknown birds. This was ancient Ngadjon country. A gust of wind brought a song, sad and monotonous, and when the last waves of the mist had lifted I saw the singers. Their dark faces with half-closed eyes were turned to the slope of Bartle Frere and I heard Jessie Calico's voice.

'DO YOU SEE A BIG GREEN PATCH OVER THERE? TREES NEVER GROW AROUND IT, it's always green, just grass. That's our sacred place up there. That's where all our people will go, up to that mountain. That is our spiritual burial-ground, where our spirits go. When our people used to die, sometimes you might have heard the older people talking about them, that they don't lie to rest, they just walked around, people have seen them. And then the older people used to sing the spirit and send it back up to there to the mountain and the spirit would not come back any more, it lie at rest.'

Flora's voice could be heard now, its placid tones blending in with the song: 'My spirit will go up there too one day'.[1] The mourning song raised and filled all the space; there was no place for my time in it, no place for us. The dead were burying their dead ...

The mist had lifted indeed. An emerald, grassy country lay below Lamins Hill. The rainforest was no longer there, revealing all the secret folds and waves of the outraged, naked land. Within the life-span of one generation tea plantations and grazing pastures have destroyed the ancient land inhabited by Ngadjon people for millennia, have ousted the mythological landscape created by Ngadjon spiritual ancestors. Jessie was the last link with them, the last who was still able to see this sacred landscape beneath the modern scene that lay in front us. She pointed to a group of trees to the north, surrounding the crater of an extinct volcano:

'AT THE GADALOFF ROAD WHERE HOMENKO LIVES, TO YOUR LEFT

you'll see a property, there's a farmhouse just below. There's Gadaloff, there's Homenko's farm out there and a little bit further down there is another farmhouse. Those people are there where the crater is. Rainbow Serpent it was there, it used to live there, we called him Yamani. He used to live there. And the old people said, in those time they wanted fire, the birds wanted fire, they were all cold, and the only one who had fire was this old Rainbow Serpent. He had his fire going there. He was keeping warm.

'And the birds were trying to get that fire, they kept saying, "You go get that wood that's laying underneath the other one, that piece of wood with the coal on it". They tried to fly down and when they got down there the old Serpent jumps up and keeps hacking them. They kept comin' back. I do not know how long they did it for, they waited and waited, kept pushing different ones. "You go, your turn, your try." They all had a go but nobody was able to get the fire, the fire-stick.

'Last one to come along was black bird Wedgetag. He said, "I'll go down for you". And they said, "Can you?" — "Yes, I'll go down for you." Then he said, "We let him go to sleep, let him sleep and then I'll go down and get that firewood". And he waited, and waited, and he waited till Yamani got to sleep. Every time he hear a noise he jumps up. And they said "Let him go to sleep, sound asleep". When he fell off to sleep, this little black bird flew down on him and he grabbed that wood. And as he was coming away with it the old Rainbow Serpent woke up and just caught him going away with the fire-stick. So he came round and he hit him on the back of the tail. That's why he has this split tail. But he took the wood. And they were all happy, so they made the fire and they sat around, they had the fire going, so all the birds had the fire and everybody was sitting around this fire.

'And the old Serpent got really angry with them because they kept picking at him all the time for that firewood. One day he said, "I'll move out of here, I'll fix them up, I'll move away". So he made up his mind he was going to move. He emptied all the water from where he was at that crater, and took off from there, and he went all the way down, right down at the bottom to Lake Barrine. He got there at the early hours of the morning before daybreak and he emptied all the water out there into Lake Barrine. Our people call that place *Barrang*, it means "early morning, daybreak". That's why we say "The ground belongs to the other tribe, Yidini [or Idindji] tribe, but the water is ours because it came from our country".'

'I heard that story about moving water from my grandma', added Jessie, and her face lit up with a smile. 'She would tell us a story and next evening we used to say "Tell us this story, grandma!" — "No, I can't keep telling that story, you already heard it." And my great-grandmother, too, told me this story, and my cousin Emma. It belongs to all of us.'[2]

Jessie Calico, this tiny, charming woman in a house-dress and cosy, knitted cardigan, who, to look at, you would hardly have associated with ancestral mythology, seemed at that moment a magician to us. From the top of Lamins Hill we could see the group of trees surrounding the crater of the Rainbow Serpent and the path the Serpent took down towards Lake Barrine along the present Gadaloff road, past Butchers Creek school and the adjoining farms. We were at the centre of the mythological landscape created by Jessie's ancestors and preserved by them as part of that mythological reality — so like a kind of mythological, virtual reality. Her art of story-telling also contributed to this strong impression. She had the ability not to question the reality of the mythological events, which we, with all our rationalism, lack. Myth, in distinction from fairy-tale or legend, is always believed by its creators to be the truth; it discusses the most basic questions of the world — the origin of the universe, man, cultural attributes, social organisation, the mystery of birth and death. Mythological events happen in mythological time — widely known as Dreamtime in Australia. Mythological time flows independently from ordinary, historical time but determines the events of historical time. The Ngadjon-ji had an even more sophisticated understanding of time. According to R. Lauriston Sharp, who recorded some facts in this area in the early 1930s, they considered that there was *tjutjapa*, the very distant past, when 'the first world' was established; this was succeeded by *ngaki*, or 'olden time', which was followed by the present.[3]

Jessie's story, unsophisticated on the face of it, is the quintessence of the different archetypes that have emerged with human beings, followed them throughout history and survived in mythology and customs till our time. A serpent or snake existed in myths all over the world. It usually had an amazing dual nature — creative and destructive — and was associated with the two opposite elements of water and fire. The element of water was connected with rain, earth and fertility, particularly the female reproductive forces; the element of fire was connected with lightning, the rainbow and, as well, with male fecundity.

Moreover, snakes often are one of the elements of another basic opposition in mythology — that of top and bottom, the upper and the lower worlds, where birds represent the upper world while snakes symbolise the lower world. The Rainbow Serpent from Jessie's story had nearly all these qualities. It acted as a cultural hero: it created the surrounding landscape, filled the lake with water, and the birds (mythological ancestors, proto-people) acquired fire from it.

It is not by chance that near the crater Aborigines had a bora ground (a place for sacred rituals), where boys were initiated into manhood.[4] The most essential element of initiation was the symbolic temporal death of the boy and his revival to a new life as an adult. This 'death' often was performed as a passage through the mouth of a monster or, in some Australian tribes, of the Rainbow Serpent.

All the above archetypes — repulsion by a snake and yet attraction to it, fascination with burning fire and lightning and terror of them, association of ourselves with the upper world supplemented with fear and attraction to the lower one, as well as personification of male and female halves in natural phenomena — are deeply rooted in our subconscious. Yet we in these modern times, with the illusion of our knowledge, often have no time to think about these basic — and most important — things and are unable to liberate ourselves from these fears and joys through words, as Jessie elegantly did in her myth. Listening to Jessie on that hill-top brought home to me in a real sense the power of Claude Lévi-Strauss's observation about Aborigines as the greatest intellectuals of the Stone Age.

If it were not for Jessie and her grandmother Polly Clarke, whose group belonged to the territory around the Rainbow Serpent crater, we would never have known its location. In 1913 a Swedish naturalist, Eric Mjöberg, heard about the crater but could not find it. He recorded that:

'ACCORDING TO THE ABORIGINES THERE WAS IN ANCIENT TIMES A THIRD, SMALLER LAKE nearby [Lake Barrine and Lake Eacham] which they call "boonoobagolamee". I could not find out in what way it had disappeared. However, they imagine that a large underground passage connects the lakes. In it floats an enormously huge cedar trunk, and, one day, it will become a giant crocodile which they call 'Canyahra'. Out of it will emerge, in its turn, the dreaded spirit of the deceased Murgalainya, the strong and mighty chief. A long way back in time when he still walked on the earth amongst his people, he had his campsite on the tallest peak of the highest mountain in Queensland, Mt

Bellenden Ker. Its crests, surrounded with mist, can, sometimes, be seen from the vicinity of the lakes.'

There was something sinister in the beauty of these tiny volcanic lakes. No water-birds lived there and the Aborigines believed the lakes to be bottomless. They considered them as dangerous, evil places, or, according to Jessie, 'Sacred to us. We'd go there but we would not swim there. We never swam in that water.'[5] It is quite possible that this fear was caused by their witnessing the volcanic eruption but probably it was also the place where they encountered the primeval Chaos.

But let's listen to Jessie and Flora first. Jessie's second myth was about the origin of the volcanic lakes.

'IT WAS TWO BOYS. AS THE YOUNG FELLAS GET OLDER THEY BECOME INITIATED. They have to go away, a little bit further away from the main camping, where the other people were all camped. So these two boys, they were there and they got their marks. The elders that were looking after them told them to rub eel oil on their bodies to somehow seal their scar. And this day the elders went hunting. They told the boys, "Now, look, we're going to leave you here, don't go out of the camp. You two stay in gunya, don't go walking around, don't do anything silly. We're going to go away for the day and we'll be back later."

'So they stayed there. And in the meantime one looked out and said, "Oh, I want to go to the toilet". He went out and came back and said to the other one, "Oh, give me a spear, bring that spear, I see a wallaby sitting there. I feel hungry, we must catch that wallaby." This other one said, "No, don't do that. We are not allowed to do that. We must not do that." He was frightened of breaking their law. But the first one said, "No, that's all right, that's all right, I want to catch it". So he threw the spear and missed the wallaby. That spear went into a flame tree. The wallaby was in front of it. And he missed the wallaby and hit the flame tree. So he went over, pulled that spear out, and when he pulled that spear out, a witchetty grub was on it. "Ai", he said, "Jambun, Jambun!" And the other one said, "What did you get?". He said, "Come on and get them, we can cook them up". They had forgotten all about that law, that the old people told them not to do. So they went ahead and got that witchetty grub, they started chopping the flame tree down and when they felled the tree they started opening them up.

'And while they were doing that, that's when that water came up there. But they were too busy. They were not worried about what was going to happen around them. All the animals start to run past them, but they were not worried about the animals, they were too busy trying to get grubs out of the tree. The elders who went away hunting, they looked back at the sky and said, "Those two boys, they must have done something wrong". They could tell by the sky, it was red. "So we'll have to go back." They were a long way from the camp. When they came back it was all gone, all gone down under water and this is now called Lake Eacham.'[6]

Flora, after listening to Jessie's myth, remembered another myth that she had heard from her Ngadjon grandmother Emily in 1940. It turned out to be the elaboration of the end of the story Jessie had just told.

'MY GRANDMOTHER EMILY TOLD ME about lakes Eacham and Barrine. She reckons it was a big clear patch in the scrub, all bare ground. And she said there was a big tribe there living on this area because it was all clear and no trees, just bare open space in the scrub. And then one day they heard a big noise and the ground started to shake. When the earth started to shake they did not know what it was. And when the earth shook, water started coming up through the ground, so they all started to run away from the ground and the ground sunk into the water. A lot of them run away but a lot of them went down into the water too. So it swallowed some of them and some of them got away. That's how the lakes come about. The ground must have been just very shallow on top of the water, the earth must have been only like a crust, and when the earthquake came it must have shook there, shook the earth and the ground went down.'[7]

Unlike Jessie, Flora told the story as if removed from it, trying even to provide a rational explanation for it. Actually, I recorded this story from Flora three times and, comparing the versions, I noticed that she always stressed that there was an empty place, and, to be more precise, provided different explanations: 'a big clear patch in the scrub', 'a big open place', 'just bare ground, no trees there', 'all bare ground, what you call bora ground, all clear'.

George Watson, Bob Dixon's informant, telling this legend also stressed that there was 'not jungle — just open scrub'. Dixon made an interesting suggestion, using geophysical and botanical data. According to this data, the volcanic lakes were formed about 10,000 years ago, whereas the rainforest appeared around the lakes only 7500 years ago, which means that when the lakes were created no rainforest was there. 'A strong case can be made for the Lakes story having been handed down, from one generation to the next, for something like ten thousand years', Dixon concludes.[8]

Nevertheless, 'the empty place' can have a quite different explanation — mythological rather than geographical — as has been suggested to me by the anthropologist Vladimir Kabo. 'Empty place' is a mythological landscape before the Creation, it is primeval Chaos, which is transformed by mythological heroes into orderly Cosmos. In Jessie's myth the boys living in this primeval landscape have broken the existing rules — worst of all, the flame tree which they hit and felled was sacred to the Rainbow Serpent[9] — and cataclysm followed. After that, the world was obviously recreated in the form of the present landscape with volcanic lakes. This new world was inhabited by people who obey the rules — the law.

Now, more than a century after the European invasion, these myths are all that remains from the former harmonious system of the universe. Yet even these fragments let us see the depth of it; they allow us to touch upon the overwhelming spirituality that imbued everyday life of the Aborigines and determined their survival for millennia in the harsh, natural surroundings. The spirituality that came from their land was no less important for them than the food which this land provided. Before the Europeans realised that these so-called 'primitive natives' were living in a quite different dimension, the fragile, mysterious world of these people had melted away as mist.

THE BARRINEAN MYSTERY

Squeezed in with Jessie, me and my young son Ralphie on the back seat of the car as we were heading towards Lamins Hill, Flora gently touched Jessie's arm: 'My mother was like that, light skin, not real dark'.[10] Flora did not suspect that this light skin-colour of her ancestors, unusual among Aboriginal tribes, was part of the problem of the origin of the Australian Aborigines, one of the enigmas still not fully resolved. Neither could she suspect that my husband, Vladimir Kabo, who was sitting in the front seat of the car, once wrote a whole book about the mystery of her ancestors' origin. Thirty years ago in St Petersburg he pondered about people from the Atherton Tablelands and Lake Barrine without at that time having any hope of seeing them, since he, a former political prisoner, was not allowed to travel abroad.[11] Luckily we came in time to meet Jessie and Flora.

It took less than a century to reduce the Ngadjon tribe of around 700 people to a handful of full-blood Aborigines who still speak the language and know the traditional culture. Only once did Flora say what the white invaders did to her people: 'They did a lot of bad, bad things, they used to shoot the black people for nothing. Just shoot them like a dog. It only came better since World War II. Before the war they didn't think they were any better than a dingo or kangaroo.'[12]

Jessie's family was captured and sent to Yarrabah Mission in the 1930s, when they came to receive their blanket rations. Only years later did she manage to return to her country. The Ngadjon, one of the most mysterious tribes, disappeared and took with them the mystery of their origin and culture, which might be the key to the settlement of Australia by humans, a key to human evolution.

In 1938 the anthropologists Norman Tindale and Joseph Birdsell described a group of twelve tribes inhabiting the rainforest on the Atherton Tablelands and neighbouring coastal area which differed from the surrounding peoples. They were distinguished by 'Small stature, crisp curly hair and a tendency toward yellowish-brown skin colour'. Their appearance so much resembled Tasmanian Aborigines that Tindale and Birdsell named them Tasmanoids and suggested an interesting hypothesis that Australia was settled by several waves of people. The Tasmanians and the north Queensland Tasmanoids were the remnants of the first, the earliest, wave. While in Tasmania their anthropological type was preserved unchanged, the inhabitants of the continental rainforest were partly influenced physically and culturally by the later waves.[13] As Lake Barrine was in the centre of the Tasmanoids' territory scholars also used another word to describe them — Barrineans. Owing to their small stature, they were sometimes called pygmoids.

It turned out that Barrineans possessed a number of distinctive features in their material culture which were not present in the rest of Australia. They used unique, large, decorated fighting-shields made from the buttresses of *Ficus* trees and flat-bladed, long, wooden fighting swords. According to Tindale and Birdsell, some rainforest tribes made 'half-hitch coiled grass baskets closely similar in their appearance and technique of manufacture to those of the Tasmanians'.[14] Some of them had a unique, cross-shaped boomerang, which was used for sport and games rather than for hunting. Furthermore, these rainforest inhabitants were the only tribe in Australia to use beaten bark blankets, which were made in a similar fashion to the tapa that is used on South

Pacific islands. Were these bark blankets a local invention or an adoption of islanders' culture? While some features in the appearance of Tasmanoids–Barrineans and Tasmanians resembled those of Melanesians, some scholars were tempted to see them as descendants of proto-Melanesians or negroids, who survived in Australia and Tasmania because of isolation.

The languages of Barrineans provided a field for further hypothesis. According to the latest research by Bob Dixon, their dialects and languages were divided into two different linguistic types. The watershed lies along the border of the Ngadjon-ji with their closest northern neighbour, the Idindji. Languages to the south of this watershed were closer to the surrounding non-Barrinean tribes than to the northern Barrinean neighbours. For instance, Ngadjon-ji had only 27 per cent of its words in common with Idindji, whose language in its turn was more related to northern non-Barrinean tribes. Moreover, the Aborigines believe that the mythological ancestors of the southern Barrineans came from the south and those of northern Barrineans from the north.[15] How to reconcile this difference with the uniformity of the Barrineans' physique and culture? One possible explanation might be derived from the fact that a similar process occurred among African pygmies; confined to the jungle area, they adopted the languages of several neighbouring tribes but have a distinctively lighter skin pigmentation than their neighbours.

The Ngadjon-ji occupied the very centre of the Barrineans' area. They, as other Aborigines, believed that their ancestors had lived in Australia forever: in Jessie's myth about the Rainbow Serpent, for instance, the birds are mythological ancestors, proto-people, that inhabited the land in the Dreamtime. Scholars operate with facts: skeletal remains, archaeological sites, geological changes. From different angles they try to find out who the Ngadjon-ji ancestors were, when they came to Australia and settled on the Atherton Tablelands. For many years it was believed that Australia was first inhabited 15–20,000 years ago. In Russia Vladimir Kabo, after comprehensive studies, suggested in the late 1960s that humans were living in Australia at least 40,000 years ago. Now, after new archaeological excavations, this date has been moved back to 60,000 years ago. European history seems only a short span in comparison with such dates. America and the South Pacific were still uninhabited 60,000 years ago; Europe, covered with glaciers, was occupied by mammoths and inhabited by Neanderthals (an extinct branch of human development) and the predecessor of *Homo sapiens*, the so-called 'archaic *sapiens*'. Thus, Australian Aborigines were correct in their own way: their ancestors settled Australia, which was at that time part of a big continent called Sahul, at a time when modern man (*Homo sapiens*) was still emerging; and from these ancestors Aborigines developed into what they are here, in Australia.

But it was the Rainbow Serpent crater from Jessie's myth that was to reveal to the world further sensational information about Australian prehistory. The snake's spirit guarded its secrets for millennia until a scientist, Peter Kershaw, began studies in this area — first of Lynch's Crater (Jim Lynch was the Illins' neighbour across the road) and then of the Rainbow Serpent crater (its official name is Strenekoff's Crater; although actually named after Strelnikoff, the official naming unfortunately incorporated this mis-spelling). Kershaw made cores of organic sediment 45 m deep. That gave the lowest date of at least 140,000 years. His analysis of the varieties of pollen and the amount of charcoal in the cores from this area allowed him to reconstruct the distant past. He discovered that, initially, wet rainforest dominated the Atherton Tablelands. Then, 80,000 years ago it became drier, *Araucaria* being the main type of vegetation. Suddenly, around 40,000 years ago, *Araucaria* was replaced by sclerophyll woodland (consisting mainly of *Eucalyptus* and *Casuarina*) while the amount of charcoal in sediments increased sharply. Kershaw argues that, along with a decrease in rainfall which took place at that time, the destruction of rainforest was caused by the fire-burning practice of the Aborigines, who burned scrub to make tracks and better hunting grounds. Between 10,000 and 6000 years ago this sclerophyll woodland was replaced by the wet rainforest, which Aborigines learnt not to destroy but to use and benefit from, and that survived until the European invasion in the late nineteenth century.[16] Thus, this discovery proves to be one of the earliest records of human interference with nature and suggests that the Atherton Tablelands have been inhabited for more than 40,000 years.

Anthropologists contributed to the solution of the Barrinean problem, too. The latest research involving different data, particularly blood tests, proves that Birdsell and Tindale's theory was not correct. The Barrineans are not related to Tasmanians or Melanesians more than other Aborigines. They acquired their unique physique as a result of genetic processes which took place in small groups isolated over a long period. While marriages were mainly endogamous (within the group), some particular features of the founders of the group might intensify among their descendants — for instance, crisp hair. In the Barrinean case the genetic evolution was enhanced by the specific rainforest environment. This might explain their light pigmentation and small stature. The Barrineans' similarity to Tasmanians, who underwent independent genetic evolution isolated on their island for 12,000 years, turned out to be only coincidental. The Barrineans' unique material culture was an adaptation to specific rainforest conditions and resources. They learnt to make sturdy domed huts — the most elaborate structures in the whole continent — that gave protection from rain and lasted for several years; they skilfully used vine-ropes for climbing trees; they developed sophisticated techniques to remove poison from tropical plants and thus increased the availability of the abundant food. As for the tapa technique used to make bark blankets, it could be a local invention suggested by the availability of *Ficus* tree bark. Thus, the Barrinean history was not just survival in isolation, it was development and adaptation to the changing environmental conditions.

The Ngadjon tribe was linguistically related to five contiguous tribes (Mamu, Jirrbal, Jirru, Gulngay, Girramay) occupying territories to the south and southwest of their territory. According to Dixon, these 'six tribes speaking dialects of what we call the Dyirbal language are all descended from a single ancestor tribe', which might live in the southern part of their present territory, in the coastal rainforest. As the size of the original tribe increased, it split into groups; these became separate tribes and moved north and northwest, occupying the emerging forest on the tableland. Ngadjon-ji was one of the first groups to split from the Proto-Dyirbal tribe and now Ngadjon is 'the most divergent dialect of the Dyirbal language'.[17]

The ancestors of Ngadjon conquered new territories, they changed the land, and they learned to live in accord with nature. Their experience suggests the methods to be adopted for current management of rainforest resources. Gradually, scholars fill Ngadjon mythological past with ever-newer facts. Alas, a hundred years ago, however, few people realised that 'the Atherton blacks' held keys to Australia's prehistory.

THE INVASION OF A VIRTUAL REALITY

In September 1910, when choosing three blocks of 'primeval tropical forest' on the map in the Land Office, Nicholas and his sons were not aware that its primeval appearance was misleading. It was permeated by another reality — an Aboriginal one. For millennia it was home to the Aborigines, their country, all of which was covered by the tracks of travels by their mythological heroes and their own hunting, gathering, trading, and ceremonial routes. Two different worlds, two different realities — of the whites and of the Aborigines — had their fragile coexistence on the same territory for several decades but remained closed to one another. The Illins discovered this other reality only after a while. They could hardly suspect that the day would come when this virtual reality would become a part of their life and, years later, include them. The first encounters, according to Flora, were very peaceful and humorous.

'ABORIGINALS CAME WITH NO TROUSERS on them, lot of them had no clothes then, and my grandmother said to Romelio, "Oh, look, give him a pair of trousers to put on and tell him to wear them all the time when he comes here". So he put them on, he's walking around with them, with the trousers, he went away back to the camp where they were. The next time he came, he'd got the trousers hanging over his shoulder.'[18]

At that time, a quarter of a century after the European invasion into this area began, Aborigines were considerably reduced in numbers but their traditional life-style was not completely destroyed. The area around Butchers Creek, adjoining the forbidding Bellenden Ker Ranges, was their last refuge. The first settlers in the Malanda-Butchers Creek area would see occasionally an Aboriginal group travelling from one camping site to another, the naked men covered with initiation scars holding fire-sticks in their hands and carrying picturesque weaponry including big decorated shields and heavy swords, and the women carrying all the household items, with babies either on their shoulders or sleeping quietly in cane dillybags hanging on their backs attached to a band round their foreheads. Some new settlers discovered that their 'primeval blocks' were already occupied by the Aborigines — there were bora grounds and big dome-shaped huts; on the paths and in the river-beds they encountered skilful traps for animals, birds and fish. The most observant of them might notice that the huge mounds in which scrub turkeys laid their eggs were marked with a broken branch by the Aborigine who found the nest and who took from it a regular supply of fresh eggs in reasonable quantities. Neither the Land Office nor the settlers worried that they were encroaching on someone's property. The Ngadjon-ji Aborigines, previously feared as cannibals, by 1910 had learned their lesson. According to Edgar Short: 'Massacres such as that at Bones Knob near Tolga and Butchers Creek between Peeramon and Boonjie, as well as numerous smaller encounters, had taught the unfortunate natives that it was suicide to oppose the white fella.'

In the best cases the Aborigines were tolerated and given handouts of food by some farmers. In the worst cases their resistance and alleged cannibalism were regarded, according to a local Boonjie miner, as a 'definite proof of a degree of savage inhumanity which put the Abo quite beyond the pale, revealing their barbarous and cruel nature, and making them fair game to be shot down like animals at any time.'[19]

The white bearers of 'civilisation' could not comprehend that 'the blacks' had had their own sophisticated civilisation — a unique model of human organisation perfectly adjusted to the surrounding land and nature. In a way Ngadjon country was a state with its own territory, borders and tracks, with its own language and laws, with sacred places and abundant natural resources that had for millennia seemed inexhaustible owing to wise use. The Ngadjon-ji's territory covered 500 km^2, spreading between the upper reaches of the Barron, North Johnstone, Russell and Mulgrave rivers on the Atherton Tablelands. Before the whites' invasion the Ngadjon-ji, according to David Harris's estimations, numbered 750. In comparison with the rest of the Australian tribes, the Ngadjon-ji had a very high population density (1 person per 0.67 km^2, similar only to coastal communities), which was made possible because of the fertile basaltic soils of the Atherton Plateau, its abundant vegetation and plentiful sources of water.[20]

As soon as the Illins, following the bed of Butcher Creek, reached the back border of Nicholas's block they discovered that it adjoined dense scrub hiding the crater of an extinct volcano. This was the Rainbow Serpent crater. Water in the tributary creeks running from its tree fern-covered slopes to Butcher Creek seemed dark-golden. Using axes, the Illins climbed up but they had no time to enjoy the feeling of being first discoverers when they stepped onto the well-beaten path which led them into the Aboriginal camp. The women were grinding nuts with stone mills, the men polished spears with pieces of broken glass (it had already replaced sharp crystals of volcanic quartz). The children were sitting around the fire waiting for a *mapi* (tree kangaroo) to be baked in the ashes. They rushed to the huts to hide but they gradually re-emerged, attracted by young Hector, who participated in the 'expedition'. When Hector tried by himself to explore one of the paths leading into the scrub, he was stopped by the older Aboriginals. The path led to the sacred place, to the bora ground: corroborees were still being held. Nicholas, by now a distinguished old man with a grizzled beard, was soon recognised by his Aboriginal neighbours as trustworthy and admitted to see the corroborees. How different they were from the long, melodic peasant songs in his native Ilinka or from the passionate, nocturnal ceremonies he had seen in Central Asia.

These Aborigines whom the Illins discovered in their 'back yard' were a unit of the Ngadjon tribe. In the precontact period the tribe was divided into ten or more communities (or 'bands'), each numbering around fifty people. Every community occupied a defined part of the tribal territory, splitting at times into family groups numbering six-to-eight people. Jessie Calico, who lived in the traditional way with her family as late as the 1930s, recalled: 'When I was little we had about seven or eight of us all together. The older ones used to go hunt, come back with a big eel, a big one ...'. During the dry season, in winter, the men would go on hunting expeditions to the edge of the scrub on the neighbouring territories. At the end of the dry season and the beginning of the wet season (November–January), when food was abundant, people from different communities would gather in big camps. Women erected huge dome-shaped huts that protected them from rain. At that time they gathered and cooked walnuts, which provided sufficient food for these big gatherings. It was a time for settling conflicts (usually about women) by fighting corroborees, and a time of social entertainment. Sometimes they had visitors from neighbouring tribes. Visits were arranged by messengers who brought the invitation in the form of message sticks. As the wet season continued and the amount of food dwindled, people separated into smaller communities and the yearly pattern was repeated.

Along with this socio-economic organisation, the Ngadjon were divided on two patrilineal totemic halves (moieties) and members of one half had to marry members of another. According to R.L. Sharp, one half was associated with water and the other one with animals. Members of each had a number of totems and these local patrilineal clans were responsible for totemic control rites. They considered themselves to be descendants of their totems and had to care for them. The Ngadjon-ji had an interesting specific feature: in some cases the whole community, whose members might belong to different totems, would care for a particular totemic sacred site on their territory:

'AMONG THE NGATJAN ... scrub turkey (*kupar*) may be increased at a tabu area known as Scrub Turkey Hole (*Kupar Kolka*) established by a scrub turkey ancestor in country near the Butchers Creek gold-diggings owned by the clan which numbers scrub turkey among its totems. The rite, consisting of stirring up the hole and throwing earth out in all directions, is conducted whenever turkeys are scarce by any man or woman of any clan who has been properly introduced to the site and ceremony by those already initiated.'[21]

That explained to me why Glenda Illin, Kitty's granddaughter, had the impression that the 'whole of the Ngadjon tribe takes the totem of scrub turkey'. Certainly, this was not correct but this misapprehension had a reasonable explanation: the popular memory of Glenda's relatives preserved a recollection of the most important totem of their particular community, the totem for which all members of that community cared, as they owned the sacred Scrub Turkey Hole. Jessie, indeed, was a scrub turkey — 'I can remember growing up and the elders used to say: "You are a turkey"'. However, she knows that other members of their community had different totems — Emma Johnston, for instance, was a native bee, and there were people belonging to the totem of possum. Jessie and Emma are both related to Flora, as second cousins, in a line descending from the children of Barry Clarke. According to Flora, her grandmother Emily, Kitty's mother, belonged to the rare totem of black cockatoo.[22]

Memory of the totems has survived up till now, and this turns out to be the strongest feature of the complicated Ngadjon social organisation. Totems have an amazing dual nature, sacred and pragmatic, through which people express their belonging to their land as well as their responsibility towards it. When I came with Flora to Ngadjon country, Flora — who, as it might seem, had grown up in isolation from her traditional culture — could express to me the most essential element of Aboriginal relationships with nature, something which she had imbibed with her mother's milk.

'I CAN REMEMBER THAT. The other dark people that was around. You did not kill a bird or break a limb of a tree unless it was for a purpose, unless you were going to use it. But if you did it for nothing, just to be destructive, you were in trouble, you'd get roused on. Not like white people that break the tree down and nothing is said. Dark people couldn't do that. They never allowed that, not even little kids. You have to have respect for your land, for your surrounding. That was a sin — to go and kill more and then throw it away. You couldn't go taking the lives of anything around unless you were going to eat it.'

Jessie supported her. 'When they used to go hunting they just caught enough for the day. Just for tomorrow. But they never killed more than they needed. They'd never waste it.'[23]

At that moment they both were proud of their Aboriginal past, of their Aboriginal philosophy, which only seems simple on the surface, and which white people still have not learnt to recognise and understand.

KITTY'S MOB

Hearing how Aborigines around me addressed Flora and other elder women as 'Auntie', regardless of their actual relationship, reminded me about a similar Russian tradition, common especially among peasants and ordinary people. Probably in both cultures it comes from a subconscious feeling that all people from one locality are related. This was true both for Australian Aborigines and Russian peasants. The Aborigines created a most sophisticated kinship system, which differed from the European model and left no one without relatives. Along with his biological father, mother, sisters and brothers, each Ngadjon considered brothers of his father as his fathers, and sisters of his mother as his mothers. Their children were his sisters and brothers (Jessie referred to that relationship as 'sister in Aboriginal law'). The system also determined whom each Aborigine could marry. Children of his father's elder sister were his potential fathers- or mothers-in-law; he could marry their children. His children in their turn could marry children of his father's younger brother. Similar laws related to his mother's relatives. These kinship laws allowed me to reconstruct the genealogical tree of Kitty's family. Like a palaeontologist who can reconstruct a skeleton from a single bone, I had only two definite facts to work on: that Emily (Kitty's mother) and Charlene were 'sisters in Aboriginal law' and they married two brothers — Willie and Jack Clarke, sons of Barry Clarke. My reconstruction was as follows:

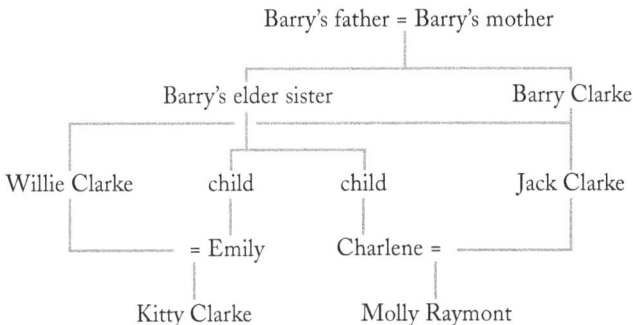

Glenda Illin recorded some more details about this family from the older people in the Atherton area. According to them, Barry had five wives and at least six children. Using materials from Glenda, Jessie and Edgar Short, it is possible to draw Kitty Clarke's family tree (see Appendix 2).

The life stories of the members of this family are connected with the particular part of the Atherton Tablelands which stretches between Butchers Creek, Lamins Hill, and Boonjie. Barry's family seems to be the patrilineal core of the community inhabiting this territory. Other members of the community could join them as a result of marriage or out of friendship, but the core clan would stay on the territory permanently. There is a lot of evidence to support this supposition. According to Jessie Calico, the Boonjie goldfield was Barry Clarke's area. There was a pocket, a clearing, known as Barry's Pocket, in Boonjie. His son, Willie, was employed by Fred Brown, who lived in Boonjie. Emily, Willie's wife, and their daughter Kitty were born on the Russell goldfield, at the upper reaches of the Russell River, which begins in Boonjie. Leandro, whose farm was between Gadaloff road and Lamins Hill, wrote about Kitty in 1915: 'My selection is right in <u>her</u> country'. (Was there any other European who wrote like that in those days?) Molly Raymont, Barry's granddaughter, was born around 1890 in Boonjie. Her daughter, Emma Johnston, remembers living in the camp near the Rainbow Snake crater in around 1920. She and Jessie knew that it was Barry's territory and preserved in their family the unique myth about the crater.

Barry's family might be the core of their community also because Barry and his son Willie were named by the first European settlers 'King Barry' and 'King Willie'. According to Harry Illin (Kitty's son), Willie even had a brass breastplate with his name engraved on it.[24] In traditional Aboriginal society there were no hereditary kings, in the European sense. Mjöberg, who lived in this area in 1913, recorded:

'I DID NOT MEET WITH ANY PARTICULAR RULING CHIEFTAINS in the tribe of Atherton ... [and] Malanda ... The tribes are led by a council chosen from the wisest and most experienced men, from those who have achieved a position of respect and consideration. Courage is valued as a virtue everywhere. Cleverness and judgment are also appreciated. As these characteristics usually increase with age, the oldest men usually have the right to supervise affairs.'[25]

Barry and Willie certainly were the most influential men in the

Butchers Creek-Boonjie area community, which led the Europeans to view them as 'kings'.

Probably Barry's high status in his community was the cause of the removal of his body out of the country after his death. According to Mjöberg and other early explorers of the area, 'The custom of preparing mummies after their death of certain men who occupied a prominent position during their lifetime, seems to exist everywhere in the districts of Malanda [and] the upper Johnstone river ...'. The early explorers hunted for such mummies for museums. Glenda Illin discovered that local elder Aborigines still remember that 'an embalmed body was taken from here'. She suggested that Barry Clarke might be the person known as 'Narcha, King of Boenje [Boonjie]', whose mummy was bought by the German anthropologist Hermann Klaatsch in 1905 and sent to a German museum. In a photo taken in 1894 of 'Narcha' with a big group of Boonjie Aborigines he is distinguished by his extremely large stature.[26]

Edgar Short, whose farm Glen-Allyn was not far from Boonjie, described Barry's son Joe, who worked on their farm, as a very tall and strong man: 'Joe had been employed by George Clarke, one of the discoverers of the Boonjie goldfield. Joe was something rare among the smallish rainforest natives, about 5 feet ten inches in height, with big chest, broad shoulders and very muscular arms and legs. He had facial features more like a Torres Strait islander than an Aboriginal.' Joe, while in his sixties, gained a victory in a traditional duel fighting with younger challengers who laid claims to his young wife Annie Kane. First they used spears and then switched to huge swords and shields.[27]

Kitty's parents, Emily and Willie Clarke, were young people when the first Europeans invaded their country. Much later on, in 1940, Emily told her grandson Harry about the first tragic encounter:

'THEY TOOK MY GRANDMOTHER IN THE EARLY DAYS from Lake Eacham. Her tribe camped at Lake Eacham. That was the main camp for them. The white men came and shot all the tribe out and took all the young people. And my grandmother was there, she was about ten or twelve years of age, so they took her. People by the name of Clarke took her. That's what she told me.'

In a brief obituary from the *Townsville Bulletin* this story was told differently:

'EMILY WAS A GIRL about 18 years of age when the first white people landed in Cairns. The blacks had a belief that one day their spirits would return as white people and when they saw them they were terrified and took to the bush for two years and did not go near Cairns for that period. She told many graphic stories of early days on the Russell River Goldfield.'[28]

I am more inclined to believe the story preserved by Harry, particularly because Cairns is too far from the territory of Emily's tribe. She might have been born around 1870.[29] According to her identity card (E–101), Emily's Aboriginal name was Darugso, her father's name was Yariha and mother's name was Nellie Acoman. Her birthplace was the Russell goldfield, and for her marriage certificate she gave her name as Emily Russell, associating herself with this particular area. Emily had a 'tribal scar on shoulder', which means that at the time of her youth the traditional customs were still observed and she was properly initiated.

Emily's husband, Willie Clarke, known as 'King Willie', obviously received his surname from George Clarke, who discovered the Boonjie goldfield in 1886 and brought the first settlers there. Part of the track that George and his mates blazed from Herberton to Boonjie is still known as Clarke's track. Emily and Willie worked for George Clarke, and Fred Brown and his wife Amelia in Boonjie. Fred Brown had a small shop, while Harry Land, his brother-in-law, started a farm there. They were both Englishmen. It was from these Europeans that Emily and Willie and their daughters Kitty and Julia first made their acquaintanceship with the world of the whites.

It is interesting that all the Aboriginal women from this family became good wives for Europeans. Emily, after Willie's death, married an English miner, Tom Denyer; Kitty married Leandro, a Russian; Julia married a French miner, Charlie Civry, an escapee from a French penal colony. According to Short, Charlie 'was looked after in every possible way. He taught his wife Julia to cook in the French manner, using it for native foods with excellent results. On one occasion a party of geologists accepted his invitation to lunch and were delighted with the dish of baked eels and native yams which Julia served. After the meal was over Charlie told them he had a confession to make, the eel was carpet snake. One of the diners promptly rushed outside and lost his meal, a couple looked a little pale, the other still said it was one of the best they had ever eaten.'[30]

However, the destiny of Willie Clarke, Kitty's father, was tragic. For reasons that remain unknown, Fred Brown took him to Brisbane. Willie never came back. Some of his descendants believe that he died in Brisbane, some think that he might be buried in Babinda.[31] Has his soul found its way to rest in peace on Bartle Frere?

'BLACK PRINCESS'

By the time twenty-year-old Kitty appeared at the Illins' farm she already had three children. Her eldest daughter, Emma, was born in around 1905 (Leandro wrote that Kitty, as was usual for Aboriginal women, had her first child when she was thirteen years old); the next one, Molly, was born in 1910 and her son George, called Ginger, in 1911. Nobody knows what happened to her first husband, an Aboriginal man called Jimmy Williamson. The Illins were among the first settlers in the area occupied by Kitty's group. She came to them in 1911, starving, and occasionally helped Alexandra with housework. By that time she must have lost her first husband. In August 1913, when Leandro returned from his travels and began to clear his selection on Cairns track, she became his de facto wife and he took care of her three young children. In July 1914 their first son, Dick, was born and, following a dramatic struggle with the authorities, Leandro and Kitty were officially married in September 1915.

Who was she, Kitty Clarke, who managed to charm this lonely Russian man, who managed to give meaning to his life? I try to see her through Leandro's eyes. A young, slim woman with a shock of thick, dark curly hair and a stern, frowning face, she seemed too reserved to attract the attention of a man at first glance. But as soon as she overcame her shyness a bright, open, white-teeth smile lit up her face. Her granddaughter Glenda seems to have inherited not only Kitty's appearance but also, miraculously, this contrast between apparent severity and overwhelming openness and joyfulness of nature. Kitty's face exhibited strong will and intelligence. Even the local policeman had to admit in his reports 'Kitty Clarke is a sensible stamp of aboriginal'; 'she is an intelligent woman as far as blacks go'. As far as blacks go ... All Leandro's upbringing must have resisted this haughty, derogatory attitude. For him the main thing was that 'she is a kind sort of a woman'; later, after Kitty's death, he wrote about her son George 'I had reared him a good honest able boy, like his poor mother was'. Although she had been in contact with the whites since her childhood, she preserved her Aboriginality, as many members of her community still lived in the scrub; for instance, she spoke only broken English, her main language remained Ngadjon. True in love, kind and honest, able to accept an alien culture but still proud of her native culture and able to make her white husband respect and appreciate it — that was Kitty Clarke, a 'little black princess', daughter of Ngadjon country.

I, brought up on European literature, was at first inclined to see the story of Kitty and Leandro's marriage as a purely romantic love-story. I tried to speak with Harry and Flora about that love, and they agreed — 'oh, yes, he loved her' — but seemed not to share my romanticism. At last Flora explained.

'WELL, I SUPPOSE HE WAS LIKE ALL THE OTHER MEN that'd come to Australia. There was not plenty of women around, not their own colour. Maybe their affair may not meant for marriage but when there was a baby came to life he was not going to run away as other white men did. He would not run away from his flesh and blood. He would not let them take my mother and brother to Palm Island. He wasn't a coward like a lot of other white men. He always thought for other people and pitied them.'[32]

Indeed, Leandro had seemed at first to treat white men's cohabitation with Aboriginal women as an inevitable drawback of life in the bush. He wrote in his report to the federal government in 1912: 'Something must be done to induce white women to come to the Northern Territory and save the poor pioneers from living with lubras'.[33] Was it having children or was it Kitty's personality that changed his attitude? Certainly, to have a son, to have children, was Leandro's cherished dream and he tenderly loved his first-born son, Dick, and he loved the second child that Kitty was expecting — this happened to be Flora, who was to preserve the story of her parents — but even at that time Kitty seems to be for him more than the mother of his son, more than a woman to live with. Was his behaviour the fulfilment of the vow made by his parents twenty-five years before, when they were shocked by Tolstoy's *Kreutzer Sonata* and its exposure of all the falsity of modern love and family life? Nicholas wrote then: 'we have to ... scrape off the dirty layers of modern civilisation's habits and customs; we have to reveal in ourselves a human being which indeed was created in God's likeness. ... [It] will be a hard struggle for ourselves but we will manage to guide our children along this pure and straight way.'[34]

Now, when the theory came to be put into practice the attitude of justice and honesty, which always dominated Leandro's world outlook, was enriched by love. How otherwise could he so deeply penetrate into

Kitty's inner world closed to Europeans, into her values of life, when he wrote so simply and so powerfully: 'My selection is right in <u>her</u> country ... It would be a very sorrowful thing if some evil happened to her in form of being taken away from her native country.' Only love could give him this dual vision — his own and his loved one's, only love could help him to understand that free food and clothes in the mission would never replace for Kitty the spiritual ties with her native land.

How far this was from the attitude of other Europeans to Aboriginal women! In 1915, for instance, only six Europeans in the whole of Queensland married women of Aboriginal descent. Many Aboriginal women were not just abandoned with children by white men. Worse than that, according to Bob Dixon — 'only two half-castes grew up in the Tully region in the first quarter of this century; many were born but all others were killed soon after birth, by their white fathers'.[35]

Leandro was one of the first Europeans to prove that it was possible to feel love for an Aboriginal woman. Nobody around him apart from his parents could understand it. Twenty years later, when he had already buried Kitty near Christmas Creek and was raising their motherless children, he read *Coonardoo*, a novel by Katharine Susannah Prichard, and was struck by the resemblances between the main character and Kitty. He recognised his lost Kitty in Coonardoo. Unlike the hero of the novel, Hugh Watt, Leandro never betrayed his love; but, like Hugh, Leandro could never overcome this love, and he never married again. According to Ric Throssell, Prichard's son, soon after *Coonardoo* was published in 1929 the literary critic Cecil Mann wrote 'that in refusing to keep off the subject of "black velvet", Katharine Prichard had tried the almost impossible task of making "the Australian aboriginal a romantic figure". So ingrained were the old racial attitudes that [Mann] could say: "With any other native, from fragrant Zulu girl to fly-kissed Arab maid, she could have done it. But the aboriginal, in Australia, anyway cannot excite any higher feeling than nauseated pity or comical contempt."'

I knew that Leandro highly valued *Coonardoo* as a true Australian book. And it was when I was thinking about the parallels between Kitty's and Coonardoo's tragic stories that a letter came from Flora. She recollected that:

'FATHER WROTE TO A LADY THAT WROTE A BOOK about an Aboriginal girl, the book called *Coonardoo*, but at the time [1933] she was going to Russia. While she was over there something happened to her husband. She did write to father when she came back from Russia. I don't know what she told him about Russia. ... You might find a letter from him to her about wanting her to come to Queensland to write a book on an Aboriginal woman up here back in 1936 or 1937.'

Might it be Kitty's story that he wanted Prichard to tell, might his letters have the key to his relations with Kitty, I thought, hopefully. Alas, I soon discovered that their correspondence did not survive, neither in Prichard's archives in the National Library of Australia, nor in Vera Ketchell's bag with Leandro's letters. Nevertheless, Ric Throssell, Prichard's son, who was only twelve when his mother returned from Russia devastated by the death of her husband, on hearing the story from me said, 'I remember the name Illin. It rings a bell. Mother told me about him, but I was too young to remember everything.' Later, in one of Leandro's letters of August 1933, I found this remark: 'I have been corresponding with the authoress of *Coonardoo* and she wrote to me she is likely to come up North for material on Abos and write a book'.[36]

One more dead end. Still, Leandro and Kitty's story is not lost. It lives on among their descendants and even gives rise to the creation of a unique modern-day mythology.

THE RUSSIAN CULTURAL HERO IN THE AUSTRALIAN LANDSCAPE

'LEANDRO AND KITTY LIVED AT BUTCHERS CREEK and at that time, in 1918, Kitty had her third child, all being half-castes, as classed by the whiteman.

'There was a Mr Blakely who was an Aboriginal Protector who wanted to send all half-castes to Palm Island. This Leandro and Kitty did not like.

'Then one day, they both started to walk from Butchers Creek all the way down Russell River and would not enter the road in fear they would be caught. They stopped at War [Waugh] Pocket and camped for the night leaving early next morning. They went on to Innisfail and when they arrived, they went straight to the Courthouse and got married.

'Seeing they were married, Blakely could not touch or do anything to their children to send to Palm Island.'

This was how Leanne Illin recorded the story of Leandro and Kitty's marriage from her father Harry in the early 1990s. Harry's son, Alec, told me a similar version of the story, the focal point being their 'coming out to Russell River and getting married in Innisfail'. When I spoke with Harry himself, in July 1996, he repeated the story nearly word for word.

'THEY WERE AFTER MY MOTHER BECAUSE MY MOTHER HAD A CHILD TO DAD. They wanted to catch her before she married my father and send her to a mission. My father said "She's got my child". They walked from up there from Butchers Creek all way down the Russell River. They came to Waugh Pocket. They camped there for the night, got up early in the morning, then got to Innisfail and got married in the courthouse. They could not touch her after that.[37]

This short text takes us into the different system of story-telling, reminiscent of an archaic myth about two cultural heroes — a man and a woman — who created new life and a new world through their journeying and overpowering of evil. Moreover, as is usual for Aboriginal mythology, the journeying of the cultural heroes is connected here with the particular features of the landscape, which acquired sacred qualities in the beliefs of their descendants. Details that are irrelevant from the modern European point of view — 'They stopped at War [Waugh] Pocket and camped for the night leaving early next morning' — acquire mythological significance in the story. Listening to it is like being present at the conception of a myth. In traditional society such a story preserved by the family would have resulted, within a few generations, in sacralisation of the landscape mentioned in Leandro and Kitty's travels.

Flora's version of the story was abundant in details and gave it another dimension.

'MY MOTHER HAD A SON BELONGING TO MY FATHER and the police were trying to get my mother and my brother and send them to a mission on Palm Island. As soon as a black woman had a half-caste baby they sent her to a mission to hide the fact that white man was carrying on with black women, the law was like that. And when my father found out that they wanted to do that, he said "No, I'll marry the mother and save my son and save her too. Why should she go over there, she never committed a crime. It's not fair. Why send her when I am willing to keep her, and look after them both." But they said that he couldn't. At that time the law was, white couldn't marry a black person.

'When my father knew that he said, "They're not going to take my son, they're not going to take her or my son". He took a gun and they went into the thick scrub, my mother and my father, he lived like a bushranger with the other Aboriginals. The policemen were looking for them, but the other tribe — there was plenty of black people there, big tribes — they would tell my father and my mother which way the police was going, and they would tell police "They went this way", but they went that way. The tribe was looking after my father and my mother and watching out for the police and tell the police the wrong direction. They were in the bush nine or twelve months.

'While they were hiding in the bush my father put his son Dick with his father and mother. And my father said, "Don't you let them take him". And my grandfather said, "They have to kill me first, before they take him". My grandfather must have been a fair man all the time, that's why he got chased away from Russia, because he could see unfair things that were done to people. And this is now his grandchild, so he is not going to let them take him away and send him to Palm Island. He wasn't worried about that he was dark, the fairness was everything that he worried about. So they looked after Dick.

'Father had to fight hard to get the permission from the Chief Protector of Aboriginals to marry my mother. Somewhere in July–August 1915 the Queensland Premier Gillies came up to Atherton to open a new railway line. Plenty of people gathered there on the station. And suddenly my father approached the premier, told him the story and asked him to help them to marry. My father never was afraid to speak to anybody. And then, when Gillies went back, he sent him the permission to marry my mother. By this time it was September and they got married in Innisfail. I was born in October 1915, a month after they got married. If father didn't worry about my mother and brother the three of us would have ended up in Palm Island mission and I would not know who my father was and where I came from, like a lot of half-caste kids.'[38]

In distinction from Harry's version, Flora's had two main focal points: the moral choice of the hero and the interference of the powerful master, who restored justice. This latter element (interference of the powerful master) was the main feature of the story which survived among Lullie's descendants as well. Nola tells what she heard from her mother, Lullie:

'She told us that they [Leandro and Kitty] got married up in Innisfail, that they had to get permission from the premier. They saw him up at the railway station, he was going through on a train, he gave all the kids two bob each.'

This 'irrelevant' detail — 'he gave all the kids two bob each' — contributes to the image of a powerful, rich master. This image was a characteristic feature of Russian fairy-tales.

For Ernie, Flora's son, who had a lot of contact with Leandro as a boy, the most remarkable feature in the story was the superman quality of Leandro: 'When he and Kitty escaped to the bush he told the Aboriginal trackers that if police had known about their hiding place the trackers would have been the first to receive a bullet from him'.[39]

'I AM DOING AN HONEST ACTION'

These stories survived in the Illin family for eighty years as an oral tradition and a historian might suspect that facts have been distorted during that period. I, however, am one who inclines to value the family tales no less than the facts. Luckily, during my visit to Townsville in 1996 and interviews with the Illins, Ernie, Flora's son, received a long-awaited bundle of documents from the Department of Family Services and Aboriginal and Islander Affairs regarding Leandro and Kitty's marriage. That provides us with a unique opportunity to compare how archival documents and oral tradition reflect the same events. Let's listen to the documents. The first in the file was Leandro's letter.

March 1915

To the Chief Protector of Aboriginals
c/o Mr A.A. Pike, Constable of Police, Yungaburra

Sir,

It is a difficult thing to write to you but a man must do it when it is necessary. I desire to obtain a permit to marry an aboriginal woman who's name is Kitty Clarke. I know her for the last four years. She used to work occasionally for my mother.

She is a kind sort of a woman and reared by whites. She belongs to one of those tribes which counted hundreds one time at the present time being reduced to a handful. My selection is right in <u>her</u> country. I hope after inquires made about me you will not deny that permission. I would like to go *and speak to you personally but it is so far to Brisbane and expensive and again there is such a lot to do. ...*

The blacks are a poor starving lot and you will do her a good turn by giving the asked permission. I could write to you plenty more but it is hardly necessary. Regarding myself I do not drink, smoke nor gamble. ... Some people advised me not to write to you but I thought different as your qualification speaks to me that you work for the best of the blacks and you could not protect Kitty in a better way. It would be a very sorrowful thing if some evil happened to her in form of being taken away from her native country. I do not know the laws of this country but thinking I am doing an honest action. I hope you will understand me and give me justice.
I have honour Sir to remain your obedient servant

Leandro Illin

Peeramon. Gadgarra. Via Cairns NQ

Note: If you thought it would be necessary to come to Brisbane I would try to raise the necessary sum, though extra expenses for a starting man on the land is a difficult thing. L.I.

The letter was accompanied by a note from the Yungaburra constable, Alfred Arthur Pike.

> 27 March 1915. ... Both parties are well known to me personally and Illin bears a very good character.
>
> The aboriginal is a full blooded Russell River black and she has three black picaninnies, she is an intelligent woman as far as blacks go.
>
> I am of opinion that Illin would be well advised to wait six months as so to insure whether he will still be of the same mind as the blacks here are not adapted to civilized living and <u>Illin</u> would <u>be</u> <u>courting</u> <u>trouble</u>.

On 29 March 1915 the Atherton Protector, George Sutton, added his opinion to the note: 'I have known this applicant for last six month, a very hard working man, I do not know of any objection to him marrying this gin.'

Ten days later the Chief Protector of Aboriginals, John William Bleakley, in Brisbane wrote his resolution on the same note.

> I am very much averse to the marriage of fullblood aboriginal women to white men and especially where as in

this case the woman has three aboriginal picaninnies. Return Illin his documents and please advise him I cannot grant his request. Perhaps it would be wiser to remove the woman and picaninnies to a reserve. 9.4.15.

Twenty days later he returned to the note once again, scribbling in the bottom corner:

Ask [Atherton] P[rotector of] A[boriginals] again if he considers it would be wiser to remove the woman and children, more secure. 29.4.15.

Thus, on the corner of a striped sheet of paper, a human destiny was cold-bloodedly decided.

John William Bleakley — that was he, the evil hero Blakely from Harry Illin's story. Born in 1879, he was nearly the same age as Leandro. One was the son of a Russian intellectual nobleman; he was a man who by his thirties had not achieved anything except hard toil on his block of land but for whom democracy and honesty in relation to all people was the only possible way in life. The other was the son of an Australian boilermaker, whose career — public servant in 1899, Chief Protector in 1914 — symbolised the Australian democracy, though he himself was far from being a democrat in the deep meaning of that word. The Russian poet Konstantin Balmont, who visited the Australian colonies in 1912, dwelt on this contradiction in the English attitudes:

'THE ENGLISH EXTERMINATED THE BEAUTIFUL, DARK-COMPLEX-IONED TASMANIAN TRIBES AND NO TRACE OF THEM REMAINS. The savagery of the English exceeded even that of the Spaniards in their subjugation of the last Mexicans. The creators of political freedom were unable to comprehend simple human freedom.'[40]

Bleakley's positive role in Aboriginal issues was recognised by his contemporaries and, moreover, he 'was considered a liberal in his day':

'BY THE LATE 1920S BLEAKLEY WAS A WELL-KNOWN AUSTRALIA-WIDE VOICE upon Aboriginal welfare. ... His professional knowledge was built on common sense, hard work and accumulated experience, not on a liberal education and training in social anthropology or native administration. Although he was affectionately remembered by both black and white for his compassion, his approach was nevertheless rigidly parochial and paternalistic. His fervent advocacy of segregation, his long-standing preoccupation with "the half-caste problem" ... and his persistent theorizing on "breed", "blood" and "race purity" show his acceptance of current racial ideas, since discredited. ... Bleakley's energetic administration encouraged greater expenditure on Aboriginal affairs in Queensland than elsewhere in Australia.'[41]

It is a historian's duty to give a balanced portrait of this personality but, for me, all his contributions to Aboriginal welfare in general will never outweigh the suffering to which he was planning to condemn Kitty and her children, and which was, at his behest, experienced by hundreds and hundreds of others, whose stories no one will ever tell.

Meanwhile, Bleakley continued to insist on his 'advice', this time on an official form.

> 5th May, 1915. To the Protector of Aboriginals, Atherton. In further reference to the aboriginal gin Kitty Clarke, for whom a permit to marry the naturalized Russian subject, Leandro Illin, was refused, please advise me if you consider it would be wiser in view of the refusal, to remove this woman and her children to a Reserve.

After the third reminder the Atherton Protector, George Sutton, who, it seems, did not undertake any actions in relation to Kitty, followed the 'advice' from above:

> 12 May 1915. [To] the Chief Protector of Aboriginals. With reference to aboriginal gin Kitty Clarke and her three children. I think it would be wiser to remove them to a mission. George Sutton.

The ball began to roll. Bleakley immediately sent Sutton's memorandum to the Home Department with a note: 'Removal to Hull River recommended'. In a few days the removal was approved and on 24 May 1915 the 'Order for Removal of Aboriginals' was issued in accordance with the Aborigines Protection and Restriction of the Sale of Opium Acts.

> To all Officers and Constables of Police, Prison Officers, and others whom it may concern. ... Now therefore, I, the Honourable Kenneth McDonald Grant [Deputy] Home Secretary of the State of Queensland, the Minister administering the above-mentioned Acts, do hereby order that the four Aboriginals hereinafter named be removed from

173

(sidebar) 'I AM DOING AN HONEST ACTION'

Yungaburra in the District of Cairns to the Reserve at Hull River for the causes stated in connection with their Names respectively ...

No.	Name	Offence, and cause for removal
1.	Kitty Clarke	For her own benefit
2, 3, 4.	her three children	To accompany their mother

The law was scrupulously observed; Leandro's appeal — 'It would be a very sorrowful thing if some evil happened to her in form of being taken away from her native country. I do not know the laws of this country but thinking I am doing an honest action' — was duly filed away.

Meanwhile, the tragedy of 'a gin' with three nameless children did not worry anybody: the removal was 'for her own benefit'. No — there was one thing about her that did worry Bleakley. The order for removal was accompanied by his memo to the Atherton Protector:

> 26th May, 1915. ... Will you please see that when removed this woman takes with her the blankets which she may have received and any other clothing which she may possess at the time the Order is executed?

Suddenly, this huge, well-functioning machinery of state fell out of step, stopped by a lonely fighter, an obscure poor Russian settler from the far north:

> 12 July 1915. Herberton. [Urgent wire to] W. Gillies M.L.A. Parliament B[risba]ne.

> I applied chief protector aboriginals for permit marry mother of my halfcast child through yungaburra police never got reply police chasing the woman sent new application who should not I take care of my child and his mother can't stand see him taken to mission kindly see protector and in debt for life yours truly reply paid Leandro Illin.

The ball now began to roll in the opposite direction. David Bowman, Home Secretary in the newly formed Labor government, wrote a minute on the wire: 'Get Home Sec[retary's Dept] suspend order for removal and [get] fresh police report. Suspend further execution of removal order and obtain fresh report. D.B. 14/7/15.'

William Neil Gillies (1868–1928) and David Bowman (1860–1916) were two men to whom Leandro was grateful all his life and he passed on this gratitude to his children. They both were members of the Labor Party and came to politics from working backgrounds — Gillies was a farmer and Bowman a bootmaker. Gillies had owned a block of land in Atherton since 1910 and won the seat of Eacham for Labor in the Queensland parliament in 1912. For several years he was minister for Agriculture; in February 1925 he became premier but resigned in October of the same year, after his administration failed to efficiently handle industrial unrest. He was remembered by contemporaries for his personal kindness and considered a fair man. Bowman was one of the founders of the Queensland Labor movement in the early 1890s. In 1907 he became leader of the Labor party in Opposition. When Labor won the State elections in May 1915, he was appointed Home Secretary but died soon afterwards. He was a man of high humanitarian ideals and, according to contemporaries, 'he had a powerful voice and a stout heart, and what he lacked in polished diction he made up in earnest vigour'.[42]

Following Bowman's resolution, Bleakley had to send a wire to the Atherton Protector:

> Removal order Kitty and three children Yungaburra to Hull River now suspended by authority Home Secretary[.] Please wire if Leandro Illin is father of half caste child of Kitty. 14/7/1915

Sutton wired the answer on the following day: 'Your wire fourteenth Leandro Illin now Babinda near Cairns supposed Kitty and children with him.'

Meanwhile, the Chief Protector's office had to send explanations to Brisbane solicitors Foxton, Hobbs & Macnish, who opened the case in defence of Leandro's application to marry. On 17 July 1915 Sutton sent a new wire stating, 'Leandro Illin now back at Yungaburra [with] Kitty and children'.

Finally, on 7 August 1915, the Yungaburra constable, A.A. Pike, recorded Leandro's statement, attempting to put Leandro's live language into a dry police document.

'LEANDRO ILLIN STATES: I AM A NATURALIZED BRITISH SUBJECT OF RUSSIAN PARENTS. I WAS BORN IN RUSSIA.

'I know an aboriginal female named Kitty Clarke who was signed on to work for my mother last year at Gadgarra.

'Kitty Clarke gave birth to a half-caste aboriginal boy last July 4th twelve months [ago] of which I am the father. I have since kept the child myself and the mother sees the child daily. I give the mother food too. I take the food into the scrub and meet the aboriginal and provide food for herself and her four children. There are three children beside the half-caste belonging to Kitty.

'The aboriginal is camped about two miles away from my house in the scrub.

'I have kept the child at my house in the scrub all the time and the mother has been to Babinda Herberton and running away from the Police all the time to prevent her being sent to a Mission.

'I have applied to marry Kitty Clarke and I am still willing to marry Kitty Clarke and keep her four children.

'I will not say I have kept Kitty Clarke on my place.

'When I had connection with Kitty Clarke I was in the scrub and it was not at my place or on my father's place.

'I think the best thing would be for me to marry Kitty Clarke and keep her.

'Kitty Clarke I believe is in the family way, in fact I am sure of it. I believe she is to have another child to me. She may be five or six months in family now. Leandro Illin.'

Obviously, Leandro denied that Kitty lived in his hut because, until they were married, that was against the law.

Leandro's statement was accompanied by Pike's own report.

'11 AUGUST 1915. ... I ATTACH STATEMENT FROM ILLIN who was very averse to giving me any information on this matter as he was under the impression I was trying to get a chance on prosecuting him on his admissions for unlawfully permitting the Gin on his premises. His impressions were certainly correct but I could not get the necessary admissions. Though he had had the aboriginal repeatedly about his place I have not been successful in catching her on the place, it being in the midst of the scrub and a considerable way from Yungaburra.

'Leandro Illin is the father of Kitty Clarke's half caste child aged eleven months. He also states he is father of Kitty Clarke's unborn child, though I think there is some doubt [if] he is the father or one of the blacks is the father. [Pike could not help trying to blacken in some way Leandro and Kitty's relationship.]

'The main point of Illin's grievance seems to be the child of his and also the unborn child which Illin thinks is his.

'If Illin was permitted to marry the Gin Kitty, he would keep these children as well as three other full blooded children of Kitty's. As long as this aboriginal is in this part there will be trouble, and as Illin is as bad as the Gin I would recommend he be allowed to marry her. If permission is refused Illin will be in trouble over the children and he threatens to shoot himself and the Gin too, so that I do not see what should prevent him marrying her if he wants to.

'Kitty Clarke is a sensible stamp of aboriginal and as his Russian neighbours state she is good enough for him.

'I think the aboriginal would be well cared for if allowed to marry Illin, in fact she would be much better off than running in the bush, the loss would seem to be on Illin's side and as he intends to marry her I think now he has two children to her it would be a fair thing if he did marry her, and I do not see the good got by send the aboriginal to Hull River.

'Neither Illin or Kitty Clarke have given me trouble before and both were apparently well behaved previously.'

On 24 August 1915 David Bowman, the Home Secretary, noted on the report: 'Under the circumstances disclosed by these reports allow the marriage to take place'.

We can imagine how unwillingly, two days later, on 26 August 1915, Bleakley had to put his instructions on the same sheet of paper, below Bowman's resolution:

> 1 Permit to P[rotector of] A[borigines] Atherton.
> 2 inform W. Gillies.
> 3 inform Comm[issioner of] Police of decision and that such cancels order for removal.

On the next day the Office of Chief Protector sent a 'permit to marry' to the Protector in Atherton, who in his turn asked constable Pike to deliver it to Leandro. In the meantime Bleakley had to send the letter with explanations to Gillies.

31st August, 1915

Sir,

With reference to your interview with the Deputy Chief Protector of Aboriginals in July last in regard to the application by Leandro Illin of Yungaburra to marry the aboriginal woman Kitty Clarke I have now to advise that the necessary permit for the marriage was forwarded to the Protector of Aboriginals Atherton on 27th inst.

Yours obediently,
Chief Protector of Aboriginals.

This letter makes clear the first-hand interference by Gillies into Leandro's case, which he kept under his personal control.

On 7 September 1915 constable Pike reported that he handed Leandro the 'Permit to marry the Gin Kitty'. A week later Protector of Aboriginals of Innisfail reported, with some amazement, to the Chief Protector:

> 14th September, 1915. Sir, Re marriage of Kitty Clarke (Abo) to Leondra Albin. A Greek or Southern Europe alien came to-day to Innisfail from Russell River way accompanied by a female Aboriginal woman named Kitty and had a permit ... to marry Kitty. They were married at Innisfail to-day by William Simpson, Esquire, a Justice of the Peace who is authorised to celebrate marriages.[43]

Leandro signed the marriage certificate, Kitty put a cross.[44] Returning to Gadgarra, they settled at Leandro's. In a month their daughter Flora was born.

* * *

Comparing the events as they survived in the memory of Leandro and Kitty's descendants and the documents from the archival file, we discover a number of discrepancies but mostly the facts complement each other. According to Flora's story, after the police attempted to remove Kitty with Leandro's son to Palm Island, Leandro made his decision to marry her and began the struggle. According to the documents it was Leandro's application to marry Kitty which provoked the order for removal. Still, I do not exclude the possibility that Leandro and Kitty were aware of a threat of her removal after their first son was born. According to the documents, he wanted to marry Kitty to be honest to a woman who had a child by him — 'I am doing an honest action'. Flora's explanation — 'I'll marry the mother and save my son' — seems not so idealistic but more worldly and understandable.

The belief that police intended to send Kitty to Palm Island (although in reality the order for removal was to Hull River mission, obviously Kitty could not know that) was due to widespread fear among the local Aborigines, who regarded Palm Island 'as the ultimate hell'.[45] Thus, the symbolic meaning of Palm Island gave Flora's story an added dimension, making it more impressive than if it had been Hull River mission, which lacks this symbolic content.

The most dramatic episodes of the story, when Leandro hid with Kitty in the scrub 'like a bushranger' for several months and approached Gillies during his visit to Atherton, are not reflected by the documents at all. We could assume that this dramatisation had emerged as a later embellishment. Moreover, it was traditional in Aboriginal love culture for lovers whose marriage was prohibited by the existing law, to run away to the bush and stay there until the conflict was settled. This ancient tradition might explain why this episode of Kitty and Leandro's marriage became so popular among Kitty's descendants. All these reservations about what was true might apply to other men but not to the Illins, who never hesitated to turn legend into everyday life. Leandro himself confirmed that the dramatic 'bushranger episode' did take place. In his later letter, of 27 April 1919, to the Home Secretary he wrote:

'HOW I GOT MARRIED AND WHY the Hon[ourable] W. N. Gillies could tell you as he helped me to do so after the Chief Protector Mr Bleakley refused to give me permit to marry and order[ed] Kitty (my wife now) to a Mission Station. Not wanting my children to be taken to a Mission I took to bush and had a very bad time of it. And only for the Hon[ourable] W. N. Gillies and the late Hon[ourable] D. Bowman I probably would had a sad end as I never would surrender my children to a mission.'[46]

Obviously, the intervention by Gillies into Leandro's case was not provoked just by the cable Leandro sent him (cited above); moreover, Gillies kept the case under his personal control till it was successfully concluded. Indeed, the local newspaper confirms that Gillies did visit

Atherton on 28 June 1915 (two weeks prior to his intervention into Leandro's case) and that he, together with a deputation of local residents, awaited on the platform the arrival of the minister for railways with a request for a branch line from Peeramon to the Boonjie gold-field.[47] This might be the moment when Leandro applied for his help. The fact that Leandro's descendants have elevated Gillies to the rank of premier (in 1915 he was a member of the Legislative Assembly, only becoming premier briefly in 1925) simply reflects the laws of the creation of a fairy-tale, when the good master should have the highest rank.

Harry's story about Kitty and Leandro's dramatic flight along the Russell River to Innisfail to marry might seem, at first glance, hyperbole for we know that by this time Leandro had the permit to marry. Still, in the report of the Innisfail Protector there is one reference — an 'alien came today to Innisfail from Russell River way accompanied by a female Aboriginal woman' — which suggests that the flight along Russell River did take place. Obviously, Leandro preferred not to go with the permit to a more accessible part of the country (such as Atherton or Tolga) because this area was under the control of the local police and of the Protector who had hunted Kitty for several months, a man whom Leandro had grounds not to trust. Formally, the order for Kitty's removal to the mission was returned by local police to the Chief Protector's Office only after they had been married.

Thus, archival documents state their truth, a supposedly objective truth, but the oral tradition, for all its inevitable distortions, has its own truth, too. The oral tradition makes an important contribution to the abundant but dry historical facts, by distinguishing, augmenting and preserving the most important points and thereby clarifying the whole story. If not for Flora and Harry, these facts would never be so memorable, would never have become part of the life of the younger generation.

...дрю, без еть...

...вной власти возвыша...

его благословенья,

...ой предковъ украшай." „Н...

<u>Омаръ.</u>

...нирасу, дѣдъ мой милый,

внуку бѣдному повѣрь,

...он, узналъ с такой я силой

душѣ смущенья, какъ тепер...

<u>Ибрагимъ.</u>

...щеньз...? Ты...? Скажи мнѣ с...

Что сердце юное гнетет...

Шевырь, в душѣ моей всеці...

...ще ласкою найдет...

SON AND FATHER

ON THE EVE

Leandro woke up first. Outside, rain was drumming upon the iron roof of his house. It was raining yesterday, and today, and it will be tomorrow; it rained nine months of the year here and this was the time of the rainy season, March 1918. He suppressed a cough, trying not to wake up the others. These severe coughs, and rain, and the forthcoming payment for the farm and cattle depressed him at times. But now in the last minutes before daybreak came with its worries he felt happy.

Kitty slept beside him holding nine-month-old Tommy. This tiny baby had quite a name: Thomas Alexander Leonidas. Thomas, to be part of the Australian world; Alexander, in honour of his Russian grandmother; and Leonidas — 'resembling a lion' — to resemble his father, Leandro, 'lion-man'. Sowing a name, he continued the game with destiny that his father began thirty-five years before in Turkestan.

Flora — she was two-and-a-half — rolled herself up into a ball on the other side of Kitty. His parents say that she looks like him in his childhood. He did not make a mistake in naming her simply Flora. Years ago, in his lonely travels in South America he met a nice little girl called Flora Nixon, and wished in his heart of hearts to have such daughter one day. And here she was, his goddess of flowers. She still did not know how hard her parents had to fight for her future but she already repaid them with the tender love and devotion that only girls can give.

Dick, who was nearly four, was a big boy already and slept with the older children. He was a copy of Kitty with a shock of curly black hair, a broad nose and dark skin. Leandro was sure that he, probably more than the others, would be his friend and supporter, a real man to rely on. Kitty's older children, Emma, Molly, and Ginger — the nameless 'three picaninnies' who were hunted by the police for removal to the Aboriginal reserve three years ago — called him 'daddy' too. He was rich, indeed; they all were his treasure that could not be bought for any money.

He slipped out of the bed but Kitty woke up too and with a smile, without many words, let him know that she would do the breakfast herself. She made a fire under the lean-to and used the camp oven to heat up the leftovers of scrub turkey that Leandro shot the day before. With a piece of damper the turkey made a nice meal. There was plenty of rainwater, no need to go down to Caribou Creek, and soon the billy was boiling. Leandro ate near the fire while Kitty was nursing Tommy. The rest of them were still sound asleep. It was so quiet that it seemed the three were alone in the world, alone and happy, at least for now. They did not have to hide any longer. They had a hut of their own, a hut that Leandro built himself of split timber, and, although their more ambitious neighbours were joking that it looked more like a native 'mia-mia', it was their home. The hut stood on the gorge between the two branches of Caribou Creek, surrounded by cleared scrub — 42 acres were grassed already and 2 acres were occupied with corn and a vegetable garden.[1] They had bought some cattle but dairying did not bring any real income yet, while the date for the payment of the mortgage was approaching. It was time for Leandro to go, to begin his daily rounds.

He parted from Kitty, slipped on an oilskin and went up along the path through the scrub to Romelio's block. There was a steep track on the other side of the creek — the Cairns mail road — but he seldom used it, especially in the rainy season, when it was impassable. The day was just starting but in the scrub it was still dark. The rain was murmuring its endless song in the lush canopy over his head when suddenly from the edge of the scrub came cheerful loud calls 'choo — choo — choo — choo'. It was a chowchilla, the scrub clock, announcing the coming of the day. In a minute the whole scrub was trilling with their chorus. Soon Leandro was at Romelio's clearing. This portion was not as rugged as Leandro's land and Romelio was doing well, he had 48 acres cleared and grassed already and planned to start an orchard. Romelio's house — it was a real house built by their friend Michael Gadaloff — was standing near the Russell road. The stock was roaming in the high grass. Leandro yoked his two bullocks, which were grazing in Romelio's paddock, to a spring cart. He attached the yoke to their horns in Latin American fashion — some people in Malanda believed that he was a Mexican because of that. That and Romelio's ability to handle a lasso and bolas, together with their strange names, all contributed to their 'Mexican' fame. The brothers greeted each other and decided to visit their father in the afternoon as it was Saturday, a time for family gathering. Leandro put the first load of cream on the cart. His team moved slowly along the muddy Russell road.

The Lamins were the first. Cans with cream were standing by the side of the road already. These former Russian intellectuals were struggling on their own but soon their Alfie will be big enough to help them in the morning with milking. Leandro felt somehow responsible for the destiny of this little fellow. A year earlier Ariadna and her new husband, Jack Mackay, had brought Alfie to Butchers Creek.

Now, eighty years later, this story is still remembered by Flora.

'MY AUNTIE ARA HAD HIM — SHE TOOK HIM FROM BRISBANE WITH JACK MACKAY when she married him. When they were boarding the train, Jack's former girlfriend — she was Greek or something like that — came to the platform holding a baby and said, "What are you going to do, are you going to send me money so that I could look after your child?". And my auntie said, "No, we'll take him". But when she took him she wasn't good to him, she was very cruel. She was a very strong woman. She could do anything that a man could do. She could build, she could cook, she could ride horses. A very strong woman. But she was also a cruel sort of woman.

'There were people, Lamins, here, they had no children. And my father said to her one day, "Look, you are too cruel to that little fellow, why don't you give him away to somebody who will look after him and be kind to him. You are terrible." And she said, "Take him away before I kill him". So my father went and saw the Lamins. And they said, "Yes, we'll have him if she wants to give him away". They named him Alfie. He was only a little fellow then. He did not know he was adopted before the Lamins died. I went to see him in Brisbane not long before his death some years ago.'[2]

After that conflict Leandro and Ara's relationship was never restored to that same friendship of an elder brother and little sister which they had in Corcovado. Moreover, she could never accept that he had married a dark woman.[3] Equality, for her, turned out to be only a word. His parents were the only ones who approved of Leandro.

Leandro thought often that, indeed, it was sometimes easier to preach to the whole world than to observe principles in your own family. Now, something else was worrying him, and it was about Romelio. Some time ago Kitty had said that in the Boonjie camp there were two kids of his but Romelio, it seemed, had no intention of marrying their mother. Well, they will grow up as Aborigines, and, who knows, maybe it is better for them to stay like that, Leandro thought, for at times he noticed the ironic smiles when he took Kitty and their children to Malanda or Peeramon. Anyway, Leandro lacked the courage to speak about that with Romelio. The only local man who followed his advice and legalised his relations with an Aboriginal woman was old Tom Denyer, a miner from Boonjie, who married Kitty's mother, Emily, in

1916. Leandro had to meet Mr Bleakley, the Protector, during his visit to Atherton, to obtain permission for this marriage. They were married in Nicholas's house by a Presbyterian minister, William Shinton. Leandro and the Frenchman Charles Civry, the de facto husband of Emily's daughter, Julia, were the witnesses.[4] These three European–Aboriginal couples openly celebrating their union — what a challenge that was to the racial prejudices which reigned around them!

He thought about all this as he was travelling along the road collecting cans of cream. Davidsons, Mailers, Lynches on the left, the Balias family on the right. Finally, he reached Butchers Creek school and turned to the right along the Gadaloff road, across the Balias Creek bridge. That school had quite a story.

In 1913 with other neighbours Leandro helped to build it: Ara's son, Hector, was nearly four and was going to start schooling soon. The first teacher was John Tait, a grey-bearded gentleman of sixty, who had evidently received a good education in his younger years. Since then he had been fossicking and mining; he was one of the discoverers of tungsten. He was a nice chap to have a yarn with around the fire, and when Leandro called at his camp nearby they sometimes did this. His usual meal was damper with billy tea. Leandro enjoyed it, unlike the school inspector, McKenna, who was shocked when Tait treated him with a generous piece of his damper during an inspection visit.

Well, damper, it was the last straw. But what was one to say about the teacher's dress, complained McKenna to Nicholas Illin one day. (Nicholas's block was next-door to the school and in this god-forsaken corner it was a pleasure for the inspector to converse with an educated man, who, when he ran out of English words, would lapse into French, German or Latin and Greek.) On one visit, related McKenna, Mr Tait had on rough boots, no collar, a coloured shirt and old coat with several holes in it. On another visit he was without a coat with his shirt-sleeves unbuttoned, his pants dirty, and his boots had not been cleaned for weeks. Added to this, Mr Tait did not know how to do the paperwork and did not teach drills to the pupils. Nicholas would attempt to object that the main thing was the teacher's ideas, his aspiration — as a Russian poet said, to 'sow what is wise, what is good, what is true' — rather than his dress, and that Mr Tait did not get a fair chance as all the children were engaged in dairying and therefore they came very late to school. Each morning and evening they had to milk around a dozen cows. Finally, McKenna had to take the side of the parents, who demanded that the Education Department dismiss this miner-'gentleman' and send them a lady teacher instead.

Several lady teachers came in succession, but none of them improved the situation. The first, Gertrude Irving, applied to resign as soon as she arrived: 'I cannot content myself to live in the bush, and this place is so very far out. Teaching in these outlandish places is far too lonely a life for a young girl.' After this failure the parents' committee appealed for 'a female teacher with bush experience' and promised 'to supply her with a horse and a saddle'. Mary Moroney took this 'tempting' offer but was unable to endure it for long and resigned in early 1917. Finally came Hanna Bennett, a lady in a desperate situation; she had left her husband and by herself was raising her three children, working as a teacher. She settled in at the Fletchers' hut next to the Illins and they felt sympathetic towards the determination of this overstrung and lonely woman.

A new school was under construction to replace the first, provisional one. All seemed fine, and at last, Nicholas hoped, these bush children had a teacher, but suddenly tension began to build between Mrs Bennett and William Fletcher's family. The tension turned into hostilities and open confrontation, which gradually involved the whole community of nearby farmers and finally the schoolchildren. Mrs Bennett moved into the old school-house, suffering constant abuse from the neighbours, probably the Fletchers. She hit back disclosing the 'filth' in the school among the rough children of these rough farmers. She saw it where it was and where it was not: she saw it in the older boys' secret society, which included the Russian children, where there certainly was 'filth'; she saw 'filth' in the children's awareness of sexual relations, as they all assisted their fathers with animals; dirty words covered slates and books; even in the seemingly innocent game of hide-and-seek behind a log Mrs Bennett discovered misconduct between one of the Russian boys and a local girl, and Leila Prochoroff was interrogated as the main witness. The hostilities in the ill-fated bush school finally involved Constable Pike, Inspector McKenna and the Education Department in Brisbane.

Hector brought news home every day about the development of events. This tiny school that symbolised for Nicholas the English aspiration for knowledge was sinking in the mire of human hatred and Russian children had somehow become involved; probably they were having to pay for the Russian revolution, which was gaining pace. Then, while pruning the trees in his young orchard, Nicholas was struck by a simple idea for stopping the squabble, not with the help of police or the school inspector, but by himself with the help of the Chekhovian cherry orchard. However rough the surrounding folk were, it could not be that they, and especially the children, would not return good for good. And so he came to school. Seventy years later Edgar Short would write about that day:

'MR ILLIN, A VERY CULTURED OLD GENTLEMAN WITH A LONG WHITE BEARD, WHO SPOKE SEVERAL LANGUAGES ... established a peach garden, and one of my best memories of Butchers Creek school is the whole school being invited to his orchard when the peaches were ripe and being told to eat our fill, which we sure did.'

What was sweeter — a peach or an encounter with generosity, a generosity which came not from wealth but from the heart? For these bush children, little slaves of the milking routine, surrounded by the prose of life alone, this was their first discovery of another level of human relations and, maybe, of the irrational Russian soul. For Nicholas himself it was a tribute to his ailing motherland, where former followers of Chekhov had now split into the Whites and the Reds, flooding the cherry orchards with torrents of blood ...

Nikifor Homenko, who always had his feet on the ground, interpreted Nicholas's message in his own way and, free of charge, erected a four-wire fence with water-gum posts around the school.[5]

Leandro's bullock-team was moving along Gadaloff road. Nikonets, Homenko, Gadaloff, Strelnikoff — they all were doing well. The latest arrival was the intelligent Prochoroff family, and even they had managed to start dairying already. Chris Fry across the road was still clearing his block and was going to enlist and go to the war. The furthest away on the track was Gysbertus de Brueys from Amsterdam with his seven children. Leandro loaded their cream and headed back to the school, and from there he turned right towards Peeramon along the Russell road. After he passed the wall of scrub still standing around the Fletchers' hut, the clearing of his parents' farm opened out in front of him. He went along the three-wire fence — it marked his and Romelio's debut in wire-fencing and now he could see some faults in it — and drew near the gates. Cans with cream were waiting for him as well as a package with pies baked by his mother this morning. Wrapped up in the towel and oilcloth, they were still warm. He took a couple to fortify himself, leaving the rest for the children. That cheered him up and even the sun appeared for a while somewhere over the high trees.

He needed to be in good spirits as the worst part of the track lay ahead. To make their living many farmers in the neighbourhood had started to sell their timber to Peeramon railway station. The logs were hauled by bullock teams that gradually turned the Russell road into deep ruts and potholes, from which water never drained. Leandro's bullocks made their way up and down slippery hills covered with red mud. In some places mud reached the bullocks' bellies and from time to time he had to stop and fill up the worst holes with logs to get along. And he was coughing and coughing under the chilling rain. At last the first houses of Peeramon appeared on the hill. Leandro passed by several shops, a blacksmith's, and the two-storey hotel, before reaching the railway yards, from where the cream was taken by rail to the Golden Grove butter factory in Atherton. The Malanda butter factory was under construction already and soon he would have to deliver cream there. Leandro collected mail at the post office — nothing from Russia as usual, just a few Australian newspapers — and headed back. Without cans it was much easier.

When, some hours later, he returned home his children surrounded him: 'Dad, can you stop the rain today?'. 'Let's try', he said, and they recited in chorus in Russian: 'If you want to stop the rain think of forty bold-headed men'. While Kitty was cooking some food it was time to play. Ginger was bubbling with excitement: 'We've found a platypus burrow at the creek, let's go down, we'll show you'. And, telling him all their news, they led him down to the left branch of Caribou Creek.

Leandro never distinguished between his own children and his stepchildren and the older ones appreciated it. He brought them something very important that was missing in their traditional culture. Up to the time of initiation there was a barrier between children and their father and other adult men; the children belong only to their own world and to the world of women. Ginger, Molly and Emma had learnt this rule well while living with the tribe. Now this big, white man brought a new relationship between the children and adults. At times he would unselfconsciously romp with them, sharing their fun and their bush skills that they had brought from the camp; at times he might be very strict and serious and treat them as adults, as equals. If he took them to do some job, they knew it would be a real job, not fun; and they did their best to please their 'Dad', not from fear but from the pride they felt in being a real help to him. And he was always honest and just. Always.

They reached the creek and, hiding among tree ferns, with bated breath watched the water below. Ginger made a sign to Leandro not to lean too far forward as his shadow could frighten the platypus. Their patience was rewarded and a platypus showed itself from the burrow. It busily swam about in the transparent water looking for some food. When it retreated to the burrow, Ginger said: 'I know what Caribou means in Ngadjon, my granny told it means "many" and there was a legend about that creek that has many branches'. 'I know a legend too, about platypus', said usually shy Emma.

But neither of them had time to tell the legend as they heard screams from the far corner of the clearing. They rushed to the rescue and discovered the Homenko brothers, Bill and John. Nearly eighty years later Bill, laughing, would tell us about that day.

'THERE WAS A BIG HOLLOW LOG where they used to have a goat. And we were only kids and went down there with dad one day and that bloody goat came running at us and oh! didn't we yell! We thought he was going to eat us.'[6]

Nikifor Homenko's clearing was on the other side of the spur by the northern branch of the creek. He would often come to Leandro's 'miamia' to have a chat in Russian or to get help with a letter in English for some office. His children, five-year-old Bill and four-year-old John, white-haired and blue-eyed like their father, only spoke Russian and when they came to Leandro's selection, Dick, who had picked up a lot of Russian words from his *Deda* and *Baba*[7], would interpret from Russian into English and Ngadjon.

After the meal Leandro told the children that they were going to go over and see *Baba* and *Deda*. Naturally, they all wanted to go, but it was finally decided that the eldest, Emma, would stay with mother to help her with Tommy, who did not feel well that day. Ginger brought their horse, a quiet mare, from the paddock and fixed a split bag behind the saddle. This was just a bag with a sewn end and a hole in the middle, which turned into two pockets on the horse's back. Soon all were ready — Leandro in the middle, Ginger in one pocket, Dick in another and Molly holding Flora on the pommel in front of Dad. They said farewell to Mum and off they went, up the gorge to Romelio's clearing and then along the Russell road. Weren't they happy! Edgar Short remembers seeing them on one such ride and it might be that it was not only the unusual utilisation of the split bag but the fact that a white man shared happiness with a troop of Aboriginal children that made it so memorable to Edgar.[8]

Soon they passed the school and the Fletchers' hut, and turned to the right to Nicholas's block. They had all worked hard on it during those first years and invested all their money brought from the Argentine and now it was one of the best farms in Butchers Creek. When, in 1916, the farm was assessed for the certificate of performance of conditions on selection — which gave the owner freehold rights — the land ranger reported that the amount of permanent and substantial improvements was more than enough to comply with requirements. Nicholas had 70 acres of scrub cleared and grassed already. The rustic house — their pride — built of timber under an iron roof with a porch, three large rooms and a big kitchen, was surrounded by flowerbeds. The vegetable garden and orchard were to the right, near the creek, while paved cattle-yard, cowshed, separator house and milking bails were situated behind the house. Their first dwelling — a slab shed built by Leandro and Romelio — was now used as a barn. It was in this shed that Leandro used to dream about Mila Daniel during the long, rainy nights but how far away that was now, as if in another life. And the real life was here — a huge water tank, 320 feet of piping and a hydraulic ram lifting water from the creek to the house and stockyard, precise wire fencing and cattle, lots of fine cows grazing on the hills. And debts to the bank for it, that too ...

Leandro unloaded his brood from the horse at the rails. Dick, Ginger and Molly were immediately carried away by Hector and Nellie, chattering in English, Russian and Ngadjon, but Flora stayed with Leandro. They went together to Nicholas's room. He was sitting at the table copying poetry from separate sheets of paper into a blue school notebook. Leandro recognised the lines from *The Orient Legend* that Nicholas had written years ago when they had just started their life in the Argentine. 'I decided to rewrite it', said Nicholas, 'isn't it about our time, about what happens in our Russia?'

> As years pass
> And death takes its toll
> Life opens light
> Hitherto hidden.
> My child, the one adoring sword,

> And war, and bloody raids,
> Has ruined his peace of mind
> Forever and irrevocably.
> Requital awaits ...

'I might die soon, but that will help you to see the right way in the modern world with all its bloodshed.' His short-sighted eyes gleamed with emotion behind his metal spectacles. Suddenly Flora who, enchanted, was looking at the pages of the notebook covered with neat beads of letters, said in Russian: 'My *Deda*, *Deda*' and hugged him. He looked into her serious dark eyes — what mystery was opened to that barefooted, delicate child who was part of him and at the same time part of that land where he would always be an alien? Could he foresee at that moment that Flora, although unable to read it, would preserve this notebook with his poetry throughout her eighty years of life full of hardships and wandering, that she would always keep it in memory of her dear *Deda*.

Romelio joined them and they remembered how, exactly a year before, when the news of the Russian revolution reached the Tablelands, they were sitting in this room discussing the first scanty and confused reports in the *Cairns Post:* 'Sensation in Russia', 'Abdication of the Czar', 'Russian epic unfolding', 'All Baulked by Revolution'. The unbelievable had happened: the great day for which Nicholas and his family had been waiting all their lives had come. Nicholas's prediction — 'We will cast down the idol from the throne and the czar will take flight' — was coming true. Now, they rejoiced, 'all the abuses, cruelty and crimes with the help of which their mother country was ruled, had come to an end'. And they believed that 'the new rule would be full of self-sacrifice, generosity, nobleness toward the conquered, and their aim would be real liberty. And so it was while Kerensky's party was in power.' They had had heated debates about going back to Russia. Luckily, they missed the moment: the first signs of this long-awaited liberty were already being swept away by the new Russian revolution and its endless atrocities.

The only thing they could say now for sure was that they had lost their darling girls, Tonia and Valia — Mania's daughters. Just before the war Mania had suffered an infection from a miscarriage and died. Wilhelm Pettersen moved to Saratov, where he had the post of chief inspector on the Ural railway line. The girls studied at the University of Saratov, one to become a doctor and the other, a civil engineer. After the fall of the Kerensky government in October 1917 the Illins did not receive any letters from their granddaughters. No news was sent either by Gabriel Ivanoff, who had returned to Russia from Queensland, when he went to see his parents in Saratov province. They would have spared nothing to have the girls safe but now they feared the worst and Leandro for the first time said, 'I do not know now if God exists but he spared the sorrow to Mania'.[9]

While the men were talking politics, Alexandra laid the table for the kids. How different they were, the tall, fair-haired Hector and Nellie and the dark offspring of Leandro and Kitty — and still they were all hers. In Hector she noticed Pusha's quiet smile, and Nellie's eyes reminded her of Valia and Tonia, lost in Russia — even now she remembered them as little girls in neat aprons — and in the dark eyes of Dick and, especially, of Flora she saw Leandro, who took after her own Tartar grandmother. But the children did not give her much time for her thoughts, devouring *Baba*'s Russian dumplings (*pelmeni*) stuffed with scrub turkey. When they were full, they fell into a more reflective mood: '*Baba*, tell how I got lost in the bush', asked Hector. 'No, better, tell how we bathed Dick', insisted Nellie. Finally, Nellie and Dick won out and Alexandra began the story.

'DICK, YOU WERE STAYING HERE, IT WAS THAT WINTER, YOU REMEMBER, when your mama was hiding from the police. Anyway, one day I had so much to do, I told you two, Nellie and Hector, to take Dick down to the creek and give him a bath. Then, what do I hear? All this yelling. You were really yelling, Dick, I thought someone was drowning. I rushed down to the creek and I can see you, Nellie, how old were you then? You must've been about four, there you were with the sandsoap and scrubbing brush and you were scrubbing Dick all over. And I said, "Nellie, what are you doing to Dickie?". And you said, "I'm just washing him, *Baba*'. Well, I said, "But can't you see, you're hurting him with that sandsoap?". And you said, "No, *Baba*, I don't mean to hurt him. I'm just trying to scrub him white".'[10]

This was followed by an outburst of laughter. Nellie even blushed from the general attention and *Baba* lovingly hugged her. How much trouble she had had with this pretty, slim girl at first! Sometimes she felt as if Nellie were her own daughter.

After the Illins came to the Tablelands Ara did not stay long in Butchers Creek. She always wanted to be independent and now she left

Hector with Alexandra and went to work as a cook in the camps for railway construction teams. Somewhere there she met a young man called Harry Dale. He was born in Ballarat, in Victoria. When they married, in July 1912, Leandro had just returned from the Northern Territory and, inspired by his tales, they left for Darwin.

Nellie, born in October 1913, was the only product of their relationship, and now, eighty years later, she tells about these painful times.

'MY MOTHER WAS A VERY DOMINEERING AND DEMANDING WOMAN, they didn't get along at all. Soon she got sick and came back to the farm. ... When I was born my *Baba* asked my mother if she wanted-ed to see me? My mother told her "No — take her away". So I was taken to *Baba* and *Deda*'s room and stayed with them till I was a 'teen. Meantime my father wrote to my mother and told her that he was glad she wasn't pregnant, because he was going to war and, as they didn't get along, it was for the best, that he didn't feel obliged to stay with her. He went to war and was killed. My *Baba* said they read in a newspaper list about his death. My grandfather wrote to his mother, [Sarah] Dale, about my birth and this, my other granny wanted them to give me to her to raise. As *Deda*'s answer was "No", that he and *Baba* would raise me, she never contacted my grandfather again.'[11]

Ara never spoke about him and for years Nellie dreamt of finding out who her father was, where he was killed, what relatives she still might have had in Australia. When I tried to find him among those killed in World War I, it turned out that, although quite a number of men with the name Harry Dale served in the army, none of them fitted the scarce data that was available about Ara's husband. A legend to be destroyed ...

Anyway, Ara soon left and the newborn Nellie stayed with Hector on *Baba* and *Deda*'s farm. Her real name was Ellen — her namesake in Greek mythology was Helen of Troy, the most beautiful woman in Greece — but somehow all used to call her Nellie. The Illins would not have managed without Kitty in those days. She had already been helping Alexandra for a while and now she took on all the hard work while Alexandra looked after the weak, tiny baby, raising her on goat's milk.

By 1916 Ara, who was working as a cook in Biboohra, near Mareeba, had met Jack Mackay; he was managing a sawmill there. Dick, Leandro's son who met up with Jack again years later in Honduras gives his portrait of the man.

'HE WAS A PRETTY HARD MAN, OLD JACK. He was a great boxer as well, and when the men at his sawmill went on strike once he had no trouble getting them back to work. He asked every man whether he wanted to work or not. Those who said they didn't, he simply took by the nose and dragged them back to their jobs. There was no further argument.'[12]

Ara and Jack both had strong personalities. But did Ara herself realise that she had been waiting all those years for the strong man who would tame her rebellious nature? This he did. She was conquered and finally felt herself quiet and happy. In February 1917 Ara gave birth to twins, a boy and a girl. The girl, named Ariadna after her mother, was so weak that she died just after the birth. The boy was named Somerled (later nicknamed Sam) after Jack's younger brother, killed during World War I. Ariadna did not want names from Greek mythology any more. In May that year Ariadna and Jack legalised their relations and married.

According to Somerled Mackay Jnr, who is the grandson of Ariadna and Jack Mackay, Jack's proper name was John Alexander Mackay. His parents, John Ronald Mackay (1856–1937) and Alexandrina Finlayson (1861–1940), came from the west of Scotland, from the picturesque island of Skye. They emigrated to Australia, where John, a naval captain, served as a master mariner. They had eleven children, John Alexander (Jack), born in Queensland in 1890, being the fifth.

The Illins, Leandro's descendants, had never been in touch with the relatives of Jack Mackay and it did not take long for a legend to be born. It was believed that Ara's husband was a son of the explorer Captain John Mackay (1839–1914). In 1860 he opened up the area south of the lower reaches of the Burdekin River, an area later to become known as the Mackay district, and the town that grew up at the mouth of the Pioneer River was named Mackay.[13] The legend that this romantic character and John Ronald Mackay, Ariadna's father-in-law, were the same person is very popular among the Australian Illins, and even among Ariadna's descendants. But, although both John Mackays came from the Scottish Highlands, they were different persons and I feel sorry having to destroy this beautiful legend.

Alexandra has just brought out a big peach-cake for the kids when new guests arrive — it is Ara with Jack and Sam. Sam has just started walking and is the centre of attention. Ara is well into the family way again, expecting a child in a few months.

Together with Alexandra, Ara laid the table for the adults and soon the whole family was gathered around it, just as in long-ago Corcovado.

Borsch soup was followed by *blini* (Russian pancakes), a traditional dish for Shrovetide — the time for winter's farewell in Russia, which was supposed to be celebrated there now. But was it? The image of white snow and merry sleigh-bells mingled in their minds with red blood on the snow, with gunshots ... But the presence of Jack made the men stop debating the Russian situation and they switched to English. The conversation was more down-to-earth — about prices for cream, and the cattle-tick, and milking machines, and the bad roads. They drank no alcohol: Jack had now got used to that unusual Russian family; before meeting the Illins, he believed that all Russians were drunkards.

As the sun sank lower they felt that the time for songs had come. Leandro took his mandolin down from the wall and began to play their favourite tune, 'La Paloma'. They all joined in the chorus and the song brought into their lonely house, lost in the Australian scrub, the happy carnival atmosphere of Buenos Aires, and the girl made as if from sun-rays was dancing, promising happiness. Romelio listened with his eyes half-closed. For the first time his thoughts did not go far away, to Corcovado, to the girl who said 'No'; now he seemed to find his 'La Paloma' in Little Siberia — it was seventeen-year-old Olga Gadaloff, but he was still afraid to believe in his dream. Jack looked at Ara. She was far away, maybe galloping across the Patagonian prairies, in her forbidden past, where she would never let him in. Only Leandro enjoyed the tune without suffering — he had learnt to recognise this girl in the smile of Kitty and her daughters ... And this sunny girl was dancing on, leading them further and further from the past into the future. They tried to sing revolutionary songs — some they had brought from Russia, some they had learnt later from their Russian neighbours. How spiritedly they sang them a year ago, after the February revolution, but now the songs were more like mourning songs, mourning for Valia and Tonia, mourning for their motherland, mourning for their life as eternal refugees. Ara, as if waking up, took the accordion and strongly and boldly began to play 'Down the Volga'. Jack listened to their singing and realised what strength was hidden in his wife, in her family. Now he was happy to be part of them, these enigmatic Russians.

* * *

Leandro, with his troop in the split bag, and Romelio were leaving their parents' home at sunset. The sky over Butchers Creek was ominously purple-red. 'I do not like this sky', Romelio murmured, 'it must be strong wind tomorrow.'

And it was. On that day, Sunday, 10 March 1918, the cyclone struck. The strong easterly wind that had been blowing since morning was gradually turning round to the west, increasing in force with each gust. By 10 p.m. it had reached hurricane force. It was hard to breathe. Rain was pouring in torrents through the constant flashes of lightning. Kitty and the children were sitting in their 'mia-mia', clinging to each other; Leandro tried to tie the roof to the slabs but all was in vain. Around midnight a strong gust unroofed their house and blew the pieces of iron roofing somewhere in the direction of Bartle Frere. The torrents of water poured in and the walls seemed about to collapse. Leandro tied a rope to one of the posts and, carrying Dick and Flora, shepherded his family down the slope. The older children followed him, holding onto the rope, and Kitty brought up the rear carrying Tommy. They stopped at the upper part of one of the cleared gullies, half-way towards Caribou Creek. The usually quiet stream was now roaring down below, carrying broken branches and debris. It was a bit quieter between the slopes of the gully but the wind continued to increase in force; it was blowing now from all directions, sweeping pieces of timber over their heads. In a flash of lightning they saw how the wall of scrub some hundred metres away was crushed and flattened in a second — venerable forest giants were snapped like matches by an unseen hand.

Leandro looked at Kitty, her wet face with wide-open, black eyes was turned towards the Bellenden Ker. 'It's him, Murgalainya, he came down from the mountain to kill us all', she whispered in Ngadjon, but Leandro understood her. At that moment he felt the same — and what is the difference if he calls it a 'primordial force'. His wife believed in animated nature and he had neglected his god for years, believing as he did in the greater strength of the human spirit — but they were equals now in their desperate hope to be spared, to survive, to protect their children. Leandro and Kitty leaned over their children and prayed together to their gods, Christian and pagan; that joint prayer was answered. The wind gradually eased and at dawn they heard the deceptively routine call of the chowchilla 'Choo — choo — choo — choo'. It was sitting on the outstretched, bare branch of the huge walnut tree, which, stripped of all its leaves, raised lonely limbs over the acres and acres of crushed and tangled scrub.

The house was flattened, pieces of roof everywhere — what a hard job it had been some years ago to carry these iron sheets the half-mile from the Cairns track! Their scanty belongings all scattered around, damp and covered with debris. Leandro's horse came up to them whinnying. Ginger was the only who did not lose heart; he made his way through the mess looking for their possessions, while Molly was weeping bitterly over the torn cloth which was all that was left of her new dress that *Baba* gave her only the day before.

They decided to make their way up to Romelio's block and met him half-way there. His new house survived the cyclone but some of the cattle had been killed by broken branches. He himself had spent a worrying night, too. Around midnight, when he saw that across the road the Davidsons' house was unroofed, he made his way there and found all the family hiding in a hollow log beside the house. He tied a rope to the trunk and, together with George Davidson, led George's pregnant wife and three children along the rope to the newly built cheese factory, which had withstood the cyclone. Then he made his way to Peter Mailer's block and with the same length of rope helped them to get to the factory.[14] He had also been to the Lamins, but did not know what had happened on their own parents' farm. Leandro left his family to have a rest in Romelio's house and they both rode to see their parents. The Russell road was covered with debris and blocked in places by fallen trunks. In some places they had to cut their way through.

Turning in to the farm, they noticed from a distance the figures of their parents. The house, their real home, lay in ruins, so did most of the outbuildings. Their parents had seemed to put on ten years in one night. Mother was just sitting. Father, as if in a daze, was wandering among the ruins. Only Hector and Nellie tried to do something practical — they picked up sheets of paper scattered everywhere and laid them out to dry. Most of the books and papers that had been on the shelf and on the table were badly damaged, only the archive that was in the trunk had survived. Wind was turning odd pages of *The Tolstoyan Diary* ...

'How is the orchard?' Romelio asked, he knew what was the most important thing for Father just at this moment.

'The crop has gone, but most of the trees seem alright, they are young and supple, they will revive', Nicholas said slowly. He looked at them lovingly through tears. Nellie and Hector, Romelio and Leandro. 'They are young and strong. They will live.'

'MEN DIE TO UPHOLD THEIR PRINCIPLE'

After the cyclone the Illins had to make decisions, decisions that involved moral choices. For Kitty, Nicholas and Leandro it was one of the hardest moments in their lives.

Kitty was the first. It was all because of Leandro's health. He did not give up after the cyclone — he rebuilt their house, he fixed the blocked roads, he helped his father. They applied to the under-secretary for Lands: 'owing to the cyclone on 10 March 1918 we have sustained such damage that required a lot of repairs which has put us to an unexpected expense. ... We have started dairying only lately and have urgent payments for cattle to comply with.' They badly needed an extension of time for payment for the farm. But the offices in Brisbane did not respond. To earn money, Leandro continued his hard job of carting cream. Flora relates:

'IT WAS COLD UP THERE and at that time very little land was cleared, it was all heavy scrub and it would rain, and rain, and rain. And he was getting wet all the time, no good for him. And he had to work carting cream. He ended up getting sick, he'd cough and cough. So the doctor told him he was best to get out of the wet climate.'

But he could not just leave; he needed money to make the payment to the bank. The day after he paid the money, he received the extension from the Land Department for which he had applied long before. He sent them a bitter message: 'Having waiting for this extension of time and being afraid I am not going to get it I have paid this at a big sacrifice and inconvenience. ... Excuse me for mentioning it but it would be to the selectors benefit if we get these notices sooner before the day of payment to know what to do.'[15]

Now he could leave the farm before it was too late. The nearest dry locality was Mt Garnet. It was not so far from Butchers Creek, just around 160 kilometres. But it was very far for Kitty. She had to confront the choice between her love for Leandro and her love for her country. It was even more than love of the country in a European sense. For her their country was a material and spiritual entity that constantly flowed from the past to the future. She herself, and her children, and all her people were an inseparable part of this entity. They didn't need any sophisticated philosophy to know that neither their country nor they could exist without each other. But now, when it came to a question of Leandro's health, she agreed to go with him. She had discovered already that along with the Aboriginal law there was another law brought to her by Leandro and his parents — the law of love and compassion. And she chose this law, however hard it was for her to leave her Russell River.

One of the first memories of Flora was her mother crying by their hut in Spring Gully, near Mt Garnet. And little Flora knew what it was about:

'MY GRANDMOTHER EMILY WAS A BLACK COCKATOO and when my mother would hear that black cockatoo singing out she used to sit down and cry. Being so far away, my mother could not go back over there. She missed her mother, she missed her country.'

For Kitty this black cockatoo was not just a reminder, it was a personification of her mother, a spirit of her faraway country. The black cockatoo, a totem, which is a subject for the refined theories of anthropologists, was a matter of life and love for Aborigines.

We were discussing totems and the Aboriginality of Kitty's children at Harry Illin's place, in Townsville. Harry is Kitty's youngest son, and his children and grandchildren surrounded him at the table, the front door was open to the peaceful, warm evening. Harry's great-grandchildren and my son Ralphie made a lot of noise in the house and finally they were sent out-of-doors. Their modern voices still managed to intrude from time to time into the stories from the past that I was tape-recording.

Flora and Harry have lived most of their lives in a world that forced them to put no value on their Aboriginality, even to abandon it. Still, seeing my interest and that of their own family, they seem to have made an effort to reveal to us their concealed connections with their Aboriginal past, something about which they did not speak before. This is a part of their conversation.

Flora: I can't remember the totem of my mother, but I can remember my grandmother's, she was the black cockatoo.
Harry: I belong to black cockatoo, you know that?
Flora: I do not know.
Harry: Dick's name was Piraj, they called him Piraj. What sort of word would that represent? I think he belong to the parrot.
Flora: I've got an Aboriginal name. I know that.
Faye: What is that, auntie Flora?
Flora: Birung.
Faye: What's that mean?

Flora: I don't know.

Harry: I do not know my Aboriginal name. Just a black cockatoo. That is my granny Emily told me that I belong to black cockatoo.

Flora: I don't think they gave Harry a name because when he was born we were away from the Tablelands.[16]

Listening to their conversation I realised that their Aboriginal names were more than names in our understanding; they were strings that tied them to the land of their ancestors. Scanty evidence that has survived about Ngadjon past confirms it. They created the most sophisticated concepts about people's belonging to their land. The Ngadjon-ji believed that their land was inhabited by spirits who had their origin in the epoch of the mythical ancestors. These spirits had special habitats, usually near the water, and when a woman was passing such a place a spirit could enter her body and develop into a child. A spirit could enter a man's body, too. In that case he would pass it to his wife by sexual intercourse or by other means — for instance, in food. To know the territory of the spirit someone would recite different localities at the time of the childbirth. The one that is named at the moment when the umbilical cord was cut off was a special territory of the spirit and, now, of the child, his home country. The father named the child by the personal name derived from the totem or this locality and 'put the name under a rock or in a cave' in the child's own country.[17]

For the whites the Aboriginal inability to connect the conception of a child with sexual intercourse was an indication of the natives' primitiveness. In reality, it was just two different world outlooks. The whites see the conception of a child as a purely physiological act involving parents alone, while the Ngadjon people saw it primarily as a spiritual act, where physiology was just a contributing factor; for the Ngadjon the main factor was the constant, unbound spiritual connection between people and their ancestors, people and their land. It was an elaborate philosophy, rather than ignorance.

When we went to the Tablelands, we spoke about the Aboriginal names again. Dick's daughters Glenda and Vera told us that they had heard from the elders that Dick's name was 'Nupi' or 'Napaj', which probably meant possum, and Tom's name was 'Pinka'. Tom's daughter Hazel had heard that his name was 'Putchety', which means little lizard with a round head. Emily's name, 'Darugso', has been returned to her great-grandchildren through the archives.[18] The meaning of these names is obscure to them but they all had inherited the feeling that names were of utmost importance on the path to a reunion with their ancestry.

Harry was born in April 1919 on the banks of G.W. Swamp, far away from Kitty's country. According to Aboriginal law he had no connection with the spirits of Ngadjon land; despite that, Kitty believed that he was part of it, that he had a spirit of a black cockatoo, a brave, strong bird, which had followed her to this place. This was her attempt to reconcile the traditional law with Leandro's law of love and compassion.

Leandro named their third son Henry Octavian, continuing his game with names. Henry, or rather Harry, was a challenge to Nicholas, who chose for his sons fanciful names — Leandr, Karterii and Romelii. Whereas, in opposition to Nicholas's trio of names, the newborn Harry was to complete Leandro's trio that symbolised ordinary, common people: 'Tom, Dick and Harry'. But this Harry had a concealed second nature, being Octavian as well — a glorious Roman emperor who gathered under his rule the vast territory from Syria and Egypt to Spain and the Atlantic Ocean. Henry Octavian Illin was born on the outskirts of another empire, that of the Atkinsons. G.W. Swamp was an outer paddock of the Gunnawarra station. Cattle roamed around the drying swamp, grazing on scanty grass and Leandro bailed water for them, day after day. There were no windmills and all water was bailed by hand. His family camped not far from the water-bail in a hut with slab walls and a corrugated iron roof. They were all alone there among endless expanses of gum-tree bush. On moonlit nights the dark shadows of dingoes emerged from behind quaint termite mounds. They came in packs howling around the hut. The frightened children clung to Kitty while Leandro went outside to fire a couple of shots to scare off the animals. Indeed, there was nothing at all around to associate with the glorious emperor's life-style. But, who knows, maybe a hidden nature of things opens up to parents when, bending over a newborn baby, they choose a name. Years passed and it was Harry who turned out to be the only one to lay claim to the title of the king of Ngadjon tribe. This is how Harry saw it.

'KING BARRY CLARKE, HE WAS MY GREAT-GRANDFATHER, then he handed down to his son Willie Clarke. My mother was his only child and when he passed away it was supposed to be handed down to my brother, the eldest one, George, he was supposed to be the king of the Ngadjon tribe. But when we left the Tablelands, it was not handed to him at all. It was to go to George, and then from George to Dick, from Dick to Tommy, and from Tommy to me. I am the only one left now. I do not know what they are going to do about it, they still talking about it, they still might put it to the government and recommend me to be king of that tribe. Whether it will come off I do not know, but I'm not very worried about it really.'[19]

Although strictly, from the point of view of the traditional law, there were no hereditary kings in the European way in Ngadjon society, if we treat Aboriginal society, not as a relic but as a living, modernising entity, Harry's belief is right in its own way.

A month after our conversation, in August 1996, Harry suddenly died. He was seventy-seven years old: nearly two millennia ago at exactly the same age of seventy-seven the Roman Emperor Augustus Octavian died in Rome ...

G.W. Swamp, where Harry was born, got its name from Ludwig Leichhardt's expedition. Somewhere near here Leichhardt left the Burdekin water-basin and turned towards the Gulf of Carpentaria, marking, according to the Atkinsons' tradition, a tree near the swamp with the letters G.W., which meant either 'Good water' or 'Gilbert's water-hole'. Local Aborigines from Warungu tribe called the swamp Minnamoolka — 'Place of many birds' — and the Atkinsons restored this name in the 1950s.[20] It was all by chance that the Illins settled in this lonely place.

In August 1918 Leandro found a buyer for his farm in Gadgarra but his health had deteriorated so much that he had no time to wait for the legal procedure of the farm's transfer and left for Mt Garnet. In the drier climate his health improved greatly. He was applying for a grazing homestead there when he met Thomas J. Atkinson, who offered him a job as a stockman in Gunnawarra. Leandro took his family there but the job involved long periods of mustering when the stockmen moved from one stock camp to another, camping on the swag. It was hard for him to leave Kitty for so long with six children and the seventh on the way. So, finally, Leandro preferred to move together with the family 40 kilometres deeper into the bush, to G.W. Swamp, where he was water-bailing, fixing fences and working as a handyman. In an official letter he would describe his position as a 'working manager' at '£2–0–0 a week and found'. The 'found' was the slab hut plus flour, tea, and sugar from the Gunnawarra store. From now, and for more than ten years to come, Leandro was part of a new world — the world of outback cattle stations.

James Atkinson (1824–99), the founder of the Atkinson dynasty, came to Australia from Ireland. According to his great-grandson Bim, James was living in Victoria when he read the description of the Valley of Lagoons in Leichhardt's diary and decided to head north, to the abundant pastures in the Burdekin River area. He joined forces with Ezra Firth and his family, and from the mouth of Burdekin covered hundreds of miles without roads to the wild country of northwest, the first graziers to reach north of Bowen. They reached the Valley of Lagoons in the upper Burdekin in around 1862 but they did not get back to register the valley properly and so missed out on purchasing it. For a while they stayed at Firth's Lagoon, moving later to Mt Surprise and Ingham, but, relates Bim, 'in about 1896 there was a big tick fever hit northern Queensland and a lot of the property on that high country went broke and James Atkinson moved in then and with three of his sons they bought up big stretches of land' in the upper reaches of Herbert and Burdekin rivers. By the 1920s their territory stretched for around 150 kilometres from Gunnawarra in the north across Cashmere (Glen Ruth), Wairuna, and Oak Hills to Wyandotte, Greenvale, and Camel Creek in the south. (What an outback poetry is hidden in the names of these first stations!) Altogether, the territory of the Atkinson empire was around 13,000 km², which nearly equals the territory of Northern Ireland. Gunnawarra with several outstations occupied over 3000 km². 'I always wondered where they got the money to buy all that', says Bim. 'Gunnawarra, Cashmere and Wairuna are probably three of the best properties in all Queensland, having the reputation of being the safest areas for grazing'.[21]

Thomas Atkinson (1869–1930), the owner of Gunnawarra, is still remembered by the local Aborigines as 'a strict but fair man'. According to Delphia, his daughter-in-law, 'He was a superb horseman, and although they bought a car in 1917, his wife always drove it, she maintained the engine, and he was never very interested in mechanics. Everybody thought very highly of him. He was considered a very good farmer and a very good neighbour to people.' In spite the immense social and wealth gap between the station owner and the labourers, particularly stockmen, their relations were quite different from those that Leandro knew about from Russia. Recently, I asked Delphia and Bim

Atkinson about this. They looked for the right words to explain to me, an outsider, this specific type of relationship and suddenly Bim found the words: 'They worked together. A stockman had a fairly difficult job and was pretty highly respected.'[22]

However hard the life was, Leandro appreciated this relationship. He also observed keenly the attitudes to the Aborigines on the station. The name itself — Gunnawarra — meant 'little home'. It was the place of yearly inter-tribal gatherings for corroborees and hunting. Thomas Atkinson's son Geoffrey said that the corroborees were still held in the 1920s. 'And then the police came and collected them all up and took them to Palm Island.' Gunnawarra's area was at the junction of the territory of several neighbouring tribes — Warungu, possibly Keramai, Djirbalngan (relatives of Ngadjon) and Ngaygungu. The attitudes towards the local Aborigines in Gunnawarra were quite patriarchal: they were well-fed, living around the main homestead, being part of this 'working together' world. Gunnawarra homestead, a tasteful piece of early colonial architecture, erected in 1878, had the aura of the 'good old days'. The station was also famous for its annual Gunnawarra Picnic Races and dances, which attracted whites and Aborigines from the whole area. Before the Aborigines were expelled to Palm Island, they used to hold a big corroboree during the races.[23] Kitty and her children felt themselves at ease in this community. But, even here, Leandro realised that the future of his children, as that of all Aborigines around, would depend on mere luck — on whether they could find 'the strict but fair master' like Thomas Atkinson or not.

Leandro was still in Gunnawarra when, in September 1918, he received a letter from his father asking him to come to Butchers Creek. It was a long way but he did not hesitate for a second. He had never seen his father so agitated. The details of the execution of the czar and his family by the bolsheviks had just reached the Queensland newspapers and Nicholas wanted Leandro to translate a letter he had written to the editor of the *Cairns Post*:

'THERE ARE MOMENTS IN PEOPLE'S LIVES WHEN INDIGNATION OVERPOWERS everything else in their souls. I am in such a condition. ... I always was an enemy of monarchy, such as existed in Russia, in Czar Nicholas' time, and that of his predecessors. I was all for the democratisation of the country and people's liberty. I hated those privileged classes that killed and tortured the blossom of the Russian people, the people who asked for liberty and reforms. ... I was a bitter enemy of Czarism, of a Czar, but not of Nicholas. This can be proved by my book of verses 'Pesny Zemly' (The Songs of the Earth).'

Whom had he tried to persuade in Cairns, who knew his book there — who besides himself? And who, if not his own guilty conscience, might reproach him, for, on nearly every page of *The Songs of the Earth*, written during the reign of Nicholas II, he accused the 'czar-criminal' who 'has destroyed a million honest people'; he predicted that 'the executioner's block' for the 'crowned butcher' would soon be erected in front of his palace, and he called to the Russian people in the epic style:

> You wake up, my people, remember the past,
> Straighten those shoulders of yours, shoulders valiant,
> Burn the tyrant up with his whole nest,
> Around you cast the blackened fire-brands,
> And let the ashes spread on the open field!

Now that his prediction had come true Nicholas shuddered. It was not what he really wanted. When he wrote his poems in Corcovado, he believed that liberated people would build 'a temple of equality and toil' under 'the star of freedom'.[24] But it turned out that 'the bloody terror' used to drive away the tyrants had snowballed, producing further 'bloody terror'. And was it not he who had awakened the Russian people to those atrocities! He turned this thought away, but it returned again and again. Involuntarily, he betrayed its presence in his letter to the paper. He childishly believed that if he said that something did not exist, it would not. He was losing his moral battle with himself. It turned out that he was unable to repent; he could only try to dissociate himself from what was happening now in Russia: the more he wrote, the more he was persuaded that all he had wanted was true democracy and that what was happening now came as if from outside.

'THE MURDER OF THE CZAR, who had abdicated and retired from political life ... is a very characteristic action to show what a mob of criminals and ignorant wrong-doers is ruling Russia at the present time. ... It is necessary to speak about the Jewish politics, introduced by Trotsky, where all the interests of the mother country are forgotten. ... The democracy, which appreciates and honours its reputation should separate themselves from the Bolsheviks. Let the dirty spot of the murders remain on them alone.'[25]

He was separating himself from the bolsheviks — 'a mob of criminals and ignorant wrong-doers'. He did not want to believe that they emerged from the Russian working-people whom he adored all his life.

Soon Nicholas's letter was published in the *Cairns Post* but his guilty conscience was not appeased and a few months later, in March 1919, he called for Leandro again and they wrote a new, long letter 'A Russian on Bolshevism', which was signed with Leandro's name alone. Of the bolshevik bosses he wrote, 'nothing will stop them, [neither] destruction, nor heaps of dead bodies. But are they sure that when they reach their goal they will make humanity happy?'; and, prophetically, he predicted that they:

'MUST DIVIDE HUMANITY INTO TWO GROUPS, GOOD AND BAD. In the first group they must include all their own, in the second all not agreeable with Bolshevism. ... [But] what if amongst the former there will be more hypocrites, cheeky abusers and perhaps, what is worse, egoists and unscrupulous self-seekers? I think in which ever party such people will find themselves they will grab the opportunity to direct things in the country. Will their main aim be the interest of the proletarians? [It] can hardly be doubted that there is no smaller percentage of individuals with doubtful morals amongst the proletarians than amongst the 'bourgeoisie', and more ignorant and therefore slaves of animal instincts.'

This was the first time that the Illins admitted that working-people — that sacred cow of Russian revolutionary philosophy — might have more vices than the 'bourgeoisie', which respects the laws. Probably, the Illins' acquaintance with Australia and, particularly with the world of the Atkinsons' cattle station, persuaded them of the values that the bourgeoisie did possess. As for Nicholas, this letter was the admission that his Patagonian reflections about Russia's destiny had been refuted by events.

Years later, when accused of communist sympathies, Leandro would recount the toll of the losses that their family experienced in the aftermath of the revolution: 'Bolsheviks have destroyed three aunties, two cousins, two nieces, a sister, a brother-in-law and two uncles'. For the moment, though, in 1919, he was worried most about the fate of his nieces Valia and Tonia who — if still alive — might have experienced the worst humiliation from the new rulers of Russia. He threw down an open challenge to the local Australian communist supporters: 'You drunken Bolsheviks of this country with your bellies full of beer, have you ever thought of such sorrows? ... God help you so-called Bolsheviks when you have the taste of the rule you want.' He would not be himself if he did not add a postscript: 'I said "drunken Bolsheviks" because I always met them that way. It may be a coincidence, though.' The gap was growing between the Illins and the majority of the Australian Russians, who sympathised with the revolution. After Nicholas's public denunciation of bolshevik atrocities, his former 'spiritual son' — the radical Zuzenko — mocked him as the 'counter-revolutionary Illin' in the Christmas performance of 1918 in the Russian Association in Brisbane.

Nicholas believed that the communist system would fall in the next fifty years, predicting that 'Bolshevism before it is destroyed will serve a great service to the most extreme reaction'.[26] The suspicion and hatred of Russians grew around them. 'I have heard many saying I am not a Russian but I am a Bolshevik', wrote Leandro. All Russians were considered now to be bolsheviks. Australians sent the following proposals to newspapers: 'Immediate internment of all Russians ..., naturalised or unnaturalised, who have not been resident in Australia over six years. ... Immediate disfranchisement of all Russians ... who have not been resident in Australia for a period of at least ten years etc'.[27] The hardworking Russian inhabitants of Little Siberia discovered that they were aliens on the land to which they had given all their strength and love.

The Illins themselves did not see their adopted country through rose-coloured glasses any longer. When Leandro read in a local paper that the Lands Department was advertising two portions in Gadgarra for soldiers 'with an honourable discharge', it made him feel indignant. The point was that since 1910 these portions had been selected and abandoned several times as they were practically inaccessible. Leandro reproached the authorities:

'DO NOT MEN WHO FOUGHT FOR US DESERVE A BETTER PRIZE than the leavings of selected land? ... To ask a disabled man to go and put in five years' residence on a block of land where he has to chop trees ten and twelve feet in diameter and sometimes more. Fancy the idea! ... Surely the Minister for Lands does not know what rubbish he offers to the soldiers. But a bit of common sense should dictate to him that if land in a settled district like Peeramon, five miles from rail, and being opened for selection since 1910, is not settled on, there is something wrong about it.'[28]

He still believed in officials at the top, but this faith was soon to vanish.

The Illins gradually came to realise that Australia was not a working-men's paradise. Nine years of honest, hard toil on their farms did not bring them prosperity; they could hardly make ends meet and pay off the debts to the banks. Romelio would later say that he just wasted nine years of his life in Australia. They all felt an urge to change the state of things. And the decision was made — return to Latin America. There were practical considerations for this: with the money that they could get for their farms they could buy a ranch there and probably would do better financially. There were other reasons as well. Nine years in Australia did not make Romelio and Ariadna feel at home, their home was in the land of their youth — in Latin America. And for Romelio there was one more reason. He was courting young Olga Gadaloff, but when he came to ask her step-father Michael Gadaloff for her hand, Michael refused, saying half-jokingly, half-seriously, that he did not want to have bow-legged children, meaning that Romelio's legs were far from perfect. That was the final blow for him. He did not want to marry an Aboriginal woman and repeat Leandro's troubles.[29] He knew how Leandro worried about the future of his children — in Australia they would always be second-class citizens.

But the main reason was Nicholas. Thoughts of Russia were burning him. He could not deceive himself any longer — the dissociation from bolsheviks which he expressed in the *Cairns Post* was not enough to expiate the mistakes of his generation; their 'noble ideas' had bred the new rulers of Russia, whose aspiration for power was camouflaged in the sacred words 'peace, liberty, equality'. He was powerless to change the situation in Russia but he could help the victims, those who fled the country as the civil war there gained momentum. A Russian colony, a new Russian colony, far away from Russia would be the remedy. They had experienced failure with the Russian colony in Australia, but in any case Australia with its xenophobic attitude to Russians was not now an appropriate place for his project. Land, spacious virgin land awaited them in Latin America. A hundred, a thousand, no, ten thousand Russian refugee families would make a home there and he, with his knowledge of the languages and the local conditions, would organise this project. He knew that it would be hard but his moral choices were always at the extreme edge, beyond the limits of Philistine commonsense.

When Leandro told Kitty about these plans, she agreed to follow him. After they left the Tablelands it was all the same to her where she lived, at G.W. Swamp or in South America her husband and children were all that she had. But the Australian authorities had a different opinion. Leandro wrote to the Home Secretary.

27–4–19
G.W.Gunnawarra
Mt Garnet N.Q.

The Honorable the
Home Secretary
Brisbane. Home Dept.

Sir,

You may pardon me for troubling you but I do not know of any other way to get out of my trouble. ... I have married an aboriginal woman some years ago and I have four children to her, one girl and three boys. As my children are growing I can see them being despised and looked down by many people and I am afraid that later having always this feeling about them they will degrade in to worse conditions. They are better than blacks and not worse than many of the whites yet they never will be able to associate themselves with whites. ...

Now it amounts to this: I have a father, mother, brother and sister. We all were brought up in South America, Argentine, and lived there for seventeen years. I know the conditions of life there better than here and made always a living easier than here. ... The people there are of colour all and everyone, so the dark blood in my children would be no objection to the people there.

All my people are also going and between the lot of us we are going to buy a ranch. We did no good here. We brought more money here than we are taking away and we lost nine years. Also we have relatives in America. Here I am working now at £2–0–0 a week and found as a working manager of an outstation for Mr T.J. Atkinson and my prospects are not great. If I happen to break my neck some day, there will be nobody to look after my children as all my relatives are going away. And of course I do not want the police protection for them. We all know what it is.

It would also be great sorrow for my father and my mother to see me stop behind (they are 70 and 59 years of age respectively). ...

What I want to know [is] if I can take my wife and children out of the country. I see there is restriction in the Protection Act. Does it apply to a married woman to a white man and his and her halfcast children? I am going this time direct to you as before when I wrote a letter to the Chief Protector he even did not answer to me but simply used the police and nearly made me a criminal. I was advised to not to write to you as I am told I would only bring trouble to myself and never get out of the country as everybody says there is a lot of red tape on the Government Offices. Yet I can not see it, and I appeal to the human feelings of which the Ministers are not deprived if I take for example the Hon. W. N. Gillies and the late Hon. D. Bowman.

Hoping I am not trespassing on your kindness. I am sir yours faithfully
Leandro Illin.

Human feelings towards Russians and Aborigines were not customary in government offices. The 'Honorable the Home Secretary' did exactly what Leandro feared — handed the letter over to the Chief Protector of Aboriginals, who was still J.W. Bleakley. He took out the old file. Well, he had lost the battle in 1915 but now he was determined to take revenge. This time he had a trump card — Kitty's full-blood children. After investigation through the local police, he wrote to the under-secretary in the Home Department on 22 October 1919.

Sir,

I submit for your perusal a request by a Russian, Leandro Illin, married to a full-blood aboriginal woman, for permission to take his wife and children to South America.

The wife has three full-blood children — 11, 9 & 7 years of age, by a previous marriage and four halfcaste children — 5, 3, 2 years and 5 months old, by Illin.

Illin was allowed to marry this woman, in 1915, by the late Hon. D. Bowman, although I had previously refused him permission, as this office is opposed to the marriage of fullblood women to white men, especially where, as in this case, the woman has three young fullblood children.

This man Illin is an erratic character and has for many years lived amongst, and made use of, the blacks for his own purposes.

I cannot regard his present request with anything but suspicion, and even though he may be legally entitled to take his wife and his own children out of the country, I am of opinion he should not be allowed to take the three older fullblood children. In another and less civilised country, three full-blood children would be valuable to Illin as labour and be doubtless nothing better than slaves.

As the woman herself wishes to go with him I cannot see that we can reasonably prevent her though I do not like the proposal.

If she and the halfcaste children are allowed to go, I consider the fullbloods should be sent to a reserve.
I would be glad of your advice.

> *Yours obediently,*
> *J. W. Bleakley*
> <u>*Chief Protector of Aboriginals.*</u>

The 'advice' from the Home Department immediately followed: 'Do not approve of the full-blooded children being taken out of the country. He may have the others. 27.10.19.' At that moment the 'erratic' Russian, whose only purpose, according to Bleakley, was to turn his Aboriginal step-children into slaves in a 'less civilised country', was writing a new appeal from Mt Garnet on 30 October 1919 to the Home Secretary.

> *... It is a matter of importance to me to know if I can now or later leave a country where my children will be <u>protected</u>? by the police. I am worrying over it. I love my children and am sorry for their future. I do not want to see them grow up and then be bullied by some policeman to be signed in to where they do not want to go. I am not in a hurry to leave while they are small but certainly I do not want them to remain here when they are grown up under the protection . . . . . .*

Finally, six months after his initial appeal, Leandro received an answer from the Chief Protector of Aboriginals:

> *24th November, [19]19.*

Sir,
Your request to be allowed to take your wife and children out of the country has been submitted to the Hon. the Home Secretary who has decided that no objection will be raised to your taking your wife and your own halfcaste children with you but on no condition will any of the fullblooded aboriginal children be allowed to leave the country.

A second copy of the letter was sent to the Mt Garnet Protector of Aboriginals with Bleakley's request to keep the movements of the family under surveillance. In the following months he did not forget to remind the local Protector to provide the results of the surveillance. The task was so disgusting that finally the local Protector, sergeant Hoey, wrote back:

> 8/4/20. ... Mr Illin seems very straight in all his dealings and I do not think that there is the slightest chance of him trying to do anything in the way of leaving Queensland and taking his family with him without first obtaining your permission.

Leandro, after the police visits, wrote a new letter to the Home Secretary.

18–5–20
Spring Gully
Mt Garnet
N.Q.

The Hon the Home Secretary
Home Department
Brisbane. Queensland

Sir,
   ... I received reply from the Chief Protector of Aboriginals that I would not get any obstacles to take my wife and my halfcast children but under no consideration I would be allowed to take the full blooded child. I only wanted to take one boy George who is too small to be parted from his mother. Well, Sir, that permit is no good to me for the time being as I do not hold with the policy of parting a small child with its mother. Therefore I am forced to stay and wait until the boy gets big enough to look after himself. ...
   Therefore I kindly ask you not to take it as settled that I am going to stay here but to make your decision stand good until such time as I am able to leave without grieving the child and his mother.

You will oblige yours faithfully
   Leandro Illin[30]

* * *

Leandro lost the legal battle but still he won a moral victory over Australian self-satisfied 'democracy'. On one side of the scales was 'a tear' of the black boy; on the other there was the future of his own children, his family, his elderly parents, and, who knows, the destiny of the new Russian colony for his suffering countrymen. The tear outweighed all the rest. The Russian writer Fedor Dostoevsky had already pondered over this dilemma — a child's tear versus the happiness of mankind — years before. Many of his readers agreed that the tears of a child were of utmost importance, yet only a few followed this belief in practical life. Leandro, the son of a Russian idealist, took on the hard task of following this advice literally. Years later he would write: 'Matters of principle are not trivial. Men die to uphold their principle.'[31]

There were principles and there was love. How indeed could he deliver a new blow to Kitty by separating her from Ginger, his devoted Kitty, who had just lost her ten-year-old Molly, a charming, boisterous tomboy. During a visit to Butchers Creek Molly was playing with Hector on a tree in *Deda*'s yard when a branch broke and she fell down, breaking her spine, fatally injured. She was buried there, near the Bartle Frere ...

Still, life went on. In March 1919 Leandro finally sold his farm at Gadgarra, to John Walker from Peeramon for £809. At the end of that year he took a selection of his own in Spring Gully, 6 miles from Mt Garnet. In August 1920 Romelio sold his farm to Alfred Wilson for £1767; in November 1920 Nicholas and Alexandra sold their farm to E.A. Brake and G.H. Williams for £1572.[32] Ariadna and Jack Mackay had been ready to go long before. Their second child, a daughter called Olga, was born in May 1918 and by now she was old enough to travel. The Illins came to Spring Gully to say farewell to Leandro, first Romelio and Hector, who drove some cattle over to him that they could not sell. Then Nellie and Alexandra came by train.

And finally Nicholas came. Leandro met him at the railway station in Mt Garnet. Nicholas brought some of his writings, old letters and photographs, his medical books and their family icon, St Peter and St Paul. It was a hot December day. They were sitting on the slope of the gully not far from Leandro's hut. The air was balmy with the scent of gum-trees, their stunted trunks seemed to dance in the hot air. Cicadas' chirring mixed with children's shouts — they were digging the sandy bottom of the gully to obtain the underground water. Leandro did not lose heart, he persuaded his father that in a few years he and his family would join them in America. But Nicholas knew that he was parting with his son forever. Kitty sat quietly beside them, fearing to look at Nicholas. She felt all that grief was her fault, and all because of her Ginger ... Nicholas understood this and tenderly smiled at her. He had come here to part with her, too. He wanted to see her. She was a mystery for him, she who had opened herself only to his son. Now, she was the only one to protect him. Maybe to protect him from himself. No, Kitty was not guilty by any means. He was the only one to blame, the father. Years earlier, in Patagonia, after Leandro had done everything possible and impossible to release him from prison, he wrote a poem 'Father and Son' that now turned out to be prophetic.

I fear, Son, that you may choose
The road that has been my ruin,
It leads to misery and grief
Enslaves you to a futile dream.

And now my mind reveals to me
That I have sown in your heart
A grain of the eternal pain
And ruined your youthful strength ...

With fatal and imperious hand
I poisoned your still growing mind,
I poured venom, drop by drop,
Not realising how far it goes ...

All wicked passions, all thirst for fame
Are not so harmful as my vice.
My venom was the search for right
And for the universal truth ...

And it will bring you to reject
All worldly joys, bring morbid thoughts,
And ruined strength and dashed hopes,
And to the grave, untimely to the grave ...

Leandro looked around. Now Ginger, Dick and Tom were running up and down the road, bowling a wheel; Flora and Emma were making a house for the doll. He remembered how Flora hugged the doll when he brought it back not long ago from Tumoulin. It was her first doll. A breeze brought the smell of a roast from the camp oven near their hut.

Well, it was not the end of life. And, most important of all, he would not hesitate for a minute to sign his own name under the words of the son from his father's poem.

> My honest Father, you alone
> Bestowed on me this noble lot.
> It makes me free among the slaves,
> Outspoken towards the false.

> I choose this thorny path of yours,
> Like you, with an open heart to good,
> Like you, with a pure soul of love,
> In admiration of the daring dream you taught ...

> All my life-long I shall await
> The day when our dreams come true.
> And when I pass away in peace
> My children follow me and you.

> Don't hesitate, my loving friend,
> To bless me on this thorny path
> Your smile serene, feeling no pain,
> With words of truth and love.[33]

... And his Father blessed him. They never saw each other again.

TWO WAYS

The flicker of the camp-fire illuminated from time to time the dark wall of jungle around their camp. It was Nicholas's turn to guard the sleep of their small party. He sat by the fire with a rifle across his legs, listening to the night sounds. This jungle differed from what they had grown used to on the Tablelands, where leeches were the main enemy. Now, the invisible danger was watching from behind the dark wall of the trees. It was everywhere. This track, the only one connecting Comayagua, lost up in the mountains, with the shore, was one of the most dangerous. Many travellers had been murdered here by banditti hiding in the jungle. Honduras, the Promised Land where he planned to settle Russian refugees from the revolution, turned out to be ruled by only one law, that of the rifle. And now he held it ready to protect his reduced family: Alexandra, Romelio — the only one of his eight children to stay with him to the end — and Hector and Nellie.

Hector and Nellie — it was their turn to receive his gift, the gift of the real world full of adventures, danger and aspirations. He had been deprived of it in his younger years and for the rest of his life could not slake his thirst for it. Indeed, there were many reasons to leave Australia, but that one — the unslaked thirst for the world — he could share now only with Nellie and Hector. He pulled them out of the narrow-minded mire of Australian materialism. They were to find the new Promised Land with him. Never mind that they had had no luck in all these months, their El Dorado lay ahead, behind these wild ridges and rapid rivers ...

The Illins and the Mackays left the Tablelands in January 1921. Years later Hector told about those times. 'The three-month journey took the family first to New Zealand and then to Panama in a freezer boat, the *Ionic*, which carried beef and rabbit meat.' From Panama they went to Barranquilla in Colombia by a dirty French ship carrying hens, cows and pigs. Here the family split. Nicholas and Alexandra, with Romelio, Hector and Nellie took off to Bogotá, the Colombian capital, hidden up in the Andes, and stayed there for about three months. He thought about taking up land somewhere in Colombia to settle the Russian refugees but when all his family fell sick with malaria it became obvious to him that this country, situated just above the equator, was unsuitable for Russians and he decided to move further north, to Central America. Ariadna, Jack Mackay and their younger children, Sam and Olga, remained in Colombia, where Jack got a job in Pato goldmines. They took one last photo together.

Nicholas and his family returned to Barranquilla, and made their way through the Panama Canal to Amapala Port on the Pacific coast of Honduras. They headed to Tegucigalpa, the capital, in a Buick car, sending on their baggage in a truck. 'We stayed there a short time', Nellie relates. 'My grandfather tried to get land to bring the Russians there to Mosquitia.' Mosquitia was swampy lowland on the eastern coast of Honduras sparsely populated by Paya and Mosquito Indians, and notorious for its fever. Finally, he had to give up this plan, too, and decided to try his luck in the more hospitable fertile valleys of the northern part of the country. The only way there was across the country through the mountain ridges. 'We then went to Comayagua by truck', continues

Nellie, 'and from there by mules and horses, as there weren't any roads or railroads. The trip was a fun trip for my brother and myself, as we rode the horses for about a week.'[34] Alexandra did not find it much fun because of the constant threat of ambush. And now her elderly husband, as before, forty-five years ago on the roads of Turkestan, had to guard them at night. But at least, this time, he had Romelio to take turns.

Nicholas added some wood to the camp-fire and lay down beside it. Suddenly he felt the burden of the years which had passed. His mother, General Kaufman, Leo Tolstoy, Nikolai Ge, Vladimir Korolenko, dozens of his opponents and friends — he was unable to prove anything to them any longer. Most of them had left this world already. Even for those who were still alive — his voice would never reach them from the Honduran wilderness. Now he was a *Deda*, nothing more than an old man venturing on a new, vain dream, a dangerous dreamer who had thrown all that was left of his family into the unknown. And there was no Leandro close by to tell him, as before, 'You are right, Father'. Ten thousand Russian refugees — he was unable to find a place for them. All he could do now was to find a place for himself to die.

He realised that his life was rapidly drawing to an end. He did not fear death. Twenty-five years before he had written:

> And I will die like all the rest. ...
> When the final hour strikes
> It will not matter, hell or paradise.
> I shall feel nothing, so I will not suffer,
> Nor be a slave to false and vain hopes.[35]

Death would be a liberation for him now, a liberation from himself, from his restless nature which had led him so many times astray. Many years ago, in Patagonia, he had written an obscure poem, which had nothing to do with his usual revolutionary poetry. It was titled 'From the depths of gloom'. Symbolically, he was to confront his final depth here, in Honduras, which means 'depths' in Spanish.

> In the stuffy casemate
> Under the pressing vault
> In the dark and dampness
> I'm confined and bound.

My heart asks for freedom,
My mind asks for scope;
But to breathe in freely
I have no hope!

I have built the prison;
I have sealed the exit;
I have blocked the sunlight
And myself have ruined ...

Have courage, my heart,
Have patience, my soul,
Freedom awaits
In a funeral mound.[36]

Yes, it was about himself. He was the captive in the prison of his passions.

Well, this wild country was the place where he would die — or, rather, the place where he would live on in his descendants. They would live here, they would become a part of this land, of its people. They would mix with the Hondurans, the dark-complexioned, simple *ladinos*. The blood of Spaniards and Indians was running in their veins. They were the descendants of the tribes of Lenca, Jicaques, and of the mysterious Maya, whose huge temples, in ruins, were hidden somewhere in these mountains. This remote land discovered by Christopher Columbus in 1502 had awakened his imagination in Ilinka all those years before, but even in his wilder fantasies he never dreamt that the day would come when he brought to the mercy of its ancient gods his most treasured possession — his own family.

Several days later they reached the Ulúa River. The sea was gleaming far ahead of them to the north. Below them stretched the green valley where the Ulúa flowed, with its sister the Chamelecón. On the other bank of Chamelecón, at the foot of the dark-green mountains, there was the small town of San Pedro Sula. They liked it, but Nicholas was not ready to give up and to settle yet. His unquenchable thirst for the world called him forth once again and he took his family on a final, desperate journey, all the way to New Orleans, in the United States of America. But they were not permitted to stay there without entry visas, and had to return to San Pedro Sula. They bought land there and had a house built. 'He showed us how to plant vegetables and flowers', relates Nellie. It was his fourth garden. His previous gardens were left behind in Ilinka, in Tashkent, and on the Atherton Tablelands; they were still flowering over there somewhere, but it was not his destiny to gather their fruits.

In 1922, six months after settling in San Pedro Sula, he was dying in his last green valley. Love and repentance filled his soul — towards his family and towards his motherland. About his love for his family, Nellie, the last one who remembers these days, said: '*Deda* was a very patient man and showed us much love, as my *Baba* did also. They both were just very, very nice people, very gentle, very sweet.'[37] About his love for the motherland, Nicholas himself said in his poem 'Confession':

> Forgive my sins, my motherland,
> As I repent committing them.
> I've paid for them all through my life —
> A hunted wolf that's doomed to die.
>
> Forgive, because in exile's vale
> I've learnt the worth of hard work and pain.
> My nobleman's hands are coarsened now
> And remain like that until I die.
>
> Not recompense, my motherland,
> To whom I'm tied by spiritual bonds,
> But mercy is all I ask of you:
> To pardon all my sins and take pity on me.[38]

The exact date of his death is forgotten and his grave in the San Pedro Sula cemetery was lost. But the time for forgiveness has come at last.

* * *

As Nicholas was making his final way, leading his family to the wide world, Leandro, his alter ego, started on his own way in the opposite direction, deeper and deeper into the Australian outback. While all Nicholas's life seems to have been a tortuous road to himself, although travelled in the name of people, Leandro's road — the one that from now on he had to take alone — was not just in the name of people but towards the people. Much still remains mysterious about it.

Nobody knows what happened to the money (£809) Leandro received after selling his farm in Butchers Creek. In those years it was a considerable capital sum: wages on the stations were between £50 and £100 a year. Yet the life-style of his family indicates that he never used this money. It is highly likely Leandro gave most of it to his father, who, for his last project to help Russians, needed capital more than Leandro. If this was so, Kitty would have accepted it — to share things is an essential part of the philosophy of her people. She would often tell her children a story about the greedy boy. Flora is the only one now to remember it.

'THERE WAS ONE BOY AND HE GOT A LOT OF WITCHETTY GRUBS. When he got a lot of witchetty grubs he took them into the camp and he cooked them all up and never shared the thing around the tribe. He ate all the witchetty grubs, so after he ate them he got all the fat from the witchetty grubs came up into his throat, so it was burning him right up into the throat, and to cool it off he ran down to the creek and drank the cold water. He drank a lot of cold water and when he walked out on the bank of the creek he turned into a stone. There must be a stone looking like a human being somewhere there on the Tablelands.'

'That's a good story, I can remember it always', adds Flora. 'The story is based on being mean and greedy, so it's told to children to share, not to be greedy. Because when they lived there in the tribe no matter what they cooked, how big or how little they got things, it must be shared in the tribe. And I put it down to that now, only since I've got older I realised what the story is based on, but when Mother told it to me, oh, I always thought about it, "funny, turned into a stone".'[39]

At the end of 1919 Leandro ceased his employment with the Atkinsons and took a perpetual lease selection 6 miles southeast of Mt Garnet with an annual rent of £5 7s 3d. The selection occupied 476 acres at the junction of Nanyeta and Spring creeks on the road from Mt Garnet to Gunnawarra. It was easy, undulating forestland with sandy soil covered by rough kangaroo and blady grasses. The forest consisted of stunted bloodwood, box, ironbark, tea-tree and occasionally cypress pine. The forest's only use was as cattle fodder. In dry months Leandro could water his stock by sinking a bore about 3 feet in the creek-bed. Flora tells about their life there.

'FATHER HAD A BIT OF A SELECTION THERE. We had goats and a few cows that Romelio couldn't sell and he brought them there. It was very dry and bare land. We had a hut built near the Spring Creek because there was water there. It was just a few corrugated irons put together up on the top and around the side. Just to stop the rain and the wind coming on to you. There was ground floor there. You make a place so you can keep your fire burning. That's all it was. It wasn't easy, no, it wasn't easy. But we were used to it.'[40]

And life went on. While Nicholas was leading his party through the Honduran jungles searching for a place for a new Russian colony, Leandro brought to their hut a drunk whom he met in a pub in Mt Garnet. The man used to work on some local stations before he took to the bottle. Leandro took him in hand and promised to cure him. He reduced the amount of spirits gradually while Kitty fed him with hot food, especially soups. And the man recovered and was grateful to Leandro for the rest of his life.[41]

The children were growing. Flora by the age of five could ride a horse. She still remembers going to the hotel in Mt Garnet to play with the children of the owner, who had six daughters. The boys were real boys. Glenda, Dick's daughter, has told me some stories that she heard from him.

'MY DAD, DICK, WAS SORT OF THE ELDEST. Sometimes grandad would take Ginger with him when he would go away working and my dad would be there at the house all the time helping grandma with all the other kids. He'd be the one like the man of the house. Oh, it must have been in Mt Garnet when uncle Ginger had his finger cut off. They had a wheel, wooden wheel. And uncle Ginger and uncle Tommy were playing with it all the time rolling it around and grandma kept saying, calling out to them to come and do something and they wouldn't. So dad volunteered to go and chop the wheel up. He said, "I'll go and get the axe, mummy, and chop the wheel". She says, "Well, right oh", and he goes over and as soon as he put the axe up uncle Ginger's hand went on it and off went his finger. Chopped his finger off!

'Another time when grandad wasn't around the boys took the branding iron. They helped grandad with branding cattle before. The branding iron grandad had was a cross and L and I. They put it on the fire. And they branded uncle Ginger on the bum, on the rump!'[42]

Here, in Spring Gully, in March 1922 their youngest daughter was born. Leandro named her Vera Araluen. Vera is an old Russian name which means 'faith'. This name was dear to Leandro; it was also the name of his sister who died as an infant in Russia. Although Leandro's descendants did not know the Russian meaning of this name, nor how it sounded in Russian, they have preserved it in their children: Dick's youngest daughter, Vera Ketchell, has this name too.

The baby's second name, Araluen, was a rare and beautiful name. Flora relates: 'People used to say to my father, "Where did you get the name Araluen?" He said, "You don't know, this is your own Australian. Don't you know there's a town Araluen in Australia." That is Aboriginal name of pretty wild flowers.' Vera Araluen's daughter Nola knows that it meant 'place of water lilies'.[43] But the location of the town of this name remained obscure.

The name Araluen seemed familiar to me but I could not recollect when I had heard it. After my family and I returned to Canberra from Townsville, our friend Keith McCombie took us for a drive to explore a desolate area to the east of Canberra. We visited ghost towns — Hoskinstown and Captains Flat. Then the road took us to Majors Creek, which seemed to preserve a lot of features of the turbulent times of the goldrush. And suddenly I saw a road sign 'Araluen'. The track to it led through the dense forest covering a mountainous slope. From a lookout we saw the Araluen valley down below. Surrounded by blue-grey misty hills, in the soft light of this spring evening the valley seemed the most beautiful place. Soon we descended to its pink, blossoming peach orchards scattered along Araluen Creek, overshadowed by casuarinas. And standing there I realised that this was the river of my childhood dreams stirred up by a poem by Henry Kendall that I had first learnt in Russian translation.

Araluen

River, myrtle-rimmed, and set
Deep amongst unfooted dells —
Daughter of grey hills of wet,
Born by mossed and yellow wells —

Now that soft September lays
Tender hands on thee and thine,
Let me think of blue-eyed days,
Star-like flowers, and leaves of shine!

Cities soil the life with rust:
Water-banks are cool and sweet:
River, tired of noise and dust
Here I come to rest my feet.

The township of Araluen grew up after gold was discovered there in 1851. It became home to the Australian poets Charles Harpur and Henry Kendall and the novelist Rolf Boldrewood. Araluen, which derives from Aboriginal words *arr-a l-yin*, meaning 'place of water lilies', is a landmark in the Australian poetic landscape. This is one of the first locations where immigrants brought up in the English aesthetic traditions felt an attraction to the Australian scenery, which differed so much from their native English countryside. Symbolising this new union, Henry Kendall named his daughter Araluen.[44]

So did Leandro. Araluen — it was an expression of allegiance to his adopted country. But it was more than that. Although Kitty could not give her daughter a Ngadjon Aboriginal name — spirits of her land were far away — she and he proudly declared the Aboriginality of their child in this new way. Araluen was a symbol, it was a dream of Aboriginality, which would not be confined by the boundaries of tribes, and it was a symbol of the emerging Australian nation absorbing different cultures, and devoting itself to the new country. A bizarre dream for the 1920s!

When I was leaving Townsville, in 1996, Flora's grandson Richard came to say goodbye with his young daughter. This fair-skinned, pretty girl with curly hair and bright eyes had the name Araluen. She was an Australian inheriting the cultures of the tribes of Ngadjon, Gugu-Badhun and Kalkadoon as well as those of her Russian, Polish, Irish and English ancestors. Kitty and Leandro's dream did come true. Their descendants pass this name from generation to generation. Dick's and Harry's granddaughters have this name, too.

Vera Araluen, born on a hot March day on the banks of Spring Creek, justified the dual nature of her name. She was the only one of Leandro's children who chose to be baptised in the Russian Orthodox Church, which she did when she was eighteen; as well, according to relatives, she was 'one of the most Aboriginal' among her brothers and sisters, her house in Ingham was open to 'all murries' of whatever tribe.[45] But that will be years later; meanwhile, the little girl was simply called Lullie.

Leandro always knew that their corrugated-iron hut near Spring Creek was only a temporary stop on his way. From here he planned to go to Honduras but after his father's death he gave up this plan. From now on he belonged totally to Australia. And again he realised that the time had come for a change. The children were growing up but, instead of attempting to enrol them in school in Mt Garnet, Leandro surrendered his selection in 1922 and began his way deeper into the outback. We do not know why. There were no real job prospects for him — just bailing water, shooting dingoes, fixing fences and driving cattle. Still he chose this way.

They were leaving in a buggy drawn by horses. For the last time they went down the gully in front of their hut where the children had spent so many happy hours playing, where they had parted with Nicholas and Alexandra forever. The horses slowly pulled up the slope and started their way along the dusty red road. Leandro rode ahead. He was leaving the place for good but he left there something very important — his name. That nameless, dry gully hidden among gum trees and boxwood, which filled with water only after heavy rains, had acquired his name — Illin's Gully.

This name does not exist on the maps, there are no signboards along the road with this name. Instead, the maps show two Spring Creeks joining each other not far from the place where Leandro's hut stood. But Frank Gertz, husband of Leandro's granddaughter Margaret, who knows the locality intimately, says, 'This gully was known under those two names — Illin's Gully and Spring Creek. Because people respected the Illins, they knew that they lived here years ago and they referred to it as Illin's Gully.' Indeed, this name does still exist. Bim, grandson of Thomas Atkinson, head of the Gunnawarra station, pointed to the right Spring Creek on the map and told me: 'That is Illin's Gully actually, they got it wrong. It flows down into Spring Creek. Illin's Gully is dry most of the year, but it flows a bit under the sand. My father always told that it starts from a spring in the swamp to the west.'[46]

It still flows under the sand. Invisible, the water is always there. But you have to know the concealed nature of Illin's Gully to dig the sandy bottom to obtain its cold water on a hot day. It never stops along its way, first it flows to Spring Creek, then to Return Creek, and finally to Herbert River, which meets the ocean in Ingham. It was there, on Herbert River in Ingham, that Leandro spent the last years of his life. Twenty-five years of his life would pass between the spring and the mouth of this river. And he would always be like this tiny creek lost in the outback — outwardly unsightly but full of life-giving water to slake the thirst of the suffering. Heed the quiet voices of his children and grandchildren and learn where to dig and then Leandro, simple and sophisticated, passionate and kind, would return to our time, to us, from the yellowish pages of newspapers, from his letters to officials and his children, from his communications to the government and through the family tales. Just dig the dry bottom of the creek on a hot day ...

172 Points rain last night
His worst away.
n and Darcy killed
ring running. Del crossed car
ry to the other side of the river
aid for cement
d digging trench. He is hung up
his work for lack of cement!

7 a.m. rain 6 points
Dick Hoolihan gone with drovers plant Camel Creek
DAY One little pig died Del, Ray,
Billy Jackson and Darcy
to cross the river. Seb came back
as there is a fresh in the river
Lunt came here on road from
going to Gainsford. George Riggs came
Lagoon ahead of H. Morgensen
ing to Ingham with bullocks. Morgensen
Willie and Riggs camping
Bullocks in tailing yard.
fixed about road toll with Otter Sing
WEDNESDAY Del, Mrs Jones Mr and Mr
Day left for Ingham. Billy fa
Darcy seen them across the river
gensen and his men left this morn
say that they will arrive J. Feitzel's pla
Mr Reece from Gordo
t to Croydon

BUSH LAWYER AND BUSH LAWS

IN THE BUSH

At Christmas in 1923 they were camped at the junction of the Burdekin River and Porphyry Creek, not far from Greenvale homestead. Flora and her brothers and sister were lying in the tent with measles, which was raging all over Greenvale and nearby stations. A group of Aborigines who came for a holiday visit and were camped not far from them had the first death. The children suffered from the sunshine and heat, which their old tent did not keep out. 'I was nearly blind', recounts Flora, 'and thought I was going to die.' But whenever she opened her eyes she could see her father's face bending over her. 'And he'd stay up half the night looking after us all the time. We could call him any time and he was always there to look after us.' He saved his family this time and many other times.

'WHEN WE WERE KIDS WE NEVER SAW A DOCTOR, ever, until we came to Ingham in 1930', Flora relates. 'Father was very responsible and thoughtful, he never neglected anything. He always carried all sorts of things, must have learned from his father. If we got sick out in the bush, he'd always have Aspros, pain-killer that was, you take it and it would calm you down. There was another thing they used to have — chlorodyne. And I can remember when we used to be sick — you can't sleep when you are sick — Father used to put one or two drops of this chlorodyne in a glass with a bit of hot tea. It would send you off to sleep, and when you'd wake up, you'd feel a lot better. And he used to carry Condy's Crystals in case you get bit with a snake. He had like a kit with all these things for the bush.'[1]

Trying to awaken Flora's memories about these early years, I asked her about the house where they lived. But, unlike my childhood, her world had not been centred on a house. It had revolved instead around water and freedom, work and mateship.

'AS LONG AS THERE WAS WATER SOMEWHERE', recounts Flora, 'on the bank of a creek they could put a camp up, a tent, we'd stop there until maybe a job come up or something. Those days wasn't like today. ... Father liked Australia. He said, "Not like other countries". Today it is like other countries. Not too good. But those days was less people and different ways. Those days people used to work and was always ready to help one another and that's what my father liked about Australia. And he said, "You can live anywhere, you can make your camp anywhere, it wasn't like you had to take land or you were prohibited from living here or there".'[2]

Years later, in the time of panic caused by the threat of Japanese invasion during World War II, when people who were planning to evacuate to the bush came to him for advice, Leandro wrote to the local newspaper:

'I HAVE LIVED IN AUSTRALIA 31 YEARS AND MOST OF THAT TIME IN VERY PRIMITIVE CONDITIONS and have learned from blacks [and] also from white bushmen most of what is to be learnt about 'makeshifts' in the bush. Any man who has an axe can get a good shelter or hut built in two or three days as long as he gets into the right locality to strip some bark and make sheets to roof the humpy and walls. Stringy bark, messmate, all the gum trees, iron bark, box tree etc., most of them will render good bark, but the stringy bark is the king of all. ... The best localities are near the big rivers (not too close to the banks in case of floods) where fish and game can be got. [The] most necessary things are: camp oven, a boiler, knife, steel and a gun, if possible. Beds are [an] encumbrance. Four logs 6in. in diameter put as a frame on the floor and filled with grass makes an excellent bed.'[3]

But let's return to Flora's story.

'MY FATHER GOT A JOB IN GREENVALE and he came to work there in 1922. I was only six-year-old when we landed there. My father worked there for Atkinsons seven years. It was very wild and deserted country, nothing — you see nobody there. We used to go around in the bush. We were living way out in this hot, terrible country, hard living. My father did fencing or bailing water for cattle. In the dry weather when there be no water around they used to dig a well in the river, but the river would be dry — put a trough that holds the water, they'll bail water out of the well into the trough to give to the cattle, that's what he used to do.'

We were travelling along the lonely road towards Greenvale township (which grew up later, after nickel was discovered in the area) when Flora suddenly recognised one of the places of their former camps.

'THAT'S WHERE WE WERE CAMPED ONE TIME IN 1924. There was nothing here, it was just like this, bush. There was a well. Father was bailing water for cattle and we all lived in the tent. We rode around here on horseback. Further up, on Miners Lake, father used to go and shoot some ducks and we'd eat them, it was luxury.

'He was a good bushman and when the work had got slack he'd go kangaroo shooting and getting their hides, and catch dingoes — you get paid for the dingo because they kill the cattle. So, might be a couple of months of the year that he'd be doing that. We went to different parts of Greenvale at that time, and then if a job come up, he'd be employed again, and go and do something around the station.

'My father rode horses too but most of the time he'd be droving. He used to take bullocks with my two brothers and drive them to the slaughter-yard, from Greenvale to Ingham. I was nine-year-old when my father took me with him to Ingham for the first time. There were Ginger, and Dickie, and myself, and him, and another old fellow. It took us about ten days to get down there — you could not drove the cattle too far every day. In Ingham there was hardly anything like houses and stores today. The train line was straight in the middle of the main street.'[4]

Just as Leandro's father had taken him, an eight-year-old boy, to Europe and America to exhibit Nikolai Ge's painting 'What is truth?', now it was Flora's turn. Leandro took Flora on the cattle-trail between Greenvale and Mt Helen, near Ingham, with over a hundred bullocks. The trail was around 170 kilometres of dry, hostile country. One of the poems — Leandro's or his mate's — about such a drive survived among his papers.

Overlander Trail

Waggon wheels are rolling on,
And the day is mighty long,
Clouds of heat-dust in the air,
Bawling cattle everywhere.

There on the overlander, overlander trail,
Where only she[er] determination will prevail,
Men of Aussie with a job to do,
So they'll stick and drive the cattle through.

And though they sweat, and curse, they know they surely must,
Keep on the trail that winds ahead through heat and dust,
Oh, sons of Aussie, and they will not fail
There on the overlander, overlander trail.

Soon the journey will be won
Tired of heat and blazing sun
Lands where friendships never fail
Overlander on the trail.[5]

Unsophisticated as it seems, this poem is a perfect sample of the unique style of Australian folk poetry which was created and performed by ordinary Australians — drovers and swagmen, stockmen and bushmen — and which fostered such talents as Henry Lawson and Banjo Paterson. The forgotten 'sons of Aussie' who wrote it were creating what later became known as 'the Australian legend', not that they realised it in those days — this 'legend' was their everyday, hard life.

Dick, years later, will write: 'My father, brother and I spent seven months from March to September taking cattle from Greenvale to Woolagran and down to Salisbury Plains and back in 1923–1924. My brother and I were not paid. My father received 25 shillings a week'.[6] It was hard this life, but could anything compare with the happiness you feel when your sons are riding beside you, your real mates and helpers, and your slim daughter, proud of her first successful handling of the cattle, flies towards you merging into one with the horse. And somewhere there behind, camped on the banks of Porphyry Creek, your wife is waiting for you with the younger children and one more on the way. And you all feel yourself children of Australia, part of this land, and you can forget for a while that your beautiful children, your pride and love, are labelled by the Aboriginal protectors and police as 'half-castes' and will have to endure a life-long battle defending their human dignity. You are free, at least for now, and happy with that ...

Once, around Christmas 1924, visiting Greenvale homestead with his family, Leandro took a photo of them. Flora, Dick, Harry, Ginger, Kitty, Lullie and Tom, unaccustomed to being photographed yet, they all tensely stared straight into the camera, as if trying to see something invisible to us. In the background are the lattices of the entrance to the manager's house. Seventy-two years later Flora and Harry brought me to the same spot. After several floods the house has partly tumbled down but the lattices were still there. And we took a new photo of Flora and Harry on the same spot.

In Leandro's second photo Kitty was with her dog — a big, half-bred kangaroo dog called Possum. 'We were all kids, we used to sit on its back and ride this dog and he'd carry us around, a big strong dog', remembers Harry.[7] These were the last photos of Kitty.

'AND THEN IN 1925 IT GOT SLACK', Flora continues, 'and we went to Christmas Creek. That's only a cattle station just further down on the Burdekin. We travelled by horse there, camped on the way down there at Thatch Creek, where it runs into Burdekin. There was no road then, just a bit of a bumpy dirty track.'[8]

We repeated this journey in July 1996 with Harry and Flora. The brick-red, bumpy road was still there, as well as numerous termite mounds scattered in dry, grey grass among sparse gum-trees. Rusty gates creaked on the post. All the rest lay in ruins. Flora's and Harry's memories gradually restored the place.

Flora: I can't see anything of the old place. Where is the big house? It crumpled up. That was the house where bosses usually lived and the kitchen was there.

Harry: Wasn't a windmill there?

Flora: That was the tank stand-down there, where they used to pump the water in there. All crumpled up now.

Harry: Oh yes, they had a big water-tank on the top, water flow to kitchen and into shower. There was a yard up the reach here somewhere.

Flora: It must be the old stockyard. There was a little yard and black smith shop here, where they used to shoe the horses, saddle them up there, they had a shed to keep all the saddles. Look, a horse-shoe here!

Harry: There is another one! A big shed was here between the main house and the kitchen, it's been pushed away into a heap there.

Flora: The house we had was somewhere there where that green bush is. A little humpy thing but it was on the ground.

Harry: Over that way from the yard there used to be a silver-leaf iron bark. It used to grow on that ridge there. Apparently they died out.

Flora: The country was more green then. The lagoon down there — it used to be full, there was plenty of water there, always. We used to be swimming over there all the time, over that end, us kids. There were plenty of ducks and geese. We used to go down there and catch perches in the lagoon.

Harry: There was plenty of lilies in the lagoon too. When we were kids we used to get these bulbs of the lilies and eat them.

The lagoon, half-dried up, was still there, and a few water-lilies blossomed in the middle of it as if to prove that seventy years ago, when the Illin kids splashed in its waters, the country was nearly the same, unspoiled, as in 1845, when it was explored by Leichhardt's expedition. Alfred Foot (1846–1925) was one of the first settlers in Christmas Creek, and it was here during World War I that tragic news came of the death of two of his sons at Gallipoli.[9] I did not know about it then but, standing with Flora and Harry among the ruins, we seemed to be enveloped by some sinister and gloomy spirit. And suddenly Harry, as if looking into himself, said quietly:

'THERE WAS A BIG LIGHT ONE NIGHT. BRIGHT LIGHT APPEARED UP THERE. Like moon rising. Do you remember that, Flora, the light that night up there? Just came up out of the grass, come up that high off the ground and it was facing us, it faced us for about two or three minutes, and then it drifted across over there and went bush over the creek that way.'

Was it an omen of the forthcoming tragedy? Soon, very soon they were to lose Kitty here.

Later, Flora told me about that time, too:

'I GREW UP RIDING HORSES. At Christmas Creek someone would saddle the horse for me and send me out into the small paddock to bring the milking cows in. While I would be riding around I used to be crying. That was before mum died. I had some sort of premonition that something bad was going to happen. I did not know what it was, but I felt lonely and sad. Christmas Creek haunted me.'

Flora's and Harry's memories continued to bring those days back again.

Flora: Burdekin from Christmas Creek was only a short way, quarter of a mile. We used to go swimming and fishing bream there, too. My mother used to cook on open fire, just make a fire outside, that's all, to cook. We had a bit of vegetable garden, and they had plenty of fruit on the station when it came on like oranges, there was a lemon tree there, they had fowls, they would kill a bullock and we had meat but they put salt on it and keep it like that, there was no fridges.

Harry: Do you remember the date tree? We used to eat dates.

Flora: Father used to work as stockman here, he did fencing and droving cattle right down to Bowen. For months you could not see anybody here, just lonely. There was a cook there, and a manager to manage the place, couple of men working and some local Aboriginal people. There was only us and them most of the time.

Our next door neighbours were the Cores from Blue Range, six miles away. They had Christmas Creek for a while, but then they sold it out to people named Beak, Robert Beak, and went down to Blue Range. Mrs Mary Core was a nice woman, all her life she rode horses and was working with cattle, she could work and do everything on the station just like a man. She was a very smart old lady in the bush. She liked Aboriginal people, she grew up with them, Mac, her son, did too. We played with Mac as kids, we were swimming in the river together.

Mac still lives in this area. We found him in Mt Full Stop in a beautiful old house on the high bank of the Burdekin. He was happy to see the Illins and memories flowed. Mary Core (1885–1980) was the daughter of one of the pioneers of this area, William McDowall, who 'owned and resold thirteen cattle stations in his lifetime'. Among them were Lake Lucy, Kangaroo Hills, Greenvale, Cashmere, and Christmas Creek. 'He would buy a place, improve it and always sold at a profit.'[10]

'MRS CORE WAS A TOUGH OLD GIRL, BUT SHE WAS KIND TOO', Flora relates, 'she was always looking after somebody, she was kind in her way.

'When my mother was dying in childbirth at Christmas Creek Mrs Core came up there, her and her sister-in-law, and she was with my mother right to the end, she hold my mother's hand when she was dying. Mother was labouring for about two days, a bad labour. It was very hard, there was no doctor to help her. Baby, a boy, was about fifteen pound weight and he was born dead. The afterbirth grew up inside, there was infection, it was blood poisoning, she was dying. Then when the doctor came he give her chloroform. In those days chloroform was a very bad thing. I think the chloroform might have done more than anything and killed her because it was too strong.

'Father would not tell us that she died. He never told us for about a month. He used to tell us that the ambulance took her away to Charters Towers. But I knew that she was dead because I saw this new grave when I rode the horse to bring the cows to milk them. I knew that that was my mother but I never said that to him. Father told us about a month after. But I knew it already. I used to say to Tommy and Harry "Mum is dead, she's not going come back", but I never said to my father that I knew. Because he was telling us she wasn't and I did not want to say, "You are not telling us the truth". I just let him think that I believed him but I didn't, I knew that she was dead.

'My mother had a dog. This dog used always to be there with us, and when my father would go away my mother used to be very frightened, so she used to put the dog underneath the bed. He was a big kangaroo dog. His name was Possum. Just before mum died that night Possum howled and howled, he must have known what was going to happen. Father took me in and show me my dead brother. Everybody in the room said "oh!" when they heard Possum howling. I was frightened too. I kissed my mum good night and went out of the room. I never saw her any more.

'And the next day, after my mum died in this little room, I went to the room to get some clothes out of it for Harry and Tom — they were smaller — to put on clean clothes. And when I went there the dog followed me in. He followed me in and he stopped underneath the bed. And the next day I went to get some clothes and when I opened the door he jumped up and he ran and he was looking at me. And I thought he had a funny look on his face. And I called him, "Possum, Possum", and he just looked at me, he kept on running, and he kept on running. I ran after him. I was nine-year-old, but I knew there was something funny about it. I was singing out to him, "Possum, Possum!" I thought he might come, but he just kept on running in front of me and looking back at me like that and kept on going. He went away and we never saw him after.'[11]

A lonely little girl in a faded dress standing on the riverbank was desperately calling out after the dog, as if it could restore the disintegrating order of things and return her mother. The old ways never came back. And this little girl never returned home either. The one who came back was nearly an adult, wise enough to understand and forgive her honest father the only lie he had to tell to his children, and kind and strong to take care of the youngest — Tommy, Harry and Lullie.

Kitty's death did not pass unnoticed in the area. By the end of July the shockwaves of it reached the *Worker* published in Brisbane. Its editor wrote to the Home Secretary inquiring about 'the case of a black woman who died recently on Christmas Creek station. It is alleged that the woman, who had 6 children, was lying on the ground in a hut for three days in childbirth, and died a few minutes after the ambulance arrived, and it is suggested that there were people on the station who might have been able to give the poor creature some attention.' For two months the police conducted an investigation, interviewing all involved in the case.

Mary Adeline Stack, the housekeeper at the station, and Isaac Jausan, the manager, stated that on 14 May 1925 Leandro Illin informed them that his wife was very sick, she was expecting to give birth to a child and 'appeared to be in great pain'. She was in labour from about 4 p.m. on that day. Leandro stated to the police that 'the wire mattress used by my wife was carried out at her request to make room for the grass bed', which was covered by clean blankets. All her children 'were born on the same kind of bed'. All witnesses stated that Mrs Illin refused to be shifted to a sofa when offered. That seemed to be the main point that interested the police inspector; meanwhile, no one explained why nothing was done before the afternoon of the 16th, when Leandro finally sent a message to Mary Ada Core at the Blue Range that his wife was very sick in labour. 'I left at once', Mrs Core stated, 'and arrived at Christmas Creek about 7 p.m. I remained with Mr and Mrs Illin all that night and as I could see a doctor was required before Mrs Illin could give birth to the child at day break on the 17th I sent to the Clarke River Post office requesting that they would send to Charters Towers for a doctor and the Ambulance.'

First, a horseman had to cover over 40 miles to reach the post office and, as it was Sunday, it took a long time for the message to reach Charters Towers. There was no direct connection and while Kitty was in agony at Christmas Creek the message was transferred by telegraph first to Mt Surprise, thence to Herberton, then through the wires which stretched now along her Ngadjon country around Bartle Frere to Innisfail, where ten years before she had married Leandro, from there to Townsville and finally to Charters Towers. But even the spirits of her country were powerless to help her by then ...

The ambulance with Doctor Gribben, superintendent I. Douglas, and nurse Morray left Charters Towers at 11 a.m. It took them more than twelve hours to reach Christmas Creek, a distance of 150 miles, 'the worst part of the journey from Maryvale Station having been negotiated at night over roads that are in a deplorable condition'. They reached the station at about 11:30 p.m., where Mrs Core told them that at about 8 p.m. that night a stillborn male child was born.

'Mrs Illin was suffering', according to the doctor, 'from severe shock following prolonged labour, she said she had lost a large quantity of blood. ... The body of the child weighed between 14 and 15 lbs [6.5 kg] and [the doctor] attributed her prolonged labour to the size of the child and probably the child was about one week overdue. On arrival the doctor removed the afterbirth ... under an anaesthetic but she was in such a weak condition that she died about half an hour later.' No questions were asked during the investigation about the possible fatal effect that Flora believes the anaesthetic may have had on Kitty. Leandro did not blame anybody, simply stating 'had we been able to get medical attention a few hours sooner in my opinion my wife would have been saved but nothing more could have been done by the people of Christmas Creek than they did'.[12]

Nobody knows why fate can be so cruel to some people. All that Leandro wanted was to earn his own bread, living quietly and honestly with his wife and children, but he was deprived even of this. He was left with six children: the eldest, Ginger, was fourteen, the youngest, Lullie — three (Kitty's eldest daughter, Emma, was by that time back on the Tablelands with her grandmother). People around did want to help Leandro but he chose to struggle on by himself. His children tell:

Harry: When mum died, there was the station owner Beak, they wanted to take us and look after us because we were all small. But father said, 'No, they are my children, I'll look after them', and he did, he never ever got married and he looked after us.

Flora: Mrs Core wanted to take us when my mother died. She used to write to my father and ask him how we were, she was concerned about us. She even used to sew dresses for me when I was a kid. We knew one another for years after, right up till she died. I came to Mt Full Stop once to see her, just before her death.[13]

The Illin family left Christmas Creek for Greenvale a couple of months after they lost Kitty. They left the lonely grave on the banks of Christmas Creek, where she was buried together with her last baby. Her sons returned to it in 1932 to make a fence, but later, after one of the floods, the grave seemed to be lost for many years. But they never forgot about this grave. Recently, local Aborigines helped Flora's son Ernie and her grandson Richard to find it again.

Now they have somewhere to grieve.

'MY DARK BROTHER'

For Leandro, to be true to the memory of Kitty was to act, not just to grieve. And there was a vast field of action that awaited his attention, which was the practical defence of Kitty's people. Working with Aborigines in Gunnawarra, Greenvale, and Christmas Creek, listening to their stories, driving cattle with them to Mt Helen, visiting local Protectors in Ingham and Townsville, he discovered the brutality of the system of so-called protection in all its details.

Kitty's son Ginger (George) was one of the first whom he had to protect from the protection laws. And again he had to apply to Bleakley.

April 7th 1926
Greenvale
Clarke River

The Chief Protector of Aboriginals
Home Secretary's Dept

Sir,

As you might remember ... in September 14th 1915 I have married an aboriginal woman Kitty Clark. On May 17th [1925] to my great sorrow she died giving birth to a little boy who was borned dead. She left me with one stepson and five children of my own.

It is about my stepson George that I am going to deal in this letter. I have reared the boy since August 1913. He was 14 years old on January, 1st last. Having reared the boy I am deeply attached to him and he is very affection-ate to his brothers and sisters. My own boy Dick is 11 years old, then follows Flora 10 years old, Tommy 8 years, Harry 6, and Araluen 4 years. I have no other help. ... I am camped out now 16 miles from the station. My poor moth-erless children stick together and although I had offers to have some of them taken of[f] we try and stick together, my poor little girl looking after smaller ones.

Mr H. J. Atkinson suggested to me to let George to work in the camp. The boy is big enough to ride and do stock work and earn a little money for him-self but I do not like him to be under agreement as if I leave the place and change employer he has to remain behind. Neither he nor I want to be sepa-rated for the sake of the other children.

Mr Atkinson proposes to give him pay and if I leave, the boy to leave with me. Now under the agreement this is rather difficult. Therefore I would like if you could do me and the kiddie a favour, that is: to allow him to work under permit to any employer where I work and live with his brothers and sisters without signing agreement for definite periods, all his wages to be paid either into his banking account or the local Protector.

I do not want the control of his money but I want to keep him and protect him (as his mother's wish always was) from being ill-treated. Children of his age are generally whipped on the stockruns. They don't dare to do it to him while he is under my protection.

I have reared him a good honest able boy, like his poor mother was, he is totally unspoiled, is reliable and smart.

If I loose control of him he might loose his honesty and be used as a tool as many boys on stations are.

Still my main reason to make this application is that I simply can't part from him on account of the other kiddies whom he loves tenderly.

Some time ago (in January last) a man in my absence swore and threatened my little boy Harry six years old. He got frightened and cleared out bush. That was in the morning. The other children missed him but called in vain. He was gone. George went and found his tracks and followed them four miles and found him in the evening at a junction of Wyandotte and Spring Creeks and brought him home in the evening. So you see I can't part with him.

I bank him a little money into the Saving Bank. I receive award wages £2 15s per week and get 15s per week toward the children's keep. If George receives wages he can cloth himself and make it easier for me for the other children. I am putting a very hard battle since the wife died and if the boy was tied up by agreement it would be a lot harder for me and the other kids and George would not like to be left behind.

... Asking you once more to do me this favour for the sake of my poor motherless children I am yours faithfully Leandro Illin

Years after slavery had been abolished in the United States and serfdom in Russia, 'democratic' Australia continued to practise actual slavery in relation to its Aboriginal population ('half-caste' as well as 'full-blood', according to the terminology of the time). Under the Protection Act, Aborigines were obliged to enter into agreement with the whites to work for them from their teenage years. The employer had to pay wages into their bank account, which was administered by a local policeman. This seemed fair enough to the European onlooker, but the problem was that the Aboriginal often could not choose the employer and was forcibly allocated to one by the police and, after signing the agreement, an Aborigine could not change his employer for one year, however harsh conditions were. What happened with his earnings administered by police we will see further on. Leandro's children after his legal marriage were exempted from this Act, but Ginger's destiny, as soon as he reached his teenage years, was to become this kind of assigned slave. The battle for him was started by Leandro in 1926 and lasted till 1940.

Bleakley this time seemed to treat the case more favourably. But, while Mt Garnet and Ingham police and Protectors discussed in whose territory 'godforsaken' Greenvale was, Leandro, not receiving an answer, wrote a new, bitter appeal to Bleakley.

May 25 1926

... All my dealings with you were so far very hard ... The trouble is that although both of us [are] most well intentioned towards the Abos we look on things from a different point. You in your official capacity have to trust and depend in everything on the police. I mistrust the police and consider them as a body privileged to do harm to the Abos. A policeman can do and in most cases does what we simple mortals are fined for. ...

Now I am enclosing 3 photos for you to see my family. You will see that my plight is real and I need George (Ginger as we call him). Please, decide one way or the other. His Granny Emily Denyer also wants him. The boy needs nothing while he is with me. I am in great suspense.

I want two of the three photos returned marked thus +. On one of them is my late wife. I suppose you are waiting for the police report to decide on the matter. ... The police is sure to report to oblige a squatter not considering that I saved the boy from all troubles up to now and reared him. I know you are humane as you was decidedly so in Denyers case in Atherton and I think you will do this for me, for the boy and my family.

Finally, in June 1926, the case was decided in favour of George. Although not exempt from the Act, for the time being he was allowed not to separate from his family.[14]

Alas, other Aboriginal boys did not have fathers like Leandro, and this did not stop troubling him. A few months after Kitty's death, in August 1925, the *North Queensland Register* published a letter to the Editor signed with a strange pen-name 'Meekolo'. Reading it, I realised that there could hardly be anybody else except Leandro in northern Queensland at that time who would so passionately raise his voice in defence of 'the son of this soil' — the Aborigine. Later 'Meekolo' disclosed his pen-name and, indeed, he turned out to be Leandro. In that first appeal he wrote:

'IN THE BEGINNING THE ABOS WERE SHOT DOWN LIKE DOGS OR WORSE. Now that they are a dying out race the Government passes laws for their so called protection. The laws in some ways are all right but in most ways are all wrong and the trouble is that the injustice to the Abo is done not by the bushman nor other private individuals but mostly by members of the institution in whose hands the Abos are and who mostly are not Queenslanders at all but big men from overseas who largely invade that particular department. The Abo's life is not his own but it belongs to his employer. He is lucky if he gets a rich employer who can afford to give him all he requires besides what is paid in to the hands of the police. ...

'I know a boy[15] with a family — a wife and three children — he has been working all his life under the one employer and has an account in the hands of the police for over £300 yet when he applied for a sum of money to buy a buggy, the protector did not grant it.

'During eight months of last year I was down to a coastal town once every month [it was when Leandro drove cattle to Mt Helen]. The second trip I came down I went with an old boy[16] to the police station to try to get some money for the boy. In August 1923, was the last time this boy was at the police station and withdrew £5. It was April 1924 when he went up with me and asked the sergeant for money. The sergeant told him "you got some money not long ago". The boy said he did not. The sergeant said he did and that he would not give him any money. So I chipped in and knowing the exact day when the boy was down last I told him when it was and on looking through the books he said, "You are right, come later on". When the boy returned he had a slip made for withdrawal of £3/13/10. I remonstrated that it was not enough for him. He wanted two flannel shirts, two pairs of trousers, hat, boots, blankets, etc. "That is all he gets", was the gruff retort. Quite enough if he buys clothes just for himself, the Sergeant said. I could see through the policeman's strategy. He was practically accusing me of trying to get the boy's money so as to hurt my feelings and make me go away. ... The boy that got the above mentioned £3/13/10 had a credit account of over £164.'

On another occasion Leandro witnessed an even more dramatic scene which obviously reminded him of the lesson he was taught in the Northern Territory when a station owner demanded, 'Don't you spoil my blacks for me!'.

'ONCE A SERGEANT OF POLICE WAS TRANSACTING SAVINGS BANK BUSINESS and had several books in his hands. He turned round to me and said, "This is not bad for an Aboriginal!" The amount showed £264 odd. I knew the boy and knew the district where he came from. I knew his old father to be starving on a creek. I told the sergeant about it and suggested that he should see the boy and give him some money to purchase tucker for this very old father. I knew the boy would be only too pleased to do it as they only looked with contempt on their money in the bank. They say always "police gets our money". The sergeant on hearing my suggestion straightened himself to his six feet odd, brushed his beautiful long moustache and answered that he knew nothing about that. That the boy was a very good boy, that he never came to ask for any money and it was no use spoiling him. Then with a great dignified and hurt air he walked away holding hard a few passbooks in his hand.'

Furthermore, Leandro disclosed numerous cases when the police released some Aboriginal earnings but used the money to buy clothes for Aborigines on the stations without their consent — the clothes were of low quality bought at the highest prices and of ridiculous sizes. Otherwise, when the boys visited the town police directed them to buy goods in a particular shop. Leandro wrote about them as a concerned friend and father who recognises their human needs.

'SPURS, SADDLES, WHIPS are articles the police in most cases do not consider as necessary for them to buy; yet every boy loves to own these articles and the money they want to spend is their own. ... They all like musical instruments and little things that we all love yet they are deprived of all but what the protectors approve.'

But the main issue that worried Leandro was Aboriginal human rights — an idea unheard of at that time.

'BOYS SIGN ON AND ONCE THEY DO SO, NO MATTER WHAT HAPPENS, THEY CANNOT BREAK THEIR AGREEMENTS. Some boys are "signed on" without having seen the agreement, they neither been in the presence of the police to put their cross or anyone else. The usual thing is "the boss said I am signed on". Every boy should be asked in the presence of J.P., besides the policeman, if he wants to sign on, or not. No Abo should be sent to a settlement on a report of a policeman alone, but should be tried publicly before he is deprived of his native land and liberty and deprived of his friends and relatives. ... To threaten boys with Palm Island to compel them to work for an employer they do not want to work for ... in my opinion is a total misapplication of the Protection Laws and against all the highest traditions of British freedom and liberty.

'In the old days when there was no protection (so the old bushmen tell me) the squatters fed the camp as a whole. Bucks[17], young gins were worked, the young, old and feeble were also provided and all were allowed to have a "walk about". Now the destitute and feeble have got to go to a prison settlement. The young ones allowed to exist on the stations and be parted from their relatives. How would you, fellow workers, like to have your earnings confiscated and only allowed to draw money at the mercy of someone who does not know your needs or does not want to know them? ... We, white workers, are deducted 3d. per week for the unemployed. The Abo has 75 per cent of his money withheld from him.

'I am an outsider and my interest in the question is only pity for my dark brother. I suggest that every district should have a honorary board for the Abos' welfare and elevation, consisted of disinterested members with country members included.'[18]

Leandro's ideas and attitudes were too greatly in advance of his time. The solutions he saw were ideas that have only recently been more generally adopted — he believed that the Aborigines should be treated as equals by the whites, should have the same rights enjoyed by all other Australians, and, moreover, he stressed the natural right of the Aborigines to stay on the land of their ancestors, together with their community. Equality, not corrupted paternalism: this was the attitude that Leandro manifested in his own life; this was the attitude which he demanded from official Australia. W.B. Sinclair, the only one who wrote to the newspaper in support of Leandro's appeal, saw the solution of the problem quite differently from Leandro. 'Segregation? Yes, and quickly', he wrote, believing that the white men living with Aboriginal women and settlers exploiting Aborigines were the main evil.[19] Sinclair was unable to look beyond that and to share Leandro's concern that the arbitrariness of police and Protectors was no less dangerous than the harm caused by the pastoralists and farmers.

An Aboriginal bush-lawyer, Leandro was also a bush doctor for the Aborigines around the station. This is just one of the cases told by Flora.

'FATHER ALWAYS WAS FRIENDLY AND STUCK UP FOR THE BLACK PEOPLE. People on the station used to come to him, looking for things, whatever there was wrong, he was the doctor around the place, all the dark people and some of the white people would ask him, especially the dark people. He always did his best to look after the sick people, always had a lot of pity for sick people.

'There was one old black fellow there and he was very sick, his legs were swollen and nobody worried about him, but my father was worrying about him. And luckily a doctor travelled through there. You could see that he was a doctor because those days if he was a lawyer, or a solicitor, or a doctor you could pick him [out] from the street. Father started talking to him and found out that he was a doctor. Father said, "Have a look at this fellow, why is he a sick man", and this doctor got him, put this thing on, he had the things with him to test you, looked at his legs and said, "Yes, he's very sick, he had dropsy, water gets into the blood". Father told the station owner, "This man is sick, should get him to the hospital". They sent him and he died later in Ingham hospital.'

Some years later, being accused that he 'associated with blacks', Leandro argued: 'My associations with them have been in no way detrimental to the blacks and if I had now in cash what I spent buying Iodine, Boracic, Quinine, Aspros, Heenzo, Castor Oil and Epsom salts, bandages, ointments etc. I would have a goodly sum'.[20]

Mac Core, when he was a boy in the 1920s, knew Leandro. Now, remembering him, the first thing he said was: 'He was very good to the younger Aboriginal people'.[21] How proud Flora and Harry were to hear this acknowledgement of their father's attitude.

There are numerous letters written by Leandro in defence of Aborigines stored in different files in the Queensland State Archives. Sometimes he wrote these letters at the request of an illiterate Aborigine; sometimes he fought alongside him, conveying facts to the Chief Protector or Home Secretary. 'I fought for every black that I seen wronged', Leandro would say about his position. They very seldom won; sometimes he would experience moments of despair but, still, he never gave up. He did not live to see the fruits of his struggle. But it was not in vain. Years would pass and his grandchildren — Ernest Hoolihan, Alec Illin, Glenda Illin and many others — put his ideas into practice, building a new society of equal opportunities for their own children and grandchildren — the Australians.

'GOOD OLD DAYS ...'

A few months after Kitty's death Leandro got a job at Greenvale on the selection of Wyandotte, and again they camped in a tent near a creek. It was here that Harry was lost and Ginger tracked him. Now Leandro could not do droving work, as the children were too young to be left alone for a long time. Ginger and Dick continued to do mustering work on the station; Flora stayed at the tent, as the eldest, with Tom, Harry and Lullie. These months in Wyandotte, after their mother's death, seem to have fallen out of Flora's life — there was nothing but heat, flies, dirty clothes to wash, food to cook, plates to clean. And loneliness ...

That was what worried Leandro most. More than material hardships, although the 25 shillings per week that he earned there as a stockman and labourer were far from enough to support the family of seven. They 'stuck together' but without Kitty their world had lost its centre; they all, including Leandro himself, felt terribly 'motherless'. Only recently Flora wrote in a letter to me: 'It still lives with me — no mother, and father had to go to work and leave us kids behind in the lonely bush. ... I was only nine-and-a-half years old ... but I grew up very fast in the mind to look after Tom, Harry and Lullie.' Years would pass but none of them would ever tell their own children about this time of despair. The outback taught them to hide their feelings. It was only at sunset, when Leandro returned to the tent after his daily rounds, that the thin faces of his children lit up. They had supper and then would sit together, and he would read them an occasional book or 'Children's corner' from the *North Queensland Register*, or tell them about his childhood in Russia and travels in North America and the Argentine, or teach Flora and Tommy letters. Seventy years later in one of her first letters to me, Flora wrote: 'I never went to school at all, my father taught me the alphabet, the letters and how to spell small things such as 'cat', 'rat', 'dog', 'pig', this and that, and make letter to write and from there I picked up the rest myself, so you see I am not a good speller'.[22]

It was on these lonely evenings that Leandro realised that they could not endure going around in the bush any longer, they needed at least some stability, a home, a community of people. This tent in Wyandotte had become the turning point in his way to the Never Never; now they had to come back to people. He had nobody to turn to but Henry Atkinson. Their relationship seems not to have been a simple one. One letter from their correspondence has survived: it was from Atkinson to Leandro.

'Greenvale'
Charters Towers
24th December 1925

Mr L. Illin
Wyandotte
Dear Sir,

Yours to hand. I can't quite understand what you are alluding to. I think you had better come in to see me and tell me all your trouble. I don't think you are right, when you say you are not wanted. Some people may not want you there, but why move to suit them.[23]

They met and Leandro received a place on the station Greenvale itself, first to bail water, then as a gardener.

For bush children this move to Greenvale was like a transfer to a capital from a country township. The Greenvale station was one of the first outposts of the whites in the area and dated back over sixty years. Henry Atkinson, whose brother Thomas had employed Leandro at Gunnawarra, was the eldest son of James and Kate Atkinson, the pioneers of this area. 'There was no homestead there then', their great-grandson, Henry Atkinson of Lucky Downs, tells us, 'they stopped their bullock team and cattle about 5 kilometres up-river at a lagoon they called Firth's Lagoon. That's where my grandfather Henry was born, at Firth's Lagoon, under a bullock wagon.' Henry Atkinson (1863–1935), his grandfather, was probably the first white child to be born on the northern Burdekin. 'Some forty years later he was to return and buy the surrounding country where he was born; in the meantime it had become Greenvale Station, running 15,000 head of cattle and 500 horses.' Henry Atkinson was a real Australian, one of the last to continue the early traditions into the twentieth century. Now, seventy years later, Flora remembers him well.

'HE WAS A KIND FELLOW, OLD ATKINSON, VERY NICE FELLOW, NOT A FLASH MAN. Yes, he was a good bloke to people with families. He always used to help us. If anybody had a big family he would give him a job, give them food, give them tea, sugar, flour, meat, whatever he could. Old man Henry Atkinson, he was brother of Thomas Atkinson from Gunnawarra, and he had one daughter but she died early, but he had three sons, Jim, Del, and Ray.'[24]

Greenvale was like a little country with its own borders, river and creeks, and with its own place-names. Flora is one of the last to remember these names — Hay Paddock, Plum Paddock, Corn Paddock — and to recall this world.

'IT WAS MOSTLY DARK PEOPLE THERE, there was very few white people, only the station owner, his sons, a housekeeper and a bookkeeper, and one or two white stockmen. There would be about thirty-five or more people on the station with kids, white people and dark people. So there was a lot of us there. It wasn't a lonely station. There was plenty of little kids, four or five dark women lived there. Some of the dark people would wander there, some of them would be working there and some of them would come from the next station, there might be a tribe somewhere around, and they'd wander there and talk to the others. Nobody chased them. They just go down to the creek and lived there. They were wandering around. Some could not speak English at all. But those on the station, they could speak English. They were cheap labour, never got paid, just working for the food and clothes. That's the way it was. But they were better off, they might not have been getting paid but they had food, they were not drunk and stupid and they lived a good, cleaner life.'[25]

Aborigines in this area belonged to Gugu-Badhun tribe. George Butcher, a stockman from Greenvale, remembers that some of them had Chinese blood, too.

Occasionally new faces appeared on the station. Greenvale station was not far from the western road to Ingham, where it crossed the Burdekin. Flora remembers:

'IN 1927 THEY MADE A SECURE CROSSING, they fixed and cemented it and dumped things in the water to lift the crossing. So old Atkinson, I suppose, he reckons "They can pay 50 cents". He used to charge them 50 cents to go through. They could not go through anywhere else, they had to go straight through here. Plenty times my father used to catch them here and collect when old Atkinson wasn't around.'[26]

When we visited the place in July 1996, Flora and Harry were the only ones to lead us back through time. Flora was telling us about the 'Square'.

'I USED TO CALL THIS THE SQUARE. All us kids used to race around here and we were playing here. Up there, where the main house is built, is Plum Paddock. This house was through three or four floods but it is still standing. It was a nice house. They had a dining room, and a big billiard room downstairs and bedrooms were upstairs. On the other side of the Square there was old Atkinson's office, he used to do all the book-keeping there.'

But Harry interrupted her with some reminiscences of more practical matters.

'UNDERNEATH, UNDER THE OLD FELLOW'S OFFICE THERE WAS THE STOREROOM, where they kept all the groceries and everything. The car shed was next to it and when we were kids we used to get through in there where a slab was missing in the wall. We used to climb over and climb down, we'd get the milk tins, suck all the milk out, and eat all the apricots and things like that. The stock went down, old Atkinson, he woke up to us, they put another slab and cut us all off.'

Flora continued to discover details of the past.

'I SEE THE OLD BUGGY SHED IS STILL THERE. But on the other side, behind the kitchen, were huts for dark people along here. There's two huts here, one for the women, one for the men, and then there was one that was for the married ones.'

The Illins, Leandro and children, found themselves between these two centres of the station — Aboriginal quarters on one side of the kitchen and manager's house on the other side. They were accepted by both of them and still they remained the Illins, with a place of their own.

One photograph has miraculously survived from those days. It was taken in Greenvale around 1924, on the 'Square', with Atkinson's storeroom and office in the background. Leandro, Dick, Flora, Tommy, Harry and Lullie are mounted on Nugget, Leandro's favourite horse. 'Just that horse would stand and put up, it was very quiet horse, and father was so proud of him, that's why he got us all on there and got the photo taken', Flora tells us. Ten years later Leandro would say in one of his speeches:

'A WRITER TO BE GREAT HAS TO DIE FIRST. ... The writer and the poet is like a good horse I had. I did not know I could not replace it until it died. I could have fed it and make it last for a few more years... but I did not and now when I have to go somewhere Nugget is not there ... and I have to walk!'[27]

Years later in their memories they return to those days. Dick, who ultimately considered himself an Aborigine, would write bitterly in a newspaper:

'OUR DAY'S WORK BEGAN AT SUNRISE AND FINISHED AT SUNSET, six days a week with Sundays off, but in the mustering camps work was every day until finished.'[28]

The mood of Flora and Harry, when we visited the place in July 1996, was quite different. As we entered the ruins of the manager's house and Flora and Harry led us though what used to be a billiard room, a sitting-room and a dining-room, Flora suddenly said:

'THE BEST DAYS OF OUR LIFE WERE HERE, in Greenvale. Here is that room, their dining-room, where the boss used to dine with his family and all the housekeeper, book-keepers. They had a big table here, and a pianola was there, they all used to sit here. We used to sing around it, we used to walk in around there, they used to play, we all used to get in and have a sing-song around the pianola. It was there, in the dining room. Good old days, that was good old days though.'

And Harry repeated as an echo: 'Good old days. I'd like to see days like that again ...'.

Flora continued:

'IT WAS QUIET, and nobody was fighting, and nobody was trying to rob one another or anything like that. Peaceful days ... Look, the ceiling is still the same. And over this side they had a billiard room, they had a big billiard table, that was their recreation room. Father used to stay here and watch others playing, he did not play but he used to watch everybody else.'

Indeed, he used to watch a lot. He wrote some of his observations of that time to Bill Bowyang's column in the *North Queensland Register*.

'I AM WORKING ON THE STATION and despite my ungainly appearance I am a keen observer. This is what I have noticed. When a swagman arrives he generally receives sufficient food to carry him on or perhaps he is offered a job for a couple of days, but as a rule, while he is at the place the sky serves him for a roof and the fertile soil is his resting place at night. He and his track companions are looked upon with suspicion. Now it is different with car drivers. They approach the homestead with the old buzzer working in fine style — sometimes there are five men in the car — and they are fairly well dressed. They ask how far it is to the next station. Then the boss or the bookkeeper almost fall over themselves in their haste to invite the visitors indoors.

Right then things begin to happen in that house. Rooms are aired and beds made. The visitors are invited to have a shower bath and are shown to their rooms. Then the whisky and soda comes to light and after a couple of shots the visitors dine with the family. After supper there is billiards or a musical evening. After that everyone goes to sleep.'[29]

Use a car — in the 1920s a novelty and a luxury in Queensland outback — was Leandro's advice to swagmen on how to receive a welcoming reception on the stations. To him, it was funny that it was the appearance that mattered, not the people themselves. The little world of the isolated station gave Leandro enough food for his reflections.

The Illins' hut stood away from the black and white poles that surrounded the Square, it was half-way down towards the Burdekin River, on the Corn Paddock. 'It was not much, just a lean-to, corrugated iron shed, that's all. Just somewhere to get into out of the rain', that is how it is still remembered by George Butcher, then a young stockman at Greenvale.[30] Leandro's first job was water-bailing. Next to his hut was a raised stand for a big water-tank. The hoses went from the Burdekin along the gully to the tank, and Leandro used a pump to lift water from the river. From the tank water went up to the main homestead — indeed, it was Leandro's responsibility to provide water for the shower for those flashy car-travellers.

But once the Burdekin River, which flowed hundreds of yards away from their hut, showed how powerful it could be. In February 1927, after the drought, the rains began to pour. The waters from the flooded Burdekin and Porphyry Creek, which met between Greenvale homestead and the gorge, could not get through the narrow passage between the two mountains fast enough and rapidly flowed back towards the station. The Illins' hut was the first on its way. The water came in the middle of the night. Flora relates what happened.

'FATHER WAS THERE, PUTTING ALL THE THINGS UP ON THE TANK STAND. Oh, he had a lot of books and papers, some medical books that were left behind by grandad. He and Dickie put them on the top so that water would not wash them away, and then they were coming up to our hut, but by that time the water was running strong and it nearly washed Dickie away. And father had to let his watch — he had his hat with his watch and everything — he had to let it go into water saving Dickie from drowning. And then we all went to the station, it was a high house, high station, but the boss of the station said, "The water is coming too fast, we best get out of here". And in the middle of the night we walked away from the station, we walked out up to the hill. There was about thirty of us, kids and everything, walking and falling over, dark, rain, and we all walked for about two miles or so. I fell over a stump, got a splinter in my leg. Somebody carried younger kids. When we looked up at the daybreak all we could see was the top of the roofs of the station. All valley was flooded, you would not believe that it can happen, but it happened three or four times since.'

The station diary recorded: '10 February 1927. ... The water at the time of departure was about three feet in depth and subsequently rose to a depth of 9 feet 6¹/4 inches. ... From 9 a.m. to 6 p.m. today the rain-gauge gave 434 points after which the gauge itself got washed away.' The waters receded from the station buildings only by midday, 12 February.[31] The Illins had their own losses after the flood: most of Nicholas's books were washed away, and their family icon — St Peter and St Paul — was damaged beyond restoration. Still, some papers and photographs did survive. Following one of the later floods the numerous buildings surrounding the 'Square' were abandoned; their ruins still stand there, gradually falling down.

After the flood Leandro got the job of gardener for the station. His wages rose to £3 per week, less £1 5s per week charged for rations. The Illins cultivated about three acres around their hut, providing a constant supply of fresh vegetables for the station. Flora relates:

'WE USED WATER FROM THE TANK TO WATER THE GARDEN, we had a lovely garden, lovely. Cabbages, potato, corn, beetroot, turnip, tomato, sweet potato — you could grow anything here. Father used to plant it and show us how to grow things. We used to help, we used to do a lot of it. We used to water it. There was a lemon garden down there with a lot of lemon trees, but it got washed away with the flood in 1927. The flood left a lot of sand out of the river on the river banks, we used to grow water melons there, they were growing all along the gully, plenty of them.'

A less enjoyable duty was tending the pigs, which were bred to provide a supply of fresh meat for the station. Besides this, the Illins provided the station with dairy products. Every morning they had to milk around twenty-five cows and Flora and her younger brothers were an essential help in doing it.

'THE CALF WOULD GET OUT WITH THE MOTHER, you think you could put them back? No way. You chased them, and belt them ... No way. When I used to go for the cows, they used to put them in the horse paddock, the night horse paddock, and that's where Tommy, Harry and me used to catch our horses, saddle them up and go out here to bring the cows. There were two bails there, where we would milk the cows.

'I used to make butter too. The separator room was next to the kitchen. I would turn the separator by hand, get the cream out, let it stay for the day, then next day make it into butter. Winter-time it was good, because the butter would be firm, in summer it was harder because it was hard to make the butter, I still made it, but you had to keep it in the cool, they did not have fridges those days. They used to have a big safe with gauze all around it. They used to put it in the middle, let the air get in to keep it cool, that's how they used to keep everything cool.'[32]

By then the Atkinsons trusted Leandro to the extent that at times he was left in charge to keep the station diary. These pages, abundant in details, with every available spot covered in his clear handwriting, are a valuable source of information for the future historian of the little world of Greenvale. At times Leandro's pages seem too personal, compared to the usually dry style of the diary: '14.12.1928. Ted Friend filling holes inside the square. Darcy and Jackson working in the flower garden. Illin cross ploughing and harrowing. Terrific heat. Nearly killing the horses'. '16.12.1928. Between pigs and separator going wrong I (L.I.) have plenty worry. All the kiddies on the station slightly sick ... The sow will not let the little ones suck'. '17.12.1928. Terrible hot. Sow killed 6 piggies after I worrying with them all day yesterday. Has only two left'. '28.07.1929. Hoolihan, Toby, Pat, Illin and his family came home from Ingham [show]. Illin and family riding from Camel Creek with drovers. Doctor, Laura and family came per lorry from Camel Creek with Dale and Darcy. Doctor fell off the lorry and got hurt.'[33] Doctor, the old Aboriginal stockman with whom Leandro was droving in 1924, was the same man Leandro helped get his money released from the Protector at the police station. He was to die not long afterwards, and was buried in a lonely grave at Grey Creek.

While the younger children were gardening and milking cows, Ginger and Dick worked as stockmen. Dick relates:

'WHEN I WAS EIGHT YEARS OLD I WORKED ON STATIONS, from 1923 to 1929, for nothing, and there were no schools for me, my brothers and sisters.

'In 1929 I was taken out of the mustering camp by my boss, who thought that I was getting too heavy for the horses, and put into another job as a dam sinker, I worked behind a scoop with three horses. I was fourteen years old. My wage was 10 shillings a week, plus keep. My keep consisted of a swag on the ground in the bush, corned beef, tea, damper and treacle. Vegetables and butter were not heard of or seen.'[34]

Harry seems to remember those days more favourably.

'BACK IN THE DEPRESSION DAYS IT WAS VERY HARD. But we had plenty to eat, everything. It did not worry us much. At the station, you see, father was milking cows, making butter, plenty of meat. When we wanted a feed of fish we went down to the Burdekin to catch fish.'[35]

The younger ones were, indeed, happy there, in Greenvale. Food in abundance produced by their own hands, and some adventures like Harry's expeditions to the storeroom for tinned milk and dried apricots, or another expedition led by Flora — 'There was a tamarind tree in front of the boss's windows, we used to climb up there on the roof and get all the tamarinds and eat them up there' — and the river, deep and quiet, overshadowed by box, gum and tea-trees. How much fun they had on its sandy shores!

'THERE WAS PLENTY OF WATERMELONS', relates Flora, 'all us kids we played with them, we would throw them into the creek and they float to the river. They float and we swim alongside with them. Then we pull them out when we got down there and go fishing and we'd cut them and eat them.'

And here, on the Burdekin they received the lesson from their father that they would remember for the whole life.

Harry: Father taught us a lot of things. He used to take us in the deep water to big water holes. When he get to the middle of the water he'd just duck and leave us there. You could not do any thing but swim by yourself. I was very young when I could swim. I was a good swimmer and Ginger called me *kviver*, that is 'fish' in Ngadjon.

Flora: Father made us get in the water and swim alongside of him. My brother Dickie, he reckoned he was frightened, my father say, 'You'll have to drown if you do not swim'. He soon swam out.[36]

Now they had their own home, even if it was just a corrugated-iron lean-to. And in the evenings they would sit listening to their father playing the mandolin, and again, like in Butchers Creek, a passionate and free 'Down the Volga' or a tender and sunny 'La Paloma' would rise to the Australian stars. On the other side of the globe, too, Romelio and Ariadna would croon the same tunes, and Alexandra would sing her Russian lullabies to her grandchildren.

Once a week Dick was despatched from Greenvale down to the post-office on Clarke River, where mail was delivered from Charters Towers. That was about a 40-mile ride and he would return the next day, occasionally bringing a letter for the Illins from Honduras post-marked with the names of far countries all over the envelope. And the children would listen to the pioneering story of the Illins and the Mackays as it unfolded overseas year by year. When Nicholas passed away, Ara with her family left Colombia and joined the rest of the Illins in San Pedro Sula. Jack Mackay started up a trucking business and was the first to bring success to the Illin family; in a few years he already owned sixteen trucks — a significant business in poor, rural Honduras, which was constantly shaken by revolutions.

Nellie, in her memoirs, speaks of them in a matter-of-fact way.

'THERE WERE A FEW REVOLUTIONS there and we had to go to Dr Gregory's cement house to get protection at night. One time one started and all the family went to the bathroom — 10 x 10 out of cement — as there was a lot of shooting. My mother tried to wake me up three times to go to the bathroom. I finally woke up. There were bullet holes in the house. Another time my sister Olga and I went to the movies and a revolution started. We both decided not to go out on account of the shooting and waited till it was quiet and the movie was over. Well, when we got out and started walking home we ran into my stepfather and mother looking for us. They had driven down to the theatre in their pyjamas and robe.

'Another time my mother was at one of the farms and the revolution started. The only way she could get home was by walking on the railroad track. She wasn't afraid of anyone, so she walked. Everyone knew her as "Mama Ara", and soldiers would shout to her to take off her red sweater, as that was the party "Reds" that had taken the town where we lived. She was lucky and made it home safely. We were much surprised to see her walking down the street.'

Nothing like that happened around Leandro's kids in Greenvale — just cows, horses and water-pumping; a sense of the romance of the trucks was the only thing they had in common with their far-off relatives in Honduras, and in that their uncle Romelio seemed the ultimate hero to them. He obtained a contract to carry mail from San Pedro Sula to the district of Santa Barbara up on the Ulúa River and, in 1926, he was the first to get there by truck. It took him one month to drive there along mountainous paths previously accessible to horsemen alone. On the way back he would carry passengers and coffee. 'Although he was short', Sam Mackay relates, 'he was well-known for his strength.' On one such trip when he had to change a flat tyre, he managed to lift the car by himself while his helper changed it. He was hard-working and sentimental, liking poetry and literature. He possessed one more quality. According to Sam, he 'liked to help people in need of his services. But he did not like to charge for his services.' And the day came when he found his true Paloma — Cristina Banegas, a sixteen-year-old girl from Trinidad de Santa Barbara. They married in 1929 and she bore him four sons.[37] The story of the Illins was unfolding now in Central America.

We explored the ruins of the old Greenvale homestead and I tape-recorded Flora's and Harry's remarks about the past. Now I knew the exact layout of the buildings and trees, of the paddocks and roads, but I realised that I was still missing the most important thing — I could not see Flora and Harry's Greenvale world from the inside. The next day, before leaving Townsville for Canberra, I was taken by Flora's son Ernie to Flora's place to say goodbye. As we were looking through old photographs, we returned to the subject of Leandro's personality once again. And suddenly Flora said:

'Well, he was quick-tempered. But he could control it, too. In Greenvale he broke two men's arms.'

'How was that?' Ernie and I exclaimed.

'With a stick one time, with a gun another time', Flora said simply.

I understood that this was what I needed — a story which would fill the setting with life. And the story followed.

'THIS FELLOW, JACK CARNEY, WAS WORKING THERE, A WHITE MAN, HE WAS. The old Atkinson was not there but the boss's son, Jim, was there. Jack wanted a drink and Jim gave him a bottle of rum. He came up to the hut where we were, he was always talking to my father, he came and they sat on the veranda, there was a table there, they sat and talked, and talked till all hours. He got pretty drunk, but not my father, he never used to touch it, but he'd sit down and talk to people. And what this fellow's idea was ... He was supposed to go to his place, there was a special place there, they called it "white men's quarters" ... I don't know when he went away, but later on in the night my father made me get up out of that room and go into his room. And he put Dickie in my bed. At two or three o'clock he heard somebody in bed pushing Dickie all around. That's what my father suspected. He got up, he was a very light sleeper, and walked to the door, "What are you doing here, Jack?" He came out and started swearing at my father and my father straightaway knew he thought that I was there. So my father was ready to bash him.

'When he came out and father started swearing at him and having a big row, of course we jumped up, too. We were standing watching the men, they were outside in front of the house. And he made to hit my father, and my father backed away, and there was a stick, he nearly fell over it — it was one of the black people's nulla-nulla that they used to fight with — and he bent down to shift the stick. The fellow, he was Britisher, he said, "Don't you pick it up, that stick, fight with your fists". Father said, "Good reminder", picked up the stick and when that fellow came to hit him, he brought down the stick and hit him right across the arm, and broke it. And he was jumping around there, singing out. Anyhow, my father said, "Well, you get out of here, before I hit your head with it". And in the morning the fellow got up and told the boss's son what my father had done to him. But Jim Atkinson said, "Well, served you right. What business did you have to go over there?" and sacked him.'

That was in 1927 when Flora was just eleven. And then, around 1928, a new ordeal followed.

'THE OLD BOSS AGAIN WAS AWAY. And there was a housekeeper there, she was that sort of woman ... she liked the men, and she was running with the boss's son Del, Jim's younger brother, she was carrying on with him. Now, there was this other fellow, he was a book-keeper. And she was carrying on with him too, when Del wasn't there. So, alright, the boss's son was away for a few days. When he was coming back, his car broke down up Sandy Creek, near Camel Creek station. He came back to Greenvale and said to this housekeeper, "Come with me, we'll go and get the car". So she gets in the car and goes with him. This book-keeper, he was an Englishman, he got very jealous because this woman went away with the boss's son, but she was all the time carrying on with the boss's son.

'So, Lullie and Dickie and me, we'd just finished milking, we'd just finished separating the milk, and put everything away, washed all the dishes, the separator, up, the buckets and everything. Then we went out and we were sitting in the kitchen-part there, talking to Essie's mother-in-law[38], she was the cook. So we were sitting down and talking to her, and this fellow came up because he's jealous and he was half-going mad or something. He comes up and said to Dickie, "What are you doing here?" — because we were living down, we had our house down the garden there. He said, "You get home", and he got hold of Dickie. "You have nothing to do here, and I'm going to run your father off the station too", this is what he said to Dickie and me.

'Now, there was one little fellow was there, a little dark boy about this high he was, so this kid heard him saying this, and he run in front down to tell my father, and when he got there, he said, "Mr Illin, Mr Illin, quick, Bob Parks coming down here to fight you, he just hit Dickie". So my father said, "Oh, is he? What's he want to hit me for?" He walked inside and got the gun. Put a bullet in it. He said, "He's not going to hit me, I'll fix him up". So my father put the gun near and he waited for him to come. When he got there he started abusing my father and going on there, and my father had never done nothing, I do not know what he was picking on him for, but he was taking it out on everybody because he was jealous of that woman. And he said, "Yes, and I'll run you off the place too", and he was standing up there and my father grabbed the gun, he said, "You get out of here, this is my place, you get back to your place, you got nothing to do with me". The fellow got so mad and he was going punch my father. When he went to punch him, my father picked up the gun, he was going to fire but instead of that he switched the gun around quick and hit him with the butt of the gun, he hit his arm and snapped it. He broke his arm. He said, "Get out of here". We could see it from the station where we were, we could see him jumping around, and going on, and singing out. And I said, "Something happened".

'And when the boss, the son, came home, he said "What's happened?". And this fellow went and told him that my father broke his arm, so the boss came down and asked my father, "What's happened? What you broke that bloke's arm for?". And my father said, "What is he coming down here and singing out at me and wanting to fight me over? I never done nothing. He hit Dickie and then he came down here and he was going to hit me, bash me, I would not let him do that." And my father told him, "Looks like he was going mad because you took the housekeeper". "Oh", boss's son said, "I'll fix him up". He came back and said, "You are finished, get out of this place", packed him off in the car and sent him to Ingham, too.'

'Non-resistance to evil by violence' — Leandro would never accept that point of Leo Tolstoy's philosophy, ever since the days when his father took a knife to protect him from a group of Irish ruffians on the ship returning from America nearly half a century before. Now, he was to defend the dignity of his own children. Several years later he would write:

'I BROKE JACK CARNEY'S ARM at 2 a.m. one night at Greenvale hunting him away (he was drunk) from my daughters door. I done the same to Robert Parks, Greenvale Bookkeeper who was interfering with my children. I broke a bottle of lemonade on a halfcaste chap Paddie Brady, exempt man, returned soldier, whom I caught trying to open my daughters door at Stoneleigh and who after ran away. There is plenty whites to mess up a halfcast girl but not many of the good men to marry them.'[39]

A bush lawyer, he also knew the bush laws.

LEANDRO ON THE TRACK OF BILL BOWYANG

At the beginning of 1926 an unusual voice sounded from Bill Bowyang's column in the *North Queensland Register*, 'On the Track'. A contributor to the column, called 'Meekolo', began his story:

'ON A FARM IN ONE OF OUR NORTHERN SCRUBS a member of a certain family brought home a little half-caste boy to his mother. He had found the dusky lad in a lonely spot and it seemed he had been deserted by his Aboriginal mother. ... Now, the white mother had other grandchildren to attend to, but still the colour of the dusky boy made no difference to her, and she treated him similar to the white children.'[40]

What followed was the Illins' favourite story of how Nellie tried to wash Dickie white; he was the half-caste boy Meekolo referred to. There could hardly ever have been another reader of this column so happy to come across this short piece as I was.

It was six months since I had discovered Leandro's note: 'I have written to Bowyang columns for years under the pen name "Meexolo" but after a bereavement in my family I knocked off'.[41] The famous Bowyang column 'On the Track' had been appearing in the *North Queensland Register* each week since 1922. It was the favourite reading of many Queenslanders, the page that they looked for first on opening a fresh issue of the paper. The column had a distinctively outback flavour, consisting of yarns and poetry contributed by the newspaper's readers, artfully intertwined with comments from the editor Bill Bowyang (a pen-name of the experienced journalist and writer, Alexander Vennard, known also under the name of 'Frank Reid'). Finding out that Leandro was not only a 'bush lawyer' but a forgotten 'bush writer' as well made me eager to search the whole paper for his contributions, but, alas, the newspaper was available only in Brisbane, not in Canberra, where I live. The Brisbane historian Nikolai Dmitrovsky generously spent his time searching for me through several years — 1922, 1923, 1924 — but, to our frustration, no sign of 'Meexolo' emerged. In spite of this, I decided to keep on trying. Months later I obtained the microfilms of the newspaper for 1925 and 1926 on interlibrary loan and discovered a contributor there with a pen-name that was similar to 'Meexolo' — 'Meekolo'.

And now, reading this story, which had to be about Nellie and Dick, and was signed by 'Meekolo', I was sure that I was finally on Leandro's tracks as a bush writer. But something else in that story struck me — these words: 'The colour of the dusky boy made no difference to [the white mother], and she treated him similar to the white children'. This was flagrantly out of tune with the usual style of humorous yarns about Aborigines from 'Track' contributors. There, 'the Abo' — an ignorant, primitive creature with hardly intelligible speech — was a subject of constant banter and mocking. The idea that colour could make no difference was, indeed, new at that time! I reread the first contribution by 'Meekolo'.

> Two young aboriginal boys were playing outside the manager's office on a Western station. ... They peered through the open door every now and then to see what the boss was doing. The manager happened to spoil a cheque before he signed it, so, tearing it out of the book, he handed it to one of the dusky youngsters. 'What this fella?' asked the boy, turning the piece of paper around in his hands. 'That is a cheque — it is your wages', said the manager with a smile. The lad walked outside where he met his dusky companion. 'What you got there?' asked the other boy. 'My wages',

was the reply. 'The boss been give me cheque'. There was a lengthy examination of the piece of paper, then suddenly the first lad's face lit up with a smile and he looked at his mate: 'You want half?' he asked. 'All right' was the reply. The cheque was immediately torn in halves and the two boys were happy.[42]

On the face of it this was a common enough yarn about an Aborigine's ignorance in financial matters. Nevertheless, the Aboriginal boy sharing the cheque with his mate — even if done in an ignorant way — won a moral victory over his educated boss.

Dignity and self-respect of the Aborigines in contrast to the whites' stereotypes made a comic effect in the following yarns as well. The first was one Leandro picked up from his 'pioneer mate'.

> In the early days this pioneer's cousin took a Queensland aboriginal to Adelaide. During their long journey the dusky youth often noticed that his boss, when departing from hotels, always wrote out a cheque and presented it to the publican. In Adelaide the aboriginal soon longed for his native land so, one day he stole a horse, saddle and bridle, and started on the return journey to Queensland. At the first township he came to he stopped at the hotel for a night. After breakfast the following morning he acted in the same way as his boss had done on the downward trip. He went into the bar and asked how much he owed. On receiving the necessary information he promptly produced his boss's cheque book which he had stolen, and securing a pen and ink, scribbled a cheque. It is hardly necessary to state here the dusky youth was soon handed over to the police and was kept busy with an axe in the jail yard until his boss was notified and took him away.[43]

The second of Leandro's yarns was probably one from his experience on the Tablelands.

> A farmer's little daughter had for playmates two aboriginal girls. Years later when they grew to womanhood

the three girls were married. One day the farmer's daughter, with her children, happened to be attending a race meeting at the township near where she lived, and she was sitting watching the horses walking up to the barrier, an aboriginal woman with three children came and sat beside her. 'Good day Mrs — ' she said. The white woman stared at the speaker for a few minutes and then suddenly recognised her as one of her dusky playmates of bygone days. 'My goodness, Bessie', she said, 'I have not seen you for years'. The aboriginal smiled. 'Yes, it is me', she said, 'and I thought I would come and see you'. 'That was indeed good of you', said the farmer's wife. 'I am told that Mary is also here. I wonder why she does not come and see me.' 'Oh', replied Bessie, 'I suppose she is ashamed. You know she did not marry properly like you and I'. 'Indeed', said the white woman, 'how is that?' 'Well you know', said Bessie, 'you married a white man, I married a black man, but she been marry a Chinaman, so I suppose she too ashamed to see you'.[44]

The trustfulness of the Aborigines, their inclination to see good in the whites' doings even when it was not the case, contributed to the comic effect in the following story; again, as in the story with the cheque and two boys, a naïve and trustful Aboriginal seemed in a way more attractive than the 'clever' white. Its characters were miners and Aborigines from Boonjie, a place Leandro knew well.

In a Northern township where there is a State battery, a miner, now dead and gone, lived with his wife and family. An ancient lubra used to visit them daily to assist the miner's wife with her housework, and she had a habit of crying and moaning whenever she wanted a nip of rum. On these occasions she used to wail, 'By cripes, missie me sick, berry berry sick'. Generally the white woman took pity on her and gave her a drink out of the bottle that was always kept in the house. However, the miner, noticing that the precious fluid which, by rights should have been kept for his own use, was fast disappearing, decided that he would teach the lubra a lesson.

He made up the following mixture which medical men have my permission to use: Castor oil, olive oil, eucalyptus oil, sewing machine oil, pepper, salt, mustard, gunpowder, sulphur, painkiller, curry, golden syrup, sugar, turpentine and ground ginger. I cannot supply the exact quantities of each ingredient that was used, but after mixing them all together he added a tumbler of rum. The following morning the lubra was sick again and she was given a nip out of the prepared bottle much against the wishes of the white woman.

The lubra did not visit the house again for several months, and the miner began to fear that she had died in the bush as a result of the decoction he had made for her special benefit. They were unable to make any special enquiries about her as, about this time, all the aborigines near the township shifted to another place where they held a big corroboree. One day the lubra again turned up at the miner's house, and strange to say, she was fat, healthy-looking and her dusky face beamed with smiles. She was leading a young sickly-looking gin about half as old as herself. 'Why it's Polly', said the miner's wife. 'I thought you were dead'. 'No plurry fear, Missus', grinned the lubra. 'Me been go longa corroboree 'noder place. Where boss, Missus?' The white woman wished to know why the lubra inquired about her husband. 'Well you see, Missus', said Polly, 'this fella gin here been my granny, an' by cripes she berry sick. Mine been thinkit if boss got any more of that medicine he been give me it might cure her. That been berry good medicine all right, Missus.'[45]

* * *

That was Leandro's last contribution for 1926. Some weeks later I received a heap of microfilm reels for the following years, 1927 and 1928, and was looking forward to the discovery of new stories by Leandro when the first 'On the Track' for 1927 gave Leandro's collaboration with Bill Bowyang an unexpected twist.

'IT IS NOT OFTEN THAT I GET A LETTER FINDING FAULT with any-thing that appears in these articles,' Bill Bowyang wrote, 'but the fol-lowing is an exception. It comes from Mr. Leandro Illin, Clarke River, Charters Towers, and I am using the writer's exact words:

"It is a while since I have written to you. I would write a lot often-er if you did not print all my yarns in a totally different style. For G—'s sake never again in your or other people's yarns put it to a nigger's mouth the words 'Mine think it'. You never heard a nigger or gin speak like that. I never did nor no one else. Your pidgeon English is not up to the nigger style. Evidently you have not been much amongst abos. You may take it to heart what I am writing to you. Well I must, as I am enti-tled to it. You have spoiled nearly all my yarns. I would rather have them rejected than printed in the way you do. I always read my yarns to my friends, who are your readers, and after they read them again in the *North Queensland Register* the usual verdict on the second reading is 'Up to putty', 'Don't sound true', 'Sounds very tame'. And they laughed at them before I sent them to you. ... You are afraid to hurt someone's feel-ings as if I myself have not got the sense to disguise the people and the localities ... I like to give you plenty yarns as I have plenty in store, liv-ing for over 16 years among abos. But give us a chance and a fair go. You are Australian, I think, and as such you should not take exception much to what I say. I would like to meet you ... You promised to write me once. You did not keep your promise. If I am a contributor do not forget I am also a reader. I send you yarns because I like to see them printed and it makes me glad to think that someone might have a little laugh. It is good to laugh some times. I am giving it to you straight off the shoulder. I like the human and humane touch in the 'Track' articles because they are the voice of the people. Don't be over scrupulous and prudent but give the people a chance to express themselves. You may print my jokes or not (as perhaps you won't after this). I may be the vic-tim to suffer as I will because I like to see my things printed, but if you give a more open hand to other people I will be repaid for my own loss. You are in the lucky position to accept or refuse or alter. Do it fairly. The fellow who only praises you is not your best friend".'

The letter was followed by Bill Bowyang's comment.

'IT MIGHT BE JUST AS WELL TO EXPLAIN for the benefit of my read-ers, that this display of fireworks on the part of Mr. Leandro Illin is owing to the fact that some months past he sent me a contribution I considered would be disagreeable to "Track" readers. There may be a place for such yarns, but it is not in these columns. The altering of this story probably offended Mr. Illin. I regret this as most of his contributions were interesting and often amusing. When he objects to the aboriginal term "Mine think it", I do not agree with him. However I invite readers to pass their opinion on this question, and their letters will be printed. If Mr. Illin is correct then Australian writers who serve out aboriginal humor are on the wrong track. Mr. Illin believes I have not been much amongst aborigines. Well, I dunno. I was born and reared on a western station where there was only a handful of whitemen, the remainder being blacks. Later on I travelled in a bullock dray, by slow stages, to Croydon and had a good deal to do with black brother for many years. Many of these natives belonged to the far-famed Kalkadoon tribe. They were splendid representatives of the aboriginal race and far removed from many wretched specimens of this dusky race who loaf around our township these days. I am sorry Mr. Illin objects to having his copy altered. If he knew my numerous pen-names he would believe me when I state I am, probably, the most prolific freelance journalist in Australia at the present time, and yet my copy is often altered — and improved — by the editors of the papers to whom I contribute. ... I hope Mr. Illin will continue to contribute to these columns, and perhaps he will yet agree to having his yarns put into shape by a writer who considers he does know something about the preparation of Australian humor for publication.'[46]

It would appear, to judge from the printed versions of the Meekolo stories, that Bowyang's 'shaping' involved not inconsiderable changes with the effect of smoothing out the distinctive tone of Leandro's voice and making it conform more closely to his own style — more changes, in fact, than Leandro mentions in his letter. But the 'Track' readers in their numerous responses were not, it seemed, able to see what was the most important point of Leandro's objections. Some of them stated that 'Aboriginals use the phrase "Mine thinkit" in answer to nearly every question'. Others argued 'I never heard any Aboriginal use the words. I have heard them use the following: "Me bin t'ink 'em" and "By cripes, I bin t'ink 'em nother one"'. Another insisted on 'I think it' or 'Me knowem'.[47] It was as if Leandro's only concern was some minor point about the correct variant of this Pidgin English phrase, but the issues that concerned him were more important. Should a writer accept alterations which contradict his style, if he aspires to be published? Should a writer distort the language of Aborigines in a way which is considered humorous, to support the established stereotype, even if it contradicts his own experience? And, the most important point of all: can there be humour that shows respect for the Aboriginal characters even when they are the subject of it — a humour that derives from a different world outlook rather than from an artificial mangling of people's speech?

* * *

I continued to search through the 'On the Track' columns year after year, but it was in vain. Leandro never returned with his yarns to these columns. I had underestimated his adherence to his principles. Did I not know that once he said: 'Matters of principle are not trivial. Men die to uphold their principle'? In 1927 Leandro Illin killed off 'Meekolo', a beginner bush-writer, in order not to give up on his principles. He chose the freedom of yarn-telling around the camp-fire, where nobody could alter his stories — not even such an experienced writer as Bill Bowyang.

...«До скораго
— конечно Да! ...
... под дождемъ ... ка
... отъ сумасшествія ...
... тому назвать, ...
... нетъ мен.. нормаль...
... не может)
... Dna ... ...
... ... — написа...
... придумать того
... разъ не жилъ ...
... каждую минуту
... либо ... ...
... радуюсь ...
...

FROM UTOPIA, FOR UTOPIA...?

UTOPIA ON THE STONE RIVER

In July 1929 Leandro took his family to the annual show in Ingham. Noise, bustle, horses, trucks, faces of acquaintances, sounds of a band and a few shillings clutched in your hand that promise such pleasure — a packet of lollies, an ice-cream or a ride on the merry-go-round. Did not Nicholas's children feel a similar excitement when they found themselves in the bustle of Paris in 1910, after a decade in the Patagonian mountains. A photographer took a picture of them at Ingham. Leandro is flanked by his two eldest, Ginger and Dick — they are already the same height as he is, real men to rely on. And how much of Kitty is in their faces! Tom and Harry — still in short pants — resemble their father more, but the two girls, Lullie and Flora, seem a mystery. Slim and tense, dressed in their best bush dresses, they seem unopened flowers that soon will blossom. And an Aboriginal boy, Kennedy — in Illin's family there was always a place for a friend.

After that visit Leandro decided to move closer to Ingham so that at least the younger children would have some schooling.

'WHEN WE COME TO INGHAM', Flora relates, 'there was a store-keeper down there. They were very rich and owned half of Ingham, properties and stores and everything. And he said to my father, "Well, I'll give you a house and you can try to milk some cows". Then we left the station and come down to Toobanna. It was a small place near the railway between Ingham and Townsville but there was a school there. We stayed there for twelve months.

'There was plenty of this fellow's cattle on the property. We had to break them in to be able to milk them. They used to put them into the bail, hold their head, tied their legs, and I used to be milking, most of the cows. Plenty times the cow kick me. Boys did not like it, my eldest brothers, about the cows, how they used to kick.

'It did not work out right, so my father said "Oh, well". He saw another man, Alston at Stone River, he was partners with people at Greenvale, Atkinsons. He had a property and he had to put somebody on it, to build on it to improve it, so they put my father there. It was all big scrub. It was hard. There were no tractors those days, you had to work with your hands, to dig ground and pull the trees out, and lantana, which was very terrible pest, prickly and poisonous and very thick, oh, and it was a big job to clean this land.

'Alstons named the property Utopia, it belonged to the Stoneleigh station, but we used to call the place Stone River. They were putting the house up just before we got here and we had to stay in the barracks at Stoneleigh for a while and then we shifted from Stoneleigh to here in 1931. And we lived here for about twelve years.

'There was scrub all around. My father and the boys used to cut and sell firewood for a living, because the people used only wood stoves in those days. They used to cut timber, load it on a cart and the horses would pull it down to the local line of the railway and then they put the timber on the motor train. So that was the way they lived down there until the war broke out. It was hard life.'

Leandro's own record of those years was quite dry: 'I am living on a property belonging to Mr Alston ... on the Upper Stone near the foot of the Sea View Range on what they call Water Full Creek. I cut wood with my boys, rear pigs, grow English Potatoes, etc.' Flora fills out the picture.

'OUR HOUSE HAD TWO ROOMS AND VERANDA ALL AROUND, we used to eat on the veranda. There was no stove or anything, no electricity, just an open fire on the other side of the house ... There was nothing, just this one house. Wild old place, wasn't it! Hard life, but in a sense much healthier than now. We worked hard and went to bed earlier. You could not have a lot of food, it was very difficult here. You had to go a long way for the food, a bit of meat sometimes — you had no fridge to keep anything. Might be a tin of jam and a tin of syrup, and a bit of potato and onion, a bit of rice. That's all. That's all we ever lived on. Never lived on a lot of good food, luxury, anything like that.

'The scrub, there was no high grass in it. Grass came after us. It was clear. We used to hunt for turkey, pigeons, cassowaries. Turkey was the luxury. There were only little wallabies and they were very sweet. Sometimes we'd catch some fish in the river, at night time you'd have a light here and spear eels.

'Oranges were here when we came here. We had a vegetable garden way down to the river. There was a lagoon and we used to water our vegetables. We used to grow a lot of vegetables there, and we took first prize with the cabbages at the show. There were plenty of stones in the river, but it was a clean-water river. Oh yes, it was clean, it wasn't like it is now. It was deep here and we used to swim. This was our bathroom. I used to walk right down there to the river, wash our clothes, boil all the clothes in a tin, carry them back and hang them up. It was hard work, it wasn't easy.'

Flora, indeed, is a woman who would never dwell on the hardships she happened to endure. Now, sixty-five years later, there are some words by Leandro himself we can add to her understated account of their life back in the depression years: 'When my daughter worked for Mrs *** washing all day hard, men's rough dirty soiled working clothes, Mrs *** paid her at the rate of 3/- per day and once gave her a bottle of marmalade for a whole day's work and no 3/-'.[1]

Dick talks about the depression years, too.

'I WAS TOO OLD TO GO TO SCHOOL. I worked in the canefields from daylight to dark six days a week just for tucker. I received no pay. My younger brothers had to get up at sunrise to round up the cows for my father (we had no mother), the youngest being six years old at the time, and milk the cows before going to school. ...

'During the Ingham Show, my father was asked if he would like to take the family to the show and was offered 30 shillings. This being the only money we had received for six months work we had done.'

Leandro himself, even though handicapped by his worsening heart disease, tackled any job. He wrote without any enthusiasm about his experience working on the almost impassable road which led from Ingham to their Utopia:

'I WAS WORKING ON THE ROAD. There were six of us doing the work, and four bosses, three of them standing over us continually and exerting us to our utmost. I think one competent Overseer and a ganger should be able to supervise the number of men working there. ... Well, the four bosses decided to economise so I left and I am not sorry.'

'FATHER WAS A TOBACCONIST, TOO', according to Harry. 'He was an agent for a firm in Brisbane, selling tobacco, and he got a commission out of it. It was in Upper Stone and when he was in Ingham, he was still selling tobacco. Right till he died.'[2]

Still, their location had its good side, as Flora relates.

'HARRY AND LULLIE WENT to Upper Stone school just for a couple of years. It was about five miles from our place and they used to get to school by bike. We had a buggy and horses as well. That's how we used to get around. Upper Stone was just a small place but down there near the school there was a dance hall. And there was a bus from Upper Stone to Ingham, it was half-an-hour drive.'

'I HAVE REARED AN AUSTRALIAN FAMILY'

Access to Ingham also greatly expanded Leandro's social contacts and, particularly, returned him to the multinational heritage of his family.

Besides Australian and Aboriginal contacts, there were more opportunities to meet Russians, Spaniards and Italians.

His Russianness always remained important for him. After ten years spent in isolation in Gunnawarra and Greenvale the opportunity to re-establish contacts with Russians was both pain and pleasure. The Russians he met near Ingham were a different type of Russian from those in Little Siberia. These were so-called White Russians, who had fought in the civil war (which swept Russia after the revolution) against the revolutionary, or Red, forces. One of these families was the Kormishens. According to Flora:

'SERGE KORMISHEN WAS SOME KIND OF ENGINEER IN RUSSIA, and his wife, Shura, was a great dress-maker. They fought the Red Army, they were in the White Army. Kormishen used to work on the railway near Toobanna. My father acquainted with them there and they were friends till his death. Shura had a sister, Lydia, who was married to Vissarion Kuznetsov. They both, Kormishen and Kuznetsov, worked on the railway line. Later on they ended up taking a farm. But they weren't young people any more, the work was very very hard, they used to work from daylight till dark, and Shura used to sew from morning to midnight, she used to work very hard, she used to have a big job, she used to have a lot of dress-making. And Lydia, oh, she killed herself by drinking too much ...'[3]

Another family which became friends with Leandro were the Jitnikoffs, Philipp and Mary. Philipp also had fought the Reds and had two bullet scars on his back. After the Whites were defeated in Siberia, the Jitnikoffs came to Australia and settled near Ingham. Philipp worked on the construction of the Ingham–Cardwell railway at first and later took a sugar-cane farm in Yuruga.[4] 'He would play chess and talk with my grandad for hours', Ernie says. What a forgotten pleasure it was for Leandro to speak his native tongue, the tongue that none of his family could understand.

His children spoke only one language — Australian English — and outwardly they seemed much like other Australian children that might have a cosmopolitan background: they didn't seem specifically Russian or Aboriginal. Leandro accepted this as inevitable. Hazel, Tom's daughter, relates: 'I asked dad why he did not learn to speak Russian and he said that Leandro, his father, said that it was an English-speaking country and he was to speak English'. Similarly, Flora's son Ernie remembers that, when his father tried to teach him his native

Aboriginal language Gugu-Badhun, Leandro did not approve of that. It might seem that Leandro accepted the policy of assimilation reigning at that time. But that would be only half of the truth. Unlike many other immigrants who chose to forget about their ethnic origin to facilitate their children's acceptance into Australian society and switched completely to English language and even culture, Leandro taught his children never to be ashamed of their Russian or Aboriginal backgrounds — this in times when these backgrounds were not highly esteemed in Australia. 'People used to say to my father', says Flora, '"Why you did not teach your children Russian?" He said, "But how could I, two people got to be speaking all the time and so the kids can pick it up". Father never taught us Russian but he used to try to tell us words, what this meant.'

Dick and Flora had some experience of Russian while they were with *Deda* and *Baba*. Now, nearly eighty years afterwards, when I asked Flora about it she suddenly extracted from the depths of her memory *moloko* (milk) and *nyet* (no). Dick, according to his daughters, once when visiting a Russian show in Townsville during his later years said that he recognised a lot of words.

It was a similar situation with the Aboriginal language, as Flora tells: 'My mother sometimes said something, some words, an animal, snake or lizard or whatever, she might rouse on us in her language'. Flora still remembers a lot of animals and words for parts of the body in Ngadjon.[5]

Still there was Russianness, which showed quite unexpectedly in Leandro's youngest daughter, Lullie. It was her own decision to be baptised into the Russian Orthodox Church. Leandro always told his children that they could choose their own religion and it seems Lullie was baptised, not because of her father's example, but because of the influence of the family of her Greek friends. At the age of eighteen she went as a nursemaid with them from Ingham to Brisbane. She felt lonely there and that further contributed to her decision to baptise. When some Russian old-timers from Brisbane heard that I was writing about the Illins, one lady suddenly remembered a surprise in the Russian community in 1941 caused by the baptism at the Russian St Nicholas Church of a girl who looked distinctively Aboriginal but had the Russian name Vera Illin. Soon, Lullie returned to Ingham. It seems she did not practise her religion later as there was no church in Ingham, where she lived for the rest of her life.

They spoke English but it did not make Leandro feel bitter — they were not turning themselves into the snobbish English from overseas. The language they spoke was Australian English, the culture they grew up into was Australian culture. It was Australianness rather than Englishness, which replaced Russianness and Aboriginality in his children. And that allowed Leandro to be proud. Australians were for him a new nation with distinctive features. He wrote: 'In over 26 years in Australia I think I have learnt what Australians are. They are hardy, self-reliant, resourceful men, capable and gamblers with nature and chances and not easily daunted by ups and downs, even if they are extravagant and not very saving while times are bountiful.' 'Australians love fair play and so do I'. He also considered them to be patriotic and mentioned their respect for their natural resources: 'no Australian, no matter what his status in society, ... will destroy water'. 'Those days', Flora adds, 'people used to work and was always ready to help one another and that's what my father liked about Australia.' Not surprisingly, he felt proud that he and his family were a part of this new nation. 'I have reared an Australian family', he would say, 'I lived 30 years happy under Australian rule and if the time comes I and my sons will defend this soil from invasion'.[6]

'DICK IS A MAN THAT LOOKS A FELLOW IN THE EYES STRAIGHT'

Life, though, never allowed Leandro's children to forget that they were Aborigines. The hardest battle they had to fight was for Flora's boyfriend. He was Richard Hoolihan, also known as Dick Shaw, from the Valley of Lagoons station. They had become acquainted at Greenvale, where he had worked. His father, Michael Hoolahan (or Hoolihan), was Irish. His mother, Lucy, belonged to Gugu-Badhun. She was one of the wives of King Lava, who received a brass plate bearing this title from the whites. Richard, born in around 1905, grew up in the Valley of Lagoons absorbing what still remained from the Aboriginal culture of his ancestors. Years later anthropologist Peter Sutton would write about him: 'Mr. Richard Hoolihan was my main informant, and the original instigator of the plan to have his language [Gugu-Badhun] recorded for posterity'.

But at the time when Richard met Flora posterity was the least of his worries. He dreamt of the world outside the station, about education. His Irish father had wanted to take him away from the station and send him to school, but Richard, because was 'a half-caste', was not allowed to leave the station. Leandro Illin was his first teacher. Richard would tell Ernie and Maud how 'Daddy Illin' showed him the letters and helped to write his first name. The rest he picked up himself looking at comics. Richard married Flora in 1932, soon after they settled at Stone River. Leandro helped him to obtain exemption from the Act. Flora tells the story.

'MY FATHER GOT A SOLICITOR TO GET AN EXEMPTION FOR RICHARD. They gave him an exemption from the Act, but they would not release his money. He had around £200 and police kept this money and did not give it to him. After Richard married me my father wanted to help him but police reckoned that my father was going to rob him for the money. In 1933 Queensland Premier Hanlon was coming to Ingham. My father took Richard and me and Ernie, he was just six months old, and my husband's solicitor, and we all went to the railway station when the premier was arriving. The solicitor went to the police and said, "This man here wants to speak to the premier", and the police went to the premier and said, "This man here wants to speak to you". And the premier looked at my father and he said, "And who the hell is he?" And my father said straightaway, "Well, if you listen to me you will know who I am". So he started listening. My father put us in front of the premier and he said, "Look, this is my son-in-law, this is my daughter married to him, this is my grandchild here". He said, "They reckon they won't release his money because, they reckon, I might take his money from him, rob him. What would I rob my daughter and grandchild for? It his money, they should release it for him." After that, the premier promised that the money would be released and Richard got the money.'[7]

Flora's story is a good example of traditional oral storytelling. It features a conflict between a hero and evil forces settled by a *deux ex machina*. It has a classical development with short introduction, rapid climax — 'Who the hell is he?' — and happy ending. The real development of the story as recorded in the documents was quite different in style: it was prolonged and exhausting, with human meanness, numerous features of the real life on the cattle stations and in police stations.

The file[8] opens in 1925 when the owner of the Valley of Lagoons, L.O. Micklem, applied to the Chief Protector of Aboriginals to exempt Dick, 'an intelligent boy, good rider and stockman'. Protector Hogan from Mt Garnet in an accompanying note asserted that Dick was unable to handle his money and was a 'flash and loud half caste'. In 1928, working in Greenvale, Dick applied for the exemption for the second time, and again his application was followed by the report of the new Protector from Mt Garnet, J.D. Lucey: 'The boy has defied the Protectors to place him under agreement and has also endeavoured to get other boys who are signed on at Gunnawarra and Cashmere Stations to refuse to work under an agreement'. It was rare indeed for such conscious civil disobedience to be practised by an Aborigine even at this stage in Australian history. Not surprisingly, he was refused exemption once again. But by this time the exemption had become an issue of extreme importance for him as there was Flora.

Leandro wrote about those days: '... he came to me and said: Old man, I want Flora! I said, it is no news to me! does she want you? She is alright! he said. And look here, he said, if she doubts me I will swim the Hinchinbrook Channel and get there or die in the attempt.'

Later, when they finally marry and Leandro is accused by the Ingham Protector of letting his daughter, 'a mere child', marry a 'black fellow' who was 'totally incapable to look after himself', Leandro wrote: 'I thought the world of Dick and my daughter. The fact of him being a halfcaste did not prevent him to be an honourable man, a first class horsebreaker and an intelligent man who can read Tolstoy or London. ... As regards my daughter's youth and her marriage she belonged to the Abo race who matured quicker and ... her mother (my wife) had her first child at 13.' Leandro was not an obstacle to their marriage, by any means. The real obstacle was that Flora, by marrying a man 'under the Act', would herself then become a slave 'under the Act'. Leandro remembered *Uncle Tom's Cabin* by Harriet Beecher Stowe, which he had read in his childhood. But even in a nightmare he could not have imagined then that the story might be repeated years later in a civilised, democratic country and affect his own family. He taught Dick spelling out of the book and it captivated both of them.

They lodged the third application for exemption and soon Lucey furnished the Chief Protector with a fresh report: 'There is a Russian named Leandro Illen at Greenvale who lived with a gin some years ago, ... he would like to see Shaw [that is, Dick Hoolihan] exempt so as he could marry his daughter and use Shaws money to his Illens advantage'. After a new refusal Leandro, in despair, appealed for help to his old friend from the time of the 1912 Russian colony project, the Labor MLA, G.P. Barber, reminding him about their 'long past meetings'. But even Barber's intervention did not help. He was cynically informed by Chief Protector Bleakley, who artfully shifted the responsibility to the local Protector:

'ALTHOUGH THE MAN SEEMS FAIRLY INTELLIGENT and probably in other circumstances would be deemed capable of managing his own affairs, the Local Protector feels he cannot in the boy's own interests recommend this freedom be given him at present. ... He also has a large sum of money to his credit and as the Russian, Leandro Illin is very anxious for Shaw to marry his daughter, it is felt that his persistency in applying for the latter's exemption is not wholly disinterested.'

Barber's support helped him, as Leandro wrote, to overcome 'the insult and pain inflicted on me and my honour by the dirty Mt Garnet Police and the Chief Protector of Abos'. He later wrote to Barber: 'I ... never a day in my life forget you and all you done for us'. Meanwhile, the nightmare continued. In 1931 the Mt Garnet Protector again reported that Dick 'has tried to cause trouble with the other natives in this District by trying to obtain exemption for most of them, and if he were to be granted exemption now he would be more cocky than ever he was'.

At that stage the Illins had left Greenvale and settled in Utopia. To marry Flora, Dick finally submitted himself to work under the humiliating conditions of an agreement as an Aborigine, which he had not done since 1924. When Dick applied for exemption for the fourth time it was done from the Ingham area, out of reach of the Mt Garnet Protector's accusations. It succeeded and finally, in February 1932, the Ingham Protector sent a favourable report to Bleakley: 'He proved himself to be a good hard working boy and capable ... He never drinks and is very intelligent and honest.' But Bleakley had a good memory and immediately reminded the Ingham Protector about 'Illin, who is a Russian, lives amongst Aboriginals and was anxious to get Shaw's money'. As a result Dick, although exempt on 4 April 1932, did not get his money, which remained in the hands of the local police. On 16 May 1932 Dick, now a free man, married Flora. But the happy ending was far away yet. Leandro wrote:

'DICK ... WAS PROMISED BY THE PROTECTOR TO HAVE HIS ACCOUNT RELEASED in 12 months. When he got married he decided to buy a runabout truck and applied for the money to the Protectors Office. ... £50 was granted. He did not wait, foolishly, in his excitement being married and borrowed £60 at 8 per cent of the friend of his childhood

J.H. Atkinson. ... Himself an honourable man it never came to any doubt in his mind that his money will not be released and that the promise will not be kept. ... Then he applied through his solicitor for the release of his account and evidently the local police has objected and so Dick did not get neither the £50 nor his money. When he went with Solicitor Clements to the Police to try to meet P[romisory] N[ote] the Sergeant told him he will have nothing to do with it and that Dick can be put back under the Act. (Nice perspective for my daughter!)

'I would not survive that. ... I am worried to death. I can't sleep for worry! My daughter is pleading to Dick to write to the Protector and take all the money as it is the bone of contention. She says any half-castes that have no money live happy. Personally I am of the same opinion.'

By that time they had a newborn, Ernie, who might get into slavery together with his parents, too. After nineteen years of Leandro's confrontation with the Chief Protector, Bleakley's chance to teach 'Russian Illin' a lesson seemed to have come. Leandro realised that he could not lose a day. On 17 June 1933 he undertook the humiliating procedure of asking his neighbours and local authorities to sign a petition to the Home Secretary stating — as in a Kafkaesque nightmare — that 'he is not a man to rob his family and son-in-law Dick Hoolihan. Leandro Illin is a very fond father of his children and son-in-law and dedicates his life fully to their welfare ...'. A few days later he, together with his family, confronted E.M. Hanlon, a newly appointed Labor Home Secretary, on the railway platform when the latter visited Ingham. Dick's solicitor was to introduce them, but, Leandro tells, 'went to pieces. ... I was not going to miss our chance and butted in'. The big boss did, indeed, promise to look into the matter but Leandro's worries were far from ending.

A few days later, on the day of the Ingham Show, Leandro and his family confronted another politician, A.W. Fadden, MLA, a former resident of Stone River district. He was favourably impressed with Dick and promised them 'hearty support'. Leandro recorded after the meeting: 'During our conversation ... black and brindle lean to us. Although the Police calls them "halfcastes", "black fellows", Mr Fadden was not afraid to shake hands with them and even with my old cobbers blacks ... [and] was not afraid to talk to "low stupid black fellows" in front of all the town folk.' That was the best characteristic for a politician in Leandro's eyes and he began to trust Fadden.

There followed numerous letters from Leandro to Barber, Hanlon and Fadden — appalling human documents. Within one month, 'half dead with flu', he wrote at least fifty pages appealing for justice for Dick, for himself and for other Aborigines. He remarked in a letter to Fadden: 'Writing such long letters might be annoying to you. It is like story writing and so it is, as it is pages out of a story of a man's life.'

Dick Hoolihan was main hero of the letters. His car — a flashy second-hand 'Pontiac' — that caused all the trouble and which he bought in Townsville against the advice of Leandro, who was 'an enemy of all cars', broke down halfway from Townsville to Ingham and after numerous repairs Dick exchanged it for a more reliable Ford utility. Still, Leandro never reproached Dick, just stating that he 'has learned his lesson about cars'. Leandro always treated Dick with love, respect and understanding. Describing Dick's confrontation with the Ingham Protector, Sergeant Collier, Leandro wrote:

'DICK IS A MAN THAT LOOKS A FELLOW IN THE EYES STRAIGHT. ... Dick came and told me: "that Sergeant can't look a man in the eyes. Every time I look at him he looks sideways or down." By the way Dick is one of them inexplicable mysteries so often described in books about native races. He suddenly tells us sometimes about something is happening away somewhere. Telepathy is very developed in him. He often reads another fellow's mind. He knows when there is a death anywhere about or someone coming. ... As a horsebreaker: the wildest of the horses start to shiver and stand still once he puts his hands on them and his face against their nostrils. ... He broke ... most of Atkinson and Alston's blood race horses. And that is the man they try to keep at 30/- per week!'

Besides praising Dick's numerous bush crafts, Leandro wrote of him in terms the like of which the Chief Protector's Department had probably never heard before from anyone about an Aboriginal person. The department, he said, asks for:

'REFERENCES FROM MEN WHO CAN READ ONLY BEER LABELS ON BOTTLES ... [for] men who read Tolstoy, Beecher Stowe, Jack London, [Richard] Dana and a host of others names of authors that most policemen never heard. There is more inside of Dick Hoolihan's woolly head than inside of a dozen full blown Sergeants (sometimes beer blown). ... Dick is the only really sober, truthful, intelligent above the average, decent fellow in town I know of. And I would not have a paddock full of whites such as they are.'

The situation arising from Dick asking for his own money which nearly resulted in his being put back under the Act, dragging with him his wife and baby, put paid to Dick's plan to apply for 8 acres on the bank of the Stone River; he wanted to build a hut there for his family, go in for poultry and be his own master. 'Why can't they help the emancipation of a man instead of keeping him down?', Leandro appealed. 'The Police if they are Protectors should not reproach a halfcaste being one. ... He is not guilty that a white man stepped into the shoes of the man who should have been his father.'

In these letters Leandro wrote about numerous cases when Aborigines were severely bashed by the Ingham police, which seemed to be a powerful institution — 'I don't want any inquiries as it is too dangerous. Once a man gets in the bad books with the Police he is a doomed man. He can be bashed about under the slightest pretext.' Even so, Leandro always gave justice to honest people whom he occasionally met among policemen: 'But I must say that every halfcaste gives a great name to Constable Lewis lock up keeper. He invariably according to their reports comes on the scene and intimidates that he does not want the boys bashed. He advises them paternally to keep sober, tells them he does not want them in the lock up, feeds them.' Such paternalism was widespread. In Dick's case, when Dick came to Sergeant McHugh asking for £1 for his wedding the Sergeant suddenly said: 'Give him a fiver, ... a man wants more than a pound when he gets married' (this being at a time when Dick had over £200 in his bank account — kind policemen, indeed!).

'As for me! Am I not only one of the fathers of 3000 odd halfcastes in Queensland?', Leandro wrote in a moment of despair in his letters to Hanlon and Fadden. 'There is 3000 more halfcastes in Queensland that have fathers who neglected them. They are men in all walks of life. There is sons of squatters, station bookkeepers, stockmen, farmers, town residents and I know even halfcastes who claim policemen and clergymen for fathers. You can meet them every day. Well to do, comfortable, successful, married to white women. Most respectfull. I am one who would not leave my load allotted to me. I carried it in the face of the world. And I get all the kicks. ... For 19 years I done my duty to my family and I fought for every black that I seen wronged. ... The Chief Protector thinks me a crook and the Mt Garnet Police also Charters Towers have slurred me. They are protected by the Maltese Cross, and it is foolish of me ever to think I will break through that wall. ... Now my spirit is broke. I only want peace for mine.'

'Better to break, my son, but never bend' — the uncompromising injunction his father had placed on him when Leandro was just eight years old seemed to have come to pass. But there were people, his black brothers, for whom things were much worse than for him, and he, crushed and maligned, would rise again and again and continue to demand from the officials real protection and justice for Aborigines, however utopian that might seem in those harsh times:

'WHY THE HON. THE HOME SECRETARY DOES NOT FORM an Aboriginal Affairs Committee locally selected and let the blacks select a man or two black or white and report to the Chief Protector. Any sick, needy, down trodden fellows could approach them and be communicated through them to the Home Secretary's office without being totally dependent on the over bearing unsympathetic insulting Police.'

Biased as I am in knowing what a crystal-clear, honest man Leandro was, I still make myself look at the situation through Bleakley's eyes. His grandson, Neville Bleakley, says about him: 'He was no power-broker. He was a quiet, dignified, bookish man who, as a public servant, wrote policies for the government of the day. He was benevolent, if very conservative. ... He honestly believed he was acting in the best interests of the Aboriginal people.'

And I ask myself — could it be that he honestly believed that Leandro married his daughter to Dick just to get hold of £200? Could he honestly believe that denying Dick's exemption and making him work under the agreement, which halved his income, protects Dick's interests? That no man would help Aborigines disinterestedly, as Leandro claimed to do? It all might just have been possible if it were not for the fact that he had known Leandro since 1914, when he, one of thousands of white men, married the Aboriginal mother of his child, and parted forever with his own parents in order not to separate his wife and his stepson, and raised six children after his wife's death ... I cannot find any reasonable explanation for Bleakley's attitude. Probably he just shared the Ingham Protector, Sergeant Collier's position: 'An Aboriginal is an Aboriginal to me'. 'To me he is a human being', Leandro commented about these words. On the National Sorry Day Bleakley's grandson said 'Sorry' on behalf of the grandfather he remembers.[9] It is for Aborigines to decide whether or not to accept this apology.

As for Richard Hoolihan, the main character in this particular story

— this first victory in defending his human rights, their win over the system, made a deep impact on the rest of his life. A relay in defending human dignity and equal rights that started with Nicholas Illin in the 1870s, passing the baton on through Leandro and his son-in-law Richard Hoolihan, reached Koiki Mabo in the 1960s, who by the 1990s turned the tide of Australian history.

Meanwhile, Leandro, a dreamer from Utopia, continued his struggle for equal rights for Aborigines. The case of his stepson Ginger (George Williamson) never stopped worrying him. A letter of 1940 to the director of Native Affairs signed by Ginger — Leandro taught him to write, too — was obviously composed and written by Leandro himself. Who else would put humiliation above financial injustice when writing to an official about an Aboriginal's problems at that time!

'IT IS VERY HUMILIATING FOR GEORGE TO RECEIVE A DIFFERENT RATE OF PAY to what his brothers receive on the same sort of work. ... George is sufficiently enlightned and capable to manage his own affairs and knows very well right from wrong.

'George is an able drover, horseman, timber cutter, lorry driver and general labourer.

'His mother died in 1925 but he [sticks] to his brothers and sisters as well as to his stepfather and he knows no other home. It is an humiliating anomaly for him to be the only member of the [family] "under the Act" and it hurts immensely his pride. His intelligence and his social outlook is in no way inferior to his brothers nor any average man. George is clean, temperant, courteous, ... very humorous and well behaved and well like[d] by all who know him well. George is no camp frequenter as camp life does not appeal to him. His social principles are very clean and sound (born in him).'

An Aborigine with a sense of humour and pride, with inborn 'clean and sound social principles' was an unusual idea for the authorities to deal with and it took them a year-and-a-half before George was granted complete exemption from the Act.[10]

Leandro's fame as a defender of Aborigines went far beyond the Ingham area — to Valley of Lagoons and Greenvale, to Blue Range and Christmas Creek. 'He had a lot to do with a lot of Aborigines there', Harry says. 'They used to go to him for help because he was an educated man.' Marnie Kennedy tells about Leandro in her book *Born a Half-Caste*:

'DADDY ILLIN, AS EVERYONE CALLED HIM, ... fought for many Aborigines whenever they got into strife with the police and they went to him with their problems and it was through this grand old man we Aborigines learnt a lot. ...

'One day I went with a few other Aborigines to get money (the police had control over money) and we waited all day. At five the police told them to come back the next day and that's how it went on. So Daddy Illin would go to the police to find out the reason for the wait. By that night they would have their money.'

Ernie, Leandro's eldest grandson, remembers those days, too.

'WHEN ABORIGINALS COME TO TOWN, THEY HAD TO GO TO THE POLICE STATION and ask for their money. It was their own money that they earned and yet they had to go and ask for it. And the policeman used to get them to sign a paper, many of them could not read or write. And some of them just put a thumb print for it. There was a lot of corruption went on. They were signing for £50 and only received half of it. Grandad Illin he travelled around that area Christmas Creek, Greenvale and got to know a lot of them. When they come to town they used to ask him to go up to the police station and see what they were signing for. And grandad Illin he used to help them ... These police, they used to try to talk over him and be smart with him or tell him off. They would tell him they would report him to people down south. They tried all sorts of things. They arrested uncle Tommy and uncle Dick one night, just as they were walking down street going home, and police came along and grabbed and arrested them, just for nothing. So grandad Illin went down to the police station and got them released straightaway as there was nothing.'

Flora put it into a nutshell: 'They said all sorts of things about my father. Because he stuck up for the black people.'[11]

Soon I learnt that 'the black people' were not the only people that Leandro stuck up for.

'RACIAL HATRED IS A POOR SENTIMENT'

We went to meet Flora's friend Ailsa in the late afternoon. Her light-brick mansion on a quiet Townsville street overlooking the sunset sea was magnificent. Ailsa seemed the personification of prosperity — well-groomed, smiling, in an elegant dress with an Aboriginal motif. She was an Italian whose parents came to Australia before the war without any capital and started a farm near Ingham. Ailsa remembered

Leandro and his family very well. 'He always defended the Italians. Yes, he used to be nice to Italians', was one of the first things she said, remembering him. My next, innocent question about Australian attitudes to Italians in those years suddenly provoked such a bitter reaction from Ailsa that I realised what a deep valley of sorrow lay behind this modern-day, outward prosperity.

Ailsa: How did they treat us? They were disgusting!
Flora: Don't you ask her! The Australians think they were far too good for any foreign people.
Ailsa: They used to call us 'black dagos', 'black bastards'!
Flora: My father could talk English but he was treated the same, they did not like him too, but they couldn't rubbish him, he was too smart for them.
Ailsa: The Italians worked hard, yet they did not like us, because we were dagos ... Terrible ...
Flora: They had to fight hard to survive. And yet the Italians used to treat the English like gentlemen.
Ailsa: We used to feed them when they came to our place.
Flora: But the British treated the Italians like nobody.
Ailsa: They would not ask you inside, give you a cup of tea like we used to give them ... A selfish mob they were! Well, it's a bit better now.
Flora: It is changed now, they even changed towards the dark people ...[12]

Ingham was rapidly developing as a centre of sugar-cane farming by the time the Illins settled nearby. After World War I the surrounding area experienced an influx of immigrants from Southern Europe, especially Italians, Spaniards and Greeks, who worked first as labourers and later as cane-farmers. They tended to live in their own communities, being often rejected by the surrounding English-speaking world, whose language and laws they did not understand. 'My Father spoke perfect Spanish', Harry remembers, and Spanish people used to say "You speak better Spanish that we do".' After settling near Ingham, Leandro easily mastered Italian, particularly the Sicilian and Calabrian dialects, and even some Greek, and became an indispensable 'adviser' and interpreter for many locals of Mediterranean descent. 'If they wanted help they used to go to him because he could understand the different rules of

Australia.' 'Grandad was friendly with all those Greeks as well, he used to help them too, he would talk a lot with them', Leandro's children and grandchildren tell with one accord.[13]

But it was more than that. In his passionate letters to the *Herbert River Express*, published in Ingham, Leandro was one of the few who raised his voice publicly against the racism that was sweeping Australia in the 1930s. The immediate cause was an article 'Deportation only solution to vendetta problem' in the *Sunday Mail* in 1937.[14] A special correspondent visited the Ingham area and particularly Stone River, where there had been some unsolved murders of Sicilians, which were labelled as the 'Stone River vendetta' and ascribed to the Black Hand gang. The correspondent went far beyond the vendetta itself, declaring 'The whole of "Little Italy" needs cleaning up'. He believed that the Italian community in this district known for its wealth lived in 'filth and squalor' in 'dirt-floor huts' and ate, 'apart from the inevitable macaroni', the kookaburras, ibises and bandicoots which they shoot with their guns. He further accused Italians of exploiting of their children and keeping them in ignorance, maintained that their women had no rights, and so on, while, according to him, their money was being wasted on flashy touring-cars, on expensive tapestries or sent to their countrymen in Italy. Creating this horrible portrait of the whole community, the correspondent did not hesitate to propose 'Here in Queensland we have only one remedy ... — deportation. Every suspect and lawless character among Italians should be given the hint: "Go straight or get out!"' As for the 'legal difficulties' which prevented such arbitrariness on the basis of pure suspicion or in relation to naturalised subjects, he did not hesitate to call for the amendment of immigration laws.

Leandro took the injustice to heart.

'THE SICILIANS ARE IN THAT ARTICLE PRACTICALLY AS THE WHOLE COMMUNITY, TREATED AS UNDESIRABLES. ... I am taking the pen to defend them. ... My residence has been in Ingham district in and out since 1923. I have met Italians and Sicilians daily in my work and dealings in town, on the road and on their farms. ... I have found both Italians and Sicilians very hospitable and courteous, good payers, proud of their homes, good gardeners and orchardists. ... Any reference to Sicilians not being clean is out of place as one only wants to peep in at their homes to see snowy white bedding, tables scrubbed, houses cemented, sinks and every comfort where they make a permanent home and can afford it.'

Leandro argued that Italians hunted just for fun and ridiculed the correspondent's statement that they starved and lived on macaroni and kookaburras:

'NO, MR EDITOR, THEY DO NOT LIVE ON JACKASSES, but on good wholesome food and plenty of it. My boys worked on several farms and tucker is plentiful and of good quality. Their fare differs from the Australian fare, and consists of much imported stuff such as expensive pastes and seasoning, Anchovy, olives, Salami, Olive oil. ... Meat is not used in quantity but quality.'

He dismissed all the allegations about the exploitation of their women and children, writing in particular:

'REGARDING CHILDREN being considered as a sort of cheap labour does not fit anywhere, as Sicilians are very proud people and love their children like anyone else. Yet the children themselves are fond of helping their parents even on holidays when the father works, but it is not a matter of compulsion. ... Strong, sturdy men, lovely, graceful children and women, who have lovely liquid full of fire eyes like those of a gazelle. ... Their women are their queens dressed expensively and often covered with jewellery.'

In his usual way he supported his general statements with facts from his own experience.

'I OWE MANY FAVOURS DONE FOR ME BY ITALIANS AND SICILIANS, such as coming with a tractor to pull out an Ambulance called to take one of my sick children. They have risen on a stormy night to pull me out of a bog where our lorry slid in to a gutter and brought us to safety and refused payment. ... Another party brought us blankets and dry clothes for five, some food and a bottle of good wine.

'A Sicilian with whom I had no end of rows on account of his trespassing and shooting on a property in my charge, when he found my son working on a job on a road and the horses were giving him trouble ... , lent stables and gave chop-chop and his cane cutters' quarters to my son to live in during the job. When offered payment he was insulted and now there is no need to say he is my friend.'

He concluded with a strong appeal for justice for all immigrants.

'RACIAL HATRED IS A POOR SENTIMENT. Take a man at his value. If people are not wanted in the country they should be told before they come. ... Once in they are members of society like the rest and racial hatred only creates clannishness and isolates the people from the community. ... People can like or dislike one nationality or another but deportation is not fair until the man is a culprit and convicted to be so.[15]

He wrote this even though his own contacts with local Italians, as with any people, were at times far from ideal. Ernie tells one story.

'ONCE GRANDAD WENT IN TO AN ITALIAN BARBER to get a haircut. The barber was a flash sort of bloke. He started talking in Italian to his mates there, making fun of grandad. He said something like "He's a big fat pig" and about his humble dress. Then grandad got up and took off the sheet around him and told him in Italian all that he thought of him. You should have seen this barber — he nearly fainted.'[16]

In 1938 Leandro raised his voice in defence of Italians once again after a new anti-Italian campaign. He argued that Italians belonged to a great civilisation with an ancient culture, from which the English have learnt a lot (in essence, Leandro wrote a little treatise on Latin culture, which he had studied in Patagonia as a teenager). Acknowledging that Italians had bought many farms around Ingham, he wrote:

'THIS WAS NOT DONE BY POLITICAL PARTIES OR LEGISLATION but by evolution. ... [Italians] were not men who went to Sydney after the cane cutting season (and in some cases only reached the first pub and handed their cheque over the counter for the publican to look after until it was cut out), but were those who saved and saved for an end, to which the proverb "the end justifies the means" is applicable.'

He demonstrated the overwhelming nature of the 'hospitality and kindness' of Italians and passionately concluded: 'The sooner sectarianism and racial hatred is abolished the sooner will the world come to universal peace and understanding. How interesting would the detractors find some of the men they despise if they could understand them.'[17]

A lonely Utopian fighter — as if by some irony of fate his articles were signed 'L. Illin, Utopia, Stoneleigh'! Who cared in those hard years about 'universal understanding', let alone about 'understanding' 'dagos' and Aborigines, Russians and Asians! Little would he have thought that with his simple, impassioned articles he once more, as it were, saved the honour of the Australian nation ... He just believed that Australians were strong enough to overcome these outbursts of racism. It might seem to us now that he conducted his struggle easily and fearlessly but only he himself knew how hard it was each time to speak up against the dominant public opinion, to stand alone against the crowd. In 1942 he would say in connection with another issue:

'MANY YEARS AGO I WANTED TO WRITE that heaps of tins in the

back yard and bread and butter and jams do not build a nation, economically nor physically. ... But I abstained as I would be abused as an alien. Most people would not understand my motives. They would say go back to Russia as some people's minds are too small to embrace the world as a brotherhood as it should be and is my ideal and some day it will be when we cease to be selfish and begin to understand that racial hate and self-conceits to our superiority provides means for the old Roman device "divide et impera" i.e. divide and rule. While we have the spirit that the other man is inferior to us we forget in our self-conceit to improve ourselves and so get behind the times. ... Now that I have spent $31^{1/2}$ years of my life here and reared a 'whole' Australian family with two sons in the Army I think I have right to be heard.'[18]

As for the Italians, they acknowledged Leandro's role in the most graceful manner. The Ingham Italian community awarded him a medal with a simple inscription[19]:

L.I.
Riconoscenza
De gl'Italiani
All'Amico
L. Illin
24.9.38

Years later copies of this medal and of Leandro's article were provided by Ernie to an Italian exhibition in Townsville.

PEOPLE'S COUNCILLOR

A provincial newspaper of the 1930s ... It is hard not to feel bored looking through it issue after issue — some advertisements, some reprints from other newspapers about international politics, a page of local sporting events and local news: weather and reports of activities of various local committees, boards, and associations. After a dozen issues you realise that all these reports have been produced year after year, seemingly unchanged, with the same several dozen surnames of the local 'élite'. Like plastic pieces moved around a games board. No matter how long you follow them from issue to issue you hardly learn anything about their personalities, let alone anything about the real life and troubles of the hundreds of their co-citizens who were never 'honoured' by being noticed in the pages of the local newspaper.

Leandro, an émigré woodcutter from Utopia, 30 kilometres away from Ingham, who had never been elected to any boards and committees, seemed doomed to remain one of these obscure persons unnoticed by the local newspaper. But he was not. In the mid 1930s the *Herbert River Express* began to receive his letters and publish them under the heading 'Correspondence'. They were quite different from the refined and sophisticated letters of the usual set of authors of this column hiding behind their noms de plume. Leandro's letters gave an impression of a fresh breeze, of a naïve child who interrupted a stuffy meeting of the adults in order to remind them that beyond the walls of the meeting-room there is a real town with real people who live a real life and speak a real language.

One of Leandro's first letters was the description of an ANZAC Day commemoration seen from the back rows of the hall.

'I AM SORRY TO SAY I WAS VERY VEXED to see that a lot of people held no reverence for the occasion and comported themselves just like if it was a Tom Mix show. There was a lot of children, both native and foreigners, unchaperoned, who did not seem to have even a notion what the occasion was ... There was a continued hullabaloo, knocking of seats, tramping of feet, walking up and down the stairs, talking, leaving and coming in during the speeches and all this made all the speeches inaudible ... I think many just went because it was free admission and expected something in the way of ordinary concerts.'[20]

A snapshot of the local manners and values unnoticed from the front rows, where 'the good men of the town' exchanged speeches as usual.

Indeed, life in Ingham provided Leandro with a lot of problems about which 'to take up the pen'. One such issue was the ostentatious 'beautification' of Ingham conducted by the local shire council at the expense of commonsense and the comfort of the ordinary people. Leandro wrote:

'A MAN CAN'T HELP SEEING THE OBVIOUS and that is the beautification scheme of the town of Ingham. The founders of the town planted the good old trees for the comfort and shade of its citizens. There were a few seats (such as they were) where people could rest in the evening coolness, and the streets were wide and free to go about. Now, the seat opposite Ramage's stationery business has been pulled down and jagged rocks are filled around the trunks of the trees and if you want to rest or wait for the bus or a date, you have to grow corns or line your pants with cushions to sit down.

'I have been a good deal over the world', continued Leandro, providing a long list of seventeen countries and over fifty towns which he had visited, 'and in any of these towns I have never seen motley, ugly, deteriorated with millions of years of age gagged basalt built into shapes that no one ever with an aesthetic eye and a sense of beauty will call beautiful. ... I wonder if the Council will be consistent and order a few wallaroos, whiptails and rock wallabies to hop on the rocks. ... I don't think one of our Councillors will miss the seats they have pulled down as I suppose they are all pretty comfortable without coming there ... Last night people were sitting on their haunches in the middle of the street calling the persons who removed the seats everything but what they really are. ...

'I voted for this Council and have a high esteem for some members of it that I know personally and it gives me pain to have to criticise the party I voted for, but I would not consider myself conscientious if I did not speak up. I tried to discuss it with one Councillor but he told me that the money was lent to the Council and it had to be spent. ... Now, the town has hardly any water and a person can't get a drink of water. If there was a fountain of water for the public benefit it would be much better than all these rocks.'[21]

This was only the start of Leandro's battle for the real needs of Ingham townsfolk. Two years later he continued with it.

'MILAN IN ITALY HAS A GREAT CATHEDRAL, London the Tower Bridge, ... Moscow has the Kremlin ... and Leningrad the Hermitage, St. Isaac's and Kazan Cathedrals. ... Ingham has the Councillors' Rockeries. I was guilty previously of criticising them, but thought they were an obstruction to the parking and traffic and I could not see any beauty in them (lack of artistic taste, I suppose). Every time I walked through the Ingham streets they hurt and offended my sight. Every time I sat on them they hurt and offended some other part of my anatomy. But still I always like to analyse things and revise and keep up to date and to my great surprise I found out that I was in the wrong. I discovered that the beds inside of these rockeries are of immense practical value to the farmers and the growing generations — they are perfect exponents of noxious ... and of all the useless plants in the district and the north. I came to think that school children as well as unscientific farmers should be taken over to them and shown at least once a week all the plants and given a lecture, explaining to them which is [which]. ... What the beds lack are a few stinging trees. Many people do not know them and really they should be planted.'

The authorities' rapid tidying up before the visit to Ingham of J.A. Lyons, the prime minister of Australia, provoked his further sarcasm: 'I was asked by various people to express our appreciation of the Council's action in cleaning the streets and the rubbish and weeds that adorned the "Rocks". It is great to see them starting to whitewashing them. ... The coming of one man (who, I suppose cares little how we conduct our "Rocks") changed the whole aspect of our life. After he goes I suppose we will lapse into lethargy again.'[22]

But he was mistaken this time. Instead of lethargy the council undertook a new step in its ostentatious 'beautification' of Ingham by erecting a fountain. But it was not the fountain that Leandro had fought for.

'I HAVE BEEN, DURING THE LAST FEW DAYS, SO MUCH TEASED about the Council building the fountain for me that I must answer this to the public. I ... did suggest years ago through the columns of your paper a fountain should have been built instead of the "Rockeries". But I suggested a drinking fountain, with a tap where we could have a drink of cool water. Every Ingham resident knows that unless we go round the back of the houses and drink from tanks, water that came down from the dusty roofs, there is no water to be had unless we cadge it from the restaurants or private people. It is not my fault that our Council looks 25 or 30 years ahead and puts an expensive work of art in a semi-swamp below flood mark, confronting the remains of the old Ingham Chinatown. ... Now I thought all day about the matter and even walked down to the fountain to have a good look at it. When I got there a fox-terrier was having a bath in it, so I thought the water would not be fit to drink. ...

'Much better use would have accrued if that money have been used for two public lavatories — one in West Ingham on the main street and one in East Ingham, opposite the De Luxe Theatre. ... Women from out of the town have a hard time with the children ... to find lavatories. At the back of the pubs the drunks render the places dirty and unsanitary for everybody. ... We can do without art fountains but not without lavatories. I don't condemn the artistic tendencies of our Council but utility comes before beauty. Even though we have a fountain we have not a tap for drinking water yet, nor a shelter for bush folk to wait for the buses in rainy weather.'[23]

As for the scoffers, Leandro always had a ready tongue to disgrace them in a way no one expected from an émigré mixing with Aborigines. E.T. Carron, an artist in newspaper polemics, took a shot at Leandro

— 'The rousing cry from Macedonia, no, from Utopia, goes up, so help me bob! ... I thought my rotund friend of Utopia was at peace with the Council since they decided to supply free gratis, the fruits of the ambrosia, or rather the crystal Adam's ale, per medium of a fountain in the Rockeries.'

'I WOULD ADVISE MR CARRON TO REVISE HIS GEOGRAPHY AND MYTHOLOGY', Leandro responded, 'before he starts to use them. Knowing that I came from Russia he writes that "the rousing cry from Macedonia". Macedonia, friend Carron, is in Greece! ... The Ancient Greeks believed that their gods' food was ambrosia which made them immortal — it was not a tree that bore fruit nor was it drink either. So how could it run through the pipes of a fountain? Read again your mythology and you will find that the drink of the gods was called "nectar".'[24]

By that time Leandro had gained considerable popularity in the Ingham area and his friends persuaded him to nominate himself as a candidate for councillor in the 1939 Hinchinbrook Shire Council elections. Although he had voted Labor all his life, he decided to stand for the elections as an independent.

'I LIKE TO ACT FREE AND SUPPORT REASON on whichever side it is. Once a man is in a party he pledges himself to support it (reason or not). ... I have not a party to pay my electioneering expenses such as the Labor party. I have not the Council and the only help I got is that the people who nominated me put up the fiver and subscription among my supporters paid for the few leaflets and advertising I got. I am not working hard to get in. I am not anxious to have an axe to grind. If I get in I will not worry and being independent I will let no one down as far as party matters go.'

His election program included public control over all Council actions, sober public entertainments on Sundays, and the protection of the interests of the underprivileged. It had this unusual conclusion:

'WHETHER PEOPLE LIKE TO ACKNOWLEDGE IT OR NOT I have been your unofficial and unelected Councillor for the last few years. Everything I fought against or for ... has been done either in the Council or other departments. ... So, ladies and gentlemen, please yourselves and give me your support or not. I will gain nothing, only moral satisfaction at the thought that I might do some good before I peg out my last claim.'

At the elections the Labor Council was re-elected and J.L. Kelly retained his position of chairman. Leandro did not receive enough votes to become a councillor. In a letter to the editor he wrote about this defeat.

'SIR, I HAVE RECEIVED MANY CONDOLENCES and expressions of sympathy at my defeat as an independent candidate for the Shire Elections. Up to now I did not worry at all, my pride being well satisfied, because even as an independent I received 1060 votes (to be exact 1059 as I voted for myself). That means I got backers although I was not a party man, who gave me their votes of their own free will.'

But, mocking the politicians, he went on to comment on the chairman's speech, in which the chairman said: 'he would like to extend his congratulation to the Councillors who had been elected and trusted their continued service to the Council would be of benefit to themselves and an advantage to the public'.

'(THEMSELVES FIRST, THE PUBLIC NEXT)', Leandro observed. '... Up to now, Mr Editor, I thought I missed only worries, disagreements, unpleasantness, and arguments, now I can see — on Mr Kelly's own statement that at not being elected I missed some benefit to myself, so I am losing sleep and am worried at seeing that in my stressed circumstances I missed my opportunity. I could not see why all the army of scrutineers, scouts, smiles to the lowest, even an army of women catching votes, meetings, speeches, dirty accusations, benzine and oil burned, candidates talked hoarse, was necessary to gain votes. I thought if people wanted a man on a job they will put him there and that it was not worth while chasing that job. I thought pride and honour were the motives, but now I see it is "benefits to themselves".'[25]

By that time Leandro seemed to be deeply disillusioned with politics. Even before that, in August 1938, when their Labor Council held a reception during the visit of Prime Minister Lyons to Ingham, he bitterly wrote:

'WE HAVE TO REMEMBER OURS IS A LABOR COUNCIL, so why make a fuss over the head of the Opposition, the man we did not vote for. ... If these receptions are held at the expense of the ratepayers it is great to be one of the 'elite' and get an invitation to these jollification reunions, where political platforms are of no account and all become ... good fellows praising each other and the ratepayer pays.'

Answering the letter of an 'Old soldier', who sneered that Mr Illin must have been 'disappointed' at not being in the gathering, Leandro formulated his attitudes to politics and politicians.

'I HAVE LIVED 56 YEARS, SEEN BAD AND GOOD, high, medium and

low. I have seen stupidity in the very highest and virtue and wisdom in the down and outs. I've seen clever tramps and stupid clergyman and others. I will derive more pleasure and learn more from a tramp and down and out than from a pampered politician and some of his followers, whose sole object perhaps is that other people see that they are near the great man... I have no 'grouch' to the different views of the political parties. Everybody is entitled to an opinion. But I have a contempt for members of parties not being consistent. ... My loyalty to the country of my adoption is not in toasting politicians but in expressing my opinions (whether they are right or wrong) openly. ...

'"Old Soldier" writes that it is trivial matters that disturb me. Not so. Matters of principle are not trivial. Men die to uphold their principle.'

He repeated this statement once again when he discovered that the Labor Council did not stick to the anti-monopoly principle in practice — in particular, giving a monopoly to one company to screen pictures in Ingham.

'MR KELLY'S EXPLANATION why they gave the monopoly doesn't hold water. Monopoly is not Labor principle. People get burnt on wood stakes, get shot, go to gaol and suffer all sorts of tortures and penuries to uphold an idea or principle. So gain should not shatter a principle. .... The £1000 that Mr Kelly says is saved on the picture goers, only amounts to a few pennies per head, and should burn holes in the pockets of any good and true principled Laborite, considering that it is degrading the Labor platform.'[26]

Indeed, he seemed to expect too much from his townsfolk. As for the fountain with drinking water, it was finally erected on the central street and this place is still remembered by Ingham's old-timers as 'Illin's memorial'. Nearby there is a public toilet, as well ...

SUNDAY CONCERTS AND THE COMMUNIST AGITATOR

After his defeat at the elections it seems Leandro decided to concentrate on the more innocent issues of the cultural leisure activities of Inghamites. He had written occasionally to the *Herbert River Express* about movies before. 'Really we are too far from Hollywood to criticise the artists there', he would say, 'yet we have the same right as we pay to see them and perhaps more than those closer to Hollywood. I am not a critic but just a picture fan ... and like to say what I think about them.' His yardstick was simple.

'I AM SURE EVERY MAN AND WOMAN felt themselves to be a bit happier after the picture, as all walked out with a smile. … I think it is a great honour to be able to see or hear something that will make us forget the dreariness of everyday life and bring a laugh and gladness into our hearts. Just try to balance the happy moments in our lives against the dreary ones and you will see that it will not balance. There is a debit in happiness.[27]

Not surprisingly, Charlie Chaplin was his favourite — 'there is more expression in one movement of Charlie Chaplin than in all one night's talk of some of the boosted talkies'. He was critical of the Americanisation of the Australian film and book market and, particularly, of misinterpreting the 'Australian legend' in the style of an American western.

The movie *Rangle River*, written by Zane Grey but depicting the Australian outback, provoked his sharp criticism: 'The whole plot of the story is ridiculous and not complimentary to an Australian character. Whatever the tactics of the American ranch owners are they must entirely differ from the Australian squatters.' Among the features he criticised as unnatural for Australia were the blowing up of the bore, the style of fights, and particularly the whip fight: 'I have been nearly 27 years in Australia, have been almost around it and across working with drovers and station hands and I have never seen a whip duel. Every self-respecting Australian uses his good (or otherwise) fists. … The indiscriminate and senseless use of whips while working the cattle and driving them in a confused and rough way is entirely non-Australian. No cattle in Australia are driven at the pace depicted.' The best remedy for such misplaced overseas fabrications would be, according to Leandro, if 'somebody will write an Australian story, "Coonardoo", by Katharine Susannah Prichard would do'.[28]

Still, he occasionally managed to find some golden nuggets in the flood of American movies screened in Ingham.

'I NEVER TOOK MY EYES FROM THE SCREEN watching Leo Carrillo in *City Streets*. … Leo Carrillo is superb. He makes you laugh till your sides ache one minute and the next he brings tears to your eyes. … It is a pity that the picture was shown to practically an empty hall. Pictures like that should be shown in Saturdays when people are all [there] to see them.'

He especially valued highly *Young Mr Lincoln* with Henry Fonda and, speaking about this film, he adopted an unusual, very personal approach.

'HAVING DECIDED TO SEE THE PICTURE, *Young Mr Lincoln*, to tell the truth I went with almost antagonistic prejudice. From my boyhood I admired Abe Lincoln more than any man who ever lived. His personality such as depicted in history and his biography impressed me so much. ... My sentiment was almost worship about Lincoln and I thought it was almost impossible, almost a sacrilege, to try to portray such a man in this century of jazz and cheap comedy. Yet I got a surprise and acknowledge my mistake and beg Henry Fonda's pardon for my prejudiced antagonistic feeling for thinking he would commit the sacrilege and cheapen the man whom I placed on such a high pedestal. ... I know these lines will never reach Henry Fonda but I appreciate his having given a glimpse of what really Lincoln was — just as I represented him.'[29]

Along with films, reading books was Leandro's favourite occupation. After years of a wandering life most of the books that Alexandra brought out from Russia were lost, but at least now Leandro could borrow English books in the Ingham public library. He remained true to his predilection for democratic writers, the predilection which was formed in his childhood and youth under his father's influence. The writer sharing the hardships of his people, the writer learning from his people was his ideal: 'Maxim Gorky, O. Henry, Jack London, Emil[e] Zola, Dostoyevsky and others did not get their philosophy and wisdom from politicians but mostly from down and outs. ... In Russia (my native land) poets such as Nekrasoff, Pushkin, Lermontov, Nadson, Koltzoff, etc lived and created in want. Prose writers like Dostoyevsky who is one of the outstanding psychologist of the world and has no end of monuments was sent during his life to Siberia for 12 years hard labour.'

Soon after Leandro settled near Ingham he discovered among his neighbours a personification of his ideal in the person of a farmer–poet, Dan Sheahan (1881–1977), an Irish émigré, who came to Australia in 1905, fought for it in World War I and later worked as a water-carrier, a contract ploughman, and a road-worker, finally settling at Elphinstone Pocket near Ingham as a cane-farmer. In between he produced numerous talented poems warmed with Irish humour but he seemed to care little about collecting and recording them. Vera Ketchell, Leandro's granddaughter, has preserved some of Sheahan's writings sent to Leandro and among them Sheahan's letter of 26 January 1938: 'Dear Andrea Illien, just a few lines hoping you got to your home safely. Your encouragement and appreciation so inspired me that I have sent four pieces of verse to "Bowyang". I started the "Sleeper Cutters Camp" in France 21 years ago and never finished until today twas just a scrap. its light. But humorous.' Leandro was the first reader of this anti-military masterpiece. Bill Bowyang soon published four of Sheahan's poems in his column 'On the Track'. Among them was a bitter satire on 'the wonder of Ingham — the Councillors' Rocks'.

> This beautiful structure of angles and curves
> Its founder, believe me, a statue deserves;
> There pigweed all twining and nutgrass in bloom,
> Are filling the air with pleasant perfume,
> But lovers and loafers, and stiffs without socks,
> Are sighing for their seats by the Councillors' Rocks.
>
> Old-timers returning shall miss the cool shade,
> That Rayne tree, Cascara and green Leichhardts made,
> Though the whisky and beer be tasting the same
> As they did in the days ere the motor cars came,
> The railings of gum where they tethered their crocks,
> Are buried deep under the Councillors' Rocks.

Sheahan continued occasionally publish his verses in the *North Queensland Register* and in other periodicals but his book *Songs from the Canefields* was not published until 1972. As early as 1938, however, Leandro was the first to attempt to raise money to publish an edition of Sheahan's poetry. In the draft of a speech, preserved in Vera's archives, Leandro declared:

'LADIES AND GENTLEMEN, I HAVE HAD THE TEMERITY to convene this meeting to try to honour a poet and a genius that lives in our midst. ... Even to me who is a foreigner it is obvious that we are committing a sin in letting a talent and a man of genius waste himself 'Pulling Cane'. ... Mr Sheahan's poems are not carefully prepared dishes like Edgar Wallace's for the mediocre mind nor like Zane Grey's for false adventures loving people. Mr Sheahan's poetries are inspirations of God. Being an Irishman we hardly want to state that there is humour in his poems. He could not throw that out, [not] even out of the bitterness. ... Mr Sheahan has seen every phase of Australian life. ... No one is more justified to sing our joys and our sorrows and if I succeed to persuade you, Ladies and Gentlemen, to ask Mr Sheahan to collect his verses, record them and publish them, I will be proud to think that this little job has justified my being in Australia 27 years. Australia is my country of adoption and I would like to think that I have been one of the stepping stones for an Irish-Australian poet to rise.'[30]

As for his other cultural interests, Leandro did not have much opportunity to visit concerts given by prominent Russian performers, such as Anna Pavlova or Fedor Chaliapin, who came to Queensland while Leandro was in Greenvale. After his family moved to Utopia, however, he occasionally managed to see a Russian concert. A keepsake of one of them survived among Flora's papers — a postcard with Cossacks signed in 1932 to 'the dear compatriot in memory of Motherland from Djigit Kuban Cossacks'. But as a rule he had to content himself with the community concerts in Ingham.

'PERSONALLY, I AM VERY KEEN on them as I think they are most wholesome and sane entertainments. ... One feels like a member of a big family and is proud even of any little achievements of fellow towns men. ... I appreciate these concerts so much that I come a distance of 23 miles to attend them.'

But, again, it was observations from the back rows rather than a traditional report of who sang what:

'IT IS VERY DEPLORABLE that some members of the audience are rowdy and a certain amount of 'hooliganism' is being developed by a section of the Ingham audience. Bad language is used and insults are hurled at some performers. ... Although not born in this country, I love the British spirit of giving everyone a chance to do their best on the stage at any social entertainments and never condemn the performer for poor performances as long as they do their best. After all the poor performer suffers the most if he does not perform well. ... We should appreciate their efforts instead of walking out on them. ... I am nearly sure that those same people would apply their ill directed energy in a better course if they tried to do something to help the cause instead of destroying it they would find themselves also happier. Come and sing or do something funny instead of booing others who are trying to give you some joy.'

A few months later, after the start of the war, he wrote with pleasure of visiting a new Sunday community concert in Ingham: 'I am pleased hooliganism had disappeared. ... As I watched the crowd I could see them pleased and supporting. I congratulate workers on their progress'.

But it was too early to celebrate the victory. Suddenly Leandro found himself severely criticised by his 'fellow townsmen' because he dared to praise concerts that took place on Sundays and to declare that 'the by-laws forbidding any paid entertainments on Sunday are to my thinking retrograde by-laws, far behind the times'.[31] Leandro was immediately attacked in high-flown style by 'Citizen'.

'THE VIEWS OF AN OLD AND EXPERIENCED WRITER MAY TEND TO MISLEAD the young. I feel certain that they will meet with the approval of those who do not love England and the British Empire. Let Mr Illin remember and realise the British Empire at present is passing through the Valley of the Shadow. ... We people of democratic institutions and ideas realise that this war is one of Paganism versus Christianity. ... Mr Illin may have been brought up in a religious atmosphere or he may not, or in all probably the nation that he claims as his homeland may have turned to Paganism. I do not know. His letter is simply the introduction of the thin edge of the wedge to wreck all that we Christians have lived for and looked up for the past 1900 odd years. Let us still maintain our Sunday as a day of rest and reminder of the faith we have in God to deliver us from the close of the beast who, void of any Christian belief, is trying to overflow Christianity. Mr Illin would have us commercialise Sunday and lose the weekly symbol of our Christian faith and thus bring about a state of existence in this land that would leave it ripe for Stalin, Hitler and Coy to come and get it.'[32]

Leandro was prompt to answer in his usual clear and witty style.

'SIR, "CITIZEN" TAKES EXCEPTION TO MY VIEWS and thinks that I am preparing and making this land ripe for Hitler and Stalin to come and get it. Considering that I have three grown-up sons, two of whom are being called up for service am I likely to want anyone to invade Australia? Besides I have daughters and grandchildren, all Australians, more Australians than "Citizen" is likely ever to be on account of their birth. "Citizen" uses a despicable political advantage and to win the argument implies that I am a pagan, a Communist and a Nazi all in one and an object approved by those who do not love the British Empire and all this from behind a corner under a "nom de plume". Now let us analyse all these implications one by one.

'Paganism. My religion is Greek Orthodox (an equivalent to the Church of England). When there is a Greek service and I happen to be in town I go to church. I believe in Christianity but I think it is not properly exercised in life as it is not enough to be going to church and listening to sermons and strictly observing a Sunday and in private life be unforgiving, intolerant, selfish and priggish of the more unfortunates. Citizen thinks I am introducing an "argument not appropriate at this particular stage of world's affairs" i.e. Sunday community concerts. What about the decision of the Fox Hunting Associations in England that despite the war they will still hunt so as not to look downhearted. Some fighting, some hunting foxes!

'As for being accused of Communistic tendencies, Citizen is travelling on flat tyres. I left Russia 47 years ago, spent 17 in South America and 30 here. In 1918 my father (the late Nicholas Illin, of Peeramon) and I denounced Bolshevism through the pages of the *Cairns Post* ... I have never preached Communism nor heresy. I believe in Christian doctrines but do not like religion commercialised nor meddling in politics. ...

'I think Citizen takes Australians too cheaply if he thinks old nondescript, nobody Illin by enticing them to community concerts will bring the downfall of the British Empire into the hands of Hitler and Stalin.'

Leandro's argument was based on commonsense: 'Wishing to get as much joy as I can on any day for myself and my fellow men I call it rest and service to God who gave us our lives to enjoy them'.[33] His battle for Sunday was part of his wider battle for legislation which would take into consideration the interests of the ordinary people rather than hypocritically observe the dead letter of the law. Leandro wrote about one such case.

'A BAKER WHO HAS TO supply us for breakfast can't move out to deliver before 8 a.m. yet we all want fresh bread and the baker is willing to deliver it. ... The town dweller can run over the road and get his bread for breakfast but country people cannot. Why not regulate their hours so that they can make their deliveries during any agreed 8 hours and not allow them to work after. ... Just think, Mr Editor, that delivering bread out of hours constitutes a serious offence, far more serious than selling grog after hours. Bread, the greatest necessity of life, and grog its greatest enemy. ... I think those who passed that act must be living next door to the baker, and perhaps long way from the pubs.'[34]

This attitude to religion in general, and to the English tradition of the Sabbath in particular, was one Leandro inherited from his father, a Russian democratic intellectual. Flora put it simply: 'Father believed in God in his own way. He always taught us to treat other people as you would like them to treat you. He never went to church, he never believed in them much, he said they were there to keep one down, blind to the facts of life'. Ernie has similar impressions.

'GRANDAD BELIEVED IN GOD, he had his own belief, that there was a God, but he was not religious, he did not like anybody to preach to him, any religion at all. He reckoned that the priests were all hypocrites. He would say, "The priest is just another man like me, why should I go to confession to him". He used to say what Lenin said "Religion is opium for the people". He just told his children they could choose their own religion.'

Maud, Ernie's wife, told another story about Leandro's attitude to Sundays.

'UNCLE DICK TOLD US that one Sunday they all were laying around, relaxing after chopping trees or cane in Upper Stone, uncle Dick laying back, and Tommy, and old Tom Sullivan and grandad. And they thought grandad was asleep. "Oh", old Tom yawned, "Oh, it's the Lord's day today, rest day." And grandad jumped up: "Right-to you boys, get back to work now". And Dickie growled at Tom, "What did you have to say 'It's the Lord's day!'. It's no Lord's day with dad around. He makes us work". He would not let them lie around like that even on Sundays.'[35]

For Leandro — a man of action — now the struggle for the freedom to enjoy pastimes on Sunday became a matter of principle. It was not long before he began to collect signatures in support of screening of pictures on Sundays, proceedings from which would go for patriotic benefits. Immediately, an 'Old subscriber' — in style, a twin brother to 'Citizen' — produced all kinds of accusations against the Russian from Utopia.

'RUSSIA HAS BECOME SO PRE-EMINENTLY NOTORIOUS in recent times for its dramatic flair for intrigue, liquidation of opposition by sinister and arbitrary methods, and the unscrupulous spreading of propaganda to gain support, that White Australians, with the innate tolerance due to their British origin, are too prone to overlook, to forget or to minimise the importance of efforts exerted by Russian agitators living in Australia to allegedly improved conditions on our free continent. During the past week in Ingham a man who admits to his birthplace being Russia ... again emerged as an Australian into the lurid limelight of local politics to flourish the cudgels in the interests of the Ingham Pictures Co. urging the holding of pictures on Sunday nights. ... This newcomer who has so diligently been appealing to patriots to sign this singular petition, now literally waves "the good old flag" in order to snare and gain support in the name of patriotism. What has this emigrant who has made such an adroit appeal to the disgruntled feelings of some and to the prejudices and patriotisms of others, ever done to help win the war for British democracy? ... Has this advocate ever purchased war savings certificates to help preserve our civilisation intact from the plundering tyrants overseas?'[36]

Leandro's answer did not stop at a proclamation of his loyalty to Australia and denial of affiliation with Russian bolsheviks — 'I became naturalized by deed and spirit in 1913. I have lost all connections with my native country and lost all my relatives during the revolution. They were butchered and worse by the Bolsheviks. What is happening in Russia now I do not know! Nor have I any chance to find out.' He went on to review his whole life.

'WHAT (THEY ASK) HAVE I DONE TO WIN THE WAR? I have reared an Australian family. Lived here for 30 years, poor, down and out. I tackled any job that came my way and never lived on charity. Never took anyone down, never profiteered, shared my tucker with all comers. I bought no War Certificates as most of the time I don't know where my next loaf of bread is coming from. I was not born to any big business, to exploit anybody. I sell nothing collecting compound interest. I am not employed on two or three jobs collecting big salaries. I have not a business to employ enemy aliens and do not do lucrative business with same beyond taking orders for a few pounds of tobacco for a company in Brisbane.'[37]

A communist agitator? Soon, in April 1942, life would put before Leandro the choice between loyalty to Australia, which he always declared, and loyalty to an old Russian acquaintance of his who expressed anti-British sympathies. It was at a time when the enemy was on Australia's doorstep, when two sons of Leandro were in the army waiting to be sent to the battlefields at any moment and he could not accept the fifth column mood. We will never know what it cost him but he chose loyalty to Australia, and informed the minister for Home Security about the attitudes of this Russian.[38]

'WHY NOT THE WALLABY IN AUSTRALIA?'

Although not a communist agitator, Leandro's attitude to Soviet Russia was never straightforward. Indeed, living in Gunnawarra, Greenvale, or Utopia, Leandro found it hard to grasp how it happened that the attractive bolshevik program and slogans — in essence, stolen from the naïve democrats of his father's generation — resulted in barbaric dictatorship and endless bloodshed. Flora felt this ambiguity of her father's attitude: 'My father wasn't really a communist-minded man. Well, in a way he was and in a way he wasn't. But when I said, "I reckon communism was good", he said, "Oh, I didn't think I had a communist daughter". As to me', Flora concluded, 'I think everybody should be equal'.[39]

It was hard to be a Russian in those years. Public opinion tended to be negative towards Russia. A snapshot from around 1939 is retained in Flora's memory. 'Mr Fraser had a big store there and he had a lot of property, he owned half of Ingham and when the war broke out he and my father used to talk a lot about World War II, a lot of discussion on Russia and America. One day Fraser came up and said to my father "Hello, Mr Molotov", and my father turned and said straight away "Hello, Mr Chamberlain".[40] They were obviously teasing each other about Russian and British attempts to negotiate separate agreements with Nazi Germany. Nevertheless, Leandro always made a distinction between Stalin and Hitler — 'although both dictators, [they] are two extremes and they never will eat out of the same trough', he wrote.

Germany's invasion into Russian territory brought to a head attitudes towards Russia. But Leandro was neither with those who continued to condemn and fear Russia nor with those who now expressed unreserved sympathy for it. His attitude was more complicated. Among his papers in Vera Ketchell's archives there is a newspaper cutting 'Soviet Quislings Hanged', describing the public execution in Krasnodar, after its liberation by the Red Army in 1943, of those who had been collaborators with the fascists. Someone wrote on the edges in Russian, 'Well done, Stalinists! That's the way to deal with traitors and betrayers', and drew a hanging traitor. Leandro wrote his comment across the lines in Russian:

'THERE IS NOTHING TO ADMIRE: pitiful, unfortunate and uncultured is the country where there are traitors and betrayers, and pitiful, unfortunate and barbarous is the ruler who is still hanging his citizens in the 28th year [of his rule]. Equally pitiful, unfortunate and dirty (legal marriage) is the family, where the wife cries and is unfaithful to her husband, and he, a pitiful man, bashes her and boasts that he has given her a good lesson. A country with traitors and a family with traitors are 'trash', or, in Russian, 'a brothel', rather than a paradise.'[41]

Yet his heart never stopped aching for the destiny of his motherland, for the sufferings of her people. He passed this attitude on to his children, too.

While the Germans were occupying more and more territory in far away Russia, the war had suddenly also come close to Australia. In December Japan began its conquest of the Pacific and southeast Asia. In February 1942 the Japanese were in New Guinea and Darwin was bombed. The rapid advance by the Japanese caused panic among Leandro's neighbours. Suddenly his bush skills turned out to be in great demand; as he wrote to the newspaper, 'I have been approached by many people asking me for advice as to localities and the best places where to evacuate their families to'. He readily shared with the readers his knowledge about the localities, how to make 'makeshifts' in the bush, what essential equipment and food would make up a survival kit. His letter provoked much interest, including his mention of flying foxes and 'opossums' as among some of the 'fair' bush food: 'A great deal of verbal chaff has been directed at me because I have mentioned flying foxes and opossums as eatable at an emergency and omitted the carpet snake, bandicoots etc. I think I have eaten every sort of bush food ...'

Still, instead of purely practical advice, Leandro decided that the time had come to reveal his own philosophy of the relations between modern man and the surrounding world.

'I HAVE LIVED IN MANY COUNTRIES and in no country have I seen the population so prejudiced to the use of foods that are not of an established standard of living and using so little local products. ... We have been living in a fool's paradise on artificial high standards, using the tin opener too much. We were ignorant to which food is more essential, and economical to a nation's health building and our politicians never foresaw the necessity of improvement.'

He argued that Australians might consume a wider range of products, including those that were used in other nations, among them some that were widely used in Russia, where 'besides sour milk sunflower oil is used and seed eaten like peanuts'; he praised the nutritional value of maize, drawing conclusions from his South American experience, and he sang an ode to South Sea Islanders and their food:

'THE BEST RACE of dark skinned natives in the Pacific are Kanakas, Samoans, Fijians and Torres Strait Islanders. Men and women are robust, have good teeth, are resistant to work, great seamen, pearlers, musical, clever in school, of jolly and happy disposition, able and capable, true friends, but foes to be feared, easily degraded by white man's civilisation and drink. Those men and women are reared mostly on coconuts, yams, and taros, fish and pork.'

He showed that a wide variety of products could be grown in Australia, which, instead of consuming expensive imports, might rely on its own resources.

It was obvious to him that modern people lack basic survival skills and are losing the essential skills required to make rational use of the surrounding natural resources:

'WE LET MANGOES AND PAW-PAWS ROT and pay 2/- and 3/- a dozen for shrivelled apples and buy all fruit that has been picked green and therefore [is] tasteless when it arrives here. ... Most people in the present generation could not bake a loaf of bread nor a damper. They all know how to bake a cake and some few can cook scones.'

Moreover, Leandro believed that under the extreme conditions of threat of war the appropriate moment had come for Australians to recognise and respect the skills of those who were prejudicially regarded as lower races: 'We want some experts ... who would teach us how to grow and use (I repeat: use) these products in a tasty palatable way, even if the instructors were Kanakas'; 'If the Government would release some Aboriginals to go bush with evacuating families they would be of much use to the welfare of women and children'.

As for meat, he offered readers the fruits of his own experience:

'WHILE REFUSING TO EAT ALL CLEAN THINGS the civilised people eat dirty (1) ducks, (2) pigs, (3) fowls (the dirtiest scavengers of the lot), (4) cattle. ... Wallabies nearly knock us down on the outskirts of the town and the people turn their noses and say Oh! I could not eat wallabies. I have fed wallaby, horse flesh, flying foxes even donkey meat and eels to many of these "could nots" and they did not know any better.'

He concluded his letter with the strong appeal: 'In America and Europe side by side with the beef hang hares, venison, quails, ducks, partridges, smoked eels. Why not the wallaby in Australia?'[42]

Throughout the war years he continued to contribute to the *Herbert River Express*. Even when he wrote about local problems thoughts of the distant war did not leave him. One such issue was vandalism towards the notorious Ingham Rockeries. Although he never approved of the Rockeries, he was indignant when some vandals began to destroy the flowers and flowerbeds 'breaking the heart' of the gardener whose loving efforts managed to make there 'a bit of paradise with lovely flowers'.

Leandro appealed to the conscience of the vandals: 'Since we have beauty let us esteem, admire and guard it. There are enough vandals in the world now destroying beautiful sacred things to all human races, without us lucky people following their steps and doing the same in this quiet, privileged [part] of the earth.'[43]

He used the local newspaper 'to ventilate [his] thoughts so that better brains may pass a judgement on them and perhaps the Government ... remedy things'. Drawing from his experience as an ex-farmer and drover in South America and Australia, he warned of 'the folly of shifting cattle inland on a big scale' under the threat of Japanese invasion. He again advocated Sunday pictures: 'All the cities in Australia are showing pictures on Sundays for the soldiers and their friends. Why not in Ingham? Surely seeing pictures on Sunday is not as sinful as getting drunk.'

After coupons for some commodities were introduced, he wrote 'A lot of people kick against rationing but I fully realise that only rationing ensures us getting certain commodities that otherwise would have been accumulated by those who have the cash and blackmarketing prices would be the result'. He argued, for instance, for the introduction of tobacco coupons for smokers, making special provisions for Aborigines: 'The rationing of tobacco for the Aboriginals and sugar workers from Palm Island settlement should be in the hands of the police as the natives are the main sufferers from the unscrupulous small storekeepers'. He even advocated tough state control over storekeepers: 'Such things as potatoes, onions and other edible commodities, everybody requires them and some unscrupulous storekeepers take advantage of the people on that account'. But what really worried him was injustice towards the ordinary people.

'SOMEHOW SOMEONE GOT IDEAS INTO THEIR HEADS THAT ONLY CHINESE PEOPLE EAT RICE and so they cut us off altogether. My family for instance (bush dwellers) used on an average four bags of rice a year. Now we get none. The idea that the Chinaman eats nothing but rice is only a wrongful credence and a legend. ... What about all the good little Australians growing and not getting one ounce per week? It is great to be courteous but charity begins at home. ... City people who have every commodity and conveniences, who never have the hardships of the bushman are favoured and can [eat out] any day they like. Where is the justice? ... Anyone that is not in profitable business is a fool to stop here for the spin we get!' [44]

'MY GOD IS MY CHILDREN ...'

Leandro's children, even after they grew up, remained the centre of his world. In the early 1930s the time came to worry about Dick. He fell in love with Alice, a fifteen-year-old daughter of Harry Williams, a friend of Leandro's from Halifax, a suburb of Ingham, who had built up a considerable capital in trade. Love flared up, they wrote to each other and, finally, an impulsive Alice decided to run away from home with him. Dick, and then Leandro himself, visited Alice's father asking for the girl, the father did not say either 'no' or 'yes' but that evening 'kicked up a stink' with his daughter and then began to threaten Dick with the police. Leandro, defending Dick, wrote to Harry Williams:

'MY BOY IS HONEST and wants to do the right thing. Perhaps him being a halfcaste lowers him in your eyes. Well! you have nothing on him in that line nor your aristocratic relations up north either. His only defect is that he has not hoarded any cash as he helped me, his brothers and sisters all this years. My boy has a good character and name. No one ever called him a boor, miser, double face and he met men always during his short life face to face. Nor would he make a pack mule of Alice if he married her, nor he would belt her either. Dick is a kind and loving man. I will admit that his letter is not first rate if it is a true copy but all lovers become silly and her letter induced him to write silly prattle. So there is flame on both sides.'

The Illins knew what love was ... From Leandro's grandfather Dmitrii, the romantic officer absconding with his future wife from Poland, from Nicholas, prophet of free love, who found his wife — a Dostoyevskian heroine — in the Tien Shan mountains, to Leandro himself who, gun in hand, defended his union with Ngadjon Aboriginal Kitty. But now Dick, instead of an honest engagement to his sweetheart had to retreat because of the colour of his skin and his poverty. The time had come for Leandro to tell his former friend, Alice's father, how things stood.

'I ALWAYS THOUGHT YOU WERE STRAIGHTFORWARD AND A FRIEND. But your friendship did not come up to standard nor your straightforwardness either. ... You say your God is money. My God is my children and grandchildren and their happiness. I think you don't understand that! So if Dick married Alice she would become my God too. She would be the mother of my grandchildren and you naturally would have a share in it too. But you say your God is £. s. d. (probably buried somewhere in a rusty tin). So you understand not what happiness is. You lived all your life like a hatter with a loaded gun within your reach. Life runs on every day and is made up of little things and when you will wake up from your boorish selfishness it will be time to die ...'[45]

To enjoy those 'little things' from which life is made up, sharing with your loved ones rather than hoarding material wealth and success — this was the philosophy that Leandro nurtured throughout his life. Summing up what he had achieved, he wrote in 1933:

'I AM JUST MAKING A LIVING AND NOT A GOOD ONE at that. I am not taking no one down. I like to see Dick [Hoolihan] get on, and all my boys. I kept them together so far even if poor but respectable. ... I have not got long to go. My health (heart) is no good. I like to see my children all with me and we all love one another. It might look that financially we are a failure but we are happy together.

'... I reared my family to honest sober workers enlightened enough to love their fellow men and beg from no one. They can drove, build yard's fences, grow potatoes, cabbage and cane, cut wood, repair roads and track a horse or a bullock with next man and ride <u>any horse</u> broken or not. I carried my duties out. My children are well liked in the district. My boy eldest got a gold medal [as] Best loser in the Ambulance [boxing] Tournament. My second was the best singer 'Solo' in his school. The youngest milks 5 cows every morning, feeds fowls, pigs, gathers chop and feed horses. Makes butter and is general manager on the farm. They are all musical. None smoke nor drink nor gamble. Fight among themselves but stick for one another to the death.

'My daughter reared all of them after the wife died and she was only $9^1/_2$. She is the light of my life, my best ... She is no more a sister to my kids; she is a mother to them.'

That was what he wrote about Dick, Tom, Harry and Flora. Lullie, his youngest, had a special place in his heart, too; her happy nature was a vital thread to connect him with the happiest period of his life, his own childhood. 'Who would not like to be a child again. ... No matter how old we are when we mix with the little people we forget we are old', he wrote after visiting Lullie's school break-up.[46] His love and understanding of a child's nature could manifest itself in the most unusual way: for instance, using a pencil to write an important letter to a member of parliament, Leandro would remark without any resentment, 'The jolly kids lost my pen for me and used half of my writing pad and they are all asleep so I have to write with a pencil'.

How they loved these happy evenings together, when the heat of the day abated with the sun setting over the soft, violet Sea View range, and father would sit on the veranda after the evening meal, with the *North Queensland Register* or the *Herbert River Express*, and, when there was no visitor to argue with him about politics, they would wind up the old gramophone and listen to Leandro's favourite songs 'Beautiful Queensland', 'Red River Valley' or 'Rose of Tralee', or even improvise a concert. 'Back in Russia they sent my father to learn music', Flora remembers. 'They sent him to learn violin, he could play violin, he could read music, but he said that his fingers were too short, he wasn't good enough to play violin. But he used to play mandolin and accordion.' Now he enjoyed teaching his children to play the accordion, and the mandolin or guitar and they all grew up musical and good singers.

Flora gratefully remembers her father's attitude.

'HE LOVED US RIGHT TO THE END. He'd do everything for us right up till he died. We were everything to him. That's all he worried about was us, he never worried about money. You can't live without money; you have to have money, but not a lot of money. He never worried about that, if you did not have it you did not have it, that's all, it did not matter. He just made anything do — go without. He reared us up and never left us behind.'

Certainly, his relations with the children were not perfect all the time. His boys were boys and to be able to say proudly that none of them 'drink, smoke, steal or gamble' he had to be strict at times. Moreover, he knew that, as Aborigines, they would have to pay for the slightest mistake which might be pardoned in a white person. His family nickname 'Little General' was indeed deserved. Harry tells: 'Of course, life was a lot stricter back in those days too, not like it is now. He was strict with us, he'd tell us right from wrong. If we done wrong we got a strap, that was it. Oh, yes, he made us obey and we never got into any trouble.' Even little Ernie had his share of grandad's 'male upbringing': 'He was very defending to disabled people and if you laugh at somebody with disability he would flick you on the ear'. This upbringing turned out to be most effective — for years Ernie would work at the Department of Social Security, helping people not just as an official but sharing with them whatever he had himself. 'We used to live from pay day to pay day', his wife Maud tells, 'but Ernie would bring home black people and white people, who had no money — "Can you make a feed, this fellow has nothing", he would say.'[47]

Leandro had a simple philosophy, which he shared with his children, as Flora tells.

'HE USED TO PUT UP WITH ANYTHING. If things came easy he would accept that, but if things were hard he accepted that too, he did not worry, he could put up with it. What was the most important for him? Well, it was to live good, honest, clean life. He was always a very fair man. He'd never try to do anybody or catch anybody or try to be dishonest to anybody, never, never. And he did not like it. He always told us: "The best way to live in life is to be honest", he said, "then you're never in trouble".'

To respect yourself and make others to respect you — it was all the inheritance that he could provide for his children; probably, it was worth more than any money.

'BECAUSE MY FATHER WAS MARRIED TO A BLACK WOMAN, some people tried to treat him the same. But he was too good for them, too clever for them, no matter how well-educated they were. He'd put them to shame, and they all respected him. White and black people respected him, because he put them to shame quick smart. Station owners and everybody, they respected him, always calling him Mister Illin, never called him by his first name. He never used to think that he was above anybody, he never thought he was much better; but never try to make him a fool, he make you a fool quick and smart. Oh, he would not allow anybody to hurt any of us or him either.'[48]

The years passed and his children grew up, then Leandro poured all his love on his grandchildren. The eldest were Flora and Dick Hoolihan's kids. Ernest, born in 1933, was a big, strong boy, nicknamed Bully by Ginger; Johnnie, born in 1934, was not so strong, and seemed always to remain a baby in the family. They nearly lost him one day when he was washed down the Stone River and Flora managed to catch him at the last moment. I met him, exhausted by kidney disease, shortly before his death. 'I remember my grandad', he said slowly, 'he would sit me on his knees and show me in an atlas where Tashkent was, his birthplace'. A smile lit his face and he seemed to forget for a moment about his suffering. The next one, Margaret, given a Russian nickname Baba, was born in 1938. Dick and Flora had their hut next to Leandro's and, as they were away working most of the time, Leandro spent a lot of time with their kids. Ernie relates:

'IT WAS A LONG WAY TO SCHOOL from Stone River and mum did

not want me to go so far, it was about 5 miles, all scrub, she did not want me to ride alone to school. And grandad Illin made school at home, he used to bring books and take me to the library. I could read and write before I went to school. By the time I went to school I had read already *Tom Sawyer* and *Huckleberry Finn* by Mark Twain, *Treasure Island*, and Jack London's *Call of the Wild*. I was nine when I started school and they put me a couple of classes up.

'The only thing Russian that my grandad tried to teach me, it was chess. At that time draughts, checkers, was more popular, all the rest of the family could play checkers, so I concentrated on that, became a very good player. Even when I was nine I was able to beat ... he used to bring adult people along to play me.'[49]

Ernie and Johnnie later went to a private boarding school — the Grammar school in Townsville — at a time when there were no other Aboriginal children there. Dick and Flora did their best to give them the education which they did not receive themselves. Their own life was not so fortunate; they separated but remained friends. Margaret remembers:

'MUM USED TO WORK HARD ALL HER LIFE. She used to clean houses, scrub floors, and wash clothes — for police, ambulance, white-collar workers. It never stopped until she nearly broke down. If anybody understands how mum felt it's me. Mum used to wash by hand and I used to hang out clothes when I came home after school and then go and deliver it. That went five days a week. And then on Sunday we did our own washing, on Monday she'd start ironing. I did the easier ironing like tablecloths and pillowcases. Mum was a tradesperson in her own right, all her washing was spotless. And nothing smelled better than freshly washed clothing ... Pay was awful but we were never hungry. Then, when I left, my younger sister Jenny carried on.'[50]

Years later Margaret would settle in Malanda, on the land of her Ngadjon ancestors, marrying Frank Gertz, a grandson of Harry Gertz (Goetz, 1887–1977), who was a famous stockman from the Valley of Lagoons, sharing German and Gugu-Badhun descent. They would raise a family of six ...

But all that will be much later on and in the meantime they were all together and in 1940 their family even enlarged when Leandro brought their granny Emily from the Tablelands to Utopia. Lullie, who must have missed a mother's love more than the elder children, always wanted her grandma to come down to live with them. Leandro himself always used to invite Emily to stay with them but she preferred to remain in her country. By now, however, Emily was nearly seventy and Leandro went to the Tablelands to bring her.

Leandro came to Butchers Creek on a cool, rainy day in June 1940. He felt a pang of sadness as he stopped near his father's farm. Dear memories of the past surrounded him — his family standing here in front of the thick scrub, full of hope ...

By now most of the land was cleared. But, together with the scrub, Little Siberia was gone too. Homenko's and Gadaloff's families were the last to remain. His own former selection looked deserted; it had changed hands several times since he sold it to John Walker in 1919 and now his clearing was overgrown, prickly lantana spread everywhere. It seemed that in a couple of years the selection would revert to scrub.[51] What were the years of his hard toil spent for!

Leandro found Emily on the Johnston farm, on Clarke's track. They had not seen each other for nearly twenty years. She seemed to have become shorter, her white hair made her face even darker, but as before she was beaming and full of energy. Years and losses, it seemed, had no power over this bright woman. After the death of her husband Tom Denyer in 1920, she stayed for a while in Boonjie, on the Russell gold-field, gardening and mining. Then, in 1922 she lost her daughter Julia, which was followed by the death of Kitty three years later. All she had by then was Kitty's elder daughter, Emma, who came to live at Yungaburra on the Tablelands. At that time Emily worked for Lancelot Johnston's family, looking after his children. She, one of the last who remembered the coming of the whites to her country, now was to witness how her people were declining in numbers because of diseases and alcohol, as well as the opium introduced by the Chinese, while those who survived were constantly hunted by police and removed to Monamona or Palm Island missions. She herself, together with Paddy Robinson, her tribal husband — as recorded in police documents — and the family of her relative, Molly Raymont, were imprisoned in January 1934, intended for deportation. They broke out and several of them, including Emily and Paddy, managed to escape and had to hide for several months in Mulgrave Gorge. Paddy was finally deported to Palm Island in 1939. 'As for Emily', reported the local Protector, '... she definitely states that she does not want to leave here, and says she will die if taken to a Settlement.' By that time Emily's granddaughter

Emma had died and Emma's daughter, thirteen-year-old Jenny, had come to stay with Emily (Paddy wanted to take her as a wife and this was one of the causes of his removal). The Johnstons employed Jenny, and Emily agreed to go with Leandro to see Kitty's children.

The six of them, from Ginger to Lullie, had outgrown Emily by then and seemed to be modern Australians rather than Aborigines. Having grown up away from the Ngadjon land, they did not realise then how important this reunion with their Aboriginal grandma would be for them in the years to come. She would tell them Ngadjon myths, travelling easily between mythological and mundane realities, and, as if instinctively, they remembered them word for word, as it was usual for the generations of their ancestors; more than half-a-century later they would tell them to me in the same manner ...

Emily told them about her first encounter with the whites at Lake Eacham as well: 'The white men came and shot all the tribe out and took all the young people ...'. But the encounter with grandma was not just with a gloomy past. One incident was retained by Ernie, then a seven-year-old boy.

'AUNTIE LULLIE HAD A HORSE, AND IT WAS REALLY FUNNY HORSE, it was a real mongrel horse, she had us chase it up the corner. We all made a line, granny Emily made the line trying to push it into the corner so she put the bridle and saddle on him. But when he looked like being bailed up he charged, of course we jumped aside. Granny picks up these sticks, we had long sticks for picking oranges, they had a hook on it. Anyway, granny said, "This has got a hook on it". Lullie says "Hook him in the back side". The horse was wild because the stick had a hook on it. And it kept running away. Then auntie Lullie said, "Hook him in the arse". Granny just lay there and she laughed and laughed.'

Emily stayed with them for about a year but, in spite of her love for her grandchildren, she felt homesick all the time and wanted to return to the Tablelands. 'So', Ernie tells, 'Johnston came down and got her, he was pretty good, the old fellow. She lived with them and they were all friends. But when the old fellow died, the police took her and sent her to Palm Island without even notifying us.' This tragic story still affects the Johnston family.

Her last night in her own country Emily spent in a cell at the Malanda police station. On 1 October 1954 she was taken to Palm Island. She knew she would soon die away from her native land but, in order not to be a burden to anybody, she did not resist. Before long her grandchildren learnt where their grandma was. Flora relates:

'LULLIE WROTE TO ME and asked me to send her some money so that she could go over to get her and bring her back to Ingham. And when she wrote to the superintendent, he wrote back to her, he said, yes, she could come over and get her. But it was wet weather time and Lullie could not go and she was waiting for the wet weather to finish and before she could go our granny died there on Palm Island.'

It was 23 February 1955. She was around eighty-five years old at that time, and probably the eldest Ngadjon. A correspondent of the *Townsville Bulletin* wrote in the obituary: 'She told many graphic stories of early days on the Russell River Goldfield. She retained a retentive memory right to the end.'[52] Alas, nobody seems to have recorded them ...

It was hard for Leandro to continue with woodcutting and farming. In 1941 he tried his luck in a new capacity — for a while he was mining for tin near Ingham but without much success. Then, in 1942, he moved into Ingham. As Flora tells it: 'He had his own little place from these Russian people, the Kormishens. Shura had a place where she used to sew, then there was two or three rooms behind, and father had one at the back of their house on Herbert Street. Oh, they all used to be talking a lot, talking in Russian.'[53]

I would like to be able to finish the story happily — a contented father lives out his last peaceful years surrounded by his children and grandchildren, who lead lives in accordance with his ideals. But, sadly, his last years brought its share of troubles to Leandro, as well. At times despair seemed to overflow in him: 'I got the pass to Brisbane', he wrote to Dick and Tom in 1943, 'but don't think I will ever go with all the sorrows and troubles of Lullie, Harry, Tom and his coming marriage and your worries, Dick. It is not worth to use science to prolong a useless and unhappy life and give troubles to doctors to cure me.' When Flora reached the point of telling about those last years, she just broke off the story: 'We lived down there at Stone River for about twelve years until the war got serious, then we left it and everybody went this way and that way ...'

Yes, it was the war, but it was something else, too — the time had come for his children to become adults, and from now on to carry the load of real life with all its troubles by themselves. And, as years before when their father would leave them in the middle of the Burdekin River to teach them how to swim, now life took them all to the deep spots and they had to swim out. All Leandro could do was to watch from the shore: 'I am that worried and powerless to do anything'.[54] They were to swim alone and yet their parents' love, their father's honesty and fearlessness in the face of injustice, their mother's Aboriginality and deep spiritual attachment to her Ngadjon land were all protecting them with invisible armour. The winged seeds sown by their parents would one day sprout in them and then, in turn, burst forth again in their own children and in their grandchildren. But in the meantime ...

Harry, his youngest son, brought Leandro not only joy but his share of troubles as well. Tall and lean — in his teenage years he shot up, overtaking his elder brothers in height — handsome, with nearly European features; after some years of schooling he started work at fourteen, first cutting timber with his family and then, for five years, working on cane farms. His teenage ambition was to break away from the misery he grew up in, a condition aggravated by the stigma that the whites forced on him of being a 'half-caste'.

'I REMEMBER AUNTIE LULLIE TOLD TO ME THAT UNCLE HARRY RAN AWAY WHEN HE WAS YOUNG', Maud tells, 'he went to Tully and grandfather went after him. And just because grandfather never worried about material things, he was a very humble man, he provided for the kids, he loved his kids, and uncle Harry was a bit ashamed of him, because he said to him, "Don't come looking for me, I want to live my own life", and that hurt grandfather a lot.'

By that time Leandro could not work as a woodcutter any longer, 'my legs are bad as usual with rheumatism', he would write to Dick. He was not getting a pension yet, and a couple of pounds from time to time for tobacco sales was all he had to live on. He, indeed, looked humble but it did not worry him a bit. Ernie remembers travelling with his grandad on trains in the war years.

'HE WAS VERY PLAIN, GRANDAD, HUMBLE SORT OF MAN, and he used always carry his food with him, his sausage, and cheese, and damper, and he used to pull it out. He even had his own little primus and put a billy on the primus. Lots of people used to shame him, "Look at him, can't he afford", they reckon he did not have to do that, they wanted him to buy the food from the shop on the train.'[55]

Leandro wrote to Dick, who was just enlisted in the army, about that visit to Harry; he bore no grudge, telling Dick how he 'found Harry much skinnier as he has been going to work without breakfast ever since he came here and very little dinner as he bought a slice of sandwiches for a 1/- and a bit of cake for dinner and a hungry supper. ... I got the primus going for him and I bought him 10/- worth of tucker. He has not been paid yet so I am sending you all I can. Harry Bunn sent me £2-0-0. I paid 10/- for fare, spent 10/- on Harry, sending you 10/- and I still got 10/-.'

He was wise enough to understand his rebellious son, and he alone knew how lonely Harry felt in this first attempt at living an adult, independent life. But suddenly luck, it seems, turned Harry's way. During a visit to Ingham he met a young, shy girl, who hardly reached his shoulder in height — Phyllis Rosendale. A few months later, in February 1942, they married in Kilcoy. Harry was twenty-one, Phyllis eighteen.

With nearly fair skin and light hair, she was 'classed as quarter-caste to the whiteman', their daughter Leanne would write years later. Phyllis brought into the Illin family the world of the Aborigines who grew up on Palm Island. They differed from Ngadjon, whom Leandro met while their traditional life-style had not yet been completely destroyed by the whites' invasion; they differed, too, from Gugu-Badhun from the upper Burdekin area, who lived on cattle stations — although their traditional life had disintegrated they remained on the land of their ancestors, close to the elders, who still preserved the traditional values. The Palm Islanders' lives were mostly stories of betrayal by the whites, of enforced segregation, the introduction of alien values to them, and then of the long, painful integration into the world of the whites as second-class citizens. This way is graphically depicted by Marnie Kennedy, a friend of Flora and Lullie, in her book *Born a Half-Caste*.

The story of Phyllis's family was no exception. Her grandmother Jimaylya, later named Topsy Brown, was born around 1892 in a Kalkadoon tribe near Mount Isa at the time of fierce resistance by the Kalkadoon people to the occupation of their land by the white pastoralists. She was very young when, at Rochedale Station, she gave birth to her first daughter, named Queenie Brown. Queenie was classed as 'half-caste'. According to Leanne: 'Queenie could not speak much [Kalkadoon] language as she was brought up on whitemen property and was taken away from her Mother when she was about seventeen or eighteen years of age. In 1923 Queenie borned her first child, a girl, and named her Phyllis, at Cloncurry.' Only recently Leanne has learnt that

Phyllis's father was a German, who, like so many white men at that time, abandoned the child. In around 1928 Queenie and her two daughters were moved to Palm Island Mission, where Queenie's third daughter was born. In 1937 Queenie married Eric Rosendale, who was, according to Leanne, 'of Singale/Melanesian and German blood coming from the Gwuggu Yalanki Tribe. ... The Rosendale family went to Church every day and night. Their religion was Church of England. They lived in a grass house made of dirt floors covered with corn bags in the kitchen, dining room and floor-boards in the bedrooms. The walls were made up of plaited coconut leaves.' Queenie and her daughters made their living by making artefacts from pandanus and coral for the tourists. For a few years Phyllis studied at school and then had to work as a cook. In 1941 the Rosendale family moved to Ingham.[56]

Their life-style at that time depressed Leandro. 'Harry is just a skeleton living mostly on ready cooked meat and fish, and the dog's life he gets. ... Yesterday morning Harry and Phyllis came home from Mum's at 8 a.m. They gambled all night.' Some moments their marriage seemed to be on the brink of collapse. 'It would be a better thing to clear out but I pity poor Gloria and the baby that is coming', Leandro wrote. Gloria was their first child and the baby was their second, Bob. The only thing for Leandro to do was to keep putting into practice his principle 'My God is my children and grandchildren and their happiness'. All he could do was love them, baby-sitting occasionally when Harry and Phyllis had their outings — Harry had to swim out by himself. And he did. He and Phyllis raised a family of eleven (seven sons and four daughters). Many of their children occupy important positions in Aboriginal organisations now. Years later their youngest daughter Leanne wrote about her mother: 'Phyllis devoted her life to her family. They were the sole reason for her existence. She was always there for them — through thick and thin. She never let them down.' When Phyllis passed away in 1993, the farewell booklet was decorated with an emu, the totem of her tribe, and at the commemorative service, along with church hymns, a didgeridoo was played. Finally, she was reunited with her Aboriginality, from which she had been forcibly segregated at her birth.

Harry, after the years of hard work cane-cutting and at a sawmill and a brief period in the army, got a better job on the railway in Ingham. 'I was a caller and shunter. Call the crew for the trains. Get to work in the morning. Get them out of bed. Light a fire, put a kettle on, so that they could have a cup of tea and a feed before the Townsville train come. And when the train came they would take over and the other mob go off, change over of the crew. It used to be all hours.' And one day, when Leandro had passed away already, a time would come for Harry to be guided by his principles: 'I had a bad boss. He was accusing everyone there of stealing stuff in the railway, pillaging, that sort of stuff, I came to station master and I said "I am not a thief", I handed in my resignation. I left there in September 1956, I went to work on the cane farm.' To defend his honour he, no longer a young man, with at this point a family of seven, preferred hard work cane-cutting to the comfortable life in a town. They moved to Townsville in 1959. Finally, he got a job as a truck driver for the Commonwealth Department of Works, where he worked till his retirement.[57]

'If the time comes I and my sons will defend this soil from invasion', Leandro declared in 1940. And in June 1941 the time had come: Dick and Tom joined the army. They served in Militia, Motor Transport, in Townsville. The boys' letters, preserved in Vera Ketchell's archives, are reserved and laconic: 'Just a few lines to let you know that I am still well'. How worried Leandro was could only occasionally be seen from their adult remarks in response to his worried letters: 'Nothing to worry about', 'Please try not to worry yourself sick'. And again, from afar, he would try to stop them from taking a wrong step: 'Keep off the shandys! It is easy to start on them with the crowd. Don't go into pubs at all, son.'[58] It was a worry for him, but not the main one. The thought that his beloved boys could be claimed by the war approaching the Australian doorstep did not let go of him for years. He lived from one letter to another, from one of their rare visits home on leave to another. Only once in a letter to the newspaper, trying to help others sharing his 'humble pie' of poverty, he revealed the piercing love and worry that enveloped him while seeing off his boys each time.

'YESTERDAY I WENT TO MEET MY TWO SOLDIER SONS coming on leave. A railway officer (whom I do not blame as orders are orders) invited me politely to obtain a platform ticket. I did not wait and got off the platform, knowing I had to be law-abiding, and as my income is very limited I thought I would give the fourpence to my little granddaughter [it was Margaret] who was with me, to buy some ice-blocks. Well now, Mr Editor, I have lived and worked over 32 years in the country and worked hard to rear a family of six, widowed, poor and handicapped. I have two sons serving their country. I see them very sel-dom and I love my sons just as any father or mother does. Our only pleasure now is to meet them and farewell them and we are charged 4d. per head to do that. There are 8 or 9 of us go to say good-bye and unless we empty our depleted pockets we have to stay outside like outcasts or animals and watch our soldier boys board the train and they go away with hurt knowledge that we could not afford to come and give them a last shake of hand like those that can afford to do so. As far as I am con-cerned I can eat humble pie in my poverty and gaze from a distance at my departing boys each time, thinking it might be the last time I will see them. There are thousands of fathers and mothers in the same boat (either buying platform tickets, paying with shaking hands the pennies they need or resigning themselves to be outcasts, like I do). Why not abolish the platform tickets? Why not give the relatives of soldiers a free pass to see their dear ones away or meet them for another painful glance?'[59]

The shortage of money, which he could put up with all his life, now aggravated his worries about the sons. Ten shillings, one pound — it was all that he could scrape together occasionally to send his boys in the first years of their service. One day, contrary to his principles, he tried gambling to get desperately needed money and frankly related the sad result in a letter to his sons: 'I had on Friday £4–0–0 and I tried to win some money to take Lullie to Brisbane ... But instead of winning I am left with about 12s. to carry on. I am very convinced now that winning comes once in a hundred cases. So it is a good place to keep out from. Ginger lost all his so I got to carry on him and myself for 11 days some-how.' Soon he got a letter from Dick 'I send you some money so that you can go with Lullie. Tom and I are sending £5 each and more later'.[60] His boys had really grown up now ...

Dick and Tom were released from the army only in 1945. Virile and independent, they were no longer 'bush boys'. The only thing that upset their reunion with their father was that Tommy had learnt to drink in the army. Dick and Tom grew up into two different personalities. Dick, serious, reserved and conscientious was the one that was most close to his father; they believed in similar things, too — while in the army he would ask his father to send him the radical newspaper *Truth*. Tom, a happy-go-lucky fellow, was different. 'Whatever life was Tom accepted it, while Dick did not', their relatives say. It took a long time for each of them to find their 'only one'. Dick met his wife Evaline Rawlins (née

Mayo) only in the 1950s. Her mother was Kalkadoon and her father, German. Tom's first and second relationships broke up and finally he married Jessie Sadler; her father was German, and her mother, a Gugu-Badhun, was a daughter of the famous King Lava, possessor of the brass plate. Tom and Jessie were a happy couple and had six children — the eldest, Alexandra, and the youngest, Nicholas, both named in honour of Tom's Russian grandparents. Both Dick and Tom worked on the railway, specialising as fettlers. While Dick finally returned to the Tablelands to live, to the land of his mother, Tom's family was constantly on the move together with his gang of fettlers between Ingham and Ayr.

Leandro's daughters Flora and Lullie had their share of troubles, too, which Leandro took deeply to heart. Their relative positions in the family after Kitty's death had resulted in two different personalities — at the age of nine Flora had taken on the full load of a mother's duties towards the other children, while Lullie for a long time enjoyed the privilege of being the baby of the family. Flora grew up responsible and reserved, a strong and rather ironic personality, prepared to carry by herself whatever life brought for her, equally demanding of herself and others. Although she never had a formal education, I was struck to find in her a perfect example of what Russians used to call *intelligentsia* — someone with an independent mind and strict moral principles. Probably she inherited this from her 'Deda', Nicholas, although she also took after him in her passion for gambling, which for such natures as Flora's is a particular 'safety-valve' to relieve the misery and strain of everyday life.

Lullie grew up different, with a feeling of security; she basked in the love and protection of her family, which in her later life she would in turn bestow on the people around her. The attitude of the two sisters to the past seemed to be different, too. While Flora's family seldom heard her talk about her bush childhood, Lullie 'always told stories how they used to be in the bush and different things as she remembers when she was kid'. They both — Flora and Lullie — married for love and the marriage of each underwent a trial in the war years, although in different ways. Flora's Dick often had to live away from the family — they moved to Ingham in 1942 — working on the stations, while Flora scrubbed floors and did washing in the Ingham hotel. These long periods of living apart resulted in jealousy and finally they separated, and Flora fell in love with Bert, a white man.

Lullie's story was different. In 1942 she married Dynzie Smallwood; his father was from the Birri-Gubba tribe, his mother from Fraser Island. Lullie and Dynzie met when he first came to Ingham to cut cane; they married and soon he joined the army. By that time they had had their first daughter, Essie. 'Essie can stand well and tries to walk', Leandro would remark lovingly about her in his letters, and when she went away with Lullie, 'I was sorry to see Essie go'. He shared with Lullie all her worries when Dynzie was sent to the battlefields in New Guinea — 'Lullie is terribly broke down. I should think she is!' — and when Dynzie was shot in the leg up there, finally contracting malaria. Lullie had health problems as well, having a tubal pregnancy. Dynzie was eventually discharged and came back to Ingham; later he became a telephone linesman working for the postmaster-general's department.

In spite of Lullie's weak health they raised a family of nine. But their house is remembered by more than that.

'SHE HELPED ANYBODY', Maud tells, 'she took abandoned kids in, they reared a lot of kids, troubled kids that parents could not handle. Auntie Lullie was a person, she was a straight-out person, she told you what she thought of you, but she did not mean to offend and she got a lot of influence from her father, too. She helped anybody, white or black, she had the biggest mob of people stay at her place all the time. All murries who used to work on stations, they used to come down, sleep at her place. They knew they could put their bag down for the night, and sleep and they would get a feed next morning. Lot of people, all Blue Range people, Lucky Downs, Greenvale, when they come to town they stayed at Lullie and Dynzie's place. Everybody can tell you in Ingham, Lullie and Dynzie had their door open for all. Very, very good people they were. And uncle Dynzie done the cooking, big stews, big pieces of corned beef, and vegetables, twenty people at a time had their meal at their house. All their married life was like that and, besides, nine kids they had. She was more Aboriginal than the rest of the Illins.'[61]

And there was Ginger. His tragedy was the last blow that Leandro had to endure in those harsh war years. Kitty's tiny black baby that, from the time he was just a few months old, Leandro treated as his own son, the boy because of whom Leandro had separated with his own parents forever — he was now grown into a strong, decent man. Always laughing and cheerful, a skilful bushman, a perfect rider, a loving and caring son and brother. 'Ginger promised to be with Tommy until I come back' Leandro wrote, going away from home for a while in 1941. 'Him and Lorna are getting sweet', he lovingly remarked in 1943. When Ginger got a good job, he would even try to help his brothers serving in the army, provoking the following comment from Tom to his father: 'If Ginger wants to send any money to me ask him to give it to you as you will need it more than I do'. Ginger would tackle any job — driving cattle, cutting wood or working in the canefields. In 1942 he joined the Allied Works Council as a truck driver, working for the army. But in March 1945 he lost his right leg in an accident. He was granted a pension but from that time his life began to fall apart. He had learnt to drink working away from home. Leandro tried to keep him away from the bottle but he realised that he was losing the battle with destiny for this boy so dear to him, at times dearer than the rest of his kids; they, he believed, would swim out without him. In 1948, when Leandro had passed away, Ingham police started a case against Ginger in an attempt to put him back under the Act and deport him to a reservation. He avoided deportation by escaping to Blue Range Station. Later he lived with Lullie and Dynzie in Ingham. He continued drinking until he got really sick and gave it up not long before his death. 'He always was in the pub. You could not have a conversation with him, he'd argue with you' — this was the sad impression that he made on the younger generation.[62] And he never spoke about the past. None would recognise in this wretched old man the former Ginger — proud heir of Ngadjon 'kings', joyful spirit of the Illin family, a loving older brother, a fearless rider. That Ginger had disappeared forever in the terrible accident ...

Before he was stricken by Ginger's tragedy, Leandro did have a bright page in his life. Thanks to the money Dick and Tom sent him, he was able to go with Lullie and visit Brisbane in 1943. One quiet day he came to Kangaroo Point on the Brisbane River, to the Immigration barracks. The city, beautiful as ever, rose before him on the opposite shore. He stood near the jacaranda tree remembering Mila Daniel, the young Russian girl from whom he parted here almost thirty-three years before. God knows where she was now and what might have become of his life had they married. He had chosen another life, harder, but his own. And if he had to choose once again, he would still have chosen that one — his and Kitty's humpy in the scrub and the first cry of their newborn son, and the chowchilla calling in the morning ... He would rewrite nothing in his life, nothing except the tragedy of Kitty's death, which never let go of him.

On the way back he lingered at St Mary's Church. That Boxing Day in 1911, they, the young Russian men entering its hall and then arguing themselves hoarse about having a Russian colony in Australia, about the Russian future ... Artem, and Rosalieff, and Manowitch — where are they now? What has happened to them all? What has happened to his Russia itself!

Manowitch was no longer there at the church, he was dead now. He died in 1925 at the time when Leandro was deep in the bush, completely cut off from the Russian community. Leandro never knew that Manowitch betrayed them all. Nor did he know that Artem had died, too, in an accident not long after returning to Russia to take his place at Lenin's side. And Rosalieff? Dead, too, just before the Stalinist purges. Leandro knew none of this. The only thing he now knew for sure was that this is his home, here, in Australia, in the country of his adoption, on the dusty streets of his Ingham.

* * *

Leandro grew more and more sick — rheumatism, heart trouble, diabetes. 'Diabetes is getting me strong. It is hard for me to walk about'. 'I am still the same, not feeling too well. I don't mind casting in when I see you free of the Army', he would write to his sons.[63] And still he found strength to continue with his duties as the people's councillor — 'somehow, when people think that something is not right, they come and complain to me and ask me to bring it to the notice of those whom it concerns'. He continued his struggle for the improvement of the world in which he was about to leave his children and grandchildren alone.

He suggested opening a canteen for kids, where unscrupulous traders would not make a fortune from their pennies. He struggled for a shed at the bus stop with a lavatory for women and children, insisting on this suggestion in spite of mockery: 'I may state that one of our smart Councillors sarcastically remarked that they would build a lavatory as a monument to myself. They can do so if they like as long as it is "Pro bono publico" (i.e. for the public's good). I will lend my name to anything that will benefit the people.' He would ring the bell about the faulty tap of a drinking fountain, which children had to suck in an unhygienic manner because of low pressure. He shamed councillors over taking so long to make a seat near the De Luxe Theatre, and over the fact that, when it arrived, it was of such a poor quality — 'the timber is cracked, inferior and ill fitted'. His struggle for that seat became the cause of his break with his former landlord, Councillor Frank Alston, and the occasion of one of his last contributions to the *Herbert River Express*.

'I ASKED CR ALSTON IF THERE WAS A BOSS IN THAT COUNCIL that enforced the orders given. I did not wait for the explanations but walked away disgusted. I have known Cr Alston for 23 years and knowing him as I do as a man that on his own estate will not let grass grow but correct the things that wanted correcting, and see it was done properly, I was his keen supporter for the Council Chairmanship. I am very disappointed now. The matter of the seat may look small to many. I do not regard it so. The people that come in want a bit of comfort.[64]

Although surrounded with people, Leandro at times felt very lonely. Now he would often think about his childhood, his parents, brothers and sisters. In faraway Honduras his mother, Romelio and Ariadna were the only ones to survive from his family. Their letters in the war years seldom found their way across the Pacific, but in December 1943 Romelio, as if answering this invisible plea from his brother, went to the British Legation in Tegucigalpa to request a British passport. He had his Australian naturalisation certificate and the Australian passport issued for him in 1921 at the time of his departure. His Majesty's Chargé d'Affaires and Consul in Tegucigalpa, instead of issuing him with a British passport, immediately furnished a report to the Australian Department of the Interior. He stressed that Romelio was of Russian origin and married to a Honduran lady and suggested revoking his naturalisation certificate 'in view of his prolonged absence from British territory'. The Department of the Interior, although aware that it should 'advise the holder of the intention to revoke his certificate in order to afford him an opportunity of resuming residence in the Commonwealth', revoked his naturalisation certificate behind his back. Romelio learnt about this deception only years later. In the meantime Alexandra, who lived with his family, passed away quietly in December 1945.[65]

Leandro received the news about his mother's death after a long delay. He knew it would happen one day but still the thought that he could not say a last farewell to his *mama* burnt him. If he could only believe, as he had in his childhood, when *mama* taught him his first prayers, that the time would soon come when they would be finally reunited in spite of all the wars, distances and borders ... But he could not. The only thing he knew was that the time for him 'to peg his last claim' was approaching fast. He did not want to cling any longer to his 'useless and unhappy life', as he put it one day. What else could he do in this world? Write his memoirs, open up sugar sacks of old letters, file away the newspaper cuttings with his articles — no, he did not feel like doing that. His children — he could do no more for them than he had done, he was sure that, however hard their life was now, they would be alright. And himself ... well, he'd better give Gloria, Bob and Essie another cuddle, or treat Margaret to one of his own hot Russian pancakes — never mind that they will not remember him, he is in them all.

Not long before his death he left the Kormishens' house in Ingham and moved to Townsville. He stayed in a boarding-house in Walker Street — to die. And on 15 August 1946 he passed away at the age of sixty-four. All his family scattered through Queensland came to his funeral in Townsville, where he died. They read his will. He left his papers and belongings to Dick, the eldest, and asked them to bury him without the church service, just wrapped up in a blanket, and without a tombstone on his grave, as if saying to them — do not look for me among the dead, do not look for me in Heaven; look for me among the living, in yourselves.

EPILOGUE

~

We went to Townsville to meet Leandro's descendants in July 1996. I was accompanied by my husband Vladimir Kabo and our four-year-old son Ralphie. I had not got a grant from the Australian Institute of Aboriginal and Torres Strait Islander Studies (AIATSIS) for the research as I had hoped, but my part-time job as a Russian tutor gave us enough money to buy the tickets from Canberra to Townsville and we decided to go. Our financial difficulties turned out to have one saving grace — the unique opportunity to see the family life of Leandro's descendants from the inside, as for ten days we enjoyed the hospitality of Maud and Ernie Hoolihan in Townsville and Margaret and Frank Gertz on the Tablelands. Ralphie, who spoke only Russian then, picked up his first Australian English words from the younger generation of the Illins — Leah, Chantelle, Majara, Taleta, Clinton, Rohan, Benjamin, Jarryd, Phyllis, and many others whose names I have not recorded — who had among their ancestors Aborigines from the Torres Strait Islands to New South Wales, and Europeans and Asians from Ireland and Germany to India and China. Well, this richness of diverse ethnicity hardly bothered any of them and they all were happy to 'Australianise' Ralphie.

As for my husband and I, the visit was a real eye-opener. Aboriginal people, about whom we had read in numerous books in far-away Russia, into whose origin and migrations Vladimir had conducted extensive research, were here, and the names of their tribes sounded like music — Gugu-Badhun, Kalkadoon, Wik, Kamilaroi ...

The diverse ethnicity of Leandro's descendants was the result of mixed marriages. The spouses of five of Leandro's children were all of mixed Aboriginal and European descent (their Aboriginal ancestors belonged to north Queensland tribes from Cairns to Mt Isa, their European ancestors were mostly of German and Irish origin). Leandro's children had thirty-four children. The origin of their spouses and partners is predominantly mixed too, but the geographical spread has increased significantly. Their Aboriginal ancestors are mainly from different parts of Queensland but some, who have traced their family history, claim to have among their ancestors people from Central Australia, and from islands in the Torres Strait and South Seas. Some spouses came from Palm Island and other missions, and associate themselves with these communities. In this generation Italian and Chinese ancestry were also added. This generation of Leandro's grandchildren has produced at least 104 children. Many of these children are married now, too, and again their spouses are mainly of mixed origin, although a few are, as in the previous generation, of purely European, or, as they put it, of 'white' origin. Aboriginal diversity continues to increase; it now includes Aborigines from New South Wales. In the present generation there is over eighty children now and their number continues to grow, bringing the total of Leandro's descendants to nearly 200.

The question that interested me was their ethnic self-identification. This turned out to be by no means a simple issue. The diversity of ethnic origin has resulted in significant anthropological differences within this huge family — they vary from Leanne (Harry's daughter), who has fair skin and golden hair, to Derek (Ernest's son) with dark skin and black curly hair. This diversity happens even within one family. Hazel, Tom's daughter, tells about her childhood.

'THERE IS ... SEVEN OF US, but myself, and Thomas, and Gladys we are the only three with dark skin, the rest are really fair. We would say, "How come I am black, dad, and you are not" — he was not, he was fair, and mum was not, she was fair. He would say, "Well, your grandmother was Aboriginal", and you would get really angry because here is your sister and your brother with green eyes and fair skin. "How come I am black? Why could not I be the same colour as them?"'[1]

In the harsh years after World War II assimilation was not only the official policy but the mood of society at large. Leandro's children and grandchildren had to struggle just to survive then, and some of them preferred not to be associated with Aborigines. But for all these years in their heart of hearts their Aboriginality never disappeared. For instance, Harry, who relatives believed hid his Aboriginality and declared himself Russian, when he spoke with me said, 'I am a bit of everything, both ways', and he turned out to be a source of interesting information on the Aboriginal past of the family.[2] And then we both happened to be in the company of an outback Queensland farmer — a nice, friendly fellow — who, not guessing that he was speaking to a man with Aboriginal ancestry, made fairly racist remarks about Aborigines. Harry bore it in silence. And I said nothing, too. It was a good lesson for me about what it was, and still is to be an Aborigine in Queensland.

For Leandro's grandchildren, who, after his death, grew up away from the Russian community and often away from the Aboriginal traditions of their ancestors, their ethnic identity became a painful issue. Hazel provides a deep insight into this problem: 'I was always aware that my grandfather was Russian. But I felt there was something missing. It's the same with my Aboriginality, you feel lost because you have not been in touch with your past. ... I felt like, where do I fit in.' But often the choice between their Russianness and their Aboriginality was made by life itself. Vera, Dick's daughter, relates: 'In the early days it was hard to take the Russian side because once you are Aboriginal, Europeans would not accept half-caste Aboriginals, and Aboriginal tribes in this area, they never outcast their half-castes, they kept them within the tribe. Even though the Russian was there we followed the Aboriginal side.'[3]

But even in their Aboriginality — and the majority of Leandro's grandchildren and their families now identify themselves as Aborigines, or murries — an important component was missing. They knew very little about their Aboriginal grandmother Kitty, some did not even know to which tribe she belonged — and it was not because of lack of interest on their side. Hazel explained the reason to me: 'Dad was not the sort of person who sits down and tells you what happened. A lot of our people are like that because they had a hard life, and I realised that it is hard for them to go back and talk about it.' Indeed, until recently when the situation in Australia changed, it was hard for the older generation to tell the young the painful story of their past. And the young patiently waited. But when the time came they realised how much they needed this reunion with their past, with the land of their ancestors, the reunion which is taking place right now. Alec Illin, Harry's son, says: 'Even though I lived for a couple of years on the Tablelands I never really knew that it was part of me. It was only recently in the last couple of years that I started to relate my granny Kitty to Malanda area because my traditional ties coming from her.'[4]

Only the eldest ones, Dick and Flora, always remembered that the Tablelands was the land of their ancestors, was their home. Visiting Dick's daughters, Glenda and Vera, who live on the Tablelands now, I heard from them about their childhood.

'DAD ALWAYS TOLD US FROM WHEN WE WERE VERY SMALL that we came from up here, this was sort of our home, he had that feeling that this was his country. Not Greenvale, not Mt Garnet, his home was up here on the Tablelands. He has passed that all to us. When we moved away from here in 1962, we went to Silkwood, but from then we always came home for holidays. He'd come back and he'd see granny Molly, and auntie Emma, and see Margie, he always came out here.'[5]

One day Flora's children, Margaret and Ernie, who is one of the Ngadjon elders now, took me to the land on the outskirts of Malanda which was recently returned to the Ngadjon people. Previously, the block was occupied by an Aboriginal reservation. Here, in 1989, died Jenny Brown, their Aboriginal cousin, daughter of Kitty's eldest child, Emma. Jenny had been kept for years in Monamona mission and had experienced a lot of hardships in her life. And she came to spend her last years here, on the land of her tribe, on the land from which in fine weather she could see the slopes of Bartle Frere, their spiritual resting-place. Jenny left no children and with her the line of Kitty's eldest full-blooded Ngadjon children finished.[6] Standing there on this land, Margaret and Ernie talked about the future, about the plans of the local Aboriginal community to care for its members, managing this beautiful block of land for their common benefit.

The Aboriginality of Leandro's descendants has received a new boost now, with the changing attitudes in Australian society towards Aborigines and as members of the younger generation have started to research the Aboriginal past of their family. Some of them continue to consider themselves to be Aborigines, without particular attachment to any specific tribal group; others do associate themselves with particular tribes — some with Ngadjon, some with other tribes in accordance with the origin of the spouses of Leandro's children and grandchildren. For instance, Dick's daughters consider themselves Ngadjon rather than Kalkadoon: 'Our mother never spoke about her side. Her mother, who was Kalkadoon, never told her'.[7] Among the young generation there is an interesting tendency to acknowledge that they belong specifically to each of the tribes of their Aboriginal ancestors while at the same time identifying more generally with their Aboriginality. For instance, Flora's granddaughter Allison has named one of her daughters Rupula Mai (Rupula is a lake on the land of her Gugu-Badhun great-grandfather and Mai means 'girl' in the language of her father's tribe, Kamilaroi); another daughter is named Minyaada (which means a desert flower among eastern Arunta on the land of Allison's great-great-grandmother); her son received the name Wharo Wurumi (which means crow's son among the Kamilaroi), and the youngest daughter's name is Yugilla Myndi (which means 'star' in Gugu-Badhun and Kamilaroi, respectively).

But along with the interest in their Aboriginal ancestors and their joyful reunion with their past there is always a painful question about their white fathers and grandfathers. Marnie Kennedy, a friend of the Illins, wrote with bitterness: 'My father was an unknown white man — the rat — making me one of the many sunburnt babies to roam our country. I am neither white nor black but of a new breed, to be punished along with our mothers for what we are.' Spouses of the Illins have brought to the family a variety of attitudes to their 'white' ancestors. Some, like Maud, Ernie's wife, who has carried out brilliant research into her family tree, seem not to hold any grudge against them. Some prefer not to mention them but not to forget — Aborigines know how to remember about their ancestors much better than Europeans, but they have been taught to keep their knowledge to themselves. For instance, one of them coming across the 'white' relatives of his Irish grandfather wanted to share the results of his research into the family tree with them but received a painful setback: 'We know about this part of the family but we are not interested in it'. This reminds us of Leandro's indignation towards the white men — 'well to do, comfortable, successful, married to white women' — who neglected their Aboriginal children in order to remain 'most respectful' members of society![8]

Still, listening to Leandro's descendants, I admired their racial tolerance. 'We never categorised anybody else', Vera says.[9] They were indeed free from any racist anti-white attitudes — unlike me, who sometimes felt ashamed of belonging to the whites. This attitude towards people, treating them on the basis of their merits, not on the colour of their skin, they inherited from Leandro. The decency and honesty of this Russian man gave the family a perfect antidote for any form of racism.

But Leandro was more than a 'white' for them, he was 'a Russian', and in rural Queensland the perception of Russia was that of a far-away land somewhere on the edge of the real world, and this increased his impact on his descendants. Although they, beginning with his children, did not preserve anything which we traditionally treat as Russianness — language, religion, customs — amazingly, they have managed to preserve their spiritual connection with Russia. Glenda Illin answered without hesitation when I asked if she thinks of herself as Russian: 'All the time. It was always there. I am Russian-Aboriginal more than Aboriginal-Russian.'[10] Alec Illin, Harry's son, provides his insight into his spiritual ties with Russia.

'I HAD NO HESITATION TO SAY THAT MY GRANDFATHER WAS RUSSIAN. I probably knew more what came from grandad's side, coming out of Russian than what I knew coming out from granny Kitty. Even if I know now that my strong spiritual ties are there, I also know that my strong spiritual ties are with Russia. I know inside of me there, in that spiritual side of me, that part of my grandfather, that's part of me, that's part of my dad. My children are part of it too.'[11]

Nola, Lullie's daughter, simply said: 'Probably because I live here — I am Aboriginal, but still my dream is to visit Russia one day, from where my grandad was'.[12]

Speaking with the new generation of Illins, I realised that, indeed, it took courage to claim their spiritual ties with the country which their ancestors left more than a century ago, four generations back. And I believe that it is their Aboriginality which allowed them to preserve their spiritual ties with Russia; their Aboriginal inheritance is their unique mentality of spiritual belonging to the land rather than owning it, and they have applied this Aboriginal spirituality to the land of their Russian ancestors. Compare this attitude to that of the grandchildren of other Russians from Little Siberia, who, to my question about their ethnic self-identification, said without hesitation that they are Australians who just have an interest in Russia. Characteristically, those members of the Illin family who have a stronger interest in their Aboriginal ancestors have an equally strong interest in their Russian ancestry. Rather than choosing between being Russian or Aboriginal they aspire to associate themselves with both.

I have discovered another unique feature in the older Illins' attitudes to their Russian past. A few material relics — an icon, photographs, letters, coins, and Nicholas's manuscripts — left by Leandro to his children have been treated by Dick and Flora as sacred rather than ordinary objects, which they carefully preserved and did not hurry to exhibit to younger generations. 'Every time I wanted to see a photo Flora said "I'll find it, I'll find it", but she never ever found it', Maud tells. It was my visit that facilitated access to these things. I am tempted here to make an analogy with Central Australian *churingas*, which elders preferred to give to the South Australian Museum to be looked after by Chris Anderson, whom they trusted, rather than to the young uninitiated members of their own tribes.[13]

The Russianness of the Illins is a living memory; they relate particular features of their own appearance or character to those of their Russian ancestors, for instance, and mention these ancestors in everyday speech. I was pleasantly surprised to see at Glenda Illin's place in Atherton a number of Russian books and artefacts. Her desire was to obtain a genuine Russian fur hat — hardly a practical object in tropical Queensland. But she is putting her dream into practice — she is learning Russian and is determined to go to Russia soon. Maud, Ernie's wife, has managed to fulfil her Russian dream — one day she came to our place in Canberra with a huge old samovar in order to read the inscription on it, and I remembered how over 120 years ago Nicholas and Alexandra became acquainted in a Turkestan inn while sharing such a samovar ...

Although Leandro's descendants had no connections with Russia and Russians for all these years their memory of their Russian ancestry was enhanced from an unexpected place — from Honduras. After Leandro's death Lullie continued to exchange letters with Romelio, her uncle, and with his son Leandro. In 1955–56 she even made an attempt to help Romelio's family return to Australia. The plan did not succeed and the correspondence ceased but the Australian Illins have never forgotten about their Honduran relatives. Hazel remembers her childhood dreams: 'Dad told us that we could have been living in America, and I thought that we would not be the same people we are now'. The contact was restored in 1978 when Alec Illin, Harry's son, went to the United States of America on an overseas study tour and found Leandro Illin's name in a telephone directory. Leandro remembers this telephone call: 'I just knew by the accent that it had to be someone from Australia. I was looking forward to meeting all the family for a long time'.[14] For both sides the reunion was like a dream. Then followed mutual visits between the two continents, an exchange of family tales and of photographs, and the discovery of each other as they are now: Honduran Spaniards and Aboriginal Australians with something Russian deep inside both.

Honduras with its rugged terrain and tropical forests reminded the Australian visitors of their native Atherton Tablelands. But what really surprised them, not rich people by Australian standards, was the poverty in Honduras. In their opinion their well-to-do Honduran relatives — Hector, Ariadna's son, was the owner of the Esso petrol stations throughout the whole of Honduras — lived like an average Australian, but, in comparison with the surrounding poverty, this was considered a high standard of living. To the Australians' surprise their Honduran relatives could afford to employ servants, paying them wages of just a few dollars a month. But there was another side of the story that devastated the Australian visitors — Hector's house was like a fortress, with a gun behind each door and a revolver by the bedside. 'If someone breaks into your room at night shoot first and then ask questions and worry about the policemen', he advised his Australian guests. He had grounds for behaving like that. In 1982 his son Nelson, who was a lawyer, went to buy the newspaper in Tegucigalpa and never returned. Twelve years later his body was found buried 150 kilometres to the south of Tegucigalpa.[15]

Listening to these stories, or watching reports from crime-stricken Colombia, where Nicholas had been about to settle, I continue to ask myself why had Nicholas abandoned peaceful Australia in favour of these turbulent places. Was it a subconscious desire to live one more completely different life through his descendants, or just an unslakable thirst for the unknown? Or maybe he could foresee the distant future and believed that the paradisaic image of a 'beloved' 'glorious' Republic of Honduras which he created in one of his last poems 'To my Country'[16] (written in Spanish) would come true one day?

And, certainly, it is not so gloomy seen from within Honduras itself. Jack Mackay, Ariadna's husband, succeeded first in the transportation business, then in farming, buying significant properties on the outskirts of San Pedro Sula, which later were used for housing. Ariadna, affectionately known all over San Pedro Sula as Mamara (which comes from Russian 'mama Ara'), seems to have found herself in this young country, too. Her grandchildren remember her as 'an extrovert woman with a strong character, sociable, happy, and hard-working. She kept the family together, always saying that a united family was a strong family. She liked travelling and quit driving her own car just two weeks before her death. She was a member of the Red Cross of Honduras and helped the orphanage. She also enjoyed playing poker and bridge.' Her children did well in sports. Hector was 'one of the founders and players of the Marathon Soccer team'; Nellie played basketball and was the tallest player for the Marathon team. Somerled (Sammy) practised boxing and became Honduran boxing champion and then won the Central American boxing championship. They all achieved professional success. Hector first owned the Hotel Roosevelt, the fanciest in town at that time, then he had a farm and the Esso gas stations. Sammy worked in his father's business. Olga, the youngest, qualified as a school-teacher and in 1969 she founded a bilingual English-Spanish school, Academia Americana, the second largest in San Pedro Sula. Nellie moved in 1948 to the United States of America, first to New Orleans, then to California. The Illins and Mackays are considered to be among the most successful and respected, hard-working pioneer families of Honduras.[17]

Romelio more than Ariadna inherited the rebel nature of Nicholas. The Australian relatives see Romelio's son Leandro, who has visited Australia several times, as a fighter for justice: 'He was for the people, Leandro. He told that those who run the country wanted to keep the poor people down and the rich people rich, and the Americans supported the rich families while Sandinistas supported poor people who wanted their own government. Leandro was in the union movement in Honduras and somebody got into him and bashed him up, breaking his legs and then he had to go to America. Nellie sponsored him. He could not go back on account of his views. He was twenty-eight and he had to learn English, he went to night school. And he became electrician over there'. Now Leandro runs an air-conditioning, refrigeration and heating service in New Orleans. And for years his ambition has been to go to Russia, to fulfil the charge his grandfather Nicholas on his deathbed gave to Romelio.[18]

Ariadna had five children, seventeen grandchildren, fifty-six great-grandchildren and fourteen great-great-grandchildren. Romelio's descendants are not so numerous: four children, eight grandchildren and three great-grandchildren. The children of Ariadna and Romelio live now in Honduras and the United States of America and consider themselves Hondurans and Americans. Their spouses are mostly Hondurans — Spaniards with some Indian blood — and, now, Americans. A Macedonian from Yugoslavia and several Guatemalans are among other nations represented in the family.[19]

Leandro's and Hector's visits to Australia, their trips to the Atherton Tablelands — where Hector met nine of his schoolmates from the Butchers Creek school — gave a big boost to the interest of their Australian relatives in the past of the family. But there was one trait of their Russian ancestors which always was there, which they never lost — their involvement in the struggle for justice.

Richard Hoolihan, Flora's husband, had experienced the strong influence of Leandro. Maud, his daughter-in-law, remembers:

'DICK USED TO SAY ABOUT LEANDRO: "Does not matter where he went, if he sees somebody being wronged, he'd stick up for him", and he said he always remembers him. He said he inspired him to get involved with the trade union and he was one of the first blacks, one of the first Aboriginals to be in the trade union'.[20]

It was in the early 1960s in Townsville that Dick befriended a young Torres Strait Islander, Eddie Koiki Mabo. They listened to communist speakers at the Tree of Knowledge in the centre of Townsville and to radio broadcasts by Kath Walker and Joe McGuinness and they realised that the time had come to form their own organisation. In 1962 they founded the Aboriginal Advancement League in Townsville. 'We had the first meeting and me and Dick became the President and the Secretary of the Advancement League', Koiki Mabo relates. The two of them became the League's regular representatives to the Trades and Labour Council, attending their fortnightly meetings, and once, in 1967, they went to the Communist Party conference. (Mabo's biographer, Noel Loos, writes that 'the Communist Party had a long history of involvement with Aboriginal people. They were the first white political party to offer them support in their struggle for justice.') At this conference Koiki and Dick were picked out by the TV cameraman and shown on the news. Soon after that Koiki, although not a member of the party, was forced to resign from his job at the Harbour Board because of his political associations.[21] But now nothing could stop them in their determination to struggle for the rights of the indigenous people. Koiki Mabo became one of the most famous Australians: he was the first to prove legally his traditional ownership of land on Mer

Island, which allowed Aborigines and Torres Strait Islanders to claim their native title on their traditional lands.

Dick contributed his share to the Aboriginal movement, as Maud relates.

'DICK USED TO GO TO CANBERRA ALL THE TIME, he and his friend Tom Sullivan [another member of the Advancement League], they used to take their holidays every Easter and go there. We used to say to him, "Why you take your holidays and go down there and spend your money, have a holiday". He said, "No, no, we go down there because all the embassies change. We have meetings there and we try to embarrass the government because Aboriginals were not treated right." And they went every year there.'

It was on one such visit to Canberra that Dick became acquainted with Yuri Yasnev, the Russian *Pravda* correspondent for Australia, and told him about Leandro Illin, his late Russian father-in-law. In 1967 Yasnev visited Townsville and Ingham and interviewed Leandro's children. He planned to write about Leandro and Nicholas but he did not succeed in his plans, probably, I guess, because he had discovered the anti-communist sentiments of Leandro and Nicholas.

Dick Hoolihan's struggle for Aboriginal rights has influenced the younger generation as well. Maud tells how: 'When Ernie and I got married, we started having kids, and Ernie was not interested in his father's involvement first, but then he started to go along to the meetings, and then I went along to the meetings with him, that's how we got involved, through dad.' While working for the Department of Social Security in Charters Towers, Ernie told many Aboriginal people of their rights, helping them to get their pensions. Working for the Aboriginal Legal Service, he conducted a painstaking investigation to prove the innocence of Kelvin Condren, an Aborigine from Mt Isa sent to jail in 1983 for life for a murder he had not committed. Ernie's determination helped him to disclose police prejudice and a cover-up and to free Kelvin after seven years in jail. The tradition started by Nicholas a hundred years ago continues ...

Maud and Ernie became founders of the housing society in Townsville, because of the sub-standard accommodation provided for Aboriginal people. As they tell it, at that time:

'NO BLACK PEOPLE COULD RENT PRIVATE HOUSES. After World War II they put all murri people in Garbut — sort of floorboards, no walls, you could hear what next door said, big community bathroom and community toilet, no doors on the toilets. There were lots of meetings, but no actual progress, the government ignored us. But when Whitlam came to power in 1972, he gave us money to buy houses. He said, if we form our own committees, societies, cooperations, he'll fund them direct, bypass the State: direct for the housing, direct for the medical, legal. So, we did all that, there was ten of us. But there was a lot of opposition then, even from our own family.'

Maud painfully remembers: 'Uncle Harry was one of the first to order me out and told me that I was troublemaker. He fought against it. He reckoned we were troublemakers, he told me "What you are going to get, a witch doctor?".' Now Maud and Ernie want to write a book telling about these turbulent years.[22]

Harry, when I met him in 1996 seemed to be fully reconciled with his Aboriginality. His own children are actively involved in the Aboriginal movement: for instance, Alec Illin, whom I met as an organiser of a merry, crowded celebration of Aboriginal and Torres Strait Islander week in Townsville. He tells about his career: 'After school I spent five years in the Australian forces, fifteen months in Malaya, twelve months in South Vietnam. I was discharged in 1970. I got a job at the Aboriginal Legal Service for about eight years, ten years I worked for the city council, after that I got my present position as the regional manager for the office of Aboriginal and Torres Strait Islanders Affairs with the Department of Family, Youth and Community care.'[23] His sister Leanne worked in Melbourne in the Aboriginal Legal Service.

Indeed, now one can meet Leandro's grandchildren and great-grandchildren in Aboriginal organisations all over Australia. In Canberra I sometimes see Ernie's daughter Allison, an artist, who, with several little kids, often goes to protest by the Aboriginal Embassy near Old Parliament House. Her sister Hilary, working as a volunteer in the National Gallery in Canberra, helped to organise a unique Aboriginal exhibition about the Wagilag Sisters. My family was proud to receive her invitation for the opening of the exhibition. At the opposite end of Australia, on the Atherton Tablelands, Glenda Illin, Dick's daughter, works in Social Security helping local Aborigines; her sister Vera became a foster-mother for many Aboriginal kids from problem families.

Certainly, I would not like to give the impression that this is an ideal family without problems. As in any family there are difficulties, there is some tension between family members, they marry and divorce, and spouses bring their own traditions and their own problems. Still one story makes me optimistic. Leanne Illin, telling me about the unhappy life and the tragic death of her brother, said with deep love, without a word of reproach: 'we lost him'. She became mother to his young, orphaned son, Leandrew Illin. These simple words 'we lost him' made me realise what we, modern urbanised Europeans, are deprived of: the feeling of belonging to a family, whatever you are like and whatever may happen to you. And, because of this sense of belonging they have, the Illins will, I am sure, overcome all troubles.

... I turn the last page and file away the papers. But the past does not disappear and Leandro, the lonely rider, continues galloping further and further along the mountain roads, and from a split bag on the back of his horse little, dark, laughing heads look out — the future of Australia.

APPENDIX 1
LIST OF NAMES

~

This lists the names of members of the extended Ilin/Illin family, in Russia, Australia, Honduras and the United States of America, who are mentioned in this book. For further information on some individuals, see the family trees in Appendix 2.

Alec	Alec Illin (son of Henry, grandson of Leandro and Kitty)
Aleksei Silin	the hero of Nikolai Ilin's novel *In the New Land*, based on (or a double for) Nikolai Ilin himself
Alexandra	Alexandra Konstantinovna Ilina (née Karlova; Nikolai Ilin's second wife); called Sasha
Allison	Allison Hoolihan (daughter of Ernest, granddaughter of Flora and Richard Hoolihan)
Ara	*see* Ariadna
Ariadna	Ariadna Mackay (née Ilina, later Illin; Nikolai and Alexandra's daughter); also called Ara and, later, Mamara (*mama* Ara)
Derek	Derek Hoolihan (son of Ernest, grandson of Flora and Richard Hoolihan)
Dick Hoolihan	*see* Richard Hoolihan
Dick Illin	*see* Richard Illin
Dmitrii Ilin	Nikolai Ilin's father
Dmitrii Sergeevich Ilin	legendary ancestor of the Ilins, hero of Battle of Çesme
Dynzie Hoolihan	son of Ernest, grandson of Flora and Richard Hoolihan
Dynzie Smallwood	husband of Vera Araluen
Ellen	Ellen Dale Flores (née Dale; daughter of Ariadna and Henry Dale, granddaughter of Nicholas and Alexandra); also called Nellie
Emma	Emma Williamson (Kitty's daughter, by her first marriage)
Emma Johnston	(née Raymond), Ngadjon Aboriginal elder and relative of Kitty
Ernest	Ernest Hoolihan (son of Flora and Richard Hoolihan, grandson of Leandro and Kitty); also called Ernie

Ernie	*see* Ernest
Evgenia	Evgenia Ilina (née Potocka; Nikolai Ilin's mother)
Flora	Flora Hoolihan (née Illin; daughter of Leandro and Kitty, granddaughter of Nicholas and Alexandra)
Frank Gertz	Margaret's husband
Ginger	George Williamson (Kitty's son, by her first marriage)
Gladys	Gladys Smith (née Illin; daughter of Thomas, granddaughter of Leandro and Kitty)
Glenda	Glenda Illin (daughter of Richard Illin, granddaughter of Leandro and Kitty)
Harry	*see* Henry
Hazel	Hazel Illin (daughter of Thomas, granddaughter of Leandro and Kitty)
Hector	Hector Mackay (né Steinkamp; son of Ariadna and Wilhelm Steinkamp, later adopted by Jack Mackay; grandson of Nicholas and Alexandra)
Henry	Henry Illin (son of Leandro and Kitty, grandson of Nicholas and Alexandra); also called Harry
Ivan Gerasimovich Ivanov	Nikolai Ilin's illegitimate, first son
Jack Mackay	*see* John Alexander Mackay
Jenny	Jenny Brown (Emma Williamson's daughter, Kitty's granddaughter)
Jessie Calico	Ngadjon elder and relative of Kitty
John Alexander Mackay	husband of Ariadna; also called Jack
Karterii	Nikolai and Alexandra's son (who died early); also called Pusha
Kitty	Kitty Illin (née Clarke), Leandro's wife
Leandr	Leandr Ilin (Nikolai and Alexandra's son); or Leandro Illin (the form of his name later adopted); also called Lena or Lenka
Leandro	Leandro Illin (the form of name subsequently adopted by Leandr Ilin)
Leandro Illin Jnr	son of Romelio Illin (named after his uncle), grandson of Nicholas and Alexandra
Leanne	Leanne Illin (daughter of Henry, granddaughter of Leandro and Kitty)
Lullie	*see* Vera Araluen
Mania	*see* Maria
Margaret	Margaret Gertz (née Hoolihan; daughter of Flora and Richard Hoolihan, granddaughter of Leandro and Kitty)
Maria	Maria Pettersen (née Ilina; Nikolai and Alexandra's daughter); also called Mania
Maud	Maud Hoolihan, Ernest's wife
Mila	Ludmila Daniel, whom Leandro met on the voyage to Australia
Molly	Molly Williamson (Kitty's daughter, by her first marriage)
Nellie	*see* Ellen
Nicholas	Nicholas Illin (the form of name subsequently adopted by Nikolai Dmitrievich Ilin)

Nikolai	Nikolai Dmitrievich Ilin or Nicholas Illin (the form of his name later adopted); also called Kolia
Nola	Nola Smallwood (daughter of Vera Araluen, granddaughter of Leandro and Kitty)
Olga	Olga Mackay (daughter of Ariadna and Jack Mackay, granddaughter of Nicholas and Alexandra)
Pusha	*see* Karterii
René	René Mackay (son of Somerled Mackay Snr, grandson of Ariadna and Jack Mackay)
Richard Hoolihan	Flora's husband
Richard Illin	Richard Illin (eldest of Leandro and Kitty's children, grandson of Nicholas and Alexandra); also called Dick
Romelii	Romelii Ilin (Nikolai and Alexandra's son); or Romelio Illin (the form of his name later adopted); also called Roma
Romelio	Romelio Illin (the form of name subsequently adopted by Romelii Ilin)
Sam Mackay	*see* Somerled Mackay Jnr
Sergei	Sergei Ilin (Nikolai Ilin's son, by Vera Tomich); also called Serezha
Somerled Mackay Snr	son of Ariadna and Jack Mackay (grandson of Nicholas and Alexandra)
Somerled Mackay Jnr	son of Somerled Mackay Snr, grandson of Ariadna and Jack Mackay; also called Sam
Thomas	Thomas Illin (son of Leandro and Kitty, grandson of Nicholas and Alexandra); also called Tommy or Tom
Tommy	*see* Thomas
Tonia	Antonina Pettersen (daughter of Maria and Wilhelm Pettersen, granddaughter of Nicholas and Alexandra)
Valia	Valentina Pettersen (daughter of Maria and Wilhelm Pettersen, granddaughter of Nicholas and Alexandra)
Vera Araluen	Vera Araluen Smallwood (née Illin; youngest daughter of Leandro and Kitty, granddaughter of Nicholas and Alexandra); also called Lullie
Vera Ketchell	eldest daughter of Richard Illin, granddaughter of Leandro and Kitty
Vera Tomich	Nikolai Ilin's first wife; also called Verochka
Wilhelm Pettersen	husband of Maria

APPENDIX 2
ILIN/ILLIN FAMILY TREES

~

1. NIKOLAI ILLIN'S ANCESTORS

1   Rurik: acceded 862, *d.* 879
2   Igor: acceded 912, *d.* 945 = Olga: acceded 945, *d.* 969
3   Sviatoslav: acceded 964, *d.* 972 = Malusha
4   Vladimir (St): *b.* 960 acceded 980, *d.* 1015 = Rogneda von Polotzk
5   Yaroslav: *b.* 978, acceded 1019, *d.* 1054 = Ingigerd (Anna) Olafsdottir: *ca.* 1001–1050 (from Swedish royal dynasty)
6   Vsevolod: *b.* 1030, acceded 1076, *d.* 1093 = Irene of Byzantium (from Byzantine royal dynasty)
7   Vladimir Monomakh: *b.* 1053, acceded 1113, *d.* 1125
8   Yurii Dolgorukii: acceded 1155, *d.* 1157
9   Vsevolod Big Nest: *b.* 1154, acceded 1176, *d.* 1212 = Maria of Ossetia
10   Yaroslav: *b.* 1191, acceded 1238, *d.* 1246 = Feodosia Igorevna of Riazan: 1194–1244
11   Constantine: *b. ca.* 1225, acceded 1247, *d.* 1255
12   David: *d.* 1280
13   Fedor: *d.* 1335
14   Ivan
15   Dmitrii: acceded 1359, expelled to Novgorod 1362
16   Vasilii
17   Boris
18   Semen OSINA
19   Boris TRETIAK
20   Liapun OSININ
21   Ivan OSININ
22   Semen LIAPUNOV: moved to Riazan Principality, early 16th century
23   Ilia Junior: the founder of the ILIN dynasty
24   Semen ILIN: *b. ca.* 1560
25   Boris ILIN: *b. ca.* 1595, owned the village of Ilina, Riazan province
26   Vasilii ILIN, ensign: *b. ca.* 1660

27 Lev ILIN, lieutenant: *b. ca.* 1695, *d. ca.* 1743 = Avdotia, daughter of Stepan

28 Aleksei ILIN (served as a dragoon): *b. ca.* 1728

29 Sergei ILIN, second lieutenant: *b.* 1757, moved from Riazan/Tambov Province to Saratov Province = Tatiana SVISHCHOVA, daughter of second lieutenant Stepan, son of Semen SVISHCHOV

30 Nikolai ILIN, second lieutenant: *b.* 1781

31 Dmitrii ILIN, lieutenant-colonel: *b.* 6.01.1811, *d.* 19.12.1853[?] = Evgenia POTOCKA, Poland, daughter of Count Ian (Ivan) POTOCKY: *b. ca.* 1827

32 Nikolai ILIN: *b.* 27.11.1852 (1849?), Ilinka, Saratov Province, *d.* end of 1922, San Pedro Sula, Honduras [for his descendants, *see* family tree 2]

NOTES

1 House of Rurik (1–15)

  1–15 are princes of the Russian ruling House of Rurik. Accession dates are to the particular princedom —

  ▓ Grand Princes of Kiev (1–8)

  ▓ Princes of Vladimir (9–10)

  ▓ Princes of Galich (11–15).

2 After Dmitrii (15), the last Prince of Galich, was expelled to Novgorod, the next two generations retained the title of prince but had no principality. Thus, Vasilii (16) and Boris (17) were the last to have the title prince.

3 Semen ILIN (24)

  Semen ILIN and his son Boris recorded in genealogies of Rurikids are identified by me as being the same persons as Semen ILIN, the first documented ancestor of our Ilin branch, and his son Boris — on the grounds of their origin from the same area of Riazan at approximately the same period.

  At this level our Ilin branch and the ancestors of Dmitrii Ilin, the Çesme hero, could be related [tree of Dmitrii is as follows: Timofei, Denis, Vasilii, Sergei, Dmitrii (1738–1802)].

SOURCES: A.V. Ekzempliarskii, *Velikie i udel'nye kniaz'ia Severnoi Rusi v tatarskii period s 1238 po 1505 g.*, vol.2, St Petersburg, 1891, pp.200–19; M.T. Iablochkov, *Dvorianskoe soslovie Tul'skoi gubernii*, vol.7, Tula, 1904; Saratov State Archive, f. 19, op. 1, d. 84. I am grateful to V. Provodina, A. Massov, A. Valdine, and N. Iudenich for their assistance.

2. DESCENDANTS OF NIKOLAI ILIN (NICHOLAS ILLIN)

Nikolai ILIN (Nicholas ILLIN) [*see* family tree 1]
b. 27.11.1852 (1849?) Ilinka, Saratov province, Russia
d. end of 1922 San Pedro Sula, Honduras
m. (1) ?
   [a peasant from Turki, Saratov province]
   (separated)
m. (2) *ca.* 1874
   Vera TOMICH
   (later divorced)
m. (3) *ca.* 1877
   Alexandra KARLOVA
   (daughter of Konstantin Ivanovich Karlov
   and Natalia)
   b. ca. 1860 Irkutsk?, Russia
   d. December 1945 San Pedro Sula, Honduras

{1.1} Ivan Gerasimovich IVANOV
   b. 17.10.1873 Turki, Saratov Province, Russia
   d. ?

{2.1} Sergei ILIN
   b. ca. 1875 Russia
   d. ?

{3.1} Maria ILINA
   b. ca. 1879 Russia
   d. ca. 1914 Russia
   m. ca. 1897
   Wilhelm PETTERSEN

     [1} Valentina PETTERSEN
     [2} Antonina PETTERSEN

{3.2} Leandr ILIN (Leandro ILLIN)
   b. 21.07.1882 Tashkent, Russia
   d. 15.08.1946 Townsville, Qld
   m. 14.09.1915
   Kitty CLARKE
   [*see* family tree 3]
   b. ca. 1890 Russell River, Qld
   d. 18.05.1925 Christmas
   Creek, Qld

     {1} Richard ILLIN
       b. 4.07.1914 Boonjie, Qld
       d. 29.06.1987 Townsville, Qld
     {2} Flora ILLIN
       b. 15.10.1915 Russell River, Qld
     {3} Thomas Alexander Leonidas ILLIN
       b. 24.06.1917 Russell River, Qld
       d. 7.06.1976 Townsville, Qld
     {4} Henry Octavian ILLIN
       b. 24.04.1919 G.W. Swamp, Qld
       d. 10.08.1996 Townsville, Qld
     {5} Vera Araluen ILLIN
       b. 31.03.1922 Spring Gully, Qld
       d. 2.08.1987 Townsville, Qld

{3.3} Karterii ILIN
   b. ca. 1885 Russia
   d. before 1897 Russia

{3.4} Romelii ILIN (Romelio ILLIN)
   b. 22.07.1886 St Petersburg,
   Russia
   d. 16.11.1976 San Pedro Sula,
   Honduras
   m. 6.06.1929
   Cristina BANEGAS
   b. 21.11.1912 Trinidad de Santa
   Barbara, Honduras
   d. 16.10.1984

     {1} Demetrio Alejandro ILLIN
       b. 10.01.1931 San Pedro Sula,
       Honduras
       d. 23.06.1960

     {2} Leandro ILLIN
       b. 14.09.1932 San Pedro Sula,
       Honduras
     {3} Somerled ILLIN
       b. 31.01.1934 San Pedro Sula,
       Honduras
       d. 5.08.1982
     {4} Romelio ILLIN
       b. 7.07.1947 San Pedro Sula,
       Honduras

{3.5} Vera ILINA (died in infancy)
{3.6} Ariadna ILINA (ILLIN)
   b. 3.06.1890 St Petersburg, Russia
   d. 16.08.1971 San Pedro Sula, Honduras
   m. (1) *ca.* 1908 Argentina
   (separated)
   Wilhelm STEINKAMP
   (German)

     {1.1} Hector [STEINKAMP]
       MACKAY
       b. 6.09.1909 Las Pampas,
       Argentina
       d. 12.02.1997 San Pedro Sula,
       Honduras

   m. (2) 6.07.1912 Australia
   (separated) Henry DALE
   b. ca. 1891 Ballarat, Vic.
   d. approx. 1916

     {2.1} Ellen (Nellie) DALE
       b. 10.10.1913 Peeramon, Qld

   m. (3) 30.05.1917
   John Alexander MACKAY
   b. 4.05.1890 Qld
   d. 24.02.1984 San Pedro Sula,
   Honduras

     {3.1} Somerled MACKAY (twin)
       b. 15.02.1917 Butchers Creek, Qld
       d. 7.02.1993 San Pedro Sula,
       Honduras
     {3.2} Ariadna MACKAY (twin)
       b. 15.02.1917 Butchers Creek, Qld
       d. 15.02.1917 Butchers Creek, Qld
     {3.3} Olga MACKAY
       b. 12.05.1918 Gadgarra, Qld
       d. 31.03.1997 San Pedro Sula,
       Honduras

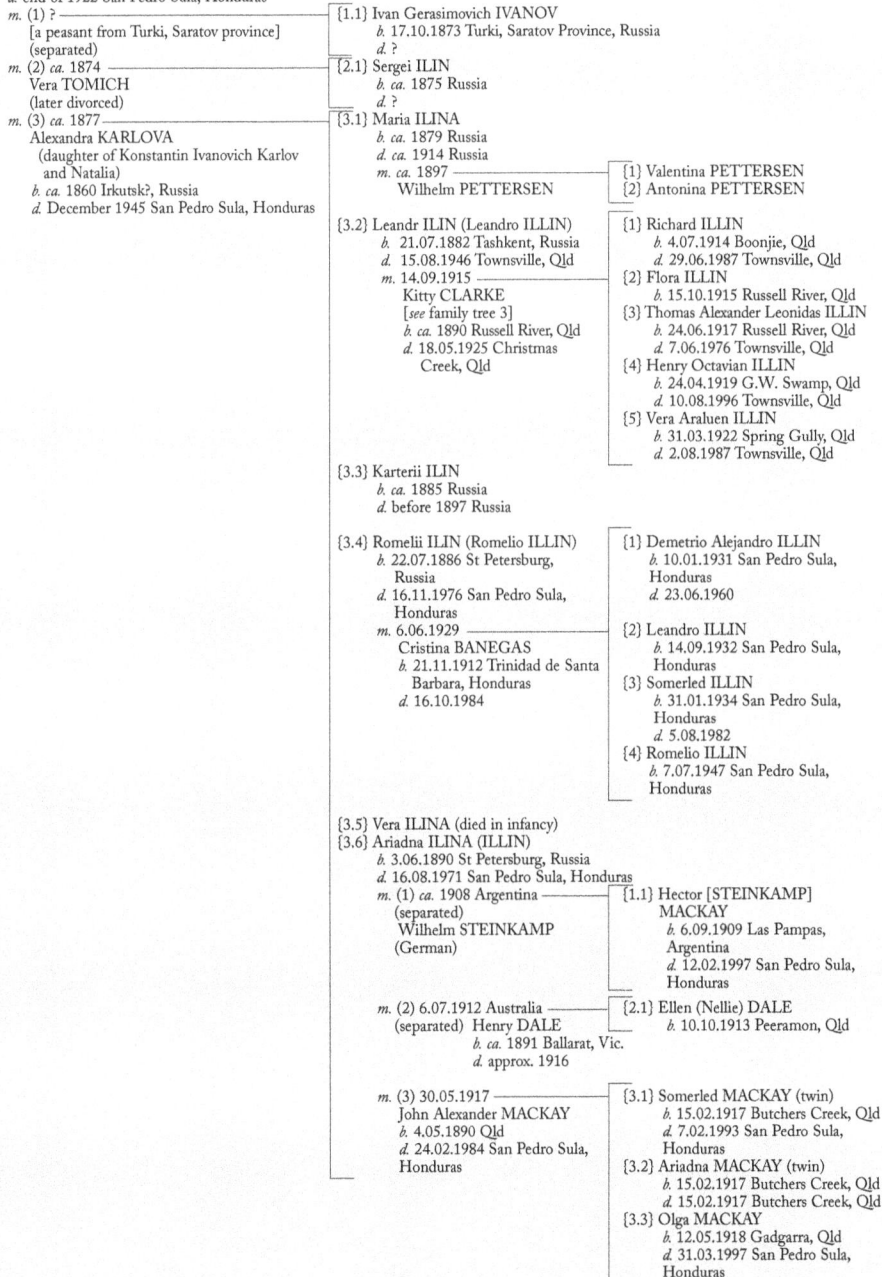

NOTES: *b.* born *ca.* circa *d.* died *m.* marriage or de facto relationship — different marriages are indicated by, for example: (1) = first marriage or relationship. Children of each relationship are differentiated by, for example: {1.1} = first child of first relationship; {2.1} = first child of second relationship, and so on.

3. KITTY CLARKE'S FAMILY

Barry CLARKE
Ngadjon
(Boonjie area)
had 5 wives
(the youngest,
Lucy)

{1} Willie CLARKE
    m. Emily RUSSELL

        Emily RUSSELL
        b. ca. 1870 Russell River
        d. 23.02.1955 Palm Island
        (Aboriginal name DARUGSO;
        father, Yariha; mother, Nellie Acoman)

        [Emily married three times:
        (2) *m.* 16.09.1916
        Thomas DENYER
        b. 1861 England
        d. 27.03.1920 Russell River
        (3) *m.* 1930s
        Paddy ROBINSON (Aboriginal)]

{2} Joe CLARKE
    b. ca. 1860
    m. Annie KANE

{3} Jack CLARKE
    m. Charlene

{4} Harry McGOWAN
{5} Polly CLARKE
    b. ca. 1880
    m. Billy CALICO
{6} Jenny
    m. Billy DENYER

NOTES
b. born *ca. circa d.* died *m.* marriage or de facto relationship. Different marriages are indicated by, for example: (1) = first marriage or relationship. Children of each relationship are differentiated by, for example: {1.1} = first child of first relationship; {2.1} = first child of second relationship, and so on. All places in Queensland, unless otherwise stated.

{1.1} Kitty CLARKE
    b. ca. 1890 Russell River
    d. 18.05.1925 Christmas Creek
    m. (1). ca. 1903 ——————————————— {1.1.1} Emma WILLIAMSON
        Jimmy WILLIAMSON   b. ca. 1905 Russell River
                                                  d. by the 1930s
                                                  m. Toby BROAD
                                                  (known as KANGAROO)
                                                  [their daughter:
                                                  Jenny BROAD
                                                  b. 7.08.1926, d. 22.10.1989]

                                          {1.1.2} Molly WILLIAMSON
                                                  b. 1910 Russell River
                                                  d. ca. 1920 Butchers Creek
                                          {1.1.3} George WILLIAMSON
                                                  b. 1.01.1911 Russell River
                                                  d. 1986 Ingham

    m. (2) 14.09.1915
        Leandro ILLIN (Russian)
        b. 21.07.1882 Tashkent, Russia
        d. 15.08.1946 Townsville
        [for details of their children, see family tree 2]

{1.2} Julia CLARKE
    d. 1922 Russell River
    m. Charles CIVRY (Frenchman)

{2.1} Jack PARKINSON

{3.1} Molly BEARD;   {3.1.1} Henry RAYMOND
        RAYMOND/RAYMONT   b. ca. 1916
    b. ca. 1890   {3.1.2} Emma [RAYMOND]
    d. 4.05.1992   SNIDER; JOHNSTON
    m. Jimmy BROWN ——————————————   b. 6.06.1918
{3.2} Polly

{5.1} Billy CALICO
    b. ca. 1905
    d. 1970
    m. Dinah LOGAN; ROSS ——————————— {5.1.1} Jessie CALICO
                                            b. 25.06.1932

NOTES

~

A NOTE ON SOURCES

To tell this story, material has been drawn from a wide range of different sources, primary and archival, published and private, from Russia, Australia, and elsewhere. In particular, this account has drawn on: the prose and poetry (translated from Russian) of Nikolai Ilin and Leandro Illin's writings in English; private and official letters and documents; material from contemporary newspapers and memoirs of contemporaries and some family members; the oral testimony of some of Nikolai and Leandro's descendants, collected by the author.

All historical and biographical reconstruction is firmly based on these sources and on the words of the two main figures themselves, Nikolai (Nicholas) and Leandro.

Edited transcripts of the oral testimony were subsequently verified by the informants themselves.

With such a variety of sources there is also a diversity of voices, many of whom may not speak or write standard English for reasons of education or dialect or non-English speaking background. Such voices include poorly educated local policemen (in official reports), the Aboriginal descendants of the Illins, Leandro himself (whose English, while good, was not always accurate in orthography or expression) and the Spanish-speaking descendants of the Illins.

For this reason, the authorial and editorial intention in this book has been to allow these voices to be heard on their own terms, in their own forms of expression. In source documents and oral testimony no attempt has been made to draw attention to linguistic or orthographic inconsistencies (for instance, by the use of *sic*) nor to tidy up or edit texts, except where clarity is in doubt. The sources have been carefully checked to ensure their authenticity.

All translations have been made by the author, unless otherwise stated.

For the transliteration of Russian names and words we have followed a modified form of the Library of Congress system of transliteration, ignoring certain more technical linguistic peculiarities (such as the use of the soft sign), as this is a book for the general reader. In the main text some names (such as Tolstoy or Kerensky) have been employed in the forms more familiar in English; other names, in the forms adopted by their owners (for instance, Illin or Gadaloff). Although this may mean some occasional inconsistencies, in the bibliography and end-notes Russian titles have been cited in full, properly transliterated for those who wish to locate them.

ABBREVIATIONS

The following abbreviations are used in the notes.

1 INSTITUTIONS/HOLDINGS/NEWSPAPERS

AIATSIS	Australian Institute of Aboriginal and Torres Strait Islander Studies
CEML	Centro de Estudios Migratorios Latinoamericanos, Buenos Aires, Argentina
EGA	Elena Govor's archives, Canberra
HRE	*Herbert River Express*, Ingham, Queensland
IRLI	Institute of Russian Literature of the Russian Academy of Sciences (Pushkin's House), St Petersburg, Russia
NAA	National Archives of Australia
NQR	*North Queensland Register*, Townsville, Queensland
QSA	Queensland State Archives
RGALI	Russian State Archive of Literature and Art, Moscow, Russia
RGA VMF	Russian State Naval Archive, St Petersburg, Russia
RGIA	Russian State Historical Archive, St Petersburg, Russia
RGVIA	Russian State Military-Historical Archive, Moscow, Russia
SSA	Saratov State Archive, Russia

2 PUBLICATIONS/WORKS BY NIKOLAI ILIN REFERRED TO

Dnevnik tolstovtsa	[*The Tolstoyan Diary*] *Dnevnik tolstovtsa*, by N.D. Ilin
Pesni zemli	[*Songs of the Earth*] *Pesni zemli*, by N. Ilin
Shest' mesiatsev	[*Six Months in the United States of North America*] *Shest' mesiatsev v Soedinennykh Shtatakh Severnoi Ameriki*, by N. Ilin
V novom kraiu	[*In the New Land. Novel-Chronicle. From the Times of Turkestan's Conquest*] *V novom kraiu. Roman-khronika. Iz vremen zavoevaniia Turkestanskogo kraia* by N. Ilin

INTRODUCTION

1 N.D. Ilin, *Dnevnik tolstovtsa* [*The Tolstoyan Diary*], St Petersburg, 1892, p.5; Ellen [Nellie] Dale Flores, 'Memoirs', 1996, EGA, p.8; Flora Hoolihan's letter to author 14.09.1995, EGA; interviews with Illin family, tape 1A499, EGA; Somerled Mackay Jnr, 'Genealogical Tree of the Illin Family', 1996, EGA, p.3.

2 I.E. Repin, *Dalekoe blizkoe* [*Far Close Past*], Moscow, Iskusstvo, 1964, p.320; I.E. Repin, *Pis'ma k pisateliam i literaturnym deiateliam* [*Letters to Writers and Literary Workers*], Moscow, Iskusstvo, 1950, p.89; *Severnyi vestnik*, no. 6, 1892, pp.75–79; V. Stasov, *Nikolai Nikolaevich Ge*, Moscow, 1904, p.346; L.N. Tolstoy, *Polnoe sobranie sochinenii* [*Complete Collection of Works*], vol.88, p.200.

3 Repin, *Dalekoe blizkoe*, p.480; V. Porudominskii, *Nikolai Ge*, Moscow, Iskusstvo, 1970, p.228.

IN SEARCH OF THE HERO

1 The facts for this chapter are based on diverse sources, particularly N.D. Ilin, 'Avtobiografiia' [Autobiography], IRLI, f. 377, no. 1347, folio 1; N.D. Ilin, *Dnevnik tolstovtsa* [*The Tolstoyan Diary*], St Petersburg, 1892, pp.256, 132; M.K. Sokolovskii, *Pamiatka 3-go gusarskogo Elisavetgradskogo ... polka*, St Petersburg, 1914, pp.29–30; Ellen [Nellie] Dale Flores, 'Memoirs', 1996, EGA, pp.2–3; Somerled Mackay Jnr, 'Genealogical Tree of the Illin Family', 1996, EGA, p.2; interview with Leandro Illin Jnr, EGA; letters of Valentina Provodina, the Director of Turki Museum, to author, 1996–98; memoirs of Ilinka's old-timers R. Fekliunin and Z.G. Sidorova, recorded by V. Provodina. Some military records concerning Dmitrii Ilin were kindly provided by RGVIA with the assistance of Anton Valdine, 'D.N. Ilin, the 6th', RGVIA, f. 395, op. 16, d. 492.

2 This date of birth seems the most reliable. It is based on Nicholas's statutory declaration for naturalisation in Australia and his official service records. He himself seemed to trick future historians, declaring both in his autobiography for the Russian biographical dictionary and in a book of poetry that he was born in 1849. Note that nineteenth century Russian documents used the Julian calendar, while in the West the Gregorian calendar is used (there being about twelve days' difference between the two). Where, as here, two dates are given, the first is the Russian, or Julian calendar date and the second date (in brackets) is the Western or Gregorian one.

3 SSA, f. 19, op. 1, d. 84 (I am grateful to the Archive and V. Provodina for giving me access to this file).

4 Flores, 'Memoirs', p.3; N. Ilin, *Pesni zemli* [*Songs of the Earth*], Paris, 1910, p.4; Ilin, 'Avtobiografiia', folio 1.

5 'Davydov, V.N.', in *Teatral'naia entsiklopediia*, vol.2, Moscow, 1963, columns 265–69; V.N. Davydov, *Rasskaz o proshlom*, Leningrad–Moscow, 1962, p.34.

6 Davydov, *Rasskaz o proshlom*, pp.35–36, 43; Ilin, 'Avtobiografiia', folios 1–1 reverse.

7 V.M. Lukin, 'Ilin, N.D.', in *Russkie pisateli. 1800–1917. Biograficheskii slovar'*, vol.2, Moscow, 1992, p.413.

8 Ilin, 'Avtobiografiia', folios 1 reverse – 2; N. Ilin, *V novom kraiu. Roman-khronika. Iz vremen zavoevaniia Turkestanskogo kraia* [*In the New Land. Novel-Chronicle. From the Times of Turkestan's Conquest*], Tashkent, 1913, vol.1, pp.295–96; tapes 3B186, 9A590, EGA.

9 N. Ilin, *Shest' mesiatsev v Soedinennykh Shtatakh Severnoi Ameriki* [*Six Months in the United States of North America*], St Petersburg, 1876.

10 *Sbornik statisticheskikh svedenii po Saratovskoi gubernii*, vol.XII, issue 1, Saratov, 1893, pp.126, 246, 507–08. Letters of Provodina to author: 17 January, 9 March, & 4 April 1997. I am grateful to Provodina and Massov for assistance with providing materials concerning history of Ilinka and its neighbourhood.

11 The Russian word *narod* signifies 'the people', that is, both peasants and proletariat, the great mass of common or ordinary people, seen as an indivisible entity and usually understood as an oppressed group. In nineteenth century Russia the word took on added significance from its use by the intelligentsia to refer to the people in this way — and retained this sense until well into the twentieth century — leading to an early form of socialism (narodism), which involved a conviction that land should be returned to the peasants. In the 1870s–80s, particularly, followers of this movement, known as *narodniks* because of their concerns about the status and condition of the people (*narod*), travelled into the country to live with, and educate the

people. Nikolai, in common with other Russians of his time and social inclinations, uses this term *narod* frequently in his writings.

12 Ilin, *V novom kraiu*, vol.1, p.296; Ilin, *Pesni zemli*, p.4. Kulak = rich peasant; probably Ilin branded with this new term all petty, unscrupulous landlords.

13 *Vedomost' spravok o sudimosti. Izdanie Ministerstva Iustitsii*, part 1, book 1, St Petersburg, 1887, p.218.

14 Ilin, *V novom kraiu*, vol.1, pp.296–300.

15 Flores, 'Memoirs', p.3. S. Mackay remembers a similar story: Somerled Mackay Jnr, 'Memoirs', 1997, EGA, p.1.

16 'N.D. Ilin. Posluzhnoi spisok [Service record]. 27.09.1882', RGVIA, f. 400, op. 9, d. 21078 (Information was kindly provided by the RGVIA, with the assistance of Stanislav Dumin); Ilin, 'Avtobiografiia', folios 2 – 2 reverse; Ilin, *Pesni zemli*, pp.22, 102.

17 Ilin, *V novom kraiu*, vol.1, pp.2–3, vol.2, p.155 and *passim*.

18 Ilin, 'Avtobiografiia', folio 3. The novel was originally published in monthly instalments in a magazine in St Petersburg.

19 Ilin, *V novom kraiu*, vol.1, pp.256, 300–04, 356–57, vol.2, pp.36, 74–75, 85–86.

20 Ilin, *Pesni zemli*, p.63.

21 Ilin, 'Avtobiografiia', folios 2 reverse – 3; Ilin, *V novom kraiu*, vol.2, pp.101, 129–35, 152–57.

22 Ilin, *V novom kraiu*, vol.2, pp.174, 194–97, 204; Mackay, 'Memoirs', p.1.

23 This, it seems, might mean any Asian nationality, particularly Buriat or Yakut, who lived around Irkutsk and members of whom the local Russians sometimes married.

24 Ilin, *V novom kraiu*, vol.1, pp.27–38, 46–55, 80–81, 128–36, 287–90, 295, 352–67, vol.2, pp.55–64.

25 Ilin, *V novom kraiu*, vol.2, pp.86–88, 187–88, 196–97, 203–06, 221–26.

26 Ilin, *V novom kraiu*, vol.2, pp.240–50.

27 Mackay, 'Genealogical Tree', pp.2–3; 'N. D. Ilin. Posluzhnoi spisok'; Ilin, *Pesni zemli*, pp.72–74.

28 A.K. Ilina to N.N. Ge, 16.11.1890, RGALI, f. 731, op. 1, d. 17; Flores, 'Memoirs', p.2.

WHAT IS TRUTH?

1 N.D. Ilin to the crew of the *Lieutenant Ilin* 22.05.1894, RGA VMF, f. 2, op. 1, d. 7, folio 73; Leanne Illin, [Family History], EGA.

2 N.D. Ilin, *Dnevnik tolstovtsa* [*The Tolstoyan Diary*], St Petersburg, 1892, pp.29–30; Ellen [Nellie] Dale Flores, 'Memoirs', 1996, EGA, pp.3–4.

3 Somerled Mackay Jnr, 'Genealogical Tree of the Illin Family', 1996, and my interviews with the Australian part of the family, all EGA.

4 N.D. Ilin, 'Avtobiografiia' [Autobiography], IRLI, f. 377, no. 1347, folio 3; Ilin to the crew of the *Lieutenant Ilin*.

5 Ilin, 'Avtobiografiia', folios 3 – 3 reverse; N. Ilin, 'V novom kraiu. Roman-khronika. Iz vremen zavoevaniia Turkestanskogo kraia' [In the New Land. Novel-Chronicle. From the Times of Turkestan's Conquest], *Knizhki 'Nedeli'*, nos 1–11, 1886; N. Ilin, 'Begletsy. Roman iz zhizni na dalekom Vostoke' [The Fugitives. A Novel from Life in the Far East], *Zhivopisnoe obozrenie*, supplement, no. 10, 1888; N. Ilin, 'Nezhdanno-negadanno' [Against All Expectations], *Zhivopisnoe obozrenie*, nos 25–27, 1889.

6 N. Ilin, 'Iuridicheskie zametki' [Judicial notes], *Sudebnaia gazeta*, 12 January 1886; V.M. Lukin, 'Ilin, N.D.', in *Russkie pisateli. 1800–1917. Biograficheskii slovar'*, vol.2,

Moscow, 1992, p.413; N. Ilin, *Pesni zemli* [*Songs of the Earth*], edited and introduced by Stepan Golub, Paris, 1910, p.4.

7   Ilin to the crew of the *Lieutenant Ilin*; interview with Ernest and Maud Hoolihan, 29.09.1996, EGA; '[Ivan Gerasimov Ivanov]', RGIA, f. 1405, op. 91, d. 3531 (I am grateful to Aleksandr Massov for discovering and copying this file). N.D. Ilin to N.N. Ge, 28.06, 7.07.1890, RGALI, f. 731, op. 1, d. 16.

8   L. Illin, 'Report of the Northern Territory' [1912], NAA (ACT): A3/1, NT1913/1156, part 3, pp.55–56.

9   Ilin, *Dnevnik tolstovtsa*, pp.8–10.

10 Ilin to Ge, 26.02, 20.04.1890, RGALI, f. 731, op. 1, d. 16; Ilin, *Dnevnik tolstovtsa*, pp.16–18.

11 Ilin, *Dnevnik tolstovtsa*, pp.25, 42.

12 Ilin, *Dnevnik tolstovtsa*, pp.5–7, 37–38.

13 Interview with Derek and Dynzie Hoolihan, June 1995; Flora Hoolihan's letters to author, 16.08 and 14.09.1995; tape 3A369 — all in EGA.

14 Flores, 'Memoirs', p.4.

15 R. Illin, 'En la Frontera (En Guarda Raya) (Hecho por el relate de mi padre, sucedido en les años de la década de 1890)', EGA, p.1; Eduardo Villanueva, 'Un poeta ruso, ignorado, descansa para siempre en San Pedro Sula', *Tiempo—El diario de Honduras*, 13 October 1971.

16 Ilin to Ge, 18.08.1890, October 1890; L.N. Tolstoy to A.M. Kalmykova, 23 or 24.09.1890, in Tolstoy, *Polnoe sobranie sochinenii* [*Complete Collection of Works*], vol.65, pp.168–69.

17 For Tolstoy's remarks about the Ilins, see: Tolstoy, *Polnoe sobranie sochinenii*, vol.65, pp.168–69, 178, 183, 210; vol.51, pp.96, 98, 223.

18 Ilin, *Dnevnik tolstovtsa*, pp.14–15.

19 Ilin to Ge, 9.07.1890.

20 Ilin, *Dnevnik tolstovtsa*, pp.60–61.

21 Ilin, *Dnevnik tolstovtsa*, pp.35, 41, 60.

22 Somerled Mackay Jnr, 'Memoirs', 1997, EGA, p.1.

23 A.K. Ilina to N.N. Ge, 13.01, 22.01.91, RGALI, f. 731, op. 1, d. 17; N. D. Ilin to A. K. Ilina, October 1890, 21.11.1890, 23.01.1891, RGALI, f. 731, op. 1, d. 62. I am grateful to Zaiara Veselaia for hand-copying the Illins' correspondence in RGALI and to the archive for providing access to these microfilms.

24 Ilin, *V novom kraiu*, separate edition: Tashkent, 1913, 2 vols, vol.2, pp.223–26; Ilin, *Dnevnik tolstovtsa*, pp.7, 41, 42, 75; Ilina to Ge, 16.11.1890; V. Stasov, *Nikolai Nikolaevich Ge, ego zhizn', proizvedeniia, perepiska* [*Nikolai Nikolaevich Ge, his Life, Works, Correspondence*], Moscow, 1904, p.333.

25 Ilin, *Dnevnik tolstovtsa*, pp.5, 11, 14, 130.

26 Ilin, *Dnevnik tolstovtsa*, p.280.

27 Ilin, *Dnevnik tolstovtsa*, pp.51–52, 194–203, 253–59.

28 Ilin, *Dnevnik tolstovtsa*, p.223.

29 Ilin, *Dnevnik tolstovtsa*, pp.131–34.

30 Ilin, *Dnevnik tolstovtsa*, pp.40, 42–43.

31 Ilin, *Dnevnik tolstovtsa*, p.48.

32 Ilin to Ilina, October 1890; Stasov, *Ge*, p.333.

33 Ilin, *Dnevnik tolstovtsa*, pp.102, 106.

34 Ilin, *Dnevnik tolstovtsa*, pp.117–20.

35 Ilin, *Dnevnik tolstovtsa*, pp.128–29, 134–35.

36 Ilin, *Dnevnik tolstovtsa*, pp.140, 147, 182–83, 226; Ilin to Ilina, 21.11.1890; Stasov, *Ge*, p.344.
37 Ilin, *Dnevnik tolstovtsa*, pp.192, 221–23, 232.
38 Ilin, *Dnevnik tolstovtsa*, pp.271–72.
39 Ilin, *Dnevnik tolstovtsa*, p.274.
40 Ilin, *Dnevnik tolstovtsa*, p.280.
41 Ilina to Ge, 1.02.1891; Ilin, *Dnevnik tolstovtsa*, pp.22, 33, 36–39.
42 Ilin to Ge, April–May 1891; Ilina to Ge, 14.05.1891; Ilin, *Dnevnik tolstovtsa*, pp.281–87.
43 Meshcherskii, *Grazhdanin*, 11 February 1892; *Russkaia mysl'*, no. 4, 1892, pp.155–56; *Severnyi vestnik*, no. 6, 1892, pp.75–79; I.E. Repin, *Pis'ma k pisateliam i literaturnym deiateliam* [*Letters to Writers and Literary Workers*], Moscow, Iskusstvo, 1950, p.89.
44 Stasov, *Ge*, pp.345–46.
45 Stasov, *Ge*, pp.365–66, 346.
46 Tolstoy, *Polnoe sobranie sochinenii*, vol.88, p.200.
47 Lukin, 'Ilin, N.D.'; V. Porudominskii, *Nikolai Ge*, Moscow, Iskusstvo, 1970, pp.228–29; E.N. Arbitman, *Zhizn' i tvorchestvo N.N. Ge* [*Ge's Life and Works*], Saratov, 1972, p.246.
48 Ilin to Ge, 28.01.1891, RGALI, f. 731, op. 1, d. 14.
49 Ilin, 'Avtobiografiia', folio 3 reverse; N.D. Ilin to S.A. Vengerov, [April] 1892, IRLI, f. 377, no. 1347, folios 6–7.
50 Flora Hoolihan, letters to author, August 1995, 14.09.1995; tapes 17A274, 1A443, 6B021, 3A369 — all EGA.
51 Flores, 'Memoirs', p.4.
52 R. Illin, 'En la Frontera'.
53 Ilin, *Pesni zemli*, pp.27–34, 102.
54 Ilin, *Pesni zemli*, p.5.
55 Stasov, *Ge*, p.365.
56 Stasov, *Ge*, p.346.
57 Flora Hoolihan to author, 16.08.1995; Mackay, 'Genealogical Tree', pp.3–4; Listado parcial de immigrantes [List of immigrants arrived on the *Mendoza* on 29 June 1897], Centro de Estudios Migratorios Latinoamericanos, Argentina. Leandro himself wrote that he left Russia for Argentina in 1893: L. Illin, 'Correspondence', *Herbert River Express*, 23 November 1940, p.6.
58 Mackay, 'Memoirs', pp.1–2.
59 P.A. Koshel, *Istoriia syska v Rossii* [*History of Criminal Investigation in Russia*], Minsk, 1996, vol.1, pp.447–52.
60 Flores, 'Memoirs', p.4.
61 Flores, 'Memoirs', p.4; Stasov, *Ge*, p.331; Tolstoy, *Polnoe sobranie sochinenii*, vol.65, p.142, vol.51, p.225 (commentaries).
62 I am grateful to A. Valdine for thorough research in Moscow archives and libraries; to N. Ryzhak (Russian State Library, Moscow); and to S. Chernov, B. Starkov, and A. Massov for their research in St Petersburg archives.

INTERMEZZO: THE CZARINA'S GOBLET

1 Ellen [Nellie] Dale Flores, 'Memoirs', 1996, p.1–2; Somerled Mackay Jnr, 'Genealogical Tree of the Illin Family', 1996, pp.1–2 — both EGA.

2 Tape 17A439, EGA.
3 General I.A. Gannibal was a son of the famous negro, A.P. Gannibal, who was brought to Russia by Peter the Great and was to become the maternal great-grandfather of the famous Russian poet, Alexander Pushkin.
4 'Ilin D.S.', in *Russkii biograficheskii slovar'*, reprint, New York, 1962, vol.8, pp.97–98; 'Ilin D.S.', in *Bol'shaia sovetskaia entsiklopediia*, 3rd edn, vol.10, Moscow, 1972, p.135; G. Gerakov, *Tverdost' dukha russkikh* [*Russians' Strength of Mind*], Petrograd, 1813, pp.50, 57–68.
5 Without going too deeply into this issue, I might note the diverse symbolism connected with goblets or cups relevant to this story — for instance, the magic golden goblet that Helios gave Hercules for his boldness (the tenth labour), or the Holy Grail with the wine used by Christ at his Last Supper, which he identified with his blood and which is treated as symbol for the remission of sins and reconciliation.
6 I am grateful to Valentina Provodina, Aleksandr Massov, Anton Valdine, and Natalia Iudenich for their thorough research (see family tree 1, Appendix 2).
7 A. Krotkov, 'O netochnostiakh publikuemykh sochinenii', RGA VMF, f. 417, op. 6, d. 83, folio 170 reverse.
8 N.D. Ilin to the crew of the *Lieutenant Ilin* 22.05.1894, RGA VMF, f. 2, op. 1, d. 7, folios 73–74.
9 Ilin, *Pesni zemli*, p.102.

FROM FARM TO COLONY

1 Somerled Mackay Jnr, 'Memoirs', 1997, EGA, p.2.
2 N. Ilin, *Pesni zemli* [*Songs of the Earth*], edited and introduced by Stepan Golub, Paris, 1910, p.45.
3 Ilin, *Pesni zemli*, pp.94–95 (poems 'To the stream' and 'Stream').
4 Ilin, *Pesni zemli*, pp.26, 38.
5 Ilin, *Pesni zemli*, pp.63, 101–102, 33–34, 62.
6 Ilin, *Pesni zemli*, p.5
7 Inscription on the photograph, Flora Hoolihan archives.
8 Ilin, *Pesni zemli*, p.33.
9 N.D. Ilin to the crew of the *Lieutenant Ilin* 22.05.1894, RGA VMF, f. 2, op. 1, d. 7, folio 74.
10 V.M. Lukin, 'Ilin, N.D.', in *Russkie pisateli. 1800–1917. Biograficheskii slovar'*, vol.2, Moscow, 1992, p.413; Ilin, *Pesni zemli*, p.5; Listado parcial de immigrantes [List of immigrants arrived on the *Mendoza* on 29 June 1897], Centro de Estudios Migratorios Latinoamericanos, Argentina; Flores, Ellen [Nellie] Dale, 'Memoirs', 1996, EGA, p.4.
11 N. Ilin, 'Pis'ma iz Avstralii' ['Letters from Australia'], *Novoe vremia*, 14 August 1913.
12 Ilin, *Pesni zemli*, p.5.
13 Mackay, 'Memoirs', p.2; Flores, 'Memoirs', p.5.
14 L. Illin, 'Report of the Northern Territory' [1912], NAA (ACT): A3/1, NT1913/1156, part 3, p.56a; L. Illin, 'Correspondence', *Herbert River Express (HRE)* — 3 March 1942, 26 November 1936, 23 November 1940.
15 L. Illin, 'Correspondence', *HRE* — 17 February 1942, 15 September 1938.
16 L. Illin, 'Correspondence. A Russian on Bolshevism', *Cairns Post*, 3 March 1919.
17 Ilin, 'Pis'ma iz Avstralii'.

18 Ilin, *Pesni zemli*, pp.1, 42, 62, 68, 75–78.
19 Ilin, *Pesni zemli*, pp.29–31, 43–45, 46–62, 84, 101.
20 Ilin, *Pesni zemli*, pp.40, 43–45, 54, 64–65, 70–71, 78, 79–81, 82–89.
21 Ilin, *Pesni zemli*, pp.17, 19, 35, 36, 60, 65, 78, 92–93.
22 Somerled Mackay Jnr, 'Genealogical Tree of the Illin Family', 1996, EGA, p.4.
23 Ilin, 'Pis'ma iz Avstralii'; 'New settlers for Queensland. Patagonian Welshmen', *Cairns Post*, 23 March 1911; Flores, 'Memoirs', p.6.
24 Ilin, 'Pis'ma iz Avstralii'.
25 Flores, 'Memoirs', p.6.
26 Ilin, *Pesni zemli*, p.35.
27 Ilin, *Pesni zemli*, p.15.
28 Register of Immigrants, IMM/132, QSA, p.115.
29 Illin, 'Report of the Northern Territory', p.71; L. Illin, 'Land for Soldiers', *Cairns Post*, 15 October 1918, p.3.
30 N.A. Kriukov, *Avstraliia: Sel'skoe khoziaistvo Avstralii v sviazi s obshchim pazvitiem strany* [*Australia: Australian Agriculture in Connection with the General Development of the Country*], Moscow, 1906, p.20.
31 Ilin, 'Pis'ma iz Avstralii'.
32 Ilin, 'Pis'ma iz Avstralii'.
33 L.E. Mellish was the Secretary of the office of the Commissioner of Public Health, while W.G. Graham was officer-in-charge of the Land Settlement Inquiry Office in the Department of Public Lands. *Blue Book*, Queensland Government, 1910.
34 Ilin, 'Pis'ma iz Avstralii'.
35 Here and below, in this section, Nicholas's quotations are from Ilin, 'Pis'ma iz Avstralii'.
36 L. Illin, 'Correspondence', *HRE*, 7 February 1942.
37 E.H. Short, *The Nation Builders*, Dimbulah, 1988, pp.42–43.
38 L. Illin, 'Correspondence', *HRE*, 17 February 1942.
39 M. Gadalov [Gadaloff], 'Russkie emigranty v Avstralii' ['Russian emigrants in Australia'], *Dalekaia okraina*, 21 August 1911, p.2.
40 QSA: LANP69A, 1545, 1546, 1547.
41 QSA: LAN/DF, 89, Atherton 1545.
42 Short, *The Nation Builders*, p.69.
43 Tape 5B401, EGA.
44 Short, *The Nation Builders*, p.30.
45 Anton Chekhov, *Five Plays*, translated by R. Hingley, Oxford, Oxford University Press, 1980, pp.269, 283.
46 N. Il[in], 'Russkie v Avstralii' ['Russians in Australia'], *Novoe vremia*, 30 July 1912; Ilin, 'Pis'ma iz Avstralii'; N.D. Ilin, 'Pis'mo iz Avstralii' ['A letter from Australia'], RGALI, f. 1666, op. 1, d. 1466. V. Korolenko to N. Ilin, 29 August 1913; N. Ilin to Korolenko, *ca* October 1913; N. Ilin to *Discourse*, 1 November 1913 — all RGALI, f. 1666, op. 1, d. 384. I am grateful to Olga Artemova for copying the materials from the RGALI for me.
47 E. Govor, *Australia in the Russian Mirror, Changing Perceptions 1770–1919*, Melbourne, Melbourne University Press, 1997, pp.166–87.
48 Illin, 'Report of the Northern Territory', p.24; 'Return of the Russian Delegates. An interesting interview', *Cairns Post*, 14 May 1912, p.8; Ilin, 'Pis'mo iz Avstralii'; Il[in], 'Russkie v Avstralii'.
49 Ilin, 'Pis'ma iz Avstralii'; Il[in], 'Russkie v Avstralii'.

50 L. Illin, 'Correspondence', *HRE*, 13 February 1937, p.4; Illin, 'Report of the Northern Territory', pp.56, 60.

51 Ilin, 'Pis'mo iz Avstralii'.

52 Ilin, 'Pis'ma iz Avstralii'.

53 QSA: LAN/DF 89, Atherton 1545.

54 NAA (ACT) — Nicholas Illin – Naturalisation certificate A1, 1913/2427; Illin, Romelio – Naturalisation file A435, A46/4/592; Leandro Illin – Naturalisation A1, 1913/17541. L. Illin, 'Correspondence', *HRE*, 17 August 1940, 23 November 1940; 'Iliny Leandr i Romelii... o razreshenii priniat' inostrannoe poddanstvo [Ilins Leandr and Romelii ... about permission to take foreign citizenship]', RGIA, f. 1412, op. 9, folios 1–2.

55 NAA (ACT) — Homenko, N.P. – Naturalisation A659/1, 1940/1/7443; Summary of Communism, vol.1, A6122/40, 111, pp.133, 138. Tape 5B220, EGA.

56 Flores, 'Memoirs', p.6; QSA: LAN/DF 89, Atherton 1545; Gadalov, 'Russkie emigranty v Avstralii'.

57 Gadalov, 'Russkie emigranty v Avstralii'; [M. Gadalov], 'We do not repent having left our native land', in: *Terse Information about Queensland. Queries and Replies*, Brisbane, 1915, pp.54–55; Gadaloff, M. – Naturalisation certificate NAA (ACT): A1, 1926/11686; QSA: LAN/DF 100, Atherton 1669; M. Gadaloff, Memoirs, 1971 (in possession of Peter Gadaloff, Southport, Queensland); M. Gadaloff, personal archives (in possession of Kathleen Gadaloff, Brisbane); interviews with Peter and Igor Gadaloff 1 and 2 May 1997.

58 Tapes 5B037–5B281, EGA; Homenko, N.P. – Naturalisation, NAA (ACT); QSA: LAN/DF 151, Atherton 2615; Sheila Gadaloff's letter to author, August 1997.

59 Michael Prochoroff – Naturalisation NAA (ACT): A1, 1915/6639; QSA: B/561–B/563; *Politicheskaia katorga i ssylka, Biograficheskii spravochnik* [*Political penal servitude and exile. Biographical reference book*], Moscow, 1934, p.520; J. Schultz, 'From Queensland with distinction', *Courier-Mail*, 12 April 1997.

60 Gabriel Mironovich Ivanoff – Naturalisation NAA (ACT): A1, 1921/18516. QSA: LAN/DF 132, Atherton 2090A.

61 Strelnikoff, Vasil – Naturalisation NAA (ACT): A1/1, 1923/27605; QSA: LAN/DF 132, Atherton 2090A; V. Strelnikoff, Memoirs, pp.77–81, in Basil Strelnikoff's archives, Mareeba; interview with Basil Strelnikoff 1.07.1997; Basil Strelnikoff's letter to author 16.12.1997; Gadaloff, personal archives.

62 Vlademir Balias – Naturalisation NAA (ACT): A1; 1914/21026; QSA: LAN/DF 85 Atherton 1508; Russians 1911–1915, QSA: file A/45328; *Atherton News and Barron Valley Advocate*, 19 June & 14 July 1915; interviews with George Balias 7.06.1997, 20.07.1997; information from Roy Phelps, Atherton.

63 John Nikonets – Naturalisation NAA (ACT): A1, 1914/3357; QSA: LAN/DF 100, Atherton 1667; interview with Peter Gadaloff 1.05.1997.

64 Lamin, V.N., NAA (ACT): A441/1, 1951/13/8524; QSA: LAN/DF 118, Atherton 1937.

65 Felemon Alexeivch Fadchuck – Naturalisation NAA (ACT): A1, 1914/11108; Short, *The Nation Builders*, pp.24–26, 32, 39, 85, 87, 109, 110, 145.

66 Illin, 'Report of the Northern Territory', pp.11, 68, 80.

67 Govor, *Australia in the Russian Mirror*, pp.213–14.

68 'Russians in Queensland', *Brisbane Courier*, 28 December 1911, p.5; Govor, *Australia in the Russian Mirror*, pp.219–20; Illin, 'Report of the Northern Territory', p.51.

69 Russians 1911–1915, QSA. Rozaliev N.P., in: *Politicheskaia katorga i ssylka*, p.815; Papers relating to miscellaneous events involving use of a red flag, NAA (Qld): BP4/1, 66/4/2165, p.360.
70 G. Barber to J. Thomas, February 1912, NAA (ACT): A3/1, NT1913/1156, part 2; Illin, 'Report of the Northern Territory', pp.6, 10, 14, 23, 43.
71 Illin, 'Report of the Northern Territory'; K.N. Vladimirov, 'Report on the Northern Territory of Australia', NAA (ACT): A3/1, NT1913/1156, part 3.
72 Illin, 'Report of the Northern Territory', pp.36, 45, 47, 50, 78, 79.
73 Illin, 'Report of the Northern Territory', pp.22, 40, 84.
74 Illin, 'Report of the Northern Territory', pp.5, 34, 63–64, 68, 73, 75–78, 81–83.
75 Illin, 'Report of the Northern Territory', pp.24–27.
76 Illin, 'Correspondence. North Australia', *HRE*, 22 December 1936; Illin, 'Correspondence', *HRE*, 13 August 1938; Illin, 'Report of the Northern Territory', pp.10, 16–17, 61–62, 87–89.
77 Illin, 'Correspondence. North Australia', p.4; Illin, 'Report of the Northern Territory', pp.22, 51, 70–72, 80, 91–92; Vladimirov, 'Report on the Northern Territory of Australia', pp.55, 59–62.
78 Illin, 'Report of the Northern Territory', pp.90–91; Illin, 'Correspondence', *HRE*, 13 August 1938; Ilin, 'Pis'ma iz Avstralii'; NAA (ACT): A3/1, NT1913/1156, parts 1–2. 'Return of the Russian Delegates', *Cairns Post*, p.8.
79 Illin, 'Report of the Northern Territory', p.9.

PRELUDE: UNTOLD LOVE STORY

1 M.'s letter in Russian, in Vera Ketchell's archives; A. Gzel, 'Pamiati Evgeniia Vasil'evicha Daniel' ['To the memory of Evgenii Vasil'evich Daniel'], *Chuzhbina*, Brisbane, 1930, no. 5, pp.18–19; Register of Immigrants, QSA: IMM/132, p.115.
2 Tape 9A487, EGA.
3 Illin, 'Report of the Northern Territory', pp.26–27.

KITTY'S WORLD

1 Tapes 4B115, 3B129 — EGA.
2 Tape 4B244, EGA. Professor Bob Dixon, who studied for many years the languages and culture of the Aborigines of this area, recorded two myths about the origin of fire by Mamu and Jirrbal, Ngadjon neighbours. They are similar to the first part of the Ngadjon myth told by Jessie, but they do not specify the particular place where Rainbow Serpent lived and they lack the subsequent story about the serpent's travel and the creation of Lake Barrine. B. Dixon, *Searching for Aboriginal Languages. Memoirs of a Field Worker*, St Lucia, University of Queensland Press, 1983, pp.187–89.
3 *Tjutjapa* was associated with the time of the totems, the time when their interrelations were established; *ngaki* was associated with the particular group of totems, those of mother's father, thus enriching the patrilineal totemic system with the female dimension. R.L. Sharp, 'Tribes and totemism in north-east Australia', *Oceania*, vol.9, no. 4, 1939, p.446.
4 Tape 4B342, EGA.
5 E. Mjöberg, *Amongst Stone Age People in the Queensland Wilderness* [original: *Bland stenaldersmanniskor i Queenslands vildmaker*, Stockholm, Albert Bonniers Forlag, 1918], translated from Swedish by S.M. Fryer (manuscript held by AIATSIS), p.73; tape 5A017, EGA.

6   Tape 5A028, EGA. I am grateful to Jessie Calico and Vera Ketchell, who further edited my tape-recorded text.
7   Tapes 1B631, 2A000, 4B411, 5A000 — all EGA. A similar myth about three volcanic lakes — Eacham, Barrine and Euramo — was recorded from George Watson and published by Dixon in *Searching for Aboriginal Languages*, pp.153–54.
8   Dixon, *Searching for Aboriginal Languages*, pp.154–55; R.M.W. Dixon, *The Dyirbal Language of North Queensland*, Cambridge University Press, 1972, p.29.
9   Dixon, *Searching for Aboriginal Languages*, p.154.
10 Tape 5A219, EGA.
11 V.R. Kabo, *Proiskhozhdenie i ranniaia istoriia aborigenov Avstralii* [*The Origin and Early History of the Australian Aborigines*], Moscow, Nauka, 1969; V. Kabo, *The Road to Australia*, Canberra, Aboriginal Studies Press, 1998.
12 Tape 2B436, EGA.
13 N.B. Tindale & J.B. Birdsell, 'Tasmanoid tribes in Northern Queensland', *Records of the South Australian Museum*, vol.7, 1941, pp.1–9.
14 Tindale & Birdsell, 'Tasmanoid tribes', p.7.
15 R.M.W. Dixon, 'Tribes, languages and other boundaries in northeast Queensland', in N. Peterson (ed.), *Tribes and Boundaries in Australia*, Canberra, Institute of Aboriginal Studies, 1976, pp.220–21.
16 G. Singh, A.P. Kershaw, R. Clark, 'Quaternary vegetation and fire history in Australia', in A.M.G. Gill, R.H. Groves, I.R. Noble (eds), *Fire and the Australian Biota*, Canberra, Australian Academy of Science, 1981, pp.23–54; P. Hiscock, A.P. Kershaw, 'Palaeoenvironments and prehistory of Australia's tropical Top End', in J. Dodson (ed.), *The Naive Lands: prehistory and environmental change in Australia and the south-west Pacific*, Melbourne, Longman Cheshire, 1992, pp.43–72.
17 Dixon, *The Dyirbal Language*, pp.24, 341, 342, 350–51.
18 Tape 5B302, EGA.
19 E.H. Short, *The Nation Builders*, Dimbulah, 1988, pp.55–60.
20 D.R. Harris, 'Adaptation to a tropical rain-forest environment: Aboriginal subsistence in Northeastern Queensland', in N.G. Blurton-Jones & V. Reynolds (eds), *Human Behaviour and Adaptation*, London, Taylor & Francis, 1978, pp.123–24.
21 Sharp, 'Tribes and totemism in north-east Australia', pp.439, 442–47.
22 Tapes 3B109, 4B115, 4B183, 2A098 — all EGA.
23 Tapes 5A100, 5A120 — EGA.
24 'George Hodges has seen at an auction sale at Yungaburra in early days a brass plate belonging to Willie Clarke. It was sold. A bloke paid quite a bit of money for it.' (tape 2A068, EGA).
25 E. Mjöberg, 'Contribution to the knowledge of the natives of North Queensland' [original: 'Beitrage zur Kenntnis Eingeborenen von Nord-Queensland', *Archiv für Anthropologie*, B. 20, 1925] (English manuscript translation held by AIATSIS), p.2.
26 Tape 3A011, EGA; H. Klaatsch, 'Mumie aus Australien und Reisebericht des Hrn. Klaatsch aus Sydney', *Zeitschrift für Ethnologie*, B. 37, 1905, pp.772–81; H. Klaatsch, 'Some notes on scientific travel amongst the black population of tropical Australia in 1904, 1905, 1906', *Report of the Eleventh Meeting of the Australasian Association for the Advancement of Science, held at Adelaide*, 1907, pp.577–92; Mjöberg, 'Contribution to the knowledge of the natives of North Queensland', p.7.
27 Short, *The Nation Builders*, pp.63–65.
28 Tapes 1A295, 7A233 — EGA; 'Death at 98', undated clipping, presumably *Townsville Bulletin*, February–March 1955 (Flora Hoolihan archives).

29 According to the obituary she was born in 1857, according to her marriage certificate she was born in 1870, according to a police report and identity card she was born in 1880. But, keeping in mind that Emily was a young girl at the time when the Europeans entered the Lake Eacham area in the early 1880s and that her daughter Kitty was born around 1890, the date 1870 seems the most reasonable.

30 Short, *The Nation Builders*, pp.7–8, 37, 43, 89, 110.

31 Tapes 2A036, 5B319, 7A334 — all EGA.

32 Tape 6A247, EGA; Flora's letter to author 18.02.1997, EGA.

33 L. Illin, 'Report of the Northern Territory' [1912], NAA (ACT): A3/1, NT1913/1156, part 3, p.19a.

34 N.D. Ilin, *Dnevnik tolstovtsa* [*The Tolstoyan Diary*], St Petersburg, 1892, p.15.

35 Dixon, *The Dyirbal Language*, p.35.

36 Cecil Mann quoted in Ric Throssell, *Wild Weeds and Wind Flowers. The Life and Letters of Katharine Susannah Prichard*, Sydney, Angus and Robertson, 1975, p.54; Flora's letter to author 18.02.1997, EGA; interview with Ric Throssell 17.09.1997, EGA; L. Illin to A.W. Fadden, 8.08.1933 — QSA: CPA, Bundle A/58692, Complaints 1933, 33/3789. Later, Flora remembered that 'Father wanted K. S. Prichard to write a book about another dark woman Nora Pope'. She was married to a European and lived in Gunnawarra area. Flora's letter to author 29.09.1998, EGA.

37 Leanne Illin, [Family History], EGA; tapes 6B087, 1A265 — EGA.

38 Flora's letter to author of 16.08.1995, EGA; tapes 2B421, 2B475, 2B564, 6A021 — all EGA.

39 My interviews with Nola Smallwood (tape 6B009) and Ernest Hoolihan 2.01.1996, EGA.

40 K.D. Balmont, 'Okeaniia', *Vokrug sveta*, no. 44, 1913, p.717.

41 R. Evans, 'Bleakley, John William', in *Australian Dictionary of Biography* [*ADB*], vol.7, Melbourne, Melbourne University Press, 1979, pp.325–26; I. Howie-Willis, 'Bleakley, J.', in *The Encyclopaedia of Aboriginal Australia*, vol.1, Canberra, Aboriginal Studies Press, 1994, pp.134–35.

42 D.J. Murphy, 'Gillies, William Neil', in *ADB*, vol.9, 1983, p.11; 'Bowman, David', in *The Australian Encyclopaedia*, vol.2, Sydney, Angus & Robertson, 1958, pp.79–80; D.J. Murphy, 'Bowman, David', in *ADB*, vol.7, 1979, pp.364–65.

43 QSA: CPA, 15/1064, 15/1543, 15/2204, 15/2212, 15/2241, 15/2536.

44 General Registry Office, Brisbane, Leandro Illin and Kitty Clarke marriage certificate 15/2266.

45 Short, *The Nation Builders*, p.61.

46 QSA: CPA, 19/1649.

47 *Atherton News and Barron Valley Advocate*, 3 July 1915.

SON AND FATHER

1 Here and below in this chapter descriptions are based on QSA: LAN/DF, 89, Atherton 1545, 1546, 1547 as well as documentation in the Queensland State Archives on the farms of the Illins' neighbours, the memoirs of the local pioneers and travellers, materials of meetings of the Eacham Shire Council, publications in the *Cairns Post*, and my own visits to the area.

2 Tapes 3B466, 6A134 — EGA.

3 It still hurts. Recently Flora mentioned this conflict in telling about those days:

'Auntie Ara and my father, they couldn't get on. She did not like him marrying a black woman. She did not approve that we were darkies. It wasn't that she was crooked on my mother, but she was on him. They were at loggerheads'. Tapes 2A399, 3B429 — EGA.

4 QSA: CPA, 16/2728; General Registry Office, Brisbane, Thomas Denyer and Emily Russell marriage certificate 16/3045. I am grateful to Glenda Illin for kindly providing the documents.

5 Facts about the history of Butchers Creek school are derived from QSA: EDU/Z 436, Butchers Creek School; E.H. Short, *The Nation Builders*, Dimbulah, 1988, p.86.

6 Tapes 4B106, 5B078 — EGA.

7 Nicholas and Alexandra are still remembered as *Deda* (grandad) and *Baba* (granny) by their English-speaking and Spanish-speaking grandchildren.

8 Short, *The Nation Builders*, p.87.

9 N. Illin, 'Correspondence. A Russian on Russia', *Cairns Post*, 4 October 1918, p.2; L. Illin, 'Correspondence. A Russian on Bolshevism', *Cairns Post*, 3 March 1919, p.7.

10 Based on tape 3B001, EGA.

11 Ellen [Nellie] Dale Flores, 'Memoirs', 1996, EGA, pp.6–7; General Registry Office, Brisbane, Henry Dale and Ariadna Illin Steinkamp marriage certificate 12/0956. I am grateful to Glenda Illin for kindly providing this document.

12 N. Naessens, 'Mackay: Dynasty behind the sleepy coastal town', *Register*, 10 May 1984, p.13.

13 Queensland birth, death and marriage records, 1850–1919; Naessens, 'Mackay: Dynasty', p.13. Somerled Mackay Jnr, 'Genealogical Tree of the Illin Family', 1996, EGA, pp.4–5; J.A. Nilsson, 'Mackay, John', in *Australian Dictionary of Biography*, vol.5, Melbourne, Melbourne University Press, 1974, pp.169–70; 'Captain Mackay's son dies in Honduras', undated newspaper cutting from Illin archives [presumably *North Queensland Register*, 1980s].

14 M. Fry, 'Memories of Mrs C.J. Fry, nee Mysie Davidson', *Bulletin of Eacham Historical Society*, no. 24, 1978, pp.1–2; J. Waters, '[Memoirs]', in Short, *The Nation Builders*, p.38.

15 QSA: LAN/DF, 89, Atherton 1545, 1546; tapes 2A456, 5B432 — EGA.

16 Tapes 2A098, 2A122, 5B468 — all EGA.

17 R.L. Sharp, 'Tribes and totemism in north-east Australia', *Oceania*, vol.9, no. 4, 1939, pp.445–46, 448; E. Mjöberg, *Amongst Stone Age People in the Queensland Wilderness* [original: *Bland stenaldersmanniskor i Queenslands vildmaker*, Stockholm, Albert Bonniers Forlag, 1918], translated from Swedish by S.M. Fryer (manuscript held by AIATSIS), pp.155, 162–63. W. Roth, 'Superstition, Magic, and Medicine', *North Queensland Ethnography Bulletin*, no. 5, 1903, pp.22–23.

18 Tape 3B075, EGA; interview with Maud Hoolihan, 29.09.1996.

19 Tapes 1A295, 7A246 — EGA.

20 Interview with Delphia and Bim Atkinson, 20.09.1997, tapes 15A011, 15A324 — EGA.

21 Interview with Delphia and Bim Atkinson, tapes 15A549, 15B004 — EGA; 'Mr. and Mrs. James Atkinson and family', *NQR*, 24 August 1930, p.30; R.L. Atkinson, *Northern Pioneers*, Townsville, 1979, pp.i–ii, 1–4.

22 Interview with Giles Atkinson, 13.09.1997; interview with Delphia and Bim Atkinson, tapes 15B082, 15B132 — all EGA.

23 Tape 15B240, EGA; R.M.W. Dixon, 'Tribes, languages and other boundaries in northeast Queensland', in N. Peterson (ed.), *Tribes and Boundaries in Australia*, Canberra, Institute of Aboriginal Studies, 1976, p.209; Atkinson, *Northern Pioneers*, pp.124–27.

24 N. Ilin, *Pesni zemli* [*Songs of the Earth*], edited and introduced by Stepan Golub, Paris, 1910, pp.35, 36, 43, 45, 61, 65, 89.

25 N. Illin, 'Correspondence. A Russian on Russia'.

26 L. Illin, 'Correspondence. A Russian on Bolshevism'; L. Illin, 'Correspondence', *HRE*, 17 August 1940; Papers relating to miscellaneous events involving use of a red flag, NAA (Qld): BP4/1, 66/4/2165, p.360; Somerled Mackay Jnr, 'Memoirs', 1997, EGA, p.4.

27 H.R. Gelston, 'Bolshevism and Disloyalty', *Cairns Post*, 15 April 1919.

28 L. Illin, 'Correspondence. Land for Soldiers', *Cairns Post*, 15 October 1918.

29 Mackay, 'Memoirs', pp.3–4.

30 QSA: CPA, 19/1649, 19/2671, 19/4041, 19/5579, 20/1840.

31 L. Illin, 'Correspondence', *HRE*, 23 August 1938.

32 QSA: LAN/DF, 89, Atherton 1545, 1546, 1547; LAN/DF, 2501A, Herberton 1065.

33 Ilin, *Pesni zemli*, pp.32, 34.

34 C. Campbell, 'Former NQ man keeps 65 y. o. vow', newspaper clipping from F. Hoolihan's archives [*North Queensland Register*, 1980s]; Flores, 'Memoirs', pp.7–8; Mackay, 'Memoirs', pp.4–5; Naessens, 'Mackay: Dynasty behind the sleepy coastal town'.

35 Ilin, *Pesni zemli*, p.38.

36 Ilin, *Pesni zemli*, p.41.

37 Mackay, 'Memoirs', p.5; Flores, 'Memoirs', p.8.

38 Ilin, *Pesni zemli*, pp.101–02.

39 Tape 1B522, EGA.

40 QSA: LAN/DF, 2501A, Herberton 1065; tapes 2A496, 4A027, 6A205 — all EGA.

41 Tapes 4A147, 6A005 — EGA.

42 Tape 4A304, EGA.

43 Tapes 2A171, 6B047 — EGA.

44 'Araluen', in P. Pierce (ed.), *The Oxford Literary Guide to Australia*, Melbourne, New York, Oxford University Press, 1993, pp.34–35; Henry Kendall, 'Araluen', in *My Country: Australian Poetry and Short Stories: Two Hundred Years*, vol.1, Sydney, Ure Smith Press, 1992, pp.124–25; L. & R. Thwaites, *The History of Araluen*, [Braidwood, 1971].

45 Tapes 6A316, 7B228 — EGA.

46 Tapes 4A042, 15A080 — EGA.

BUSH LAWYER AND BUSH LAWS

1 Tapes 8B397, 9A657, 9B001 — all EGA.

2 Tapes 9A094; 1B191 — EGA.

3 L. Illin, 'Correspondence', *HRE*, 7 February 1942.

4 Tapes 1B001, 2B326, 8A628, 8B082, 8B640, 9A107 — all EGA.

5 Vera Ketchell's archives.

6 R. Illin, 'Aborigines', *Townsville Daily Bulletin*, 6 January 1982.

7 Tape 7A304, EGA.

8   Here and below tape 8A, EGA.
9   'Mr. and Mrs. Alfred Foot', *NQR*, 22 March 1930, p.30.
10 Tapes 9B281, EGA; 'Life's end for grazing pioneer, Mary Ada Core', *NQR*, 23 February 1980; M. Core ['Memories'], *NQR,* 26 July, 2, 9, 16 August 1980.
11 Tapes 9B305, 8A120, 9B270, 3B520; Flora's letter to author of 15 July 1998 — all EGA.
12 Correspondence — Home Office, QSA: HOM/J564, no. 6629 of 1925.
13 Tapes 7A113, 8A149 —EGA.
14 QSA: CPA, 26/2404, 26/2483, 26/3270, 26/3388.
15 In those times it was customary to call all male Aboriginals 'boy', regardless of their age.
16 Leandro is writing about the Greenvale Aboriginal stockman known as 'Doctor'. Greenvale Station Records, Mt Helen diary, 12.04.1924.
17 Aboriginal male.
18 'Meekolo' [L. Illin], 'Correspondence', *NQR*, 10 August 1925, p.16.
19 W.B. Sinclair, 'The Aboriginal', *NQR*, 17 August 1925, p.16.
20 Tapes 1B252, 3A107, 9B034 — all EGA; QSA: CPA, Bundle A/58692, Complaints 1933, 33/3789 Re: Dick Hoolihan.
21 Tape 8A091, EGA.
22 Flora's letters to author of 15 July 1998, 16 August 1995, EGA.
23 Vera Ketchell's archives.
24 Interview with Henry Atkinson Jnr, 1.02.1998, tape 16A245, EGA; G. Pike, 'Foreword', in R.L. Atkinson, *Northern Pioneers*, Townsville, 1979, p.ii; tapes 9A101, 9B384 — EGA.
25 Tapes 1B240, 1B333 — EGA.
26 Here and further in the chapter, tape 8B — all EGA.
27 L. Illin, ['Draft of speech about Dan Sheahan's poetry'], *ca.* 1938, Vera Ketchell's archives.
28 R. Illin, 'Aborigines'.
29 'Meekolo' [L. Illin], [Contribution to 'On the Track'], *NQR*, 11 January 1926, p.98.
30 Tape 16A004 — EGA.
31 Tapes 1B273, 3B180, 8B099, 9A144 — all EGA; Greenvale Station Records, Greenvale diary, 10–12.02.1927.
32 Greenvale Station Records, Greenvale diary, 7.02.1927; tapes 8B, 9A156 — EGA.
33 Greenvale diary.
34 R. Illin, 'Aborigines'.
35 Tape 1A232, EGA.
36 Tapes 8B606, 1A380 — EGA.
37 Somerled Mackay Jnr, 'Memoirs', 1997, EGA, pp.5–7; Ellen [Nellie] Dale Flores, 'Memoirs', 1996, EGA, p.8; Somerled Mackay Jnr, 'Genealogical Tree of the Illin Family', 1996, EGA, pp.16–17.
38 Essie is Lullie's eldest daughter. Flora, Lullie and the cook (who was scarcely older than they were) worked together at Greenvale, and years later the cook's son (William Morganson) married Lullie's daughter Essie.
39 Tape 9B065, EGA; L. Illin to A.W. Fadden, [July 1933], QSA: CPA, Bundle A/58692, Complaints 1933, 33/3789.
40 'Meekolo' [L. Illin], [Contribution to 'On the Track'], *NQR*, 25 January 1926, p.80.
41 L. Illin, 'Correspondence', *HRE*, 23 August 1938.

42 *NQR*, 12 December 1925, p.102.
43 *NQR*, 25 January 1926, p.80.
44 *NQR*, 6 September 1926, p.41.
45 ibid.
46 *NQR*, 3 January 1927, p.69.
47 *NQR*: 17 January 1927, p.74; 31 January 1927, p.23; 7 February 1927, p.91.

FROM UTOPIA, FOR UTOPIA ...?

1 Tapes 1B087, 1B125, 2B026 — all EGA; L. Illin to A.W. Fadden 1.08.1933 & 7.08.1933 — QSA: CPA, A/58692 (33/3789 complaints; Re: Dick Hoolihan).
2 R. Illin, 'Aborigines', *Townsville Daily Bulletin*, 6 January 1982; Illin, 'Correspondence', *HRE*, 7 December 1935; tape 7A014, EGA.
3 Tapes 2B403, 9A402 — all EGA; S. Kormishen – Naturalization certificate, NAA (ACT): A1, 1932/771.
4 Jitnikoff, P. – Naturalization certificate, NAA (ACT): A1, 1928/10997.
5 Tapes 1B450, 1B492, 3B056, 7B548 — all EGA.
6 L. Illin, 'Correspondence', *HRE* — 22 December 1936; 13 February 1937; 17 June 1937; 23 November 1940; 17 August 1940. Tape 1B191, EGA.
7 P.J. Sutton, 'Gugu-Badhun and its Neighbours. A Linguistic Salvage Study', Canberra, Sydney, 1973 (AIATSIS manuscript collection), p.21; tapes 14B368; 7B098; 2B491 — all EGA.
8 All of the following detail is based on the official correspondence and Leandro's letters to officials from the file located at QSA: CPA, Correspondence files 1901–1944; Bundle A/58692, Complaints 1933, 33/3789 Re: Dick Hoolihan. I am grateful to Dr Noel Loos, James Cook University of North Queensland, for providing me with information about the location of the file and to Ms Margaret Reid, archivist, Queensland State Archives, for help in obtaining access to it.
9 G. Cooke, 'Grandson of "Stolen Generations" architect sorry', *Canberra Times*, 24 May 1998.
10 QSA: Department of Native Affairs, 8G/18, George Williamson, 40/1255.
11 Tape 7A210, EGA; M. Kennedy, *Born a Half-Caste*, Canberra, Australian Institute of Aboriginal Studies, 1985, p.27; tapes 7B006; 3A107 — EGA.
12 Tape 9B479, EGA.
13 Tapes 7A192; 7B278; 6B116 — all EGA.
14 'Deportation only solution to vendetta problem', *Sunday Mail*, Brisbane, 10 January 1937.
15 *HRE*, 13 February 1937.
16 Tape 7B053, EGA.
17 *HRE*, 15 September 1938.
18 *HRE*, 17 February 1942.
19 The inscription reads: 'L.I. In recognition from Italians to their friend L. Illin. 24.9.38'.
20 *HRE*, 30 April 1936.
21 *HRE*, 26 November 1936.
22 *HRE*, 12, 28 July 1938.
23 *HRE*, 17 January 1939.
24 *HRE*, 23 August & 27 August 1938.
25 Illin, 'To the electors of the Hinchinbrook Shire', *HRE*, 14 March 1939; *HRE*, 28 March & 2 May 1939.

26 *HRE*, 9, 13, 23 August 1938; *HRE*, 28 March 1939; 'Old Soldier', 'Correspondence', *HRE*, 11, 20 August 1938.
27 *HRE*, 3 June & 28 September 1939.
28 *HRE*, 3, 17 June 1937.
29 *HRE*, 3 June & 19 December 1939, 11 April 1940.
30 *HRE*, 13 August 1938; L. Illin, ['Draft of speech about Dan Sheahan's poetry'], *ca.* 1938; Dan Sheahan to Leandro Illin, 26 January 1938 — both Vera Ketchell's archives; Dan Sheahan, 'The Councillors' Rocks', *NQR*, 19 February 1938, p.66. Dan Sheahan, *Songs from the Canefields*, Ingham, 1986.
31 *HRE*, 28 September 1939; 2 July 1940; 13 August 1940.
32 *HRE*, 15 August 1940.
33 *HRE*, 17 August 1940.
34 *HRE*, 30 April 1938.
35 Flora Hoolihan's letter to author, 16.08.1995; tape 7B298, EGA.
36 *HRE*, 19 November 1940.
37 *HRE*, 23 November 1940.
38 Minister for Home Security to Leandro Illin, 21.04.1942 — Vera Ketchell's archives (I prefer not to mention the Russian's name for reasons of sensitivity, especially as no further details of the case are available.).
39 Tape 9B456, EGA.
40 Tape 9B419, EGA.
41 The text is not signed by Leandro but the handwriting seems to be his. Probably it is a paraphrasing of someone's aphorism.
42 *HRE*, 7, 17 February 1942.
43 *HRE*, 20 November 1941.
44 *HRE* — 3 March 1942; 15 September 1942; 31 August 1944; 5 October 1944; 13 March 1945.
45 L. Illin to Harry Williams, Vera Ketchell's archives.
46 L. Illin to G.P. Barber, 8.07.1933, 21.07.1933; to A. W. Fadden, 8.08.1933 — QSA: CPA, A/58692; file 33/3789. *HRE*, 19 December 1936.
47 Tapes 3B288, 6A270, 7A084, 9B581, 14B188 — all EGA.
48 Tapes 6A217, 6A230, 2B445, 9B257 — all EGA.
49 Tape 7B098, EGA.
50 Tape 17A375, EGA.
51 QSA: LAN/DF 89, Atherton 1546.
52 QSA: CPA, 8P/27, Paddy Robinson; CPA, 8E/335, Emily Robinson; CPA, 8J/454, Jenny Brown; tapes 1A295, 1B631, 7A233, 7B179, 7B208 — all EGA; 'Death at 98', undated clipping, presumably *Townsville Bulletin*, February–March 1955.
53 Tape 9A444, EGA.
54 L. Illin to T. and R. Illin, 25.11.1943, Vera Ketchell's archives; tape 1B152, EGA.
55 Tape 14A251, EGA; L. Illin to R. Illin, 24.07.1941, 30.07.1941 — Vera Ketchell's archives; tapes 7B063, 14A352 — EGA.
56 '"Topsy" born during time of bloodshed', *Northern Territory News*, 26 March 1988, p.18; *Phyllis May Illin (née Rosendale). 20.11.23–6.9.93* [Commemorative booklet, compiled by Leanne Illin, Townsville 1993]; interview with Leanne Illin 28.02.1996, EGA.
57 L. Illin to R. and T. Illin, 13.11.1944, 25.11.1943, Vera Ketchell's archives; tape 7A023, EGA.

58   L. Illin to R. Illin, 30.07.1941, Vera Ketchell's archives.
59   *HRE*, 1 October 1942. For further discussion of the issue of platform tickets, see *HRE*, 14, 24 November 1942.
60   L. Illin to R. and T. Illin, 25.07.1943 & R. Illin to L. Illin, 6.09.1943 — Vera Ketchell's archives.
61   L. Illin to R. and T. Illin, 25.11.1943, Vera Ketchell's archives; tapes 7B228, 14A312 — EGA.
62   L. Illin to R. Illin, 24.07.1941, L. Illin to R. and T. Illin, 25.11.1943, T. Illin to L. Illin, 16.10.1943 — all Vera Ketchell's archives; QSA: Department of Native Affairs, 8G/18, George Williamson; tape 14B131, EGA.
63   L. Illin to R. and T. Illin, 25.07.1943 & L. Illin to R. Illin, 26.09.1944, Vera Ketchell's archives.
64   *HRE* — 18, 20 December 1941; 15 July 1943; 9, 27 October 1945; 3 November 1945, 8 December 1945.
65   Illin, Romelio – Naturalization file, NAA (ACT): A435, A46/4/592.

EPILOGUE

1   Tape 9A052, EGA.
2   Tape 7A210, EGA.
3   Tapes 7B554; 3A300 — EGA.
4   Tape 7B590; 6B198 — EGA.
5   Tape 4A352, EGA.
6   QSA: CPA, 8J/454, Jenny Brown.
7   Tape 3A300, EGA.
8   M. Kennedy, *Born a Half-Caste*, Canberra, Australian Institute of Aboriginal Studies, 1985, p.3; QSA: CPA, Bundle A/58692, Complaints 1933, 33/3789.
9   Tape 3A300, EGA.
10   Tape 3A252, EGA.
11   Tapes 6B198, 6B251 — EGA.
12   Tape 6B037, EGA.
13   Personal communication from Dr Chris Anderson, December 1990.
14   Tapes 9A019; 6B059 — EGA; 'Leandro impressed with city lifestyle', an undated newspaper clipping.
15   Tapes 6A070, 14A043 — EGA; Somerled Mackay Jnr, 'Genealogical Tree of the Illin Family', 1996, EGA, p.7.
16   Somerled Mackay Jnr, 'Memoirs', 1997, EGA, pp.7–8.
17   Mackay, 'Memoirs', pp.6–9; 'Romelio Illin: Primer contratista para el aseo de nuestra ciudad', *Tiempo—El Diario de Honduras*, 29 June 1976; F.F. Paz, 'Sammy, el inmortal del pugilato', *La Prensa*, 26 May 1985, p.21.
18   Tapes 14A000, 14A063 — EGA.
19   Mackay, 'Genealogical Tree'.
20   Tape 7B070, EGA
21   N. Loos, K. Mabo, *Edward Koiki Mabo: His Life and Struggle for Land Rights*, Brisbane, University of Queensland Press, 1996, pp.xxiii, 9, 50–51, 107, 111, 128–29.
22   Tapes 7B070, 7A644, 17A000, 7A544 — all EGA.
23   Tape 6B406, EGA.

BIBLIOGRAPHY

~

PRIMARY SOURCES

A CHRONOLOGICAL LIST OF PUBLICATIONS BY NIKOLAI ILIN (NICHOLAS ILLIN)

Ilin, N., *Shest' mesiatsev v Soedinennykh Shtatakh Severnoi Ameriki* [*Six Months in the United States of North America*], St Petersburg, 1876 (183 pp.).

Ilin, N., 'Iuridicheskie zametki [Judicial notes]', *Sudebnaia gazeta*, 12 January 1886.

Ilin, N., 'V novom kraiu. Roman-khronika. Iz vremen zavoevaniia Turkestanskogo kraia [In the New Land. Novel-Chronicle. From the Times of Turkestan's Conquest]', *Knizhki 'Nedeli'*, nos 1–11, 1886. Separate edition: Tashkent, 1913, 2 vols [quotations in the text are based on this edition].

Ilin, N., 'Begletsy. Roman iz zhizni na dalekom Vostoke [The Fugitives. A Novel from Life in the Far East]', *Zhivopisnoe obozrenie*, supplement, no. 10, 1888, pp.3–100.

Ilin, N., 'Nezhdanno-negadanno [Against All Expectations]', *Zhivopisnoe obozrenie*, 1889: no. 25, pp.402–03, 406; no. 26, pp.418–19, 422–23; no. 27, pp.2–3, 6.

Ilin, N.D., *Dnevnik tolstovtsa* [*The Tolstoyan Diary*], St Petersburg, 1892 (289 pp.). [Reviewed: Meshcherskii, *Grazhdanin*, 11 February 1892; *Russkaia mysl'*, no. 4, 1892, pp.155–56; *Severnyi vestnik*, no. 6, 1892, pp.75–79].

Ilin, N. 'Oshibsia [Mistaken]', *Vestnik Evropy*, no. 9, 1898, p.99.

Ilin, N., *Pesni zemli* [*Songs of the Earth*], edited and introduced by Stepan Golub, Paris, 1910 (104 pp.).

Il[in], N., 'Russkie v Avstralii [Russians in Australia]', *Novoe vremia*, 30 July 1912, p.2.

Ilin, N., 'Pis'ma iz Avstralii [Letters from Australia]', *Novoe vremia*, 14 August 1913, p.4.

Ilin, N. 'Snova osen' i snova toska! [Again autumn and again sadness!]', *Parus*, no. 1, 1915, p.4.

Illin, N., 'Correspondence. A Russian on Russia', *Cairns Post*, 4 October 1918, p.2.

A CHRONOLOGICAL LIST OF PUBLICATIONS BY LEANDRO ILLIN

— in *Cairns Post*, Cairns, Queensland

Correspondence: 'Land for Soldiers', 15 October 1918, p.3; 'A Russian on Bolshevism', 3 March 1919, p.7.

— in *North Queensland Register*, Townsville, Queensland

Correspondence (under pseudonym 'Meekolo'), 10 August 1925, p.16.

Contributions to 'On the Track' (under pseudonym 'Meekolo'): 12 December 1925, p.102; 11 January 1926, p.98; 25 January 1926, p.80; 9 August 1926, p.67; 6 September 1926, p.41;

Letter to 'On the Track', with Bill Bowyang's comments, 3 January 1927, p.69.

— in *Herbert River Express*, Ingham, Queensland

Correspondence: 7 December 1935, p.6; 30 April 1936, p.4; 26 November 1936, p.4; 19 December 1936, p.4; 'North Australia', 22 December 1936, p.4; 13 February 1937, p.4; 'Advocate of silent pictures', 3 June 1937, p.4; 17 June 1937, p.6; 30 April 1938, p.4; 12 July 1938, p.6; 28 July 1938, p.6; 9 August 1938, p.4; 13 August 1938, p.6; 23 August 1938, p.4; 27 August 1938, p.6; 15 September 1938, p.4; 17 January 1939, p.4; 'To the electors of the Hinchinbrook Shire', 14 March 1939, p.5; 28 March 1939, p.6; 30 March 1939, p.6; 2 May 1939, p.6; 3 June 1939, p.6; 18 July 1939, p.5; 'Rowdyism at Band Concerts', 28 September 1939, p.6; 19 December 1939, p.6; 11 April 1940, p.6; 2 July 1940, p.6; 13 August 1940, p.6; 17 August 1940, p.6; 23 November 1940, p.6; 'Garden vandalism', 20 November 1941, p.5; 18 December 1941, p.6; 20 December 1941, p.6; 7 February 1942, p.6; 17 February 1942, p.6; 3 March 1942, p.6; 15 September 1942, p.3; 1 October 1942, p.4; 14 November 1942, p.3; 24 November 1942, p.4; 15 July 1943, p.4; 'An open letter to Mr C. G. Jesson, M.L.A.', 31 August 1944, p.4; 'An open letter to Mr C. G. Jesson', 5 October 1944, p.4; 13 March 1945, p.4; 9 October 1945, p.4; 27 October 1945, p.4; 3 November 1945, p.4; 8 December 1945, p.4.

ARCHIVES

1 AUSTRALIA

NATIONAL ARCHIVES OF AUSTRALIA [NAA]

NAA (ACT): A1, 1913/2427, Nicholas Illin – Naturalization certificate.

NAA (ACT): A1, 1913/17541, Leandro Illin – Naturalization.

NAA (ACT): A1, 1914/3357, John Nikonets – Naturalization.

NAA (ACT): A1, 1914/11108, Felemon Alexeivch Fadchuck – Naturalization

NAA (ACT): A1, 1914/21026, Vlademir Balias – Naturalization.

NAA (ACT): A1, 1915/6639, Michael Prochoroff – Naturalization.

NAA (ACT): A1, 1921/18516, Gabriel Mironovich Ivanoff – Naturalization.

NAA (ACT): A1, 1926/11686, Gadaloff, M. – Naturalization certificate.

NAA (ACT): A1, 1928/10997, Jitnikoff, P. – Naturalization certificate.

NAA (ACT): A1, 1932/771, S. Kormishen – Naturalization certificate.

NAA (ACT): A1/1, 1923/27605, Strelnikoff, Vasil – Naturalization.

NAA (ACT): A3/1, NT1913/1156, pts 1–3 – Russian Emigrants for Northern Territory. 1911–1913.Illin, L., 'Report of the Northern Territory' [1912] (92 pp.). Vladimirov, K.N., 'Report on the Northern Territory of Australia', 1912 (63 pp.).

NAA (ACT): A435, A46/4/592, Illin, Romelio – Naturalization file.

NAA (ACT): A441/1, 1951/13/8524, Lamin, V.N.
NAA (ACT): A659/1, 1940/1/7443 Homenko, N.P. – Naturalization.
NAA (ACT): A6122/40, 111, Summary of Communism, vol.1.
NAA (Qld): BP4/1, 66/4/2165, Papers relating to miscellaneous events involving use of a red flag.

QUEENSLAND STATE ARCHIVES, BRISBANE [QSA]

QSA: A/45328, [785M], Russians 1911–1915.
QSA: B/561–B/563.
QSA: CPA, 8E/335, Emily Robinson.
QSA: CPA, 8J/454, Jenny Brown.
QSA: CPA, 8P/27, Paddy Robinson.
QSA: CPA, 15/1064, 15/1543, 15/2204, 15/2212, 15/2241, 15/2536.
QSA: CPA, 16/2728
QSA: CPA, 19/1649, 19/2671, 19/4041, 19/5579, 20/1840.
QSA: CPA, 26/2404, 26/2483, 26/3270, 26/3388.
QSA: CPA, Correspondence files 1901–1944; Bundle A/58692, Complaints 1933, 33/3789 Re: Dick Hoolihan.
QSA: Department of Native Affairs, 8G/18, George Williamson.
QSA: EDU/Z 436, Butchers Creek School.
QSA: HOM/J564, no. 6629 of 1925, Correspondence—Home Office.
QSA: IMM/132, Register of Immigrants.
QSA: LANP69A, 1545, 1546, 1547.
QSA: LAN/DF 85, Atherton 1508.
QSA: LAN/DF 89, Atherton 1545, 1546, 1547.
QSA: LAN/DF 100, Atherton 1667, 1669.
QSA: LAN/DF 118, Atherton 1937.
QSA: LAN/DF 132, Atherton 2090A.
QSA: LAN/DF 151, Atherton 2615.
QSA: LAN/DF, 2501A, Herberton 1065.

OTHER AUSTRALIAN ARCHIVES

Australian Institute of Aboriginal and Torres Strait Islander Studies manuscript collection [AIATSIS]:
Mjöberg, E., *Amongst Stone Age People in the Queensland Wilderness*, translated from Swedish by S.M. Fryer (manuscript held) [Original: Mjöberg, E., *Bland stenalders-manniskor i Queenslands vildmaker*, Stockholm, Albert Bonniers Forlag, 1918].
Mjöberg, E., 'Contribution to the knowledge of the natives of North Queensland', (English manuscript translation held) [Original: Mjöberg, E., 'Beitrage zur Kenntnis Eingeborenen von Nord-Queensland', *Archiv für Anthropologie*, B. 20, 1925].
Sutton, P.J., 'Gugu-Badhun and its Neighbours. A Linguistic Salvage Study', Canberra, Sydney, 1973 (AIATSIS manuscript collection).
General Registry Office, Brisbane:
Henry Dale and Ariadna Illin Steinkamp marriage certificate 12/0956.
Leandro Illin and Kitty Clarke marriage certificate 15/2266.
Thomas Denyer and Emily Russell marriage certificate 16/3045.
Queensland birth, death and marriage records:
Birth 1850–1914; death 1850–1919; marriage 1856–1919.

2 RUSSIA
INSTITUTE OF RUSSIAN LITERATURE OF THE RUSSIAN ACADEMY OF SCIENCES (PUSHKIN'S HOUSE), ST PETERSBURG [IRLI]

N.D. Ilin, 'Avtobiografiia [Autobiography]' [1892], f. 377, no. 1347, folios 1–3.
N.D. Ilin to S.A. Vengerov, [April] 1892, f. 377, no. 1347, folios 6–9.

RUSSIAN STATE ARCHIVE OF LITERATURE AND ART, MOSCOW [RGALI]

N.D. Ilin to N.N. Ge, f. 731, op. 1, d. 16 — 26.02, 20.04, 28.06, 7.07, 9.07, 18.08 & October, 1890; April–May, 1891.
N.D. Ilin to N.N. Ge, f. 731, op. 1, d. 14 — 28.01.1891.
N.D. Ilin to A.K. Ilina, f. 731, op. 1, d. 62 — October & 21.11.1890; 23.01.1891.
A.K. Ilina to N.N. Ge, f. 731, op. 1, d. 17 — 16.11.1890; 13.01, 22.01, 1.02 & 14.05, 1891.
N.D. Ilin, 'Pis'mo iz Avstralii [A letter from Australia]', f. 1666, op. 1, d. 1466.
V. Korolenko to N. Ilin, 29.08.1913; N. Ilin to Korolenko, *ca.* October 1913; N. Ilin Letter to *Discourse*, 1.11.1913 — all f. 1666, op. 1, d. 384.

RUSSIAN STATE HISTORICAL ARCHIVE, ST PETERSBURG [RGIA]

'[Ivan Gerasimov Ivanov]', f. 1405, op. 91, d. 3531.
'Iliny Leandr i Romelii... o razreshenii priniat' inostrannoe poddanstvo [Ilins Leandr and Romelii ... about permission to take foreign citizenship]', f. 1412, op. 9, folios 1–2.

RUSSIAN STATE MILITARY-HISTORICAL ARCHIVE, MOSCOW [RGVIA]

'D.N. Ilin, the 6th', f. 395, op. 16, d. 492.
'N.D. Ilin. Posluzhnoi spisok [Service record]. 27.09.1882', f. 400, op. 9, d. 21078.

RUSSIAN STATE NAVAL ARCHIVE, ST PETERSBURG [RGA VMF]

N.D. Ilin to the crew of the *Lieutenant Ilin* 22.05.1894, Colón, Argentina, f. 2, op. 1, d. 7, folios 73–74.
A. Krotkov, 'O netochnostiakh publikuemykh sochinenii [About inaccuracies of published works]', f. 417, op. 6, d. 83.

SARATOV STATE ARCHIVE [SSA]

'Delo po prosheniiu poruchika Sergeia Alekseeva Ilina o vnesenii ego v dvorianskuiu rodoslovnuiu knigu [File on application of Lieutenant Sergei Alekseev Ilin concerning his inclusion into the Noblemen family register]', f. 19, op. 1, d. 84.

3 ARGENTINA
CENTRO DE ESTUDIOS MIGRATORIOS LATINOAMERICANOS, BUENOS AIRES [CEML]

Listado parcial de immigrantes [List of immigrants arrived on the *Mendoza* on 29 June 1897].

4 PRIVATE ARCHIVES
ELENA GOVOR'S ARCHIVES, CANBERRA

Flores, Ellen [Nellie] Dale, 'Memoirs', 1996.
Illin, Leanne, [Family History] (typescript, 2pp).
Illin, Leanne, *Phyllis May Illin (née Rosendale). 20.11.23–6.9.93.* [Commemorative booklet, compiled by Leanne Illin, Townsville 1993].

Illin, Romelio, 'En la Frontera (En Guarda Raya) (Hecho por el relate de mi padre, sucedido en les años de la década de 1890) [On the border (Border-guard) (based on my father's account, of events of the 1890s)]' (manuscript provided by Illin-Mackay family, Honduras/USA).

Mackay, Somerled Jnr, 'Genealogical Tree of the Illin Family', 1996.

Mackay, Somerled Jnr, 'Memoirs', 1997.

Interviews:
   with the Atkinson family (tapes 15A–16B)
   with George Balias (tape 12A).
   with the Gadaloff family (tape 10AB).
   with the Illin family (tapes 1A–9B, 13A–14B, 17A).
   with Basil Strelnikoff (tape 11A).
   with Ric Throssell, 17.09.1997.

Letters to author:
   from Flora Hoolihan, 1995–99.
   from Basil Strelnikoff, 16.12.1997.
   from Roy Phelps, 16.03.1997.
   from Valentina Provodina, 1996–2000.

FLORA HOOLIHAN'S ARCHIVES, TOWNSVILLE, QUEENSLAND

Illin, N., *Vostochnaia Legenda* [*The Orient Legend* (poem)] (41 pp.).

Illin, N., poetry.

Family photos with inscriptions (1880s–1960s).

Postcards to N. Illin and N. Rosalieff, 1910s.

VERA KETCHELL'S ARCHIVES, MALANDA, QUEENSLAND

[Daniel, Ludmila] to L. Illin, 1910.

Illin, L. to Harry Williams, early 1930s.

Illin L., [Draft of speech about Dan Sheahan's poetry], *ca.* 1938.

Minister for Home Security to Leandro Illin, 21.04.1942.

Sheahan, Dan to L. Illin, 26.01.1938.

Correspondence between L. Illin, R. Illin, T. Illin, and H. Illin, 1939–45.

Family photos with inscriptions (1890s–1960s).

OTHER PRIVATE ARCHIVES

Gadaloff, M., 'Memoirs', 1971: in possession of Peter Gadaloff, Southport, Queensland.

Michael Gadaloff's archives: in possession of Kathleen Gadaloff, Brisbane.

Greenvale Station Records: in possession of Henry Atkinson, Lucky Downs, Queensland (microfilm copy at Queensland State Library).

Strelnikoff, V., 'Memoirs': in possession of Basil Strelnikoff, Mareeba, Queensland.

SECONDARY SOURCES

BOOKS

'Araluen', in P. Pierce (ed.), *The Oxford Literary Guide to Australia*, Melbourne, New York, Oxford University Press, 1993, pp.34–35.

Arbitman, E.N., *Zhizn' i tvorchestvo N.N. Ge* [*Ge's Life and Works*], Saratov, 1972.

Atkinson, R.L., *Northern Pioneers*, Townsville, 1979.

'Bowman, David', in *The Australian Encyclopaedia*, vol.2, Sydney, Angus & Robertson, 1958, pp.79–80.

Chekhov, A., *Five Plays*, translated by R. Hingley, Oxford, Oxford University Press, 1980.

Dixon, R.M.W., *The Dyirbal Language of North Queensland*, Cambridge, Cambridge University Press, 1972.

Dixon, R.M.W., 'Tribes, languages and other boundaries in northeast Queensland', in N. Peterson (ed.), *Tribes and Boundaries in Australia*, Canberra, Australian Institute of Aboriginal Studies, 1976.

Dixon [R.M.W.] Bob, *Searching for Aboriginal Languages. Memoirs of a Field Worker*, St Lucia, University of Queensland Press, 1983.

Evans, R., 'Bleakley, John William', in *Australian Dictionary of Biography*, vol.7, Melbourne, Melbourne University Press, 1979, pp.325–26.

[Gadalov (Gadaloff), M.], 'We do not repent having left our native land', in: *Terse Information about Queensland. Queries and Replies*, Brisbane, 1915, pp.54–55.

Gerakov, G., *Tverdost' dukha russkikh* [*Russians' Strength of Mind*], Petrograd, 1813.

Govor, E., *Australia in the Russian Mirror, Changing Perceptions 1770–1919*, Melbourne, Melbourne University Press, 1997.

Harris, D.R., 'Adaptation to a tropical rain-forest environment: Aboriginal subsistence in Northeastern Queensland', in N.G. Blurton-Jones & V. Reynolds (eds), *Human Behaviour and Adaptation*, London, Taylor & Francis, 1978, pp.112–34.

Hiscock, P., & Kershaw, A.P., 'Palaeoenvironments and prehistory of Australia's tropical Top End', in J. Dodson (ed.), *The Naive Lands: prehistory and environmental change in Australia and the south-west Pacific*, Melbourne, Longman Cheshire, 1992, pp.43–72.

Howie-Willis, I., 'Bleakley, J.', in *The Encyclopaedia of Aboriginal Australia*, vol.1, Canberra, Aboriginal Studies Press, 1994, pp.134–35.

'Ilin D.S.', in *Bol'shaia sovetskaia entsiklopediia*, 3rd edn, vol.10, Moscow, 1972, p.135.

'Ilin D.S.', in *Russkii biograficheskii slovar'*, Reprint, New York, 1962, vol.8, pp.97–98.

Kabo, V.R., *Proiskhozhdenie i ranniaia istoriia aborigenov Avstralii* [*The Origin and Early History of the Australian Aborigines*], Moscow, Nauka, 1969.

Kabo, V., *The Road to Australia: Memoirs*, Canberra, Aboriginal Studies Press, 1998.

Kendall, H., 'Araluen', in *My Country: Australian Poetry and Short Stories: Two Hundred Years*, vol.1, Sydney, Ure Smith Press, 1992, pp.124–25.

Kennedy, M., *Born a Half-Caste*, Canberra, Australian Institute of Aboriginal Studies, 1985.

Koshel, P.A., *Istoriia syska v Rossii* [*History of Criminal Investigation in Russia*], vol.1, Minsk, 1996.

Kriukov, N.A., *Avstraliia: Sel'skoe khoziaistvo Avstralii v sviazi s obshchim pazvitiem strany* [*Australia: Australian Agriculture in Connection with the General Development of the Country*], Moscow, 1906.

Loos, N., Mabo, K., *Edward Koiki Mabo: His Life and Struggle for Land Rights*, Brisbane, University of Queensland Press, 1996.

Lukin, V.M., 'Ilin, N.D.', in *Russkie pisateli. 1800–1917. Biograficheskii slovar'*, vol.2, Moscow, 1992, p.413.

Murphy, D.J., 'Bowman, David', in *Australian Dictionary of Biography*, vol.7, Melbourne, Melbourne University Press, 1979, pp.364–65.

Murphy, D.J., 'Gillies, William Neil', in *Australian Dictionary of Biography*, vol.9, Melbourne, Melbourne University Press, 1983, p.11.

Nilsson, J.A., 'Mackay, John', in *Australian Dictionary of Biography*, vol.5, Melbourne, Melbourne University Press, 1974, pp.169–70

Politicheskaia katorga i ssylka. Biograficheskii spravochnik [*Political Penal Servitude and Exile. Biographical Reference Book*], Moscow, 1934.

Porudominskii, V., *Nikolai Ge*, Moscow, Iskusstvo, 1970.

Repin, I.E., *Pis'ma k pisateliam i literaturnym deiateliam* [*Letters to Writers and Literary Workers*], Moscow, Iskusstvo, 1950.

Repin, I.E., *Dalekoe blizkoe* [*Far Close Past*], Moscow, Iskusstvo, 1964.

Sheahan, D., *Songs from the Canefields*, Ingham, 1972; Rev. edn, Ingham, 1986.

Short, E.H., *The Nation Builders*, Dimbulah, 1988.

Singh, G., Kershaw, A.P., Clark, R., 'Quaternary vegetation and fire history in Australia', in A.M.G. Gill, R.H. Groves, I.R. Noble (eds), *Fire and the Australian Biota*, Canberra, Australian Academy of Science, 1981, pp.23–54.

Sokolovskii, M.K., *Pamiatka 3-go gusarskogo Elisavetgradskogo ... polka* [*Booklet of the 3rd Elizabetgrad Hussar ... Regiment*], St Petersburg, 1914.

Stasov, V., *Nikolai Nikolaevich Ge, ego zhizn', proizvedeniia, perepiska* [*Nikolai Nikolaevich Ge, his Life, Works, Correspondence*], Moscow, 1904.

Throssell, R., *Wild Weeds and Wind Flowers. The Life and Letters of Katharine Susannah Prichard*, Sydney, Angus and Robertson, 1975.

Thwaites, L. & R., *The History of Araluen*, [Braidwood, 1971].

Tolstoy, L.N., *Polnoe sobranie sochinenii* [*Complete Collection of Works*], Moscow: vol.51, 1952, pp.98, 223; vol.65, 1953, pp.168–69, 178, 183, 210; vol.88, 1957, p.200.

Tolstoy, L., *The Kreutzer Sonata and Other Stories*, N.Y., Penguin Books, 1985.

Vedomost' spravok o sudimosti. Izdanie Ministerstva Iustitsii [*Register of Convictions Published by the Ministry of Justice*], part 1, book 1, St Petersburg, 1887.

Waters, J., '[Memoirs]', in Short, *The Nation Builders*, pp.36–38.

PERIODICALS, NEWSPAPERS

Balmont, K.D., 'Okeaniia', *Vokrug sveta*, no. 44, 1913, pp.716–18.

Campbell, C., 'Former NQ man keeps 65 y. o. vow' [undated clipping, presumably *North Queensland Register*, 1980s].

'Captain Mackay's son dies in Honduras' [undated clipping, presumably *North Queensland Register*, 1980s].

Carron, E.T., 'Correspondence', *Herbert River Express*, 23 August 1938, p.4.

'Citizen', 'Correspondence', *Herbert River Express*, 15 August 1940, p.6.

Cooke, G., 'Grandson of "Stolen Generations" architect sorry', *Canberra Times*, 24 May 1998, p.4.

Core, M., [Memories], *North Queensland Register*, 26 July, 2, 9, 16 August 1980.

'Death at 98' [undated clipping, presumably *Townsville Bulletin*, February–March 1955].

'Deportation only solution to vendetta problem', *Sunday Mail*, Brisbane, 10 January 1937, p.4.

Fry, M., 'Memories of Mrs C.J. Fry, nee Mysie Davidson', *Bulletin of Eacham Historical Society*, no. 24, 1978, pp.1–2, no. 25, 1978, p.1.

Gadalov [Gadaloff], M., 'Russkie emigranty v Avstralii [Russian emigrants in Australia]', *Dalekaia okraina*, 21 August 1911, p.2.

Gelston, H.R., 'Bolshevism and Disloyalty', *Cairns Post*, 15 April 1919.

Govor, E., 'Il'iny iz plemeni Ngadzhan [Illins from Ngadjon tribe]', *Avstraliada*, Sydney, no. 10, 1997, pp.5–9.

Govor, E. 'Po sledam Nikolaia Manovicha, pervogo russkogo sviashchennika v Avstralii [On the track of Nikolai Manovich, the first Russian priest in Australia]', *Avstraliada*, Sydney, no. 13, 1997, pp.1–3.

Govor E. 'Sviashchennik-sotsialist ili samozvanets-donoschik. K biografii Nikolaia

Manovicha [Priest-socialist or impostor-informer. Towards a biography of Nikolai Manovich]', *Avstraliada*, Sydney, no. 16, 1998, p.7.

Govor E. 'Malen'kaia Sibir' na plato Aterton [Little Siberia on the Atherton Tablelands]', *Avstraliada*, Sydney, 1999: no. 20, pp.5–9; no. 21, pp.10–13.

Gzel, A., 'Pamiati Evgeniia Vasil'evicha Daniel [To the memory of Evgenii Vasil'evich Daniel]', *Chuzhbina*, Brisbane, 1930, no. 5, pp.18–19.

Illin, R., 'Aborigines', *Townsville Daily Bulletin*, 6 January 1982.

Klaatsch, H., 'Mumie aus Australien und Reisebericht des Hrn. Klaatsch aus Sydney', *Zeitschrift für Ethnologie*, B. 37, 1905, pp.772–81.

Klaatsch, H., 'Some notes on scientific travel amongst the black population of tropical Australia in 1904, 1905, 1906', *Report of the Eleventh Meeting of the Australasian Association for the Advancement of Science, held at Adelaide*, 1907, pp.577–92.

'Leandro impressed with city lifestyle' [undated clipping, presumably *North Queensland Register*, 1980–81]

'Life's end for grazing pioneer, Mary Ada Core', *North Queensland Register*, 23 February, 1980.

'Mr. and Mrs. Alfred Foot', *North Queensland Register*, 22 March 1930, p.30.

'Mr. and Mrs. James Atkinson and family', *North Queensland Register*, 24 August 1930, p.30.

Naessens, N., 'Mackay: Dynasty behind the sleepy coastal town', *Register* (Townsville), 10 May 1984, p.13.

'New settlers for Queensland. Patagonian Welshmen', *Cairns Post*, 23 March 1911.

'Old Soldier', 'Correspondence', *Herbert River Express*, 11 August 1938, p.6; 20 August 1938, p.6.

'Old subscriber', 'Sunday night picture shows', *Herbert River Express*, 19 November 1940, p.6.

'On the Track', *North Queensland Register*, 17 January 1927, p.74; 31 January 1927, p.23; 7 February 1927, p.91.

Paz, F.F. 'Sammy, el inmortal del pugilato', *La Prensa*, 26 May 1985, p.21.

'Return of the Russian Delegates. An interesting interview', *Cairns Post*, 14 May 1912, p.8.

'Romelio Illin: Primer contratista para el aseo de nuestra ciudad', *Tiempo — El Diario de Honduras*, 29 June 1976, p.11.

Roth, W., 'Superstition, Magic, and Medicine', *North Queensland Ethnography Bulletin*, no. 5, 1903.

'Russians in Queensland', *Brisbane Courier*, 28 December 1911, p.5.

Schultz, J., 'From Queensland with distinction', *Courier-Mail*, 12 April 1997 (weekend supplement, p.5).

Sharp, R.L., 'Tribes and totemism in north-east Australia', *Oceania*, 1939: vol.9, no. 3, pp.254–75; no. 4, pp.439–61.

Sheahan, Dan, 'The Councillors' Rocks', *North Queensland Register*, 19 February 1938, p.66.

Sinclair, W.B., 'The Aboriginal', *North Queensland Register*, 17 August 1925, p.16.

Tindale, N.B, & Birdsell, J.B., 'Tasmanoid tribes in Northern Queensland', *Records of the South Australian Museum*, vol.7, 1941, pp.1–9.

'"Topsy" born during time of bloodshed', *Northern Territory News*, 26 March 1988, p.18.

Tranter, H., 'The Russian Settlers of Butcher's Creek', *Bulletin of Eacham Historical Society*, no. 222, 1997, pp.1–2.

Villanueva, E. 'Un poeta ruso, ignorado, descansa para siempre en San Pedro Sula', *Tiempo — El Diario de Honduras*, 13 October 1971, p.18.

INDEX

~

NOTE

†indicates that one or more of the photographs in the picture section refers to this entry

www.ingramcontent.com/pod-product-compliance
Lightning Source LLC
Chambersburg PA
CBHW030856270326
41929CB00008B/437